Before the vote was won

WOMEN'S SOURCE LIBRARY

Series Editors:
Dale Spender and Candida Ann Lacey

This series brings together some of the most important, but still too little known, written sources which document the history of women's struggles for liberation. Taken from the principal women's archive in Britain, The Fawcett Library, and reprinted in full wherever possible, these pamphlets and papers illustrate major debates on a range of issues, including suffrage, education, work, science and medicine as well as making the words of individual women widely available for the first time. Each volume contains a historical introduction to the material and biographical details of those campaigners who sought to improve the social, economic and legal status of women. The series was devised in collaboration with Catherine Ireland and David Doughan of The Fawcett Library, both of whom greatly assisted in the selection and compilation of material.

Other volumes in this series:

Barbara Leigh Smith Bodichon and the Langham Place Group edited by Candida Lacey
The Sexuality Debates edited by Sheila Jeffreys
The Education Papers: Women's Quest for Equality in Britain, 1850–1912 edited by Dale Spender
The Non-Violent Militant: Selected Writings of Teresa Billington-Greig edited by Carol McPhee and Ann Fitzgerald
Suffrage and the Pankhurts edited by Jane Marcus

Forthcoming volumes include:

Women's Fabian Tracts edited by Sally Alexander
The Lily edited by Cheris Kramarae and Ann Russo
The Revolution edited by Cheris Kramarae and Lana Rakow
Sex and Social Order, 1660–1730 edited by Carol Barash and Rachel Weil

Before the vote was won: arguments for and against women's suffrage

Edited by
Jane Lewis

Routledge & Kegan Paul
New York and London

First published in 1987 by
Routledge & Kegan Paul Ltd
11 New Fetter Lane, London EC4P 4EE

Published in the USA by
Routledge & Kegan Paul Inc.
in association with Methuen Inc.
29 West 35th Street, New York, NY 10001

Set in 10 on 11pt Bembo
by Columns of Reading
and printed in Great Britain
by T. J. Press (Padstow) Ltd
Padstow, Cornwall

Library of Congress Cataloging in Publication Data

Before the vote was won.

(Women's source library)
Includes index.
1. Women – Suffrage – Great Britain – History –
Sources. I. Lewis, Jane (Jane E.) II. Series.
JN979.B44 1987   324.6'23'0941   87–4634

British Library CIP Data also available
ISBN 0–7012–1101–5

Contents

Contents

Contents

Contents

Introduction

WHEN feminists call attention to the use of sexist language and in particular to the use of only male pronouns, they are often accused of pettiness. But in 1868, Mrs Lily Maxwell found to her cost that in the matter of the franchise, 'he' most certainly did not also mean 'she'. Mrs Maxwell was a widow living in Manchester who supported herself by keeping a small crockery shop. Somehow, her name had been included on the voters' register and she duly recorded her vote in a by-election in 1867. However, in 1868 the Court of Common Pleas ruled that 'every woman is personally incapable' of exercising a vote. The decision came as no surprise. When the franchise was first reformed and extended in 1832, the phrase 'male person' had been used for the first time to make it clear that there was no intention of including women. There was nevertheless some residual doubt about the issue, for women had not been explicitly excluded from the very limited franchises existing before 1832. The franchise underwent major reform again in 1867 and Mrs Maxwell's case made it absolutely clear that nineteenth-century legislators did not intend to give women the vote. With the third major extension of the vote in 1884, somewhere between 63 and 66 per cent of adult men were entitled to vote, and as the franchise widened so it was inevitable that women felt the injustice of their exclusion more deeply.

The agitation for women's suffrage is usually dated from John Stuart Mill's 1865 campaign to be elected for Westminster, although the subject had been discussed for some years by feminists, as the first document in this volume indicates. Mill made votes for women part of his platform and three pioneers of the early women's movement, Barbara Bodichon, Emily Davies and Bessie Parkes, took the unheard of step of campaigning on his

1

behalf. Barbara Bodichon called together the first women's suffrage committee in 1866 and they presented a petition to Parliament during the debates over the 1867 Reform Act. These women were all middle-class and for the most part moved in the same Radical circles. They had already been involved in organising a petition to reform the married women's property laws, setting up a Women's Employment Bureau, and founding *The English Woman's Journal*. Nevertheless, the novelty of public speaking and campaigning on a major issue like the vote should not be underestimated. Ray Strachey stressed this point in her account of the early suffrage campaign, recording the embarrassment of the women who presented the first petition for female votes to Parliament in 1867 and the trepidation with which Millicent Garrett Fawcett faced her first public meeting in 1869. She was publicly reviled for her appearances, one MP objecting strongly to her 'disgraceful' conduct.[1] These women had given occasional papers to the National Association for the Promotion of Social Science (which took up the case of married women's property rights), but had no other experience of public life. They were few in number, had no role models to follow and risked being socially ostracised. Their goal was first, to establish the right to be heard and second, to persuade male opinion of the justice of their cause. Their style and even the tone of their speeches and writings was more often than not very similar to that of their male opponents. This does not mean that they did not hold firmly-based feminist views on a wide variety of subjects, but the terms on which they ventured into the public sphere allowed little space for the development of a distinctively different voice.

The first Women's Suffrage Bill requiring that 'wherever words occur which import the masculine gender, the same shall be held to include females for all purposes connected with and having reference to the right to be registered as voters'[2] was brought before Parliament in 1870 by Mr Jacob Bright. Bright was the first of a long line of supporters in the House of Commons, on whom the suffragists relied to introduce private members' Bills. A Bill was introduced every year during the 1870s except 1875. Jacob Bright, his wife Ursula and his two sisters, were strong supporters of both women's suffrage and the feminist campaign for the repeal of the Contagious Diseases Acts, which forced women prostitutes in garrison towns to submit to medical examination for venereal disease. But his more famous brother, John Bright, also a Radical MP, fiercely opposed votes for women, largely because he believed that women would prove an overly religious and conservative influence on politics. His opposition undoubtedly counted for more than Jacob Bright's support. Reliance on private members' Bills was in any case unlikely to meet with success, but this together with petitioning and parliamentary lobbying, constituted the bulk of the activity of the early suffragists.

The suffragists developed a range of arguments to promote their cause. They searched the historical record for evidence of women's right to citizenship; argued for the vote on the basis of need and of justice; and spent considerable time demolishing the arguments of their male opponents. However, the early suffragists' claim to the vote was grounded in the rather narrow argument that women property owners should have as much right as male property owners to exercise the franchise. As Helen Taylor put it: 'property represented by an individual is the true political unit among us' (p. 26). This was correct in so far as the qualifications for voting were concerned, although the Victorian theory of political representation stressed the importance of the fitness of any particular individual – by virtue of his (sic) education, material wealth or political knowledge – to represent the whole community. From this they were able to derive the idea that non-electors could be adequately represented by the leading men of the community. The suffragists nevertheless argued that those relatively few women who owned sufficient property to qualify for the franchise should be able to exercise it. As the property qualification was lowered in the 1867 and 1884 Franchise Reform Acts, so rich women became more incensed as they watched increasing numbers of working-class men getting the vote. There were, in 1884, for example, some thirty thousand women tenants who themselves farmed their land; the male labourers they hired were enfranchised under the Act, but they were excluded.

The early call for the vote was therefore by no means democratic. In 1870 a very few rich women would have been enfranchised by the Bill introduced by Jacob Bright, although of course by 1884 many more women would have been included with the lower property qualification. The demand for votes for women on the same terms as men also effectively discriminated against married women. The Married Women's Property Act of 1870 gave women control of their earnings and was intended to benefit primarily working women. Other forms of property were controlled by husbands under the doctrine of couveture, which was the idea that 'the very being or legal existence of the wife is suspended during the marriage or at least incorporated and consolidated into that of the husband under whose wing, protection and cover she performs everything'.[3] Thus any property a woman brought to her marriage became her husband's and the propertyless married woman could not qualify for the vote. The suffragists were aware that their call for votes for women on the same terms as men effectively excluded all married women, but they hoped that once the suffrage had been granted women would be able to secure the abolition of couverure. Certainly many of the women represented in this book played an active part in the campaign to reform the married women's property laws. This achieved a large measure of success in 1882, when married women were given control over any wealth they might acquire, although their liability in respect to the property was restricted to a proprietary rather than a personal one, which meant that they had but a limited capacity to sue and contract and were therefore unable to take part in the wider world of business. When the 1874 Bill to enfranchise women was introduced in the Commons by Mr Forsyth (Jacob Bright having been defeated in the election of 1873), he decided that a clause explicitly excluding married women should be inserted in an effort to make the idea of votes for women more acceptable. Although not entirely united on the issue, most suffragists opposed him strongly, not wishing to see married women disqualified by statute law as well as by the common law disabilities of marriage, and the clause was dropped in 1876 when the Bill was reintroduced.

Thus the early women's rights campaigners sought a relatively restricted franchise and based their claim firmly on what they identified as inconsistencies in the law. They stressed that they were law abiding and, being convinced of the justice of their cause, were also initially naively optimistic as to its rapid success. But the fundamentally conservative nature of their arguments is explained in large part by the kind of opposition they faced. As Frances Power Cobbe remarked in 1874 (p. 179), it was something of a triumph to make votes for women a public question at all; when the issue was first raised in the Commons, it was treated as a great joke. The suffragists chose their ground carefully and argued their claim as tightly as possible in order that they might be taken seriously.

Above all, they deliberately avoided any appeal to sentiment. Millicent Fawcett correctly perceived very early on in 1871, that the most powerful force motivating the opposition to women's suffrage was the belief that 'the exercise of political power by women is repugnant to the feelings and quite at variance with a due sense of propriety' (p. 114). Put simply, most men felt that votes for women were unnatural and therefore wrong. But as

Helen Taylor remarked (p. 34), their arguments showed remarkably little clarity of thought and relied heavily on abstract notions as to the true 'nature of woman'. John Bright's powerful speech against women's suffrage in 1876 was full of references to the idea that women were by nature unfit to vote. Because male opponents relied so heavily on sentiment, their arguments were often inconsistent. Few things angered suffragists more than this. In a letter to John Bright, an anonymous suffragist wrote that his speech was so riddled with inconsistencies 'that if it had been spoken by a woman it would have been used by our opponents as a perpetual peg on which to hang the charge of the logical incapacity of the sex' (p. 261). Male opponents to the women's vote argued either that women were inferior and therefore unfit to vote, or that their interests were the same as those of men and therefore adequately represented by men. Lydia Becker, the editor of the *Women's Suffrage Journal* and a central figure in the Parliamentary lobbying of the 1870s and 80s neatly pointed out the illogicality of their position: if women were really morally and intellectually inferior, then they warranted political representation as a separate 'class' within the community; if on the other hand the interests of propertied women were the same as those of men, then there could be no harm in giving women the vote. Feminist logic fell on stony ground, and in the early twentieth century the suffragettes were to abandon patient rational argument as a strategy altogether. However, in the 1870s and 1880s feminists were convinced that the only answer was to show themselves to be as capable as men on men's terms, whether in debate, or in their general conduct. The conviction of these early feminists that they had to 'prove' themselves made their writings often stern and unbending. In particular, they tended to be impatient with those middle-class women who took no interest in public life and, doing as they had been socialised to do, simpered in the company of men, thus reinforcing the male view that women were charming, silly creatures.

While the early claim to the vote was based on narrow legalistic arguments – albeit with good reason – the early suffrage campaigners had a much larger view of what the vote would mean to women. Some, like Rhoda Garrett (p. 159) and Julia Wedgwood (p. 269), emphasised the needs of working women. Since 1851, the Census had revealed there to be considerably more women than men in the population. It followed that there would inevitably be women who would be unable to find a male 'provider' in the shape of a husband and who might, in the absence of material support from male relatives, be forced to rely on their own earnings. It was in order to help such women that Barbara Bodichon and her friends had set up the first Women's Employment Bureau. By the early 1870s, the range of occupations open to women was beginning to widen, for example, women were appearing as clerks and telegraphers in the Post Office, but as Rhoda Garrett pointed out, after 'years of faithful work' they could only expect to earn a maximum of £200 a year. In stating the case for employing women in the civil service to a government inquiry in 1888, Sir Algernon Edward West of the Inland Revenue said simply: 'they are cheap and there is no superannuation [because women left work on marriage].'[4]

The preoccupation of the early feminists was very much with the plight of single women, hence the reluctance of some to take up the cause of married women in the controversy over the wording of the 1874 Women's Suffrage Bill. Nevertheless, many early suffragists were also keen to point out that married women were desperately in need of rights within the private sphere of home and family: to property and to guardianship over children. A very few women argued that the vote would also promote a single moral standard for men and women, but the majority of early women's rights campaigners were wary of this issue in the 1870s, because of its association with Josephine Butler's campaign against the CD Acts, which was felt to be potentially harmful to the suffrage movement's respectability. Echoing Frances Power Cobbe's campaign on the issue of domestic violence towards women, Lydia Becker claimed that women needed the vote as 'a protection for women from the uncontrolled dominion of the savage passions of men' (p. 137).

Thus early suffrage campaigners were clear that the vote represented a means to a larger end, but as Constance Rover has pointed out, they were less clear as to whether woman was 'the strong possessor of many talents, which needed wider scope for their realisation, or . . . [was] so weak that she needed additional means of protection'.[5] On the whole, the early suffragists unhesitatingly believed that middle-class women needed the vote to give greater scope to their talents and working-class women needed its protection. Thus they argued that the vote would enable middle-class women both to broaden the range of occupations open to them, and allow them to help frame the laws that affected the poor, whom it was their bounden duty to visit and care for. Isabella Tod referred to the importance of aiding middle-class women's constructive work of philanthropy in 'elevating the classes who naturally come under their care' (p. 399). Indeed, legislators were in broad sympathy with middle-class women's charitable endeavours and to this end were prepared to grant women's claim to the local franchise. Thus by 1875, single women could vote for municipal councils and both single and married women could act as Poor Law guardians and sit on School Boards.

Julia Wedgwood declared that men dealt with the suffrage issue as if it were one of protection, while feminists demanded it as a matter of justice (p. 281). But Frances Power Cobbe clearly envisioned the vote as a protective device for battered women, who were believed by definition to be working-class women. Feminists also talked about poor women shirt makers' need for protection against exploitation and believed the vote to be a much more effective weapon in this respect than protective legislation, which the vast majority of nineteenth-century feminists strongly opposed on the grounds that it restricted women's employment opportunities. The whole case for women's rights was constructed around the idea that women were asking for 'a fair field and no favour', meaning equality with men necessarily on men's terms. It was a case geared primarily to the middle-class woman's desire to gain entry to the public sphere. Above all the early middle-class feminists wanted to establish the principle of equality and they saw the vote as the most significant symbol in their struggle.

In the documents that follow, we glimpse the views of male opponents of votes for women chiefly through the women's eyes. Inevitably, both political parties feared that women would vote for their opponents if enfranchised, although the prevalence of the view that women would prove a conservative force made some Conservative MPs look more favourably on their cause for a brief period before the 1884 Reform Act. However, after 1884, the Conservative Party enjoyed two decades of almost unbroken rule and had little reason to consider the enfranchisement of women as a counter-weight to the votes of working-class men. Broadly speaking, while leaders of the Conservative Party expressed some sympathy with the feminist cause and the rank and file were implacably opposed, the reverse was true of the Liberal Party. The Liberal leader, Gladstone, belonged to the school who thought women too pure to be sullied by the business of voting. He felt that their 'personal attendance' at elections would constitute a 'practical evil not only of the gravest, but even of an intolerable character' (p. 67). Women's place was in the home. Ladies, it was argued, wanted chivalrous protection and not votes.

Such a view was only marginally less offensive than the opinion that women should not vote because they were stupid and incapable. Feminists pointed out time and again that, to use the words of Anne Isabella Robertson (p. 155), men 'first deny them the means of cultivating their intellect, and then declare they have no intellect to cultivate'. This circular reasoning developed by scientists as well as politicians, underpinned the opposition to women's rights in the nineteenth century. Victorians used their own society as the model from which they formulated their ideas, which in turn justified the position of women as they found it. Having stopped women acquiring certain capacities, science provided the justification for refusing rights on the grounds that those capacities were 'naturally' absent.[6]

Underneath the either sentimental or openly dismissive opposition to enfranchising women ran an unmistakable current of hostility and contempt. This came as a surprise to Arabella Shore, writing in 1870,[7] but it was to become increasingly characteristic of the bitter struggle for women's votes. As Millicent Fawcett observed, the opposition to the 1892 Women's Suffrage Bill was a 'curious mixture . . . of sentimental homage and practical contempt for, and distrust of, women' (p. 435). An explanation as to why this should have been so is crucial to our understanding of why it took women so long to achieve the vote.

Victorian writers idealised married love and the role of the wife and mother. The home was portrayed as a sanctuary in which the wife reigned as 'guardian angel' in the words of Coventry Patmore, or a 'Queen' in Ruskin's imagery. Law and custom as well as literature told women unequivocally that they should confine themselves to their sphere of home and family and this view was legitimated by Victorian science which held that the psychological and cultural differences between men and women, such as women's stereotypically greater tenderness, generosity and intuition, were biologically based. Women's sphere was judged to be 'naturally' different from that of men. Women therefore challenged the whole gender order when they demanded the vote, for their desire to cross the boundary between the private and public spheres was considered to run against the dictates of nature. As the eminent physician Henry Maudsley wrote in 1874, 'sex is fundamental, lies deeper than culture, [and] cannot be ignored or defied with impunity'.[8] Victorian scientists, men of letters and legislators viewed any attempt to change the sex-role system with horror.

It was very difficult for feminists to attack the concept of separate spheres supported as it was by Victorian science, and impossible for them to question the importance attached to the traditional role of wife and mother. They usually contented themselves with acknowledging that there were natural differences between men and women, but in denying that this rendered women necessarily inferior. Both Millicent Fawcett and Emily Pfeiffer argued strongly that women needed a greater say in the nation's affairs as mothers. To Millicent Fawcett, 'the mother-hood of women, either actual or potential, is one of those great facts of everyday life which we must never loose sight of' (p. 419) and as mothers women needed to be able to force legislators to consider the domestic as well as the public sphere by the exercise of their votes. But while MPs were prepared to acknowledge that women could play a role locally, for example, as Poor Law guardians inspecting the conditions of children in the workhouse, they denied their capacity to judge matters concerning diplomacy or empire. Women's role in local government could be viewed as an extension of their domestic role, but affairs of state were firmly located on the other side of the private/public divide. Thus men firmly defended their public space in the polling booth and in the House of Commons, although after the passing of the Corrupt Practices Act in 1883, which set effective limits to spending during election campaigns, both the Liberal and Conservative Parties welcomed the voluntary work women did in the (Conservative) Primrose League and the Women's Liberal Federation, fund-raising and canvassing. This was conveniently regarded as an acceptable extension of their philanthropic endeavour.

By 1892, the date of the last document in this collection, Millicent Fawcett had been actively campaigning for women's suffrage for 33 years. It was to be another 26 years before women over thirty gained the vote, and a further nine years on top of that before all women over 21 were enfranchised. The early twentieth-century campaign for the vote is better known than the early struggle covered by this book, dominated as it was by suffragette militancy, a well-organised opposition to women's suffrage and growing violence on the part of the authorities. As Martha Vicinus has recently remarked,[9] brutality and aggression were the 'sexual consequences of women's attempting to enter a male domain'. Millicent Fawcett was one of the few early suffrage pioneers to see the campaign through to its close and she maintained her steady pursuit of a constitutional strategy – persuading and lobbing – to the end.

The early suffragists wanted above all to join in public life on equal terms with men. By so doing they hoped that public life would be morally elevated, but they had no plan to radically reform its substance. However, before subjecting their goals and strategies to criticism, it is important to remember how courageous it was in 1869 for a woman to speak in public and to understand the extensive framework of oppressive beliefs, customs and legal constraints under which feminists were forced to operate. Furthermore, a small number of suffrage pioneers of the early 1870s built a well-organised movement based on a network of women's suffrage societies. Nevertheless, the suffragists' lobbying tactics suffered a severe defeat when the 1884 Franchise Reform Act failed to include women and by the 1890s the movement was running out of steam and was facing a much better organised opposition, which included a well-publicised group of women 'antis', organised by Mrs Humphry Ward, a popular novelist (see pp. 409–19). The part played by the militant suffragettes in achieving the vote is a source of historical controversy, but, notwithstanding the importance of its contribution, there is no doubt but that the early campaigners badly needed new impetus by the turn of the century.

NOTES

1 Ray Strachey, *The Cause* (London: Bell, 1928), p. 117.
2 PP, 1870 (31), IV, 799, 'Women's Disabilities Bill'.
3 For more discussion of the concept of couveture and the reform of the laws affecting married women's property, see Jane Lewis, *Women in England, 1870–1940* (Brighton: Wheatsheaf, 1984), pp. 119–23.
4 Hilda Martindale, *Women Servants of the State, 1870–1938* (London: Allen & Unwin, 1938), p. 66.
5 Quoted in Constance Rover, *Women's Suffrage and Party Politics in Britain, 1866–1914* (London: Routledge & Kegan Paul, 1967), p. 35.
6 For further discussion see, Elizabeth Fee, 'The sexual politics of Victorian anthropology', in *Clio's Consciousness Raised*, eds. Lois Banner and Mary Hartman (New York: Harper Torchbooks, 1976); Susan Sleeth Mosedale, 'Science corrupted: Victorian biologists consider the "Woman Question" ', *Journal of the History of Biology*, 11 (Spring 1978); and Janet Sayers, *Biological Politics* (London: Tavistock, 1982).
7 Arabella Shore, *An Answer to Mr John Bright's Speech on the Women's Suffrage* (London: by the author, 1870), p. 6.
8 Henry Maudsley, 'Sex and Mind in Education', *Fortnightly Review*, XV (1874), p. 477.
9 Martha Vicinus, *Independent Women* (London: Virago, 1985), p. 265.

Part I
A woman's voice

I wonder, Mr Editor,
    Why I can't have a vote,
And I will not be contented
    Till I've found the reason out.

I am a working woman,
    My voting half is dead;
I hold a house, and want to know
    Why I can't vote instead.

I pay my rates in person,
    Under protest, tho', 'tis true,
But I pay them, and am qualified
    To vote as well as you.

I like my neighbour very well,
    But still I like what's fair,
And paying a rate for him to vote,
    Is neither fair nor square.

My 'compound' rate was heavy enough,
    But this qualification's worse;
If the franchise will not have my voice,
    Let it do without My Purse.

FROM THE *LEEDS EXPRESS*

The English Woman's Journal

Editorial: The Enfranchisement of Women

1 July 1864

AMONG the numerous papers which have appeared in magazines and reviews, during the last few years, on the condition of women, few, if any, have equalled in calm philosophical reasoning and exhaustive treatment an article entitled 'The Enfranchisement of Women,' which appeared in the *Westminster Review* for July 1851. As its contents are as interesting and important now, as at the time of its publication, and as it is by no means well known to the general public, we hope to do some service to our readers by bringing before them some of the leading ideas and principles which it enunciated, while at the same time warning them that no abstract can do justice to its masterly handling of the subject, and that our object is rather to stimulate curiosity to examine the original essay than to lead any one to rest satisfied with the cursory view here given of it, coloured too as that may be by our own thoughts and feelings.

The enfranchisement of women, or in other words, their admission in law and in fact, to equality in all rights political, civil, and social, with the male citizens of the community, is not a new question to thinkers, nor to any one by whom the principles of free and popular government are felt as well as acknowledged.

As a question of justice the case seems too clear for dispute. As one of expediency the more thoroughly it is examined, the stronger it will appear. Those who advocate universal suffrage

13

must grant it to women or be guilty of the flagrant contradiction of terming that universal which they deny to half the human species.* Again, those who do not regard the franchise as a matter of personal right, yet usually uphold some principle of political justice which is inconsistent with the exclusion of all women from this participation in the rights of citizenship; as, for instance, that taxation and representation should be co-extensive. There are many unmarried women who pay taxes. Such a division of mankind into two castes, one born to rule, the other to serve, cannot be justified on the ground of expediency, as will be presently proved, and must result in the demoralization of both, and in hindering the development of the best qualities of our nature.

The great impediment in the way of a calm discussion of this subject is *custom*. *Custom* is still our law, although no longer the insuperable obstacle to all improvement that it once was. Its sanctity was urged against freedom of industry, against freedom of conscience, against freedom of the press, but these liberties have triumphed, as the freedom of women must ultimately triumph, by the law of progression. How custom took its form in early ages in regard to women, is easily explained – it was by the right of physical force. We have not space to enlarge upon this point, but doubtless many illustrations will at once present themselves to the mind of the reader in confirmation of the fact that the domination of physical force was the law of the human race until a comparatively recent period. And 'of all relations, that between man and woman, being the nearest and most intimate, and connected with the greatest number of strong emotions, was sure to be the last to throw off the old rule and receive the new'.

'When a prejudice, which has any hold on the feelings, finds itself reduced to the unpleasant necessity of assigning reasons, it thinks it has done enough when it has reasserted the very point in dispute, in phrases which appeal to the preexisting feeling. Thus, many persons think they have sufficiently justified the restrictions on women's field of action, when they have said that the pursuits from which women are excluded are unfeminine, and that the proper sphere of women is not politics or publicity, but private and domestic life. We deny the right of any portion of the species to decide for another portion, or any individual for another individual, what is and what is not a proper sphere. The proper sphere for all human beings is the largest and highest which they

---

* The chartist who denies the suffrage to women, is a chartist only because he is not a lord: he is one of those levellers who would level only down to themselves.

are able to attain to.' Only complete liberty of choi[ce] [will] determine this. It is as certain that after a short period of ti[me] [the] majority of women will pursue only those avocations for which they are fitted by Nature, as that men do not now follow the legal profession when their talent is for medicine, or enter the church when they have a genius for painting. Of course we meet with exceptions, with men who are not in their right places, and who have discovered this too late in life to change, but that these *are* exceptions we believe every unbiassed person will allow.

We do not enter here into the alleged differences in physical and mental qualities between the sexes, because the field of enquiry on this subject is too wide for our present purpose; but to be assured that there is no inherent difference so great as to preclude women from the studies and pursuits of men, we need but to recall the names of such female rulers as Elizabeth of England, Maria Theresa, Catherine of Russia, and Jeanne d'Albret, mother of Henri Quatre; of such artists as Rosa Bonheur and Harriet Hosmer; of such a poet as Mrs Browning, of such a writer on science as Mrs Somerville.

But the objection is more likely to be made that politics and other public pursuits are unfit for women, than that women are unfit for these occupations, and this objection will turn mainly upon these three points; first, the incompatibility of active life with maternity, and with the cares of a household; secondly, the inexpediency of making an addition to the already excessive pressure of competition in every kind of professional or lucrative employment; and, thirdly, its alleged hardening effect on the character.

The maternity argument can apply only to mothers, and when we consider that the ranks of single women are becoming larger year by year; that there are numerous cases of widows, whose children are old enough not to need the mother's constant supervision; that there are childless wives and women who marry so late in life as to have passed ten or fifteen years of *ennui* and uselessness previous to their marriage, are we not losing sight of the claims of a large minority?

By allowing no other scope for a woman's energies but the duties of a wife and mother, we force thousands to enter upon these at an early age before the judgment is formed or the feelings matured. Impelled by no high affection, but happy for the time in the discovery of an object in life, how many rush precipitately into marriages of convenience, to taste their bitter fruits when repentance is too late.

Those who are mothers, and who seek to discharge faithfully

the sacred responsibilities which maternity entails, will never be drawn from these duties by finding the paths to professional distinction and commercial industry laid open to them. Surely, it is late in the day to have to repeat Sydney Smith's often quoted words; 'What,' he says, 'can be more absurd than to suppose that the care and perpetual solicitude that a mother feels for her children depends on her ignorance of Greek and mathematics, and that she would desert an infant for a quadratic equation?' As for the question of competition, if we take the worst possible result of the introduction of female labour into those fields now occupied by men alone, it can be only that a man and woman jointly would not earn much more than a man now earns separately, and even this would be but a passing state of things – a transition. Even in this case great benefits would arise from the woman's acquiring a pecuniary independence. She would at once be treated with more consideration by men, and, what is of still more importance, would acquire that self-respect, in which, in its higher forms, she is now so often wanting. Ultimately, the increase of productive labour, and the proportional decrease of unproductive consumers, must augment the wealth of the country, and thus tend to the welfare of individuals.

Thirdly, as to the hardening effect of these proposed changes upon the nature of women. The objection would be valid were we in a ruder state of society, where supremacy could be maintained only by physical force. But in the present age, men have to fight with circumstances only; and in this warfare, women already bear their part. Every man who has any woman dependent upon him for support, every man who possesses any woman's love or sympathy, and who is oppressed by the circumstances against which he is making war, must know that she is exposed to their hardening or other influences with him. We all suffer now – men and women – more from what is *said* than from what is *done*, and nothing but complete seclusion from society can shield any of us from this evil.

But the real point to be judged is, whether it be wise or just, to doom one half of the human species to a state of forced subordination to the other half. The only reason to be given for the continuance of this state of things is that men like it; and they have succeeded in educating women into the belief that only those qualities which are useful or convenient to men are to be regarded as virtues.

Civilization has mitigated some of the evils arising from the dependence of woman upon man, but it has brought with it others which did not exist in a ruder state of society. It has enforced the claims of the weak upon the strong, of the governed upon the ruler. As when the divine right of kings was still acknowledged, but the opinion of mankind condemned the selfish use of power, monarchs were no longer actuated by mere passion and caprice in their conduct towards their subjects; so, while custom still keeps women in subjection, men, whose minds are refined by intellectual cultivation, own the obligation to treat them with kindness and with that deference which the strong owe to the weak. Civilization, however, has also, while altering, and to some extent ameliorating the condition of women, produced a most serious evil by this very change. At a time when women performed manual labour for their lords, and at a later date when, though treated with greater gentleness and consideration, they led a life apart from their husbands, who only returned home as to a resting place from pleasure or business, men were not affected in their intellectual progress by the influence of women. Their moral nature might suffer, but their intellectual character depended on a different class of influences. Since, however, men have ceased to find pleasure and excitement in violent bodily exercises, and in rude merriment and intemperance, they have few tastes which they do not possess in common with women. This sympathy draws them into ever closer companionship, so that the best men are becoming more and more devoted to private and domestic interests, and as they fall daily more under these influences, they are in danger of losing all sense of the importance of a wider range of ideas and of the cultivation of that public spirit which can alone make them pioneers of progress and benefactors of their species.

When we speak of the deteriorating influence of women as they now are, it must not be supposed that we consider them intellectually inferior to men, but that the want of a proper education and the constant employment of their faculties upon petty cares and pursuits produce, except in rare instances, a certain pettiness of character incompatible with high tastes and aims. Men who are in constant association with women who are their inferiors, must suffer from this companionship. 'If one of the two has no knowledge, and no care about the great ideas and purposes which dignify life, or about any of its practical concerns save personal interests and personal vanities, her conscious, and still more her unconscious influence, will, except in rare cases, reduce to a secondary place in his mind, if not entirely extinguish, those interests which she cannot or does not share.'

But there is now a large class of moderate reformers who would educate women to be the companions of men; that is to say, would give them a knowledge on a variety of subjects sufficient to enable them to be interested in the conversation of educated men, while they are not to pursue such studies for their own sake. Knowledge sought with such an aim, must necessarily be superficial, as indeed the result has proved it to be. We meet on all sides, women who have a smattering of science, of art, of history, of politics, but except accomplishments, they are taught nothing thoroughly. The consequence of this is, that a man who has such a companion acquires a dictatorial habit, having to decide all questions which arise between them. In this case there is merely the contact between an active and a passive mind, while the only mental communion which is improving is that between two active minds.

And until stronger incentives are given to women, this state of things must continue. 'High mental power in women will be but an exceptional accident, until every career is open to them, and until they, as well as men, are educated for themselves, and for the world – not one sex for the other.'

It is also to the hope of seeing this change gradually effected, that we must look for reform in our system of parliamentary representation, or rather to that portion of it which it is most difficult to touch by any act of legislation. We allude to the tendency which exists towards a lowering of the class of representatives for our large cities, and especially for the metropolis. The best men will not truckle to the mob, therefore the mob (that portion of it which possesses the franchise) must be improved before a better class of representatives will offer themselves. And here female influence, rightly directed, could do more than all else. Women of the higher and middle classes are brought into more immediate contact than men with those whom we may call the lower-middle-class, and such influence as they exercise is even now often good in its effects; but how immeasurably would it be increased and improved by their own greater cultivation!

Women's influence also upon their own class in the matter is of great importance. It exists already for evil. The political opinions of an Englishwoman are at present upon the side by which censure is likely to be escaped, or worldly advancement secured; and, having no political vote, she is not restrained by that sense of responsibility which the actual possession of such a power must give to all reflecting and conscientious minds. Acting by her counsel, the husband satisfies himself that he is but sacrificing a lower to a higher duty when he neglects the welfare of his country for the advancement of his children in worldly honors – honors which in no way bring them happiness, and which are often but the excuse for his own greed of money or for an unworthy ambition.

There is a prevalent belief that, though the present position of women may be a hindrance to the intellectual development of men, their moral influence is always good. We are even told that married life is the great counteractive of selfishness in men. This view of the case is a superficial one. The very fact of a man's being placed in a position of almost despotic power over his wife and children must give him a sense of his own importance eminently calculated to promote selfishness. The exceptions are in cases of high and generous minds, with whom the feeling of responsibility in being made the arbiter of another's destiny and happiness produces a disposition to be too lenient in judging all cases between them submitted to his discretion, and thus the weaker side is enabled to take an ungenerous advantage of generosity. In average cases, however, if the wife succeeds in gaining her object, it is by indirect means. 'We are not now speaking of cases in which there is anything deserving the name of strong affection on both sides. That, where it exists, is too powerful a principle not to modify greatly the bad influences of the situation; it seldom, however, destroys them entirely. Much oftener the bad influences are too strong for the affection, and destroy it. The highest order of durable and happy attachments would be a hundred times more frequent than they are, if the affection which the two sexes sought from one another were that genuine friendship which only exists between equals in privileges as in faculties.' If such unions were more frequent we should not have to lament the utter absence of mental progress so often observable in men who marry at an early age. All social sympathies which have not an elevating must have a lowering effect, and we see an exemplification of this truth here. We find many men who began life with wide sympathies and high aspirations which under favorable circumstances would have widened and grown to produce good fruits in their season, becoming utterly careless of their earlier interests and devoted merely to the love of gain and selfish ease. We cannot, therefore, in the interest of men as well as in that of women, allow the condition of women to remain as it is. Men are no longer, if they ever were, independent of it, and women have been raised just high enough to have the power of lowering men to their own level.

There is one other popular objection to the emancipation of women which is generally urged with great effect: – women, it is said, do not care for or seek freedom for themselves. If this were true it would constitute no fair reason for excluding them from those rights and privileges which would contribute to their progress.

The only good for every human being is the highest cultivation of *all* the faculties with which he is endowed. The indifference of Asiatics to political freedom, and of savage races to civilization does not prove that these are not desirable for them, or that they will never enjoy them. But we assert that it is not true that women do not desire freedom. Nearly every woman wishes it for herself, but she has been so educated that she fears to appear unfeminine, and to be disgraced in the eyes of men – her tribunal – if she openly express her wishes or opinions on the subject.

Literary women are not blameless in this matter. Their success depends so much upon their obtaining the good will of the other sex, that they servilely flatter men into the belief that they are satisfied with their position. They believe that there are few men who do not dislike strength, sincerity, or high spirit in a woman. 'They are, therefore, anxious to earn pardon and toleration for whatever of these qualities their writings may exhibit on other subjects, by a studied display of submission on this: that they may give no occasion for vulgar men to say (what nothing will prevent vulgar men from saying) that learning makes women unfeminine, and that literary ladies are likely to be bad wives.'

Let all honorable paths to distinction be open to both sexes, and the event will prove whether women really desire and have within them the capacity for that intellectual and moral development, which hitherto has only been attained by individuals, and in the face of difficulties which only genius or an almost superhuman perseverance could have overcome.

Helen Taylor

The claim of Englishwomen to the suffrage constitutionally considered*

1867

AMONG the demonstrations of opinion which the discussions on Parliamentary Reform have drawn forth during the past session, no one was more remarkable than the petition signed by fifteen hundred ladies, which was presented to the House of Commons by Mr J. Stuart Mill. This petition is comprised in a few short sentences, and sets forth that the possession of property in this country carries with it the right to vote in the election of representatives in Parliament; that the exclusion from this right of women holding property is therefore anomalous; and that the petitioners pray that the representation of householders may be provided for without distinction of sex.

This claim, that since women are permitted to hold property they should also be permitted to exercise all the rights which, by our laws, the possession of property brings with it, is put forward in this petition on such strictly constitutional grounds, and is advanced so entirely without reference to any abstract rights, or fundamental changes in the institutions of English society, that it is impossible not to feel that the ladies who make it have done so with a practical purpose in view, and that they conceive themselves to be asking only for the recognition of rights which

*Originally published in the *Westminster Review*.

21

flow naturally from the existing laws and institutions of the country.

That a considerable number of ladies should think it worth while to examine into their actual political status, and finding it to all appearance inconsistent with the principles of the British Constitution, should proceed to lay what they term the 'anomaly' before the House of Commons, is assuredly an important symptom of our national condition; an evidence that the minds of English people, men and women, are actively at work in many directions where they might have been but little expected to penetrate. It is, at the same time, a sign of that disposition which various causes (partly political and partly philosophical) have tended to foster of late years, to seek the reform of existing evils rather in the development than in the overthrow of the present order of things.

It may appear, at first sight, as though in proportion to the millions of Englishwomen who live happily under our laws, or who groan under all the miseries of wife-beating and other social evils, without a thought of how their condition might be affected by legislation, fifteen hundred women are too small a number to be worthy of a moment's consideration. But if we reflect a little on the peculiar position of women, and their usual ways of thinking – on their habitual reticence on all subjects which they are accustomed to consider as beyond their own sphere, their timidity and dread of exposing their names to public observation, their deference even to the most unreasonable prejudices of those who have any claim on their affections, their clinging to old associations, and their regard for the opinion of all who are even remotely connected with them – we shall see reason to think that these fifteen hundred ladies, who have not hesitated to affix their names to a public document, and to pronounce a decided opinion, open to the controversy and criticism of all the world, must represent an extraordinarily important phase of thought. It is not going too far to say, that for one woman who can and will pronounce openly on such a subject, there must be at least ten whom family hindrances or habitual timidity will prevent from expressing an opinion, even if they have formed any. And the number must be still greater of those whose minds are only partially prepared for any ideas on such subjects, who are little in the habit of arriving at any definite conclusions at all on political matters, but who, as they have passed through much of the same experience, and lived in the same state of society as their more energetic or more active-minded sisters, must have been liable to the same influences, and are not at all unlikely to adopt the same way of thinking, when it is put before them in so plausible and so little startling a form as we find it in this petition. The peculiarly dependent position of women is another circumstance which must add much to our estimate of the number really represented by these fifteen hundred petitioners. There is scarcely a family in the kingdom where a mother, or a widowed or unmarried sister, or one married to a kind husband, is not the intimate friend and confidant of a daughter, a mother, or a sister in a less fortunate position. Those who have been brought up together, who have learnt from one another's experience, or who have imbibed from one another the same ways of feeling, are often separated in appearance by the political or religious opinions of their fathers or husbands, or by a domestic despotism which only allows one person to express openly what many think. Moreover, when we remember that few women are able both to form and to express political opinions at all, without the assistance and encouragement of some at least among their male relations, it becomes evident that every woman who does form such must be looked upon as the representative of a considerable body of opinion. And when the thought thus expressed is so comparatively new as to meet with little external encouragement, it must be strongly rooted in many unseen ramifications before it can have grown vigorous enough to show itself in a clear, definite, and conspicuous shape. But even independently of any of these considerations, it is impossible to glance down the list of signatures appended to this petition without seeing that it includes a proportion large for the actual number of names, both of the intelligence and the property of Englishwomen. With all these facts before us, we think we are justified in repeating that the appearance of such a claim, supported in such a manner, is a significant indication of the direction public opinion is taking.

What we find asked for, then, in this petition seems to be that Englishwomen shall be included in that measure of political freedom which the wisdom of Parliament sees fit to grant to Englishmen. This amount of political enfranchisement is asked for by the means by which men and women have for ages been accustomed, in this country, to make their wants known to the legislature; namely, by petition to the House of Commons. It would appear as if the election to Parliament of a member who, before his election, distinctly enunciated his opinion that women ought to have votes, has, in the judgment of the petitioners, opened for them a new prospect of getting their claims heard. That a writer of the scientific eminence and political ability of the member for Westminster holds such an opinion, and moreover

23

openly proclaiming it he has been returned to Parliament by a constituency influenced only by public motives, is certainly a fact that may very justly encourage these ladies to think that the political representation of women is really a question ripe for discussion; and it may fairly give them reason to hope that if they can advance any rational grounds for their claims, they will receive reasonable attention.

This being the case, we propose to examine, in some degree, not merely into the general purport of this petition, but also into the specific reasons assigned in it for the claim which it puts forward. For although it would be in itself a remarkable thing that so many Englishwomen are now prepared to ask for some sort of political representation, yet more or less increase of the liberty allowed to women has been recommended by men and asked by women, both in this country and others, for a long time past. Some relaxation of the restrictions under which the female sex has hitherto laboured is indeed a natural and inevitable consequence of the advancing freedom and civilization of the other sex; but this movement is marked by what appear to us some novel and especially national characteristics. It is interesting to observe what form this general tendency towards freedom assumes when it shows itself among a large body of Englishwomen; by what means they propose to work it out, and by what train of reasoning they seek to recommend it to their countrymen.

The petitioners ground their request on the principles of the British Constitution. They assert that certain facts in our existing system establish that women cannot be considered to be without the pale of the Constitution, for that there are precedents to show that its general principles have already been applied to women in some particular cases. They point out that in this country the franchise is dependent upon property, and that the acknowledgment of women as sovereigns among us shows that women are not considered disqualified for government. From these two principles, both of which are undoubted parts of the British Constitution as it stands at this day – the representation of property, and government by female sovereigns – the petitioners draw the evident inference that where the female sex is no bar to the higher, it cannot reasonably be to the lower privileges of political life, when those privileges are dependent upon conditions (such as the possession of property) which women actually fulfil. And they characterize the exclusion of half the human race from any share in self-government as an 'anomaly' in our representative system.

Whether this way of treating the subject arises from the

petitioners themselves only looking at it from this peculiarly English point of view, or whether it is adopted as the one likely to meet with the most general support and the smallest amount of dissent, it is equally a sign of the times. If the idea of the political representation of women has now made its appearance among us in a peculiarly English dress, and one adapted to the exigencies of the reform discussions of the past session (which have turned so specially on the representation of property, and a suitable property qualification), we cannot refuse to admit that it is all the fitter to take its place among the political ideas of the day; and that it has thereby assumed a more practical character than if it had been attempted to establish it on the grounds of any more general or philosophical systems of representation. Without attempting to go at length into the subject, it will be easily seen that the representation of women might be urged with considerable force on almost any of these systems; but it is itself more in harmony with our present institutions than they are. Nothing can be more entirely foreign to our whole English system than Universal Suffrage, or than either Personal or Class Representation. All these systems, whether we hold them to be in the abstract pernicious or beneficial, are so entirely unable to coalesce with that already prevailing among us, that if they are to be tried it would be a wise policy to introduce them *parallel*, so to speak, to our present institutions, of which they are not the development, but properly and literally a re-form. But if any of these systems be admitted, either partially or entirely, either in theory or in practice, women would find a place under them equally with men. Universal Suffrage by its very name includes them; personal representation, if carried out on principle, has for its necessary consequences the representation of women, since the leading idea of personal representation is the effort to secure a hearing to every individual interest or opinion in the nation, however insignificant or obscure. And the totally opposite principle, of class representation, is in the highest degree favourable to the political interests of women, who, if considered as a class, are the most numerous class in the country. Indeed, no advocate of the system of class representation can for a moment refuse in consistency to recognise the claims of so important a class, and of one which is certainly bound together by a community of interests in many of the largest branches of human affairs. Those who disapprove of all attempts at class representation, and believe them to be a lingering remains of an effete state of society, and those who disapprove of special legislation grounded on difference of sex and enforcing by law the exclusion of women from all masculine occupations or privileges, may consistently object to consider women as a class, or to make any claim for them as such. But this is not possible for those who group all women together, as actual or potential wives and mothers. They, on the contrary, must in consistency admit that the wives and mothers of the nation, regarded as a class, form one before whose vital importance, and overwhelming numbers, all other classes shrink into insignificance. For independently of the consideration that women are in this country more numerous absolutely than the sum of all the many classes into which men are divided by their occupations, it is evident that if women are permitted no other interests than those which they hold in common with all women by virtue of their sex, these interests must be of proportionately greater consequence to women than the equivalent interests are to men, since men have other interests in life as well.

If therefore the lady petitioners had chosen to urge their claims simply as women, and not as English women, they would, on the theory of class representation, have been able to take up very strong ground. But, apart from all consideration of the abstract truth of this theory, it seems to us that they have done well to leave it aside. For it is, as we have indicated, diametrically opposed to the English political system, and indeed more fundamentally so than personal representation. For if the English system refuses to recognise the mere individual as a political unit, and if it insists that he must have palpable evidence that he requires protection for something more precious (we presume) than life or honour, before it admits him to any share in protecting himself; still more does it refuse to protect interests which do not belong to any one in particular, but which are diffused over vast numbers of men, grouped together under the merely ideal definition of a class. Property represented by an individual is the true political unit among us; and in this we recognise the influence of those mediæval habits of thought, which, putting forward living persons as the representatives of rights supposed to be inherent in particular functions or particular localities, was itself practically an advance on those Oriental ideas of caste which survive in the privileges of class, sex, or colour. This mode of thought was due partly, no doubt, to the influence of the Church, which gave and still gives examples of it in the 'incumbent' and 'parson' or 'persona,' who derives his rights neither from privilege of birth nor even from his functions as priest, but from the induction into the enjoyment of certain property for his life, of which he has the management; and of which he becomes, so to speak, the bodily expression, the 'persona,' responsible for the due payment of all charges. It was diffused and perpetuated by the arrangements made under the feudal system for the protection of property in times of war and against an illegal violence; and it seems to have been held, that as only those possessing property could be obliged to furnish a contingent share towards the expenses of government, they alone had any direct interest to protect against the central authority, which, in so far as it preserved peace and order in lawless times, must have stood in the position of gratuitous benefactor towards the unpropertied portion of the people. However this may be, there can be no doubt that the principle underlying our English system of government, is that men are endowed with the privilege of voting in the election of members of the Legislature, in order to enable them to protect their property against undue taxation, or other legislative enactments that might injuriously affect it. So deeply is this idea rooted in the English mind, that long after the separation of the American colonies we find American politicians arguing against conferring votes on negro slaves, upon the express ground that slaves, not being able to hold property, do not require political representation; and for authority for this point of view we find them referring to the acknowledged principles of the British system of law, which, it is well known, is considered as the foundation of the institutions of the United States, wherever not abrogated by the American Constitution or by special legislation.

Lord Somers, in 1703, speaking in the name of the House of Lords, lays it down that 'The Lords . . . conceive that giving a vote for a representative in Parliament is the essential privilege whereby every Englishman preserves his property; and that whatsoever deprives him of such vote, deprives him of his birthright.' The line of thought, or train of reasoning, plainly to be traced here, is certainly very favourable to the claim of the ladies. The 'birthright' of an Englishman is defined by this high authority as the privilege of preserving his property. He is refused any birthright inherent in himself, but it is laid down that by the possession of property he comes into possession of a privilege attached to property; a privilege which is a '*birthright*' apparently, because it is 'essential' to the system of law under which he is born. It is observable that this way of considering a *birthright* as not of *natural* but of *legal* origin, is in conformity with modern habits of thought in regard to civilized men, the natives of civilized societies; but exactly in proportion as it is opposed to any *à priori* theories of the rights of man, it is also opposed to any attempt to give or withhold privileges for merely *natural* reasons, such as difference of sex. It is hard to see how, if the law of England endows a woman with property, it can, consistently with this legal dictum, deprive her of the 'essential privilege' (which, as we understand Lord Somers, must be her 'birthright' if she is born in England) whereby her property is to be preserved. Undoubtedly, Parliament may make special enactments excepting particular classes of English subjects from the rights they would otherwise enjoy in common with the rest of the community; and from this point of view the adoption of the word 'male' in every Act of Parliament which confers the suffrage, must be looked upon as the adoption of an exceptional form, used (as Lord Somers would seem to say) to 'deprive' Englishwomen of property of their 'birthright.' Now, it is assuredly in harmony with all our institutions that any class of persons, labouring under an exceptional disability as a consequence of special legislation, should petition Parliament for its removal, and should appeal against it to the general principles of the Constitution; while the burden of adducing sufficient reasons for such an exceptional disability must, in justice, lie with its supporters.

In pointing out the quite peculiar position occupied by female possessors of property, the lady petitioners have undeniably touched upon a weak point in our present political system, a kind of gap, where in political life there exists no equivalent for what we have in social and civil life. It is an 'anomaly,' as they assert. For who else among us, entitled by law to hold property to a certain amount, is nevertheless deprived of the vote which the British Constitution looks upon as the safeguard of property? The answer will be – Minors, idiots, lunatics, and criminals. These, and these only, are classed politically along with women. But none of these are so classed in anything but in politics. In no other respect can their standing among us be compared with that of women. We do not mean to compliment the ladies by asserting that they may not be as weak, as foolish, as mad, or as wicked as any of all these classes of the community; but we might be as enthusiastic a woman-hater as ever wrote in the *Saturday Review*, and still a moment's reflection on the legal position of these classes would show that it has nothing in common with that of women administering their own property. However incapable these latter may be, our institutions do actually permit them to administer their property for themselves. Women do actually undertake the responsibility and enjoy the privileges of property, excepting only the privilege of voting. They are liable for debts; they can enter into contracts; they can alienate or they can purchase at their own free will and pleasure; they can devise by will or gift; they can sue or be sued in courts of law in vindication of their rights or in punishment of their shortcomings; they can release others from legal obligations towards themselves, and they can incur legal obligations towards others in regard of the property they hold. But minors, idiots, lunatics, and criminals can do none of all these things. They merely hold the right to the possession of property at some future time when they shall have become different from what they now are, along with the right to transfer it to their heirs. Upon them the law bestows no power of dealing with their possessions as seems good to themselves; no power of vindicating their own doings before a legal tribunal; no power of prosecuting those who attack their pecuniary interests; no power, in short, of 'preserving their property' before the civil law.

Nor is this all. The legal powers of women in regard to property are no dead letter. These powers are not an obsolete right known only to antiquarians, hidden away among the curiosities of the Constitution, exercising no influence upon the world around us; a mere chance survivor of effete customs, an anachronism in the society in which we live. So far from it, the exercise of these powers is an established part of our social system, and every day becoming a more prominent part. It awakens no surprise by its novelty; it shocks the prejudices of no one among us; on the contrary, he who should propose to deprive maiden ladies of their little independence, and put it into the hands of their nephews, or who should recommend a law to place all widows' property under the control of their deceased husband's brother, would be universally looked upon as un-English, and as either a fanatical admirer of exploded absurdities, or a would-be introducer of Oriental ideas. Not only, therefore, do our laws permit women to exercise all the rights of property, but it is customary with us for women to do so, and public opinion regards their doing so as usual and proper. Nor is it any novelty among us. Although we know that in the more disturbed and lawless periods of our history it was necessary to make haste and marry rich unmarried girls and widows (unless they were willing to retire into convents), in order to secure protection for their riches, still we cannot point to any precise date when this state of things came to an end, and when advancing civilization and general respect for law relieved rich women from the fear of outrage, and made it possible for them to dispense with a male protector. It is very possible that the dispersion of the monastic houses may have hastened this stage in the emancipation of women; it is still more probable that the rise of the middle classes had much to do with it; but from whatever cause it originated, it has long been an established thing with us that no woman is obliged to hand over her property to any one unless she so pleases, and that if she does not so please, law and custom allow her the fullest liberty, and an absolute equality of right with men, excepting only in the single instance of political right.

Whence, then, comes this exception? Why, when they possess the necessary property, are women, alone among citizens of full age and sane mind, unconvicted of crime, disabled by a merely personal circumstance (that of sex) from exercising a right attached by our institutions to property and not to persons? What is the historical origin of this anomaly? For an historical origin there must be, and it appears to us shortsighted to attribute it to any of those general theories about the natural functions of women which it might be necessary to have recourse to in explaining a similar anomaly in a system based on universal suffrage. The explanation must, we think, be sought in our own history, and is not far to seek. It is probably the very fact to which we have referred, that, during the earlier period of our constitutional history, society was in so unsettled a state that women could not practically administer their own property, which led to women's not being included among the voters in the elections of members of Parliament. While women did not actually fulfil the other functions of owners of property, the political functions were naturally not attributed to them. Even though it might be by no fault of their own that women could not govern their own property in those times, still it was not likely that they should be admitted to a share in the political government of property which was not actually under their management. The Constitution was perfectly consistent in permitting the feminine nominal owners of the property to derive as much benefit from their civil ownership as they could manage to do, while it ignored all personal claims on their part to political influence derived from property which they were not (from whatever causes) practically competent to administer. Many centuries elapsed after our electoral system had been brought into tolerably regular operation, before the progress of law and order enabled women, as a matter of course, to exercise openly the civil rights which the law attaches to property. It is in the natural course of things that now, after one or two centuries of the practical enjoyment of their civil rights, intelligent women begin to ask why the political rights should not accompany them.

To this question, there can, we apprehend, be but one answer in the negative, at all consistent with the general principles of English law and institutions. It may be said that society is still in too uncivilized a condition to be able to protect women in the enjoyment of their political rights; for that it is still beyond the power of the Government to prevent them from being molested by riotous proceedings at polling-booths, or coerced by undue interference on the part of their male relations. It is evident that, even if this statement had a broader foundation in fact than we believe it has, this foundation would be diminished by the natural progress of every year that passes over our heads. But it can scarcely be seriously maintained that the central authority which can preserve Hyde Park, against the whole working population of London, for the recreation and health of ladies and children of the upper classes, is incompetent to preserve order in and around polling-booths on the exceptional occasion of an election. And if neither the troops, nor the police, nor any number of special constables could prevent women from being subjected to insult on these occasions, it would still be perfectly easy to afford to them the same immunities as are already accorded to non-resident members of the Universities of Oxford and Cambridge, and to permit ladies also to record their votes by means of voting papers.

The notion that the possession of a vote would expose women to improper coercion on the part of their male relations, will still less bear examination than the theory that our Government is not strong enough to protect any class of its subjects in the exercise of whatever rights it may see fit to accord them. The strength of the motives that would be likely to induce men to interfere with their female relatives in the disposal of their property, is incalculably greater than the strength of the motives that, even in times of political excitement, would urge men to try to overawe women in the exercise of the suffrage. The law has for centuries ruled that women possess sufficient strength of mind to protect their own pecuniary interests; and it has left them to seek the same redress as men, if they find themselves subjected to force or improper influence in doing so. The will of an elderly lady is not cancelled because of the possible influence her son may have used to induce her to make it in his favour, any more than the will of an old gentleman is set aside on account of the possible interference of his daughter. The law very properly refuses to consider whether men are likely to domineer over women, or whether women are likely to cajole men, and in either case it requires ample proof before proceeding to act on particular instances of either disposition. The law, which has, most properly, left women to fight their own battle (and the battle of their heirs) against private greed, cannot be required in these days to provide exceptional protection for them against the comparatively mild force of political enthusiasm.

No candidate for parliamentary honours ever more ardently desired them, than a spendthrift nephew desires that his rich aunt would leave her comfortable fortune to him, rather than to her favourite minister; nevertheless, we none of us dream of depriving the poor lady of all control over her property, in order to protect her against the unprincipled importunities either of the minister or of the nephew. Yet how great is the prize that either of these may hope from the weakness of only one woman, compared to the triumph of the parliamentary candidate, even if every qualified woman in his constituency could be persuaded or compelled to vote for him! To say that such danger of undue coercion as women might be exposed to by the possession of a vote, however small, is wanton, inasmuch as women seldom care for politics, is to overlook the drift of the constitutional claim made by the petitioners, and which it has been the purpose of this paper to follow out. The English representative system, such as it is, good or bad, represents not persons but property. By holding property women take on the rights and duties of property. If they are not interested in politics, their property is. Poor-laws and game-laws, corn-laws and malt-tax, cattle-plague compensation Bills, the manning of the navy, and the conversion of Enfield rifles into breechloaders – all these things will make the property held by Englishwomen more or less valuable to the country at large of this and the succeeding generations. It is on the supposition that property requires representation that a property-qualification is fixed by the law. It is not the mere personal interests of the rich man that a property franchise is supposed to protect; were it so, the injustice of giving the franchise to the rich man only would have been too grossly palpable to have endured so long, or to be capable of as good a defence as the English Constitution; for the rich man's person is no dearer to himself or to the nation than the poor man's. Nor is it granted to him because he is supposed to be, by some mysterious dispensation of providence, endowed by the possession of a 10*l* house with a special capacity to understand and care for the personal happiness of himself or others. The law acts upon the supposition that he who is in actual possession of property will be keener and more efficient to protect it than any other person. The abhorrence of our ancestors for allowing land to fall into *main-morte* proceeded in part from this mode of thought; a habit of considering it as at once the general interest that land should be efficiently managed and protected, and as the most effectual way of providing for its being so, to place it under the guardianship of an individual personally interested in it. It is to us almost indubitable, that the same legislators who enacted the

Statute of Mortmain would, if as much English property had been in the hands of women as at the present day, either have deprived them of the right of holding property at all, or else have invested them with the power of protecting it in Parliament, rather than have permitted it to remain unrepresented as it now is.

The next question that will probably be asked by such of our readers as have accompanied us thus far in the consideration of the peculiar line of argument of the Ladies' Petition, is – Supposing this petition be granted, and that Parliament were to extend the suffrage to duly qualified women, what good would it do to them or to the country in general? And, on the other hand, what harm might be expected to arise from it? And, looking at the matter from the point of view in which it is placed by the petition, these two questions are perfectly reasonable; it is indeed in our eyes one of the merits of this point of view that it brings us so directly and so logically to the consideration of these really practical questions, and enables us to leave aside all those considerations either of abstract right or of accidental custom and sense of fitness, the discussion of which is certain to be as difficult as it is usually indecisive. For if we acknowledge with the petitioners, that the exclusion of women from the right to vote in the election of members of Parliament is an anomaly, the question of right may be granted, but the question of expediency is not. We may acknowledge that their exclusion is exceptional, the result of exceptional legislation, producing an invidious distinction under which they alone labour; and yet we may think it desirable to impose such a distinction, and to establish such an exception. But then we must be prepared with reasons for doing so. What this petition appears to us to have pointed out is, that no one who accepts the principles upon which the British Constitution and English society are established, can consider the exclusion of women from political privileges as a matter of course. On the contrary, he must look upon it as the result of anomalous legislation, requiring to be justified either by its urgent necessity or by its evident advantages.

Unfortunately for anything like clearness of thought, it is very seldom that we find people willing to look at the subject in so simple and practical a manner; too often, on the contrary, the very persons who would most object to importing theories of the abstract rights of man, into a discussion on the franchise, will go off into vague generalities on the nature of women, and fancy that some such universal axioms can be somehow applicable to the legal position of particular classes of Englishwomen in the nineteenth century. Now we are far from denying that general principles must underlie not only all theory, but also all practice. We readily admit that most people do in reality either accept or reject the abstract theory of the natural equality of all men, just as they do in reality talk either poetry or prose; and so, in like manner, most people have their own theory as to the special aptitudes of women. But the theory that 'all women are destined for family life' is about as applicable to any practical settlement of the franchise in this country, as the somewhat equivalent one that 'all men are born free and equal.' We may assent to either assertion, or we may dissent from it, without being one whit further advanced in the question under discussion; for in fact they have nothing whatever to do with it, unless we propose to pull down the whole fabric of English law and society altogether, and build it up anew from its foundations. Whether or not all women are destined for family life, all Englishwomen do not live it; whether or not women are fitted by nature to be anything else than wives and mothers, many Englishwomen are something else; whether law ought or ought not to recognise women as anything else, the law of England does so recognise them. Marriage may or may not be the only good, the only ideal existence for all women; but the law of England has long ago refused to drive women into marriage, as sheep are driven into a fold, by shutting every gate against them but the one they are intended to go through. Even if all unmarried women ought to be looked upon as stray sheep, still, as we have already seen, both law and custom in this country, have bestowed upon them abundance of rights and privileges; and the assertion that such people have no right even to exist, is out of place in answer to the question, whether the rights they already possess do not naturally imply one right more?

It seems to us, therefore, that no abstract ideas of woman's mission can reasonably be brought forward as proof of an urgent necessity for the exclusion of women from the franchise under our existing system; and that if the question is asked – What good would be gained by their admission? the answer is very plain – Whatever good is to be gained by the British Constitution. If that be a good, it is evident that the carrying it out must be good. The perpetuation of an omission which originated in circumstances that have long since passed away, must do as much harm to those who are omitted as would have been done to their countrymen if the British Constitution had not existed. If it be an advantage to be able to protect one's property by the power of voting for members of Parliament, the possession of this advantage must be a good for all those who live and own property under Parliamentary Government. The good that would be done to women themselves is, in fact, not open to dispute, unless we dispute the advantage of Parliamentary Government and representation of property; and in that case we must dispute the advantage of the English system of government altogether.

If, continuing to confine ourselves to a strictly constitutional point of view, we ask what would be the advantage to the country in general of the political representation of female holders of property, on the same conditions as men, we think, as we have already indicated, that the reply is equally clear. If the representation in Parliament of those who are interested in property is a national good, tending to the preservation and fostering of all property interests, to the increase of our national wealth, and to the handing down to our descendants of the national property under favourable conditions, then the disfranchisement of any class of holders of property must be an evil proportioned to their numbers, and their enfranchisement an advantage in the same proportion. Whatever may be the causes, there can be no doubt that the class of independent women is a continually increasing one in this country, and their admission to the franchise is therefore continually becoming, by the natural course of events, a question of greater practical importance.

Turning now to the question, what harm could be done by their admission? we are embarrassed by the difficulty of finding any answer whatever, unless we go out of the bounds we have prescribed to ourselves, and get beyond the limits of the constitutional point of view. Revolutionary violence is out of the question from them, and their numbers are not such as to give rise to any of the apprehensions of a disturbance of the balance of power which have been excited in some minds by the claims of the working classes. There would probably be found some duly qualified female voters in every rank of society, and among them some members of almost every religious system or political party, so that the existing interests of no single class or party or religious body could have anything to fear from them. It seems difficult to imagine a case where the principles of the Constitution could be applied with more absolute freedom from the slightest shadow of danger.

Can it be said that, although there would be no danger to the State, nor to anybody within the State, yet that private interests might suffer? We confess we do not see how this is to be maintained. If we consider the private interests of men, they cannot be concerned in the political action of independent women. Their political interests may be; but we have just seen that for these there is no danger. If it be urged that the power of voting

35

may make women more independent than it is thought they ought to be, it appears to us, once again, that English law has already decided that women may be independent, and that a woman who is absolute mistress of her own life, person, and property, will not be rendered more independent of men by the power of giving an occasional vote for a member of Parliament. There are some who think that by giving to any women whatever the power politically to protect their own interests, we should diminish that generous, disinterested, and romantic character which is so charming in women, and which indeed we all like to see in others, and most of us even to encourage in ourselves, so long as it does not expose us too defenceless to the selfishness of the selfish. Yet the remarks we have already made on the legal ability of women to defend their own pecuniary interests will apply even more appositely here. For if the sole responsibility of all their own private pecuniary affairs does not unsex spinsters and widows, and make them coarse, worldly, avaricious, grasping, and selfish, the addition of a vote, giving them a very slight direct influence on public affairs, is not likely to have so extraordinary an effect upon the most gentle and amiable half of mankind; on the contrary, as we find that the names of ladies abound on all charitable and philanthropic subscription lists, showing how kindly and generous a use they are disposed to make of their property, so we might reasonably expect that such little direct influence on politics as the possession of a vote would give to women, would probably be chiefly used in the direction of what we may call philanthropic legislation; in any case, politics in themselves certainly afford more scope for exalted and generous feeling than private business affairs. Ladies accustomed to the government of households and the management of their families, will scarcely find political affairs petty, or calculated to exercise a narrowing influence on their sympathies. Whether we consider that women ought to be especially devoted to what is beautiful or to what is good, there is much work in the interests of either to be done in politics; and if the ladies were only to take schools, workhouses, public buildings, parks, gardens, and picture galleries under their special protection, and try to send to Parliament a few members who would work efficiently at such subjects, the rest of the community would have cause to be glad of their help, without their being themselves in the smallest degree vulgarized by such a task.

But, in fact, as we have already pointed out, it is too late to be afraid of letting Englishwomen share in the life of Englishmen. We cannot shut up our women in harems, and devote them to the cultivation of their beauty and of their children. We have most of us long ago acknowledged that a perfect woman is

> Not too bright and good
> For human nature's daily food.

The fear that a womanly nature could be corrupted or hardened by politics, would strike at the root of our Western and Christian civilization, which owes much of its progress to having devolved upon women a share of the commonplace practical cares and duties which go to make up the sum of ordinary human life, whether domestic or political. The ingenuity, the love of luxury, the taste, and the housewifely instincts of women, have contributed much to the comforts of modern civilization; a more rapid and efficient adaptation of these same comforts to prisons, schools, barracks, and workhouses, would be a useful and probable result of the extension of women's energies to political life. It is, indeed, remarkable how large a part of the subjects which occupy most attention in modern politics are of this quasi-domestic character; and how growing a tendency there is for them to become ever more so. The homes of the working classes, education, Factory Acts (regulating the labour of women and children), sanitary laws, water supplies, drainage (all municipal legislation in fact), the whole administration of the poor-laws, with its various subdivisions – care of the pauper sick, pauper schools, etc. – all these are subjects which already, by common consent, are included in the peculiarly feminine province of home and charity. If the possession of a vote should induce more women to extend their interest to the comfort and happiness of other homes beside their own, it will certainly not have exercised a deteriorating influence on their character.

Barbara Leigh Smith Bodichon

Reasons for and against the enfranchisement of women

1869

THAT a respectable, orderly, independent body in the State should have no voice, and no influence recognised by the law, in the election of the representatives of the people, while they are otherwise acknowledged as responsible citizens, are eligible for many public offices, and required to pay all taxes, is an anomaly which seems to require some explanation. Many people are unable to conceive that women can care about voting. That some women do care, has been proved by the petitions presented to Parliament. I shall try to show why some care – and why those who do not, ought to be made to care.

There are now a very considerable number of open minded, unprejudiced people, who see no particular reason why women should not have votes, if they want them; but, they ask, what would be the good of it? What is there that women want which male legislators are not willing to give? And here let me say at the outset, that the advocates of this measure are very far from accusing men of deliberate unfairness to women. It is not as a means of extorting justice from unwilling legislators that the franchise is claimed for women. In so far as the claim is made with any special reference to class interests at all, it is simply on the general ground that under a representative government, any class which is not represented is likely to be neglected. Proverbially, what is out of sight is out of mind; and the theory that women, as such, are bound to keep out of sight, finds its most emphatic expression in the denial of the right to vote. The direct results are probably less injurious than those which are indirect; but that a want of due consideration for the interests of women is apparent in our legislation, could very easily be shown. To give evidence in detail would be a long and an invidious task. I will mention one instance only, that of the educational endowments all over the country. Very few people would now maintain that the education of boys is more important to the State than that of girls. But as a matter of fact, girls have but a very small share in educational endowments. Many of the old foundations have been reformed by Parliament, but the desirableness of providing with equal care for girls and boys has very seldom been recognised. In the administration of charities generally, the same tendency prevails to postpone the claims of women to those of men.

Among instances of hardship traceable directly to exclusion from the franchise and to no other cause, may be mentioned the unwillingness of landlords to accept women as tenants. Two large farmers in Suffolk inform me that this is not an uncommon case. They mention one estate on which seven widows have been ejected, who, if they had had votes, would have been continued as tenants.

The case of women farmers is stronger, but not much stronger, than that of women who, as heads of a business or a household, fulfil the duties of a man in the same position. Their task is often a hard one, and everything which helps to sustain their self-respect, and to give them consideration and importance in the eyes of others, is likely to lessen their difficulties and make them happier and stronger for the battle of life. The very fact that, though householders and taxpayers, they have not equal privileges with male householders and taxpayers, is in itself a *deconsideration*, which seems to me invidious and useless. It casts a kind of slur on the value of their opinions; and I may remark in passing, that what is treated as of no value is apt to grow valueless. Citizenship is an honour, and not to have the full rights of a citizen is a want of honour. Obvious it may not be, but by a subtle and sure process, those who without their own consent and without sufficient reason are debarred from full participation in the rights and duties of a citizen, lose more or less of social consideration and esteem.

These arguments, founded on considerations of justice and mercy to a large and important and increasing class, might in a civilised country, and in the absence of strong reasons to the contrary, be deemed amply sufficient to justify the measure proposed. There remain to be considered those aspects of the question which affect the general community. And among all the reasons for giving women votes, the one which appears to me the strongest, is that of the influence it might be expected to have in increasing public spirit. Patriotism, a healthy, lively, intelligent interest in everything which concerns the nation to which we belong, and an unselfish devotedness to the public service, – these are the qualities which make a people great and happy; these are the virtues which ought to be most sedulously cultivated in all classes of the community. And I know no better means, at this present time, of counteracting the tendency to prefer narrow private ends to the public good, than this of giving to all women, duly qualified, a direct and conscious participation in political affairs. Give some women votes, and it will tend to make all women think seriously of the concerns of the nation at large, and their interest having once been fairly roused, they will take pains, by reading and by consultation with persons better informed than themselves, to form sound opinions. As it is, women of the middle class occupy themselves but little with anything beyond their own family circle. They do not consider it any concern of theirs, if poor men and women are ill-nursed in workhouse infirmaries, and poor children ill-taught in workhouse schools. If the roads are bad, the drains neglected, the water poisoned, they think it is all very wrong, but it does not occur to them that it is their duty to get it put right. These farmer-women and business-women have honest, sensible minds and much practical experience, but they do not bring their good sense to bear upon public affairs, because they think it is men's business, not theirs, to look after such things. It is this belief – so narrowing and deadening in its influence – that the exercise of the franchise would tend to dissipate. The mere fact of being called upon to enforce an opinion by a vote, would have an immediate effect in awakening a healthy sense of responsibility. There is no reason why these women should not take an active interest in all the social questions – education, public health, prison, discipline, the poor laws, and the rest – which occupy Parliament, and they would be much more likely to do so, if they felt that they had importance in the eyes of members of Parliament, and could claim a hearing for their opinions.

Besides these women of business, there are ladies of property, whose more active participation in public affairs would be beneficial both to themselves and the community generally. The want of stimulus to energetic action is much felt by women of the

40

higher classes. It is agreed that they ought not to be idle, but what they ought to do is not so clear. Reading, music and drawing, needlework, and charity are their usual employments. Reading, without a purpose, does not come to much. Music and drawing, and needlework, are most commonly regarded as amusements intended to fill up time. We have left, as the serious duty of independent and unmarried women, the care of the poor in all its branches, including visiting the sick and the aged, and ministering to their wants, looking after the schools, and in every possible way giving help wherever help is needed. Now education, the relief of the destitute, and the health of the people, are among the most important and difficult matters which occupy the minds of statesmen, and if it is admitted that women of leisure and culture are bound to contribute their part towards the solution of these great questions, it is evident that every means of making their co-operation enlightened and vigorous should be sought for. They have special opportunities of observing the operation of many of the laws. They know, for example, for they see before their eyes, the practical working of the law of settlement – of the laws relating to the dwellings of the poor – and many others, and the experience which peculiarly qualifies them to form a judgment on these matters ought not to be thrown away. We all know that we have already a goodly body of rich, influential working-women, whose opinions on the social and political questions of the day are well worth listening to. In almost every parish there are, happily for England, such women. Now everything should be done to give these valuable members of the community a solid social standing. If they are wanted – and there can be no doubt that they are – in all departments of social work, their position in the work should be as dignified and honourable as it is possible to make it. Rich unmarried women have many opportunities of benefiting the community, which are not within reach of a married woman, absorbed by the care of her husband and children. Everything, I say again, should be done to encourage this most important and increasing class to take their place in the army of workers for the common good, and all the forces we can bring to bear for this end are of incalculable value. For by bringing women into hearty co-operation with men, we gain the benefit not only of their work, but of their intelligent sympathy. Public spirit is like fire: a feeble spark of it may be fanned into a flame, or it may very easily be put out. And the result of teaching women that they have nothing to do with politics, is that their influence goes towards extinguishing the unselfish interest – never too strong – which men are disposed to take in public affairs.

Let each member of the House of Commons consider, in a spirit of true scientific enquiry, all the properly qualified women of his acquaintance, and he will see no reason why the single ladies and the widows among his own family and friends should not form as sensible opinions on the merits of candidates as the voters who returned him to Parliament. When we find among the disfranchised such names as those of Mrs Somerville, Harriet Martineau, Miss Burdett Coutts, Florence Nightingale, Mary Carpenter, Louisa Twining, Miss Marsh, and many others scarcely inferior to these in intellectual and moral worth, we cannot but desire, for the elevation and dignity of the parliamentary system, to add them to the number of electors.

It need scarcely be pointed out that the measure has nothing of a party character. We have precedents under two very different governments, those of Austria and Sweden, for something very similar to what is now proposed. Now, let us calmly consider all the arguments we have heard against giving the franchise to women.

Among these, the first and foremost is – women do not want votes. Certainly that is a capital reason why women should not have votes thrust upon them, and no one proposes compulsory registration. There are many men who do not care to use their votes, and there is no law compelling them either to register themselves or to vote. The statement, however, that women do not wish to vote, is a mere assertion, and may be met by a counter-assertion. Some women do want votes, which the petitions signed, and now in course of signature, go very largely to prove. Some women manifestly do; others, let it be admitted, do not. It is impossible to say positively which side has the majority, unless we could poll all the women in question; or, in other words, without resorting to the very measure which is under discussion. Make registration possible, and we shall see how many care to avail themselves of the privilege.

But, it is said, women have other duties. The function of women is different to that of men, and their function is not politics. It is very true that women have other duties – many and various. But so have men. No citizen lives for his citizen duties only. He is a professional man, a tradesman, a family man, a club man, a thousand things as well as a voter. Of course these occupations sometimes interfere with a man's duties as a citizen, and when he cannot vote, he cannot. So with women; when they cannot vote, they cannot.

The proposition we are discussing, practically concerns only single women and widows who have 40s. freeholds, or other county qualifications, and for boroughs, all those who occupy, as owners or tenants, houses of the value of £10 a year. Among these there are surely a great number whose time is not fully occupied, not even so much as that of men. Their duties in sickrooms and in caring for children, leave them a sufficient margin of leisure for reading newspapers, and studying the *pros* and *cons* of political and social questions. No one can mean seriously to affirm that widows and unmarried women would find the mere act of voting once in several years arduous. One day, say once in three years, might surely be spared from domestic duties. If it is urged that it is not the time spent in voting that is in question, but the thought and the attention which are necessary for forming political opinions, I reply that women of the class we are speaking of, have, as a rule, more time for thought than men, their duties being of a less engrossing character, and they ought to bestow a considerable amount of thought and attention on the questions which occupy the Legislature. Social matters occupy every day a larger space in the deliberations of Parliament, and on many of these questions women are led to think and to judge in the fulfilment of those duties which, as a matter of course, devolve upon them in the ordinary business of English life. And however important the duties of home may be, we must bear in mind that a woman's duties do not end there. She is a daughter, a sister, the mistress of a household; she ought to be, in the broadest sense of the word, a neighbour, both to her equals and to the poor. These are her obvious and undeniable duties, and within the limits of her admitted functions; I should think it desirable to add to them – duties to her parish and to the State. A woman who is valuable in all the relations of life, a woman of a large nature, will be more perfect in her domestic capacity, and not less.

If we contemplate women in the past, and in different countries, we find them acting, in addition to their domestic part, all sorts of different *rôles*. What was their *rôle* among the Jews and the Romans? What was it in the early Christian churches? What is it amongst the Quakers? What is it in the colliery districts, – at the court of Victoria, and the Tuileries? We can conjure up thousands of pictures of women performing different functions under varying conditions. They have done and do, all sorts of work in all sorts of ways. Is there anything in the past history of the world, which justifies the assertion that they must and will do certain things in the future, and will not and cannot do certain other things? I do not think there is.

But to return to my argument, and supposing that there were enough data in the past to enable us to predict that women will never take sufficient interest in politics to induce even widows and single women to wish to vote once in several years, should we be justified in realising our own prediction, and forbidding by law what we declare to be contrary to nature? If anyone believes, as the result of observation and experience, that it is not a womanly function to vote, I respect such belief, and answer – only the future can prove. But what I do not respect, is the strange want of toleration which says – 'You shall not do this or that.' We do not want to compel women to act; we only wish to see them free to exercise or not, according as they themselves desire, political and other functions.

The argument that 'women are ignorant of politics,' would have great force if it could be shown that the mass of the existing voters are thoroughly well-informed on political subjects, or even much better informed than the persons to whom it is proposed to give votes. Granted that women are ignorant of politics, so are many male ten-pound householders. Their ideas are not always clear on political questions, and would probably be even more confused if they had not votes. No mass of human beings will or can undertake the task of forming opinions on matters over which they have no control, and on which they have no practical decision to make. It would by most persons be considered a waste of time. When women have votes, they will read with closer attention than heretofore the daily histories of our times, and will converse with each other and with their fathers and brothers about social and political questions. They will become interested in a wider circle of ideas, and where they now think and feel somewhat vaguely, they will form definite and decided opinions.

Among the women who are disqualified for voting by the legal disability of sex, there is a large number of the educated class. We shall know the exact number of women possessing the household and property qualifications, when the return ordered by Parliament has been made. In the meantime, the following calculation is suggestive. In the 'London Court Guide,' which of course includes no houses below the value of £10 a year, the number of householders whose names begin with A is 1149. Of these, 205, that is more than one-sixth, are women, all of whom are either unmarried or widows.

The fear entertained by some persons that family dissension would result from encouraging women to form political opinions, might be urged with equal force against their having any opinions on any subject at all. Differences on religious subjects are still more apt to rouse the passions and create disunion than political differences. As for opinions causing disunion, let it be remembered that what is a possible cause of disunion is also a possible cause of deeply-founded union. The more rational women become, the more real union there will be in families, for nothing separates so much as unreasonableness and frivolity. It will be said, perhaps, that contrary opinions may be held by the different members of a family without bringing on quarrels, so long as they are kept to the region of theory, and no attempt is made to carry them out publicly in action. But religious differences must be shown publicly. A woman who determines upon changing her religion – say to go over from Protestantism to Romanism – proclaims her difference from her family in a public and often a very distressing manner. But no one has yet proposed to make it illegal for a woman to change her religion. After all – is it essential that brothers and sisters and cousins shall all vote on the same side?

An assertion often made, that women would lose the good influence which they now exert indirectly on public affairs if they had votes, seems to require proof. First of all, it is necessary to prove that women have this indirect influence, – then that it is good, – then that the indirect good influence would be lost if they had direct influence, – then that the indirect influence which they would lose is better than the direct influence they would gain. From my own observation I should say, that the women who have gained by their wisdom and earnestness a good indirect influence, would not lose that influence if they had votes. And I see no necessary connexion between goodness and indirectness. On the contrary, I believe that the great thing women want is to be more direct and straightforward in thought, word, and deed. I think the educational advantage of citizenship to women would be so great, that I feel inclined to run the risk of sacrificing the subtle indirect influence, to a wholesome feeling of responsibility, which would, I think, make women give their opinions less rashly and more conscientiously than at present on political subjects.

A gentleman who thinks much about details, affirms that 'polling-booths are not fit places for women.' If this is so, one can only say that the sooner they are made fit the better. That in a State which professes to be civilised, a solemn public duty can only be discharged in the midst of drunkenness and riot, is scandalous and not to be endured. It is no doubt true, that in many places polling is now carried on in a turbulent and disorderly manner. Where that is unhappily the case, women clearly must stay away. Englishwomen can surely be trusted not to force their way to the polling-booth when it would be manifestly unfit. But it does not follow that, because in some disreputable places some women would be illegally, but with their own consent, prevented from recording their votes, therefore all women, in all places, should be, without their own consent, by law disqualified. Those who at the last election visited the polling places in London and Westminster, and many other places, will bear me out in asserting, that a lady would have had no more difficulty or annoyance to encounter in giving her vote, than she has in going to the Botanical Gardens or to Westminster Abbey.

There are certain other difficulties sometimes vaguely brought forward by the unreflecting, which I shall not attempt to discuss. Such, for example, is the argument that as voters ought to be independent, and as married women are liable to be influenced by their husbands, therefore unmarried women and widows ought not to vote. Or again, that many ladies canvass, and canvassing by ladies is a very objectionable practice, therefore canvassing ought to be the only direct method by which women can bring their influence to bear upon an election. Into such objections it is not necessary here to enter.

Nor is it needful to discuss the extreme logical consequences which may be obtained by pressing to an undue length the arguments used in favour of permitting women to exercise the suffrage. The question under consideration is, not whether women ought logically to be members of Parliament, but whether, under existing circumstances, it is for the good of the State that women, who perform most of the duties, and enjoy nearly all the rights of citizenship, should be by special enactment disabled from exercising the additional privilege of taking part in the election of the representatives of the people. It is a question of expediency, to be discussed calmly, without passion or prejudice.

In England, the extension proposed would interfere with no vested interests. It would involve no change in the principles on which our Government is based, but would rather make our Constitution more consistent with itself. Conservatives have a right to claim it as a Conservative measure. Liberals are bound to ask for it as a necessary part of radical reform. There is no reason for identifying it with any class or party in the State, and it is, in fact, impossible to predict what influence it might have on party politics. The question is simply of a special legal disability, which must, sooner or later, be removed.

Part II
The debate in the House of Commons on the Women's Disabilities Bill

3 May 1871

The debate in the House of Commons on the Women's Disabilities Bill

3 May 1871

ON the order of the day for the second reading of this Bill, Mr
JACOB BRIGHT observed that when the question of the removal of
the electoral disabilities of women was first brought before the
House in 1867 it was regarded with feelings of curiosity, and
probably most of those who remained to hear the debate did so in
the expectation that they would get some amusement from it.
When the Bill, of which he was about to move the second
reading, was last year submitted to the House its opponents
somewhat under-estimated the amount of Parliamentary support
it would receive. They had no idea that in a House of between
two hundred and three hundred it would be read a second time by
a considerable majority. Such, however, was the fact, and when it
was borne in mind, in connexion with that fact, that there were
170 members of the present Parliament who had, at one time or
another, given their sanction to the principle of the Bill, he
thought he might state that they now approached the discussion
of it with a feeling that they had a subject before them as serious
and important as any which had ever occupied the attention of the
House or country. He had no means of knowing whether the
House would read the Bill a second time to-day; but if he might
judge of the future by the past, he could say if they did not read it
a second time to-day they would do so at no distant period.
Whatever measures had been generally supported by the large

49

Parliamentary boroughs had found their way to the statute book. The great towns had recently decided in favour of household suffrage for men; and they had now decided, not with entire unanimity, but with a remarkable approach to it, in favour of this Bill for giving household suffrage throughout the country without any distinction of sex. Edinburgh and Birmingham, Manchester and Bristol, Leeds and Brighton, Oldham and Sheffield, Halifax and Bolton had given an undivided vote in favour of the Bill. He would not go into the general question of unequal legislation as between men and women. He believed the House pretty well understood the whole subject. Women asked for the Parliamentary suffrage because they bore in common with men all the burdens of the State, and because they believed they had a constitutional right to influence the making of the laws which they had to obey. The great and oppressive inequalities in the laws as between the sexes supplied them with a practical motive of the very strongest kind to endeavour to obtain the franchise, from a knowledge of the fact that only those who could influence the legislative body had any chance of getting their grievances redressed. Two recent cases might be quoted as illustrating the state of the law between men and women. One was the case of a grandchild of Lord Mount-Cashell – a child taken away from the guardianship of its mother by its father. The case was most severely commented on by the Judge, and the Court would have liked to give a decision entirely opposed to that it gave. He did not say that the child, instead of being the property of the father, should be the property of the mother; but in a matter of this kind there should be some just decision, and if there was any choice certainly the child should go to that parent who would best do a parent's duty by it. Another case came before the Courts the other day, and the question was whether in this country a widow had any right to bring up her child in the religion she professed. The father was a Roman Catholic, the mother a Protestant, and the child was eight years of age. The father had left no instructions as to the religion in which the child should be trained; but the relatives of the dead father absolutely controlled the mother, who was obliged to have her child brought up in the Roman Catholic religion, although she herself entirely disbelieved it. Women had discovered that whenever a class of persons hitherto debarred from the franchise were admitted within the political pale, a very decided change soon occurred in the legislation affecting them. Until working men got votes the House had looked with considerable suspicion on Trades' Unions, and would gladly have suppressed them; but now they had legislated for them in a spirit of justice, and probably even of generosity. He did not believe this change was owing to the fact that working men could now meet them at the polling-booth and there assert their powers. He attributed it to a much better motive. When working men were enfranchised the House had been compelled to look at every question which affected them, and were likely, therefore, to arrive at more truthful and just decisions. If women had the franchise the House would get to know their opinions and feelings, and legislation affecting them would be more successful. Had they possessed the franchise, would the Women's Property Bill have met the fate it did? It passed that House and reached the other Chamber, where the voice of justice was not always heard unless its demands were in harmony with the supposed interests of those who assembled there. What was done with it? The Peers destroyed the Bill and created another. During that process the Government, so far as he recollected, were inactive, and did not lend the slightest assistance to the admirable Bill sent up by that House. He did not blame the Government. They were overweighted with business, having three times more on their hands than they could possibly get through. They must choose what measures they could give attention to, and must do the work of their masters – those who made and could unmake them. To suppose they could give attention to the interests of the unenfranchised was to suppose what was impossible. That Bill came back with the principle knocked out of it – a thing of shreds and patches, very good for the lawyers, but very difficult for any one else to understand; and to this hour confiscation of property at marriage was the law for women in this country. The Government had been obliged to take up the subject of university tests, especially during the last two sessions, the object being not to enable Nonconformists to obtain an academical education, but to enable them to enjoy certain emoluments they could not otherwise reach; but how was it with women? A struggle was going on among women for a higher education. At Edinburgh University some half-dozen women of great ability, high character, and industry desired to become qualified as medical practitioners – not seeking emoluments and honours, but simply the education which such institutions were supposed to give; but nobody came down to that House for their relief; no great party was set in motion; the Government was silent while half-a-dozen women were heroically fighting their own battle against a high class trades' union in that city. (Hear, hear.) In the course of the discussion on the Bill for legalising marriage with a deceased wife's sister several Hon.

Members referred to what was said to be the opinion women entertained of that measure. The Hon Member for Boston (Mr Collins) had read a passage from the *Women's Suffrage Journal* to show this. That journal, conducted by a woman, was as ably conducted as any journal in the kingdom – (hear, hear) – and more than any other paper represented the suffrage associations of the country. Women, however, were not satisfied with that sort of irregular representation in this House. What they said was that if their opinions were of any value, if their condition was to be studied at all, they ought to express their views by the constitutional method – through the polling-booth, precisely as men did. With a conscientious desire to lessen infanticide, the Hon Member for Salford (Mr Charley) had introduced the Infant Life Preservation Bill. If it affected anyone it affected women, and it was natural they should consider it. These women's suffrage societies were becoming vigilance committees which watched the legislation of the House with regard to women. They agreed with the Hon Member for Salford in his object, but they differed from him in regard to the means by which he proposed to attain it. They had presented a memorial to the Home Secretary against the Bill, and they had sent it to every member. Was it not of some use to Hon Members to see the criticisms of women upon the Bill? And if it were, was not their demand a reasonable one, that they should be allowed to express their opinions at the polling-booth? If political disabilities ought to exist at all, it would be more fair to place them on men than on women; if either men or women should be without votes, it ought to be men; and his reason for that opinion was that men had ten times the means of influencing the Legislature of any country apart altogether from votes. They had physical strength, combative qualities, opportunities of meeting, and the almost entire control of the press, the platform, and the pulpit; they were the masters of all the great professions in this country; they had the command of the purse; and when all these things were considered it appeared to him that Hon Members sitting on that side of the House, who had always been in favour of representation, could hardly enter the lobby to vote against this Bill without feelings of discomfort almost akin to shame. Among those who opposed the Bill last Session were the Right Hon Member for Kilmarnock (Mr Bouverie), the noble lord the member for Haddingtonshire (Lord Elcho), and the Hon Member for North Warwickshire (Mr Newdegate), and, if he could have selected his opponents, he would have picked out these three members. From the names of his opponents he should expect that they would bring forward arguments drawn from prejudices rather than from reason; and he found that the arguments which did service a few years ago in opposition to the extension of the franchise were disinterred. As it was said that men did not want the franchise, and men were produced who did not want it, so with respect to women now; but during this Session there had been presented to Parliament in favour of the Bill 420 petitions, to which 150,000 signatures were attached; and 150 meetings, of varying character but many of them crowded, had been held in support of it in the United Kingdom, but mainly in Scotland and England. It was said that the franchise would be a curse to women; but it might be assumed that women were the best judges of that; and there had recently been presented to the Prime Minister, a memorial in support of the Bill signed by women and headed by the names of Florence Nightingale, Harriet Martineau, Miss Carpenter, and several ladies of title. He now came to the pedestal or pinnacle argument, which was that women stood in too high a position to be subjected to the dirt and mire of politics; but everything in this world had its baser side, including religion, literature, and art, and we did not attempt to exclude women from them on that account. Those who used this pinnacle argument were members of aristocratic families, and belonged to that privileged order in which women stood on high social pinnacles; but he did not come there to advocate the claims of women who stood upon any pinnacle or pedestal whatever, he came to plead the cause of those who, less powerfully armed by nature, less favoured by law, had to do the rough work of the world in the face of obstacles more formidable than ever beset the path of men. He did not underrate the importance of adding 14 or 16 per cent to the constituency, but what he regarded as serious was the neglect of this demand for enfranchisement, because Parliament could not legislate successfully for a community with so large a portion of which it had no relation. If the Bill passed no demand for a dissolution would come from women, who would know that from that time the question in which they were concerned would assume a different aspect, because they would have votes at the next election. The present government in its first Session enabled women to vote at municipal elections; an eminent member observed to him at the time 'That vote means the other,' and the public had made up their minds that it did. Last Session women were enabled to vote for members of School Boards, and to be members of them, too, as they were in several places. As women could not be elected by large communities without being known to them, and as they had been encouraged to present themselves to constituencies, it appeared to be impossible for a

Government which had gone so far to justify itself in preventing women from voting once in four or five years at parliamentary elections. Last year, the Government being neutral on this question, the House passed the second reading of the Bill by a large majority, and then there came over the scene a remarkable change, which he never could understand; but there was a panic, and in a state of panic men always saw that which did not exist. There was set to work machinery which more than once he had seen employed to upset just decisions; and on that occasion this result was achieved. He cared very little about the party aspects of this Bill; but if, as was alleged, the political power of women would be Conservative, it was a question for the grave consideration of the Government whether they would make it more Conservative by promoting its closer alliance with the Conservative party. Last year the Home Secretary did not conceal, but rather attempted to avow, that if he had been left unfettered he would have voted for it; the Solicitor-General voted for the Bill, and had spoken warmly in its favour before his constituency; the Solicitor-General for Ireland voted for it; and the Secretary of the Poor Law Board was a supporter of it; the Secretary to the Admiralty voted for Mr Mill's resolution in favour of the enfranchisement of women. There were other members of the Government who had never availed themselves of any opportunity of voting against the Bill. The Attorney-General had not done so; the Vice-President of the Council, who had admitted women to the membership of School Boards, would hardly be likely to do so; the Under Secretary at the Home Office and the Secretary to the Treasury had not voted against it; and without inferring that all these were in favour of the Bill, he must conclude that there was something favourably suspicious in the fact that they had not voted against it. The great principle of the Liberal party was that taxation and representation should go together; and with so many members of the Government favourable to the Bill and others not hostile to it, it would not be a very unlikely thing that they should on this occasion leave this an open question, and allow the House to dispose of it free from their influence. ('Hear, hear,' from Mr Gladstone.) He rejoiced that the Prime Minister would co-operate with them so far as to allow the House to dispose of the question according to its own view. Parliament had made the home the political unit, do not let it maintain disabilities in those homes bereft of the father, and where the support to be derived from the presence of men was not to be found. (Cheers.) The Hon Member concluded by moving that the Bill be read a second time.

Mr EASTWICK, in seconding the motion, said that, as he had had no opportunity of speaking in the debate on this question last year, although his name was then as now on the back of the Bill, he naturally felt desirous of stating the grounds on which he supported the Bill, and had placed his name in a somewhat prominent position with regard to it. He was the more anxious to speak because he differed in some respects from the views of the Hon Member who had just spoken. However his health just then was not such as to encourage him to address the House, and he should not have done so had he not taken a real interest in the Bill, and did he not feel it to be an imperative duty to do all in his power to support it. He must begin by saying that he was surprised at the extreme and even dangerous importance which some attached to the enfranchisement, not of women, but of the comparatively few women who possessed the qualifications which entitled men to vote, and whose claims had not been voluntarily surrendered by marriage. Our common law looked upon husband and wife as one, and we might, therefore, set aside all married women, even those who enjoyed the income of property settled on themselves without the intervention of trustees. If we did so, and also eliminated all women except unmarried householders and lodgers qualified as males were required to be, and took the remainder only, the number of female voters placed on the list, according to the best information he could obtain, would not equal one-fifth of the number of voters added by the last Reform Bill. The peril of this addition, if there were any, was still further diminished by the fact that women were not turbulent, corrupt, and revolutionary like men, and that any changes their influence might introduce would be of the mildest and most beneficent character. He was astonished, therefore, when he heard the Right Hon gentleman, on whose motion the Bill was thrown out last Session, speak of it as a measure which ought not to be carried without an appeal to the country, and a dissolution of Parliament. If the passing of this Bill were to involve a dissolution, we might as well have one about the encroachments on the Thames Embankment. The enfranchisement of some myriads of women would no more affect the nation at large than those encroachments, and if they chose to call that enfranchisement an encroachment it was at all events a beneficial one, while those others were mischievous. Another futile objection which he had heard in the last year's debate was that women could not be admitted to the suffrage without conceding to them also a seat in Parliament. It was a sufficient answer to that objection that the clergy possessed the suffrage but could not sit in Parliament, and had never agitated for the privilege. A more absurd objection still was that the enfranchisement of a small minority of women would alter the character of the whole sex, who would invade the occupations, habits, and lines of thought which formed the peculiar domain of man, and sweeping like a torrent, as it were, *per fas atgue nefas* obliterate the boundaries which Nature herself had set up between the sexes. Were it not for the extreme respect in which he held a candid opponent, he should catch himself inwardly exclaiming, –

The force of folly could no further go.

If we wished to know what change admission to the suffrage would make in women, we could not do better than consider what it made in men. He did not deny the advantage of enfranchisement, but he did not believe that it consisted in an immediate change of character. Was any man, he asked, the wiser, the merrier, the better, the worse (he would not say till the Ballot Bill passed, perhaps not even then, the richer, the poorer), for obtaining the right to vote? He should be curious to hear any one explain the physiological or psychological changes which he had detected in himself after he had obtained the suffrage. Thousands were indifferent about the possession and use of their privilege as voters, and many women would be as indifferent, though more conscientious, perhaps, than many men, when they did vote. But it was unnecessary to argue that the electoral suffrage would make no change for the worse in woman's character, because there was a practical demonstration of the fact in that the municipal suffrage had been given to women, and the educational, without in the slightest degree detracting from the feminine softness of women, or disturbing their *rôle* in life's great drama as wives and mothers. Women meddled neither more nor less in politics than they did in the days of Margaret of Anjou, of Queen Elizabeth, or of those contests when a beautiful duchess canvassed for Charles James Fox. Some few high spirits entered the political arena then, as they might do now, but the vast majority contented themselves with elevating and depressing their eyebrows, as the Roman ladies did their thumbs, for or against the combatants; and so, he thought, things would remain. He dismissed the thought that any very portentous changes, political or social, would be effected by carrying the measure; but then the question arose, if the measure were likely to be so inoperative, why press it at all? The answer was that it completed the representation of property and of intelligence. The intelligent views of women were no more to be disregarded than those of men; and, as it was our constitutional theory that property ought to be represented, there was no reason why it should not be represented when it was in the hands of women who discharged the duties connected with it, and were, therefore, entitled to its privileges. In the next place, it was only just that women should have such a political *status* as to enable them to obtain an equal share of educational endowment and other social advantages which were at present denied them. The Hon Member for Sheffield last year spoke of many women as being but 'fair savages;' the reason was that the unfair savages, men, took the lion's share of education; and the same unfairness prevailed in other matters, and he agreed with Mr Mill, when he said 'all that education and civilisation are doing to efface the influences on character of the law of force, and replace them by those of justice, remains merely on the surface as long as the citadel of the enemy, (that is the unjust treatment of women) is not attacked.' Lastly it appeared to him that to imply the inferiority of women by withholding from them the suffrage was detrimental to their character, whether that inferiority were or were not wholly and absolutely true; and an illustration of this was to be found in the results of the policy of the Spaniards towards the Indians in America. He had lately read in the work of a distinguished French traveller, a passage which seemed to him to bear on this point. It was this, 'The special code and ordinances sent out by the council of the Indies unintentionally, perhaps, but effectually, favoured the spread and perpetuation of the popular prejudices as to the real inferiority of the Indians, by speaking of them and providing for them as minors in all civil matters. Habituated for so long a period to contempt and pity, they have come to regard themselves as inferior beings, and their self-respect can never be restored, except through a series of efforts as prolonged as those which have humbled them have been continuous.' For these reasons he supported this Bill, but he also thought there was a special reason why this country should be the first to adopt the enfranchisement of women. That reason was the immense influence which the example of England must exert upon the 200 millions of Asiatics in India, among whom, with a few brilliant exceptions, woman had been degraded to a state little better than slavery. How could we expect that Indian women would be emancipated from the imprisonment of the zenanah or be admitted to the full privileges of education, so long as we continued to proclaim the inferiority of women in this country? If for no other reason, he should support this measure as a blow dealt at the slavery of women in the East, and as a reply to the besotted demand of the Chinese Government that schools for female education should be dissolved. (Cheers.)

Mr BOUVERIE apologised for intruding himself as an opponent of the measure, and said he abstained from giving notice of opposition almost up to the last hour in the hope that some other member would come to the front. He was unwilling to put himself forward in a matter which interested a great number of his countrymen and countrywomen, but the House would do him the justice to admit that he had always had the courage of his opinions – a merit not always conspicuous in ministers or members. He had always given his vote in favour of the extension of the franchise, and though he criticised the Bill of 1866, his suggestions were accepted by the Government. (Hear, hear.) But his hon. friend raised a question of a different kind by the Bill he had introduced, and argued as if it were a mere complement to the measure he had himself passed two years ago, contending that, in logic, the House of Commons was bound to confer the parliamentary suffrage on women, because it had entrusted them with the municipal franchise. For his own part he believed that extension was made inadvertently and almost by surprise – (hear); but however that might be, he for one would be no party to any further extension of that measure. He must remind the House that the experience we had had of the measure on which his honourable friend based his argument was not of a very satisfactory kind. One of the points he insisted upon last year in his opposition to the present measure was that mixing up women in contested elections would be to contaminate the sex. (Hear.) On that occasion he also urged upon the House that if we conferred the Parliamentary franchise on women we should not be able to protect those who were unwilling to take part in politics. They would be driven to the poll whether they liked it or not, their lives would be made a burden to them during a contested election, and there was no woman who would not be assailed, bothered, annoyed, and persecuted to give her vote. (Cheers.) Therefore, unless the great bulk of our countrywomen asked for the franchise – which they did not – the House ought not to impose such a *damnosa hereditas* upon them. The struggles of parties in political life stood on a very different footing from the minor affairs referred to by his hon. friend. About a month ago there was a discussion in the Manchester Town Council as to whether that body should petition in favour of this Bill, and a majority agreed to do so. He would read, however, the statements made by two gentlemen who took part in this debate. Mr Alderman Murray said: – 'With regard to the question before them, though he supported it last year, he felt bound to vote for the amendment on this occasion, and he would tell them why. At the last municipal election it was his duty to preside at one of the booths in Ardwick, and he must say that more unseemly sights took place on that occasion than he ever witnessed at any previous election, either municipal or Parliamentary. Women in a state of semi-drunkenness were hustled into public houses by men in the same state, and he made up his mind then that before the Parliamentary franchise was extended to women they ought to have the ballot.' (Hear, hear.) Well, he had always voted for the ballot, but how could the ballot prevent scenes of that kind? Again, Mr Alderman Lamb was reported to have said that, – 'He would ask whether any gentleman present would like to see his wife, daughter, or sister taking part in the disgraceful scenes which were witnessed at the last municipal election. (Hear, hear.) Staggering women, supported by staggering men – not their husbands – were seen going up to vote, both sexes boisterous and obscene in their language.' He thought, therefore, that the experience of the measure which gave the municipal franchise to women did not suggest the expediency of extending the principle. But he based his opposition to the present Bill on a much wider ground. No more serious question could be raised in Parliament than this. It was so serious, indeed, that he was astonished to hear his right hon. friend intimating that it was considered an open question for members of the Government. His hon. friend, by his proposal, raised in a practical shape a question which had been often raised before by philosophers in their closets – viz. 'Why are half the human race excluded from political privileges?' No, this was not a new question, albeit it was a very portentous one; but his hon. friend, in attempting to solve that question, was in reality disturbing the whole foundations of society and obliterating the distinction of sex, and the functions of the sexes in society which have always existed in every civilised community. (Hear, hear.) The issue now raised by his hon. friend originated in a country which was fertile in strange notions and ideas, the United States of America, and which was often extolled by his hon. friend and those who acted with him as furnishing an example of everything wise and expedient in political life. Now, what had our practical kinsmen on the other side of the Atlantic done in reference to this question? Why, they had repudiated the notion of woman suffrage, and the American women themselves had also repudiated it. The New York correspondent of a daily newspaper in this country said: – 'I am afraid it must be confessed that the woman suffrage movement in the United States is pretty well "played out." It has become unmistakably evident of late that the women

of the country do not want the suffrage.' The same correspondent, after quoting the letter of a lady who exposed the
unbusinesslike way in which women managed their societies in
America, said: – 'I agree with this lady that it is not surprising that
under this state of things the sensible women of the country have
become disgusted with the agitators and with their agitation, and
have exercised the influence which they have with their brothers
and husbands to knock the whole thing on the head as soon as
possible. In Illinois, the other day, 1,400 women of a single town
petitioned not to be allowed to vote; in Massachusetts an
amendment to the Constitution, allowing women to vote, has
been rejected in the Legislature by a large majority at the request,
as it appears, of the women themselves; in Minnesota, a Women's
Suffrage Bill, which had passed the Legislature, has been vetoed
by the Governor, who says that he is satisfied the women of the
State would be more annoyed than gratified by the suffrage; and
in Utah, where the women have the suffrage, they refuse to go to
the polls.'

Mr HUNT asked whether it was proposed there to give the vote
to married as well as to single women.

Mr BOUVERIE believed it was. His hon. friend's Bill would
tend to obliterate the practical distinctions which the experience,
the wisdom, and the habits of mankind in all ages had established.
It had been said that the Bill was a very small affair, and that the
House need not go much further; but if we conceded electoral
power to women, how could we refuse them a share in
legislative, judicial, and administrative power? (Hear.) This was a
state of things which this House ought seriously to contemplate if
it intended to pass the Bill. His hon. friend, no doubt would be
prepared to go that length, but he felt sure such a view was not
entertained by a great bulk of the women of England. His hon.
friend assumed to speak in the name of all the women of England,
but, in fact, he spoke in the name of only a very few of them.
(Cheers.) The great bulk of the women of England had an
instinctive horror of this measure, for they were aware of the evil
which would ultimately ensue to their sex if they entered into
rough competition with men in all the pursuits of life. Women
were physically weaker than men. They were protected by the
habits and ideas of society generally from oppression. There was
scarcely any man above 40 years old who was not identified in his
happiness and interests in life with one woman or with more than
one woman. (Laughter.) The happiness and interests of wife and
daughters were far dearer to the head of a family than his own.
(Hear.) His interests and theirs were entirely wrapped up together;

and he maintained that this was the real protection of women against oppression and injury, and not the electoral power which his hon. friend proposed to confer on them. To his mind, his hon. friend struck at the very foundation of society – namely, the family. (Hear, hear.) Was the head of the family the man or the woman? Was the head of the family to be the master of the family or was he not? Was it nature's intention, and was it our Maker's intention, that when society was founded on the family the man should be at the head of the family and should rule? Strange notions were spread abroad at the present day by those whose views his hon. friend advocated in that House. The existing state of things was to come to an end. He was not speaking without book, but would quote some passages of not inordinate length to show that the persons who with great ability promoted the views advocated by his hon. friend aimed their blows at the existing state of society and at marriage in particular. (Hear.) These were socialistic views, and he was glad to say they were not entertained by the great bulk of our countrymen and countrywomen. They were, however, entertained by philosophers and fanatics in ancient times, and they had been much written about during the last half century, so that there was a large literature on the subject by many writers, and especially by French writers. He dared say his hon. friend had not studied much of the literature on this subject. He, on the contrary, had; and he knew that the logical results of what his hon. friend advocated were the socialistic views of those who asserted that the existing foundations of society were altogether wrong, and that the laws of property and marriage ought to be entirely revised, they being at present an abuse of the rights and privileges of mankind. Marriage was represented by these writers as a state of intolerable bondage and slavery. He would quote a passage from a work by Mr John Stuart Mill, a gentleman who was called by some a great philosopher, although in his judgment he was rather a crude sophist than a philosopher. ('Hear, hear,' and laughter.) In his essay 'On the Subjection of Women' Mr Mill said: – 'The wife is the actual bond-servant of her husband, no less, so far as legal obligation goes, than slaves commonly so called. She vows a life-long obedience to him at the altar, and is held to it all through her life by law.' That was the complaint. In another passage Mr Mill said: – 'I am far from pretending that wives are in general no better treated than slaves; but no slave is a slave to the same lengths and in so full a sense of the word as a wife is.' Again, Mr Mill said: – 'If married life were all that it might be expected to be, looking to the laws alone, society would be a hell upon earth.' (Laughter.) And again: – 'The law of servitude in marriage is a monstrous contradiction to all the principles of the modern world, and to all the experience through which those principles have been slowly and painfully worked out. It is the sole case, now that negro slavery has been abolished, in which a human being in the plenitude of every faculty is delivered up to the tender mercies of another human being, in the hope, forsooth, that this other will use the power solely for the good of the person subjected to it. Marriage is the only actual bondage known to our law. There remain no legal slaves except the mistress of every house.' Was that a just representation of married life, and the relations between husband and wife among the great bulk of our countrymen and countrywomen? (Hear, hear.) Mr Mill was not even original in these views. In the year 1825 this subject was handled by Mr W. Thompson, a gentleman of the same school of opinion as Mr Owen, the Socialist, who gradually drifted into extraordinary notions, and held that there ought to be no morality, no laws, no property, and no marriage. (Laughter.) Among Mr Owen's chief apostles was this Mr Thompson, who wrote a book, entitled, *An appeal of one-half the Human Race against the Pretensions of the other Half*. In this work he said: – 'Even under the present arrangements of society, founded as they all are on the basis of individual competition, nothing could be more easy than to put the rights of women, political and civil, on a perfect equality with those of men. It is only to abolish all prohibitory and exclusive laws statute, or what are called "common," the remnants of the barbarous customs of our ignorant ancestors, particularly the horrible and odious inequality and indissolubility of that disgrace of civilisation the present marriage code.' Again he said: – 'Woman is, then, compelled in marriage by the possession of superior strength on the part of men, by the want of knowledge, skill, and wealth, by the positive cruel, partial, and cowardly enactments of law, by the terrors of superstition, by the mockery of a pretended vow of obedience, and, to crown all, and as the result of all, by the force of an unrelenting, unreasoning, unfeeling, public opinion, to be the literal unequivocal slave of the man who may be styled her husband. . . . A domestic, a civil, a political slave, in the plain, unsophisticated sense of the word, in no metaphorical sense, is every married woman.' It would thus be seen not only that Mr Mill was a sophist in regard to this matter, but that he had not the advantage of being an original sophist. (Laughter.) Such were the views on which were founded the operations of those persons outside the House who asked for an extension of the franchise to women owners of property. Another of the modern philosophers,

Mr M. D. Conway, said in a work entitled *The Earthward Pilgrimage*: – 'That which is now called morality directly and deliberately stunts or even ruins the faculty of man, and on principle. This will appear to those who consider its standards of nobility, commercial success, Sabbath keeping expediency; but beside the grave at Bournemouth' (the writer was here referring to the grave of Mary Woolstonecraft, one of the originators of this school.) 'I revert only to that point upon which our hereditary monastic morality is most stern and uncompromising – marriage. Nothing but superstition ever sacrifices human beings to institutions. The origin of the marriage superstition is pagan. . . . Like every other superstition, it is suicidal. Permitting the *minimum* of freedom in its regulation and duration, marriage finds the young already dreading it. . . . Formosa now excites sympathy, she will presently gain respect. When finally she shall deserve respect, when she also shows she can be faithful as lover and mother, the lock and bolt system will break down. Society will before long be glad enough to assimilate contracts between man and woman to contracts between partners in business.' He thought he had shown to the House by these extracts that there was a school who ardently supported the member for Manchester's measure, but who aimed their shot higher than he, and made an attack upon the very foundations of society. (Hear, hear.) There was a book far more esteemed by our countrywomen, if not by our countrymen, than the writings of Mr Mill, and it said: – 'Her desire shall be to her husband, and he shall rule over her.' (Cheers.) Now they were told that all this was to come to an end, and that women were to engage in men's pursuits – to be politicians, to become members of that House, and to take part in the administration of the country. His hon. friend the member for Cork (Mr Maguire) had just written an entertaining book, in which he contemplated what would occur thirty years hence, and described a House of Commons, most of the members of which were women, the whips being two remarkably engaging and captivating young ladies. (Much laughter.) This was a condition of affairs to which he for one strongly objected, for he maintained that the pride and glory of woman were her modesty and her purity. (Hear, hear.) Women could not be brought into contact with the rough occupations of men without defiling their modesty and purity. He did not know whether his hon. friend the member for Manchester was a classical scholar, and had read the *Sixth Satire of Juvenal* respecting the state to which society was reduced in Rome after the women there had been struggling for what they called their emancipation. He did not, of course, say that a similar state of things could be brought about in a civilised country in the present day, but still the tendency of human nature would be the same as it was in the time of Juvenal, and he believed that the great English divine of 200 years ago was right when he said that 'fear and blushing were the girdles of innocence.' If the weaker part of the human race were to enter into the active occupations of men they would be sure to go to the wall. Some of the greatest French writers had complained that in their country the family had almost disappeared from the lower strata of society, and were we prepared to exchange our domestic morality for that which existed in France? He would take the liberty of reading part of a letter which had been placed in his hands since he entered the House, and which was written by an accomplished and educated lady. She wrote to him as follows: – 'I find that you purpose moving the rejection of the Women's Suffrage Bill when it comes on for the second reading to-morrow. As the upholders of this Bill have had their hands strengthened by the voices of a small number of very demonstrative women, it seems scarcely right that not a voice should be raised to aid you in urging the rejection of the measure. I consider myself to be in exactly the position which enables me to express opinions which may be regarded as a fair exponent of the feelings of my countrywomen on the subject. I am middle-aged, unmarried, and live in my own house, and under the new *régime* should be entitled to a borough and a country vote. I have a keen appreciation of politics, and am intensely interested in everything connected with the well-being of society, but I am strongly opposed to the extension of the franchise to women, not because I think they are not wise enough to use the privileges aright, but because they have other and more genial duties. I feel myself able to give an opinion on this subject, having an immense circle of acquaintances, including no inconsiderable number of single ladies, not one of whom has ever expressed the least desire to be endowed with the boon which Jacob Bright and its other advocates would have one to suppose was the blessing above all others to be desired. As a rule, unmarried Englishwomen are perfectly satisfied with the position and privileges which the Legislature confers. The noisy few will ever be heard above the quiet many, while the latter would almost rather be burdened with the weight and responsibilities of the franchise than make an effort to protest that they do not desire it.' That letter, he believed, succinctly expressed the ideas of the great bulk of our educated countrywomen. (Hear, hear.) He clung to the conviction he expressed last year, that if this so-called boon was given it would prove a curse to them, and, therefore, he entreated the House to support him in negativing the motion of his hon. friend. (Cheers.) In conclusion the right hon. gentleman moved that the Bill be read a second time that day six months.

Mr SCOURFIELD cordially supported the amendment, but would not detain the House long, as all the ground had been travelled over by his right hon. friend. He was firmly convinced that the great mass of the women of this country did not desire to have this so-called privilege conferred upon them. This measure would put in the thin end of the wedge, to use the ordinary phrase, although he never heard of anyone endeavouring to put in the thick end of the wedge. (A laugh.) The House had no right to force upon women a privilege which only a very limited number of their sex asked for. As a means of testing whether the women of England really wished for the power of voting, he would suggest – and commend the suggestion to the attention of the Chancellor of the Exchequer – that every person signing a petition in favour of the extension of the franchise to women should be instructed to accompany the signature with a photographic portrait, and that Mr Darwin or Professor Owen, who could distinguish the sex of animals from very trifling signs, should be retained to decide from an examination of the pictures as to the sex of the person represented, for he could not help suspecting that many of the signatories were not women, but men in women's clothing. (Laughter.)

Mr GLADSTONE: Both the mover of the second reading of the Bill and the mover of the amendment having referred to the position of the Government on this question, I desire very briefly to explain to the House what that position really is. The Government abstain from taking any part whatever as a Government in this discussion – not upon the mere ground that their mind and time are overcharged with public business, but upon the more comprehensive and positive ground, that it is neither desirable nor advantageous that the Government should make a rule of interfering – as a Government – with every discussion at its earliest stages; and for this plain reason – that we wish in this country to have legislation founded on mature and on free consideration. That mature consideration of subjects is much impeded by considerations of party which it is hardly possible to keep out of subjects of this sort, after, by the adoption of one view or another, they have become the property of the executive government. With a view to that free consideration, it seems to me far more desirable, while we need not shrink as individuals from expressing our opinions, that we should leave to members of our own party to take an independent course on this question –

not because it is an unimportant question, but because our intervention as a body is premature and inexpedient. Now sir, I am not prepared to vote with my hon. friend in favour of this Bill; and I may state the reasons which disincline me to take that course. But I must congratulate my hon. friend on the ability with which he has stated his case. The presence of the hon. member here – I might even say the tones of his voice – agreeably remind me of the absence of his distinguished relative. I will not say that it consoles me for the loss we sustain, but at least if my right hon. friend and late colleague cannot be with us, I rejoice that the name of his family is so worthily represented. (Hear, hear.) Now, sir, my main reason for declining to vote for this Bill is that, although I do not think our present law is perfect, I am unwilling to adopt, by the second reading of the Bill, the principle of a measure for its amendment until I have some better prospect as to the satisfactory nature of the particular amendment about to be proposed than I perceive at the present moment. Proceeding to state my view of the case, in the first place I would set aside altogether the question whether the adoption of such a measure as this is likely to act in any given sense upon the fortunes of one political party or another. (Hear, hear.) It would be what I may call a sin against first principles to permit ourselves to be influenced either one way or the other by any feeling we might entertain on such a point, and therefore into that part of the subject I will not, for one moment, undertake to inquire. When I look at the particular proposals of my hon. friend I am encountered by the particular reasoning on which the opposition has been based. The mover and seconder of the amendment opposed the Bill on the specific ground that they are opposed to these revolutionary changes in the relative positions of men and women. These they do not allege to be included in this Bill, but of which they say, and I admit with some semblance of truth, that the Bill savours more or less. I entirely agree with my right hon. friend the member for Kilmarnock in his opposition to these revolutionary changes. But I must speak of Mr Mill in terms of much greater and warmer respect that the right hon. gentleman has used. The Bill itself is somewhat remarkable in one point of view, namely, in its avoidance of any statement of reasons for the change it contemplated. My hon. friend has dispensed with the preamble altogether, as if he were unwilling to commit himself to any limited purpose. With regard to the specific objections to the measure, I was well pleased with a portion of the speech of the hon. member who seconded the amendment. He based his objection on the direct operation of the measure as it stands, and I have no assurance from my hon. friend (Mr Jacob Bright) of any disposition to modify the measure in committee in that important respect. The hon. member placed his objection in a great degree on its demanding the personal attendance of women, and involving them in the general proceedings of elections. That appears to me to be an objection of the greatest force. It may be that when we adopt the principle of secret voting we may ensure that tranquility of elections which has been achieved in other countries. I remember to have been in Berlin on the day of a general election, and to have been totally unable from any sign or note whatever in the streets to discover the fact that the election was going on. We are told that the same tranquility prevails on the day of election in Australia; and whether that state of things arises from the simple adoption of secret voting or not, I hope we shall labour to attain tranquility in election procedure. All the pomp and glory of elections in this country, which I am old enough to recollect, has now disappeared. I must say there was in it something of a national character. (Hear, hear.) But while we have got rid of all that was attractive, we retain much that is dangerous and demoralising. Speaking generally, however, I am inclined to say that the personal attendance and intervention of women in election proceedings, even apart from any suspicion of the wider objects of many of the promoters of the present movement, would be a practical evil not only of the gravest, but even of an intolerable character. I am not quite sure that my hon. friend, in excluding married women, has adopted a perfectly consistent course. It is quite clear that married women, if they possessed the qualification, ought not to be omitted from any privilege conferred upon single women. The question with regard to the recognition of women's rights – I use the expression very largely without intending to express any opinion upon it – is, after all, a question of degree. The ancient law recognised the rights of women in the parish; I apprehend they could both vote and act in the parish. The modern rule has extended the right to the municipality, so far as the right of voting is concerned, and I hope our municipal elections will receive some reform with regard to order and tranquility; or else we must admit that the intervention of women under circumstances like those just described by my right hon. friend is a matter of regret. With respect to School Boards, I own I believe that my right hon. friend the Vice-President of the Council was right in the course he took last year, and that we have done wisely, on the whole, in giving both the franchise and the right of sitting on the School Board to women. Then comes a question with regard to Parliament, and we have to ask ourselves whether we shall or shall not go farther. Now, I do go so far as to admit that my hon. friend has a presumptive case for some change in the law, although, for my part, I will go no further until I know more of the nature of the change to be effected. With reference to the nature of that change, I am sorry my hon. friend has not noticed the subject of the representation of the property of women at elections by their actual exercise of the franchise, provided it is not done by means of personal intervention and attendance. I will not give any positive opinion on that subject, but I have never heard any conclusive reason why we should not borrow a hint from the law now existing in Italy, under which a woman is allowed to exercise the franchise if she is possessed of a qualification, subject to the condition that she shall only exercise it through a deputy, some friend or relative, especially chosen for the purpose. That may be found on examination to be a good or a bad plan, but it is one worthy of discussion. I admit, at any rate, that as far as I am able to judge, there is more presumptive ground for change in the law than some of the opponents of the measure are disposed to own. I think my right hon. friend the member for Kilmarnock perhaps fell into an error on this subject, which is very common in our discussions, I mean the error of making the social rules and considerations which govern and determine the constitution of the upper class of society, the rules and considerations which should apply to the whole. (Hear, hear.) It is very easy to deal with this case as regards the upper class. I am disposed without giving a positive opinion, to say that, so far as grievance is concerned, so far as practical mischief to be removed is concerned, with regard to the higher circle, to those who are familiarly called the 'upper ten thousand,' there is no case at all for entertaining a measure of this kind. There is not even a presumptive case. But when we look at the whole of society the case is different. In the first place, we are encountered by a great social fact. My right hon. friend rests upon the old law of the human race – the law under which to the woman falls the domestic portion of duty, the care of the household, and to the man the procuring of subsistence. But that great and world-wide and world-old fact is one which the return of every census shows us to be undergoing a somewhat serious modification. The number of absolutely self-depending women is increasing from year to year, especially in the great towns of the country. My right hon. friend speaks truly, when he says that the head of the family is the person naturally charged with the interest of his unmarried daughters: but when we go downwards in society we find that, almost as a matter of necessity, at any rate as a matter of practice, it now very frequently happens, especially in this vast metropolis, that cases arise where, when the girl approaches womanhood, it becomes almost a necessity for the father, under the limited conditions of his existence and his habitation, irrespective of the lot of marriage, which is the normal or ordinary condition of woman, to say to his daughter that she must begin to think for herself, and set about providing for her subsistence. If it be true that there is a progressive increase in the number of self-dependent women, that is a very serious fact; because these women are assuming the burdens which belong to men; and I agree with the hon. member for Manchester that when they are called upon to assume those burdens, and to undertake the responsibility of providing for their own subsistence, they approach the task under greater difficulties than attach to their more powerful competitors. Now, sir, I cannot help thinking that, for some reason or other, there are various important particulars in which women obtain much less than justice under social arrangements. It is to me a matter of astonishment to observe in London the distribution of employments as between men and women. I scarcely ever see in the hands of a woman an employment that ought more naturally to be in the hands of a man – (hear, hear), – but I constantly see in the hands of a man employment which might be more beneficially and economically in the hands of a woman. I may be told that there is no direct connection between this and the parliamentary franchise, and I admit it; but at the same time I am by no means sure that these inequalities may not have an indirect connection with a state of law in which the balance is generally cast too much against women, and too much in favour of men. There is one instance which has been quoted, and I am not sure there is not something in it – I mean the case of farms. (Hear, hear.) The not unnatural disposition of landlords is to see farms in the hands of those who, sympathising – as the English tenant is ordinarily and honourably disposed to do – with his landlord, can give effect to that sympathy by voting at the poll, and I believe to some extent in the competition for that particular employment women suffer in a very definite manner in consequences of their want of qualification to vote. I go somewhat further than this, and say that so far as I am able to form an opinion of the general tone and colour of our law in these matters, where the peculiar relation of men and women are concerned, that law does less than justice to women. (Hear, hear.) The right hon. gentleman has said truly that some enthusiasts or fanatics are set on modifying or subverting the law of marriage. I confess I am one of those who think that we struck a serious blow at the law of marriage when we passed the Divorce Act; but I have never yet been able to satisfy my mind as to the reasons why, in framing and passing that Act, we chose to introduce a new and gross inequality against women and in favour of men. (Hear, hear.) The subject which I am now on the verge of is rather painful, and not necessary to enter upon in detail, but I may say that in the whole of this chapter of legislation, especially where the irregular relations of men and women and the consequences of those irregular relations are concerned, the English law does women much less than justice, and great mischief, misery, and scandal result from that state of things in many of the occurrences and events of life. (Cheers.) I may be told that it is not to be supposed that women would in any circumstances, if in a majority, exercise a preponderating influence in public concerns. They will not and they cannot. But the question whether it is possible to devise a method of enabling them to exercise a sensible influence, without undertaking personal functions and without exposing themselves to personal obligations, inconsistent with the fundamental particulars of their condition, as women, is a question which, in my opinion, is very worthy of consideration. Although, therefore, I am unable to give a vote for a Bill with respect to which there is no promise of its modification, if we cannot adopt it in its present form, yet I am not sorry to think that some activity of thought in these busy days of ours is directing itself to the subject of the relations which actually prevail between men and women; and if it should be found possible to arrange a safe and well-adjusted alteration of the law as to political power, the man who shall attain that object, and who shall see his purpose carried onward to its consequences in a more just arrangement of the provisions of other laws bearing upon the condition and welfare of women, will, in my opinion, be a real benefactor to his country. (Cheers.)

Lord JOHN MANNERS said he had not hitherto voted on this measure, because, while on the one hand unable to discover any logical reasons against it, he had on the other been restrained by that which was properly called sentiment, but which was an element that ought not to be shut out from view in considering questions of this kind. And he was prepared to admit that if there were any proof on the present occasion that the majority or any reasonable portion of the women who would be affected by the Bill were hostile to the measure he should be glad to allow sentiment rather than reason to prevail, and withhold his support from the Bill; but on reference to the parliamentary papers he found that up to that morning no single petition had been presented against the measure, while a considerable number had been presented in its favour. Therefore, he was bound to ask what were the practical arguments against the measure, and having listened to the speeches of the mover and seconder of the amendment, and of the Prime Minister, he was unable to perceive that there were any arguments possessing validity against the second reading of the Bill. (Hear, hear.) The right hon. gentleman the member for Kilmarnock took exception to the speech of the Hon Member who moved the second reading of the Bill on the ground that it was too narrow. He (Lord J. Manners) confessed that if he were to find fault with the speech it would be in precisely the opposite direction, but the right hon. gentleman himself could not be accused of narrowing the issue, for his speech was directed to almost every subject under the sun except the Bill the House was now called upon to discuss. (Hear, hear.) He told the House with perfect truth that he had studied every branch of the subject, and produced most voluminous evidence that his statement was correct, with the single exception that he had not studied the Bill itself. He dilated upon the laws of marriage and of property, the state of affairs in America, and the writings of every philosophical writer on the question from Payne Knight to Mill, denouncing the theories of the latter; but he did not say one word to show that the female ratepayers of this country ought not to have the suffrage accorded to them. (Hear, hear.) He could not tell from the speech of the right hon. gentleman at the head of the Government whether he was in favour or against the measure. (Cheers.) He thought, however, he might venture to say that, whatever might be the opinions of the right hon. gentleman now, he would before long be numbered among the supporters of the measure. (Cheers and laughter.) The principal objection which the right hon. gentleman appeared to take to this measure was that it had no preamble, but he did not know that in these days that was a serious objection. (Hear, hear.) He had himself passed a measure, while in office, that had no preamble. Then the right hon. gentleman had objected that there was nothing in this Bill to prevent the personal attendance of the female voters at the poll; but that objection, if valid, might be equally urged against women voting at municipal elections and elections for the School Boards and local boards of health. The right hon. gentleman had suggested that by going to Italy we might borrow a mode by which we could surmount this difficulty; but he would suggest that the difficulty would be removed without travelling so far by resorting to the plan already in use in respect to the elections for the universities, where voters are permitted to record their votes by deputy. But, whether it were advisable to adopt that plan or not, the subject was one pre-eminently for the decision of the House, when they got into committee. (Hear, hear.) What he contended was that if the principle of enfranchising women ratepayers was sound in relation to other elections it was equally sound in relation to the election of members of Parliament. Did his right hon. friend, the member for Kilmarnock, mean to contend that women had no interest in the subjects brought before that House? Were they not interested, for example, in the subject of education, or were they not interested and did their interests not deserve to be represented in the Deceased Wife's Sister Bill – a measure which had so long been the shuttlecock of the two Houses of Parliament? (Hear, hear.) His right hon. friend appeared to say by his argument that women might be permitted to vote for such inferior bodies as Poor Law Guardians, Boards of Education, and Municipal Councils, but that they had no right to share in the election of so august a being as a member of the House of Commons. Now, he (Lord J. Manners) was prepared at all times to vindicate, if necessary, the rights and privileges of that House, but to assert that female ratepayers were not worthy to form a part of the constituencies of members of parliament was an arrogation of personal dignity and superiority which he was by no means able to support. Under all those circumstances, he confessed he was unable to see any reason why the female ratepayers should be any longer excluded from the exercise of the franchise at parliamentary elections – (hear, hear) – and he should therefore give his support to the second reading of the Bill.

Mr BERESFORD HOPE thought that the right hon. gentleman the member for Kilmarnock in opposing the Bill gave the House an elaborate, but a very truthful, *exposé* of the policy of women's rights, in his Bill of indictment against the strong-minded phalanx, for whom he personally had a great respect and no little fear. It was only the previous morning that he had received a speech from a lady belonging to that body, in which he was charged with comparing certain noble women to dancing dogs. He had a high respect for the virtues and the capacity of women, and he therefore looked upon a woman's tongue, sharpened by debates and journalism, as a very formidable weapon, and one that was highly dangerous to encounter. The speech of the Prime Minister was satisfactory to him in one point, for it showed that, however much his right hon. friend's opinions might have changed with respect to other parts of the marriage law, his opinions in relation to the subject of divorce were exactly what they were 14 years ago. He (Mr Beresford Hope) also fought by his side, as well as his noble friend who had just spoken, in opposition to the Divorce Act of 1857. Recollecting those days he listened with much interest for the arguments which his noble friend should adduce. In supporting the measure of the Hon Member for Manchester, he was bound to traverse the able reasoning of the right hon. gentleman the member for Kilmarnock, but he did nothing of the kind. He simply contended that because women were allowed to exercise the franchise at municipal and School Board elections, they should be allowed to vote for members of that House. This was assertion and not argument until the identity of the two cases was shown, and when that was done his noble friend must in consistency range himself with the supporters of the ballot. He was astonished to hear his noble friend allege as any argument that no women had petitioned against the Bill. These words should have come from any mouth but his, for it was equally true that they had never petitioned against the Divorce Bill, although it was well known that the women of England were righteously opposed to the passing of that measure. He (Mr Hope) honoured the women for not having done so, because that innate modesty which was the great attribute of the sex prevented them putting themselves forward on such occasions. Their not petitioning was indeed an argument against the change, for it proved that women shrank from thrusting themselves forward into the noisy turmoil of politics. No doubt women had sometimes petitioned Parliament – they had even crowded that table with petitions on a certain question which should have been the very last to attract their attention. So far from that fact being a reason for conferring this franchise upon women, as showing that they took a deep interest in the proceedings of the House, he thought that the disgusting appearance of the petitions to which he alluded greatly strengthened the arguments of those who were conscientiously opposed to the principle contended for by the advocates of the present measure. He was opposed to the Bill, because he wished to protect women from being forced forward into the hurly-burly of party politics, and obliged to take part in all the disagreeable accompaniments of electioneering contests and their consequences. The right hon. gentleman, the First Minister of the Crown, referring to the upper ten thousand, said that they had not an appreciable shadow of grievance to complain of in this respect, whilst he observed that the class of self-dependent women was increasing very rapidly, and seemed to regard this fact as a reason for the change. The right hon. gentleman indeed stated that he would not vote for the Bill of the hon. member for Manchester, but his sibylline tones left the impression that there was such doubt lurking in his mind that in another session he would be found in the ranks of those who were in favour of women's suffrage. The fact of the class of self-dependent women increasing so much was in his mind a reason for withholding the franchise from them. There were a few women who obtained a great influence in society by their genius and their capacity for work, and he honoured them for it. They had, however, as much power already in their way as the exercise of a vote for members of that House could give them; but the great majority of the self-dependent class were persons who by many sacrifices and ceaseless industry just succeeded in realising competence sufficient with great thrift to support them in a moderate and quiet way. The extension of the franchise to such women would not only disturb the peaceful character of their lives, but might seriously endanger that competence by forcing them into the arena of political excitement where they would be exposed to the animosities, the bickerings, and the resentments which are so unhappily inherent in the rough work of electioneering. Taking then this self-dependent class as they really were and not as philosophers painted them, he thought that Parliament would do them a great wrong by exposing them to the temptations inseparable from the franchise whether those who possessed it took an active part in politics, or refused to exercise the franchise which had been conferred on them. All who were familiar with contests knew that it was often as troublesome not to vote as to give a vote; and yet Parliament was asked to put the helpless female lodgers, seamstresses, and such persons, in this dilemma. The very nature of women called for sympathy and protection, and for the highest and most chivalrous treatment on the part of the men, but, instead of this being accorded for the future, it was now proposed to thrust them into a position which they were by their sex, by their condition in life, and by their previous training totally unqualified to grapple with. It would be said that the proposal was only to enfranchise unmarried women, but he was not a believer in such illogical finality. If this Bill were passed did his right hon. friend behind him (Mr Russell Gurney) believe that the distinction contemplated in it between married and unmarried women would long continue to be upheld? And, without going so far, why should not those ladies who were temporarily independent be invested with these privileges? There was, for instance, he would not mention any names, a lady who had recently been remarkable for an act of great daring, and who had subsequently escaped in consequence of admirable management. Would it not be right that she should be invested with these privileges for some eight years or so? The lady in question was one whose ability had been proved and her innocence decided in the face of the world. If this Bill should pass, and the number of emancipated women were found to produce no appreciable change in the quality of the representation in the House, then he would say that they had made a great disturbance to gain something very small indeed; but, on the other hand, if it were found to cause any serious alteration in the character of the representation, then, with all due respect to all the new constituencies, he believed that the alteration would be shown in the deterioration and not in the improvement of the quality of Parliament. On this head he desired to speak plainly. It was not a question whether the male or the female intellect were the superior one. He simply said that they were different, and that the difference made man more capable of direct government and woman more fitted for private influence. There were in the world women of a manlike-mind – a Mrs Somerville or a Miss Martineau, and there were now and then men of feminine softness; but he reasoned from the generality and not from marked exceptions. Reason predominated in the man, emotion and sympathy in the woman, and if the female vote made any noticeable difference in the character of our constituencies, the risk would be that they would have in the House an excess of the emotional and sentimental element over the logical and reasoning faculty. Though emotion and sentiment were admirable qualities in their way, he maintained distinctly that reason ought to govern emotion, and not emotion govern reason. If, indeed, our existing constituencies were exclusively composed of bachelors and widowers, it might be argued that the reason was not sufficiently tempered by sentiment. But with the large bulk which they contain of family men, he felt quite satisfied that the womanly nature had quite as much play in making up the national minds as could be healthfully desired. The character of the legislation of a woman-chosen Parliament would be the increased importance which would be given to questions of a *quasi* social or philanthropic character (viewed with regard to the supposed interests, or the partisan bias of special classes, rather than to broader considerations of the public weal) in excess of the great constitutional and international issues which the Legislature was empanelled to try. We should have more wars for an idea, or hasty alliances with scheming neighbours, more class cries, permissive legislation, domestic perplexities, and sentimental grievances. Our legislation would develop hysterical and spasmodic features, partaking more of the French and American system than reproducing the tradition of the English Parliament. On these grounds he should vote against the second reading of the Bill.

Dr LYON PLAYFAIR said that the House would observe that the opponents of the Bill had brought forward no objections to the question of right and wrong involved in it, but had treated it simply as a matter of convenience and expediency. They were told that there would be a considerable innovation in the social habits of the people if this Bill passed into law, and to that view the right hon. gentleman the member for Kilmarnock had given powerful expression. Last session the objection received support from the First Minister of the Crown, when he described it as uprooting the landmarks of society. He was glad to find that that argument was not now repeated by the right hon. gentleman, although it had to a certain extent been re-echoed by the right hon. gentleman the member for Kilmarnock. When he had heard that expression fall from a Liberal Minister with regard to a Liberal measure he felt certain that the right hon. gentleman would be on their side before long ('hear' and laughter), for there was a fine extinct Tory roll about the phrase. (Cheers and laughter.) The phrase used to be brought forward to accompany the doctrine of the divine right of kings; it was urged against the negro emancipation, and had served as stage thunder on similar occasions from time immemorial whenever there was a question of extending suffrage among the people. The whole argument of the supporters of the Bill was contained in one sentence – that the law imposed upon women the burdens of citizenship, and that if sex was no reason for preventing the imposition of those burdens, so also sex should be no justification for withholding from them the rights which attached to citizenship. (Hear, hear.) The fact was that one-sixth to one-seventh of the taxpayers, being females, were not represented in that House. No person had said in the House that the average woman was not able by her intellect to carry out the smallest function of political duty – the voting for a member of Parliament. While they actually did give this privilege to the most ignorant and debased men, and refused it to the most cultivated and virtuous women, the only reason that could be urged against the enfranchisement of women was their sex. The argument employed by his right hon. friend the member for Kilmarnock amounted to this – that women had no business to interfere in politics. But his definition of politics was the meanest and lowest view that could be taken, and referred not to the science of government, which was the true meaning of the word, but to the struggle of parties for power. Politics, properly understood, meant the government of the people in equal and fair relations to each other, with a view to their happiness and to the security of their property and persons. Why should one-half the human race be cut off from such a noble study? His right hon. friend had expressed his opinion that the concession of the municipal franchise was a mistake, and had instanced one or two cases in which votes were given in an unhappy state of intoxication. But all that showed was that there were degraded men as there were degraded women, and no doubt there would always be degraded female electors as there were degraded male electors. If his argument were worth anything it only implied disfranchisement of the unworthy of both sexes. (Cheers.) If his right hon. friend, in accounting for the interest which women took in the School Boards by the fact that the voting was secret, had promised this measure his support after the Bill for secret voting had been carried, his position would at least have been logical. It had been urged that women already possessed a vast amount of political influence. There could be no doubt that that was true, as they had lately witnessed in relation to a matter which was very repugnant to their feelings. His own opinions on that subject were well-known, so he was not likely to be misunderstood; but there could be no doubt that the women on this subject had exercised so much influence, whether rightly or wrongly, as to endanger the seats of many members of that House who did not take their views. If the opinion of these women was right the Act ought not to have been passed without greater regard being paid to their interests and feelings – if they were wrong the responsibility of rejecting the Acts ought to be shared by those who induced its rejection. Ultimately it was still the fault of those who, by excluding women from politics, had allowed them to act in a natural feeling of sympathy for the fallen of their sex, and not to subjugate their feelings to the exigencies of public polity. (Hear, hear.) But then the objection is made that women are not educated for politics. Quite true this, and whose fault is it? The same objection was brought forward at the late extension of suffrage to men; but experience has shown that actual responsibility was a wonderfully rapid educational power. The want of political education among women was the fault of the House in not having already given them the franchise – the greatest political educator at command. The old argument that the exercise of the franchise carried to its legitimate conclusion would result in the presence in the House of representative women did not alarm him. If the Bill passed, the men would still number six to every single woman on the register, and although he was not sure that even now any law existed for disqualifying women from seats in the House, he was prepared to oppose any measure conferring such power, not on the ground of mental but physical incapability. The Hon Member for Cambridge University and those who supported him acted on the traditional idea of women being subject to men, the old 'rib' theory. It had been said by the Hon Member for Pembroke, in the true 'rib' spirit of the question, that the avocation of women was a high one – to make life endurable; the Hon Member for the University of Cambridge had more elegantly put it that the avocation of women was to guide, to influence, to moderate, to regulate, and to suffer – not to govern. But convert his verbs into nouns, and why were guidance, influence, moderation, and endurance to be regarded as qualities opposed to government? The Prime Minister had said that to justify the denial of the franchise to any person it was necessary to prove personal unfitness or public danger. That was a perfectly sound political axiom; and judged by it the Bill should pass, especially as it was on all hands admitted that women exhibited a higher moral tone than men, which increased their aptitude, while their quiescence of character did not involve political danger. The Right Hon Member for Kilmarnock (Mr Bouverie) had read them passages from the writings of eccentric authors of socialistic proclivities, as evidence that the suffrage should not be extended to women. He might as well have adduced the ravings of Red Republicans and Communists as an argument for refusing the suffrage to men. He also had alluded to the opinions of a distinguished constituent of himself (Dr Playfair) John Stuart Mill. He read passages from his writings, and implied that these were calculated to dispute the sanctity of marriage. These passages, however, had no such bearing. They simply referred to the theory of subjection implied by the law, when it dealt such unequal justice to the two sexes. At Avignon there is the grave of an Englishwoman, on whose tomb there is a beautiful tribute to her high excellencies. She was the wife who had adorned the life of John Stuart Mill, and any one who had read these touching words would have known the veneration which that philosopher had for woman, and would blush to accuse him of desiring to destroy the sanctity of marriage. (Cheers.)

Mr JAMES, although dissenting from the supporters of the Bill, could not discuss the question in the spirit in which it had been dealt with by the Prime Minister, or dwell on the trivial point of the absence of a preamble. Although the matter should not be treated technically, it was clear that every married woman who might choose to be rated would be entitled under the Bill to a vote as well as the unmarried; but there were more important considerations than this. The natural consequence of granting the franchise was that all women were eligible to sit in the House of Commons, and they could, of course, claim their right to be represented in the House of Peers, to act as jurors, and even to sit on the episcopal bench. (Hear, hear.) Under these circumstances it was sufficient if the opponents of this Bill established that there was no precedent in the past or practice in the present to justify its passing; and having done this they had a right to stand on the defensive and say, 'On what grounds should this Bill pass?' The speech of the Prime Minister upon the measure had given the greatest dissatisfaction, and some had heard it with sadness. To introduce the question of the ballot into such a grave matter as this was almost an insult to those who supported the ballot. (Hear, hear.) He assured the Prime Minister, with all respect, that he would get little support for the ballot if the moment it became law this measure would be regarded as unobjectionable by him. On hearing such arguments as those the Prime Minister had used for the Bill, and finding in the end that he would vote against it, he was disposed, with all respect, to remind him that while we were told Fame had no present, it was equally true that popularity had no future. (Cheers.) Supporters of the Bill on the other side of the House advocated it on the ground that property should be represented whether held by a woman or a man. But those who used that argument had overlooked the causes which had led to the possession of property being regarded as a qualification for the franchise. The possession of property had been made a qualification because it was held to indicate capacity and fitness in the holder. If the property itself were the thing to be represented, why should not minors vote? It had been formally resolved elsewhere, in language he did not accurately remember, that every person governed should take part in the Government, and the Hon Member for Edinburgh University had said that those who bore the burdens should enjoy the rights. What did this convey? Universal suffrage and something more, for children and minors bore the burdens of the State. Mr Mill, however, had rested his argument solely on the fitness and capacity of the person for whom he was speaking; but although it might be true that women in some mental qualities were stronger than men – in learning languages, for instance – in political matters they were decidedly not so. (Hear.) The sympathetic element in the mental constitution of women absolutely blinded them to all logic. (Hear, hear.) It might be that it was a gain to men that they were not judged day by day by those who could strictly hold the balance. Of course there were exceptions to this rule, just as there were exceptions to the rule that men generally were superior to women in physical strength. On the question of fitness to govern, he asked whether it was not true that in all matters connected with the army, the navy, and matters commercial, diplomatic, and legal, women would have to judge on the basis of information obtained second-hand, and not from practical experience? It might be answered that all these things would come, but before they could come not only the whole character of our social life, but the very nature and passions of mankind, would have to be changed. What father would send his daughter, at the age of 19, into the world to fit her for a political life, saying, 'I know dangers will await her, but the Hon Member for Manchester says she has a political function to fulfil, and I must send her forth to fit her for its fulfilment?' There were other arguments based on matters about which men felt more strongly than they could express, but on the question of the practical effect such a measure would have upon constituencies he remarked that the measure was objectionable, not so much because of the influence it would give to women as to the undue influence it would give to men. The ballot was about to be adopted to prevent the exercise of undue influence over men; but if this Bill passed how enormous would be the power of the priest in one country and the clergyman in the other, to say nothing of the influence of the well-selected canvasser. Surely it could not be expected that women, if endowed with the franchise, would give an unbiassed vote, the result of political convictions? There was one other argument of which much had been made by those who lectured on the subject – namely, that our Sovereign was a woman. Possibly it would be useless to suggest that the possession of negative political qualities was regarded as a virtue in the Sovereign of these realms; but there was another answer to this argument which might have more weight. It was well known that Her Majesty had been fully prepared for her high office by wise statesmen, and that she was an Englishwoman with a full knowledge of the English character; but when it pleased her to take beneath her roof one of her own age, a stranger and a foreigner, and one who had little knowledge and experience of the English people, Her Majesty chose to receive the guidance and direction, the counsel and assistance, of that foreigner simply because she was a woman and he was a man. (Hear, hear.) The few itinerant, restless ladies – (cheers) –

who passed from town to town giving utterance to the oft-repeated sentiments of Lady A and Miss B alleged that the women of England were on their side, but although he had read the periodical advocating their views he had never found that in any of the meetings any lady rose and endorsed the views expressed by the lecturers. Their auditors, occupying their true position, preserved silence, and because of their courteous attention the advocates of women's suffrage assumed they endorsed the lecturer's views. There were other arguments which might be used against this measure – arguments which carried one back to one's first instructress, arguments which received strength in the minds of those who had felt the sympathy and support of a pure woman's love, and he could not doubt that there were many in the House who, in consideration of these arguments, would long resist any attempt to upset what nature had ordained and custom had ratified as the natural place for woman in the State. (Loud cheers.)

Mr W. HUNT, having complimented the hon. and learned gentleman on the force and eloquence which characterised his argument, said: – I do not, however, think the argument irrefutable. From the speech of one of the chief supporters of the amendment he must have thought that this Bill was of the same kind as that withdrawn at Massachusetts, and which did not receive popular support in Utah, because the arguments he used were such as might be brought against a Bill proposing to revolutionise in this country the relations between the sexes. But the Bill proposes nothing of the kind. What it does propose is, that any woman who is placed in the position which gives a man a vote should be entitled to exercise the franchise. It does not propose to divide the vote in the case of a man and wife, and therefore all the arguments of my right hon. friend appear to me to be entirely out of place. Then he used what may be called 'the hobgoblin argument.' He said this was the first step towards socialism. If I thought that would be the effect of this measure, I should be very loth to give it my support. I confess I have always thought the female part of the population showed great reverence for law and order, and was more deeply imbued with religious feelings than the rest of the community – (hear, hear) – and I believe there could be no more certain means of checking the growth of socialism than by giving greater power to women. The right honourable gentleman (Mr Bouverie) says he does not wish the female character to be contaminated by possessing and exercising the suffrage. According to that argument we have done great injustice to those whom, in the years 1867 and 1868, we thrust into the suffrage. It seems we have been contaminating them. But to pass to the speech of the hon. and learned gentleman who has just sat down. I understand he accepts the position of the Hon Member for Cambridge, and says that if the female part of the community bear the same burdens as the male, and also pay rates, there is no reason – unless they are personally unfit – why they should not have a vote. He accepts the conditions, adding that the female is personally unfit. And here, I think, he takes too low a view of the female intellect. In the latter part of his speech, where he speaks of maternal love, and of love of another kind, he seemed to forget that he might attribute other qualities than those of the heart to women. He says they are led away by their sympathies and are incapable of calmly exercising their reason, and that the female mind can rarely follow a logical argument. But if we were to go into the question who is able to follow a logical argument – ('hear, hear,' and laughter) – I fear we should have to bring in Bills of disfranchisement. (Cheers.) A great many of those whose opinions we in this House represent could not, I am afraid, put their opinions in a logical shape, and few, I apprehend, follow a logical argument when we go to the hustings. (Hear, hear.) He says that on political subjects it is notorious that women are not capable of forming independent judgments. I want to know is this not because they have not been entrusted with political power. (Hear.) We know that in some countries so low is the opinion of the female sex they are shut up with their families, while in other countries, and I fear in some parts of our own, they are treated as beasts of burden. The habits of mind of women, as in the case of men, must depend on their training; and I believe no greater means of education could be conceived than entrusting them with political power. My hon. and learned friend says they are unacquainted with subjects such as the army and navy, and other subjects upon which women in this country are supposed to have no opinions. But what did the Right Hon Member for Kilmarnock (Mr Bouverie) say? That they were very usefully employed in hospitals and working charities, and that that was their proper work. But is not this House concerned in a great many social questions on which the opinions of women might be most usefully brought to bear? Such questions as the proper management of hospitals, and kindred subjects, might be thus dealt with most profitably. Some questions have come before this House, notably of late years, in regard to which it would be impossible for men to understand the feelings of the other sex. There is the question which was alluded to by the Hon Member for Cambridge – the question of the

Contagious Diseases Act. Who could say that men are capable of entering into the feelings of women on this question? It has been said that women were going about in an itinerant manner agitating on this subject. But I say, in any case, they have a right to their opinions. But why do they go about? It is because they have no legitimate mode – (cheers) – of giving effect to their opinions, and, therefore, they are compelled to resort to itineracy as the only means open to them. (Renewed cheers.) Supposing that this Bill were passed, and that female ratepayers were allowed to give their votes for the election of members of Parliament, I believe that that itinerant agitation would subside. But with regard to another question which has been before the House – that of altering the marriage laws – is not that a question in which women are entitled to take an active part? Is the opinion of women of no value upon that? During the present and in other sessions this House has passed a Bill containing an alteration of the marriage law which I believe to be repugnant to 99 out of every 100 women in the country. And I ask again, is not this a question upon which they have a right to be heard. Can we assume to ourselves the right to alter the whole state of the marriage law, while more than half the population of the country are regarded as having no voice in the matter? I have never before recorded my vote in favour of this measure, and lately I have not voted at all upon the question, because when changes occur in one's opinions one does not like to commit oneself to such changes on a sudden, or without mature deliberation; but having considered the matter calmly, I have come to the conclusion that it is no longer right to refuse to accede to the principles contained in this Bill. (Hear.) It is not often that measures coming from that quarter of the House receive my support, but this particular measure commended itself to my reason. I believe that the feeling against granting the franchise to women is the result of old prejudice and not of reason, and therefore I shall with great pleasure support the second reading of this Bill. (Cheers.)

Mr NEWDEGATE said: Sir, in common with many other members of the House, I have been gratified by hearing the able and eloquent speech of the Hon and learned Member for Taunton. I rejoiced in it the more on account of the manliness with which the Hon and learned Member, whilst acknowledging the ties of party, lamented the want of force in the speech of the right hon. gentleman, the First Minister of the Crown. But if Hon Members on the Government side of the House, who acknowledge the bonds of party, have some reason to complain that their leader did not repeat emphatically the sentiments to which he gave expression last session in these words: – 'I must say that I cannot recognise a necessity or desire for this measure, which would justify such an unsettling, not to say uprooting, of the old landmarks of society;' if, I repeat, hon. gentlemen opposite, while acknowledging party obligations, lament that those words were not repeated or the equivalent of these strong words by their leader, what must be the feelings of hon. gentlemen on this side of the House, who in like manner acknowledge the obligations of party? Had not they much more reason to be dissatisfied, when they heard the ex-Chancellor of the Exchequer of a Ministry who professed Conservative opinions, adopting this ultra-radical measure? (Loud cheers.) I regret extremely that the House was not fuller, when my right hon. friend, as I hope he will allow me to call him, the member for Kilmarnock, spoke in opposition to this Bill. That right hon. gentleman is true to all the best traditions of his party. He is an old Whig and something more; and he remembers that at the close of the last century and at the commencement of the present century, during the long war, the Whig party became involved by their acceptance of the Encyclopædist opinions, which were then prevalent in France; and he remembers their long and just exclusion from office, and that, at last, they wisely receded from those dangerous opinions, as did that great Sovereign, Frederick of Prussia. Acquainted, therefore, as he is with the history and the traditions of his party, the right hon. gentleman is, perhaps, one of the most competent as well as safest witnesses, who can warn this House against the consequences of accepting this dangerous measure, for I fully agreed with the right honourable gentleman, the Prime Minister, in what he said last session when he declared that it tends to the uprooting of all the relations of society. (Hear, hear.) The least that can be said is this – that if such a law were to be enacted, it would be established without reference to, if not in defiance of, the natural relations of society. I wish Hon Members had been here in greater numbers to have heard the speech of the right hon. gentleman, the member for Kilmarnock; and I would express a hope, that a speech, which is no less worthy of perusal than it was worth hearing, may reach the country through the usual channels of communication. It appears to me, that the division which is about to be taken on this Bill, will establish a clear distinction between those who are sound constitutional and those who are unsound and unconstitutional reformers; between those who would effect changes in the constituencies, and therefore, in the constitution of this House and in the course of our legislation, consistent with the great traditions of the country, traditions which are reflected across the Atlantic, in the United States, and those, who, disgusted with the popular privileges, to the concession of which they have been forced, now seek to degrade this assembly, which has been elected by household suffrage. I do not say this lightly – I say it because I know that this measure has been promoted out of doors by those who look upon that state of this country with disgust, and are prepared to adopt any measure to force a change. Indeed, where could be found an expression of more intense disgust than is conveyed in the description given of England by Dr Manning, when he deliberately described this country as the 'sentinagentium,' the cesspool of nations? Such is the expression which Dr Manning thought fit, in 1864, to publish in a sermon. I shall look with suspicion upon every vote given in favour of this Bill by those who are known to be Dr Manning's followers, because I am convinced that such votes will be actuated not by the desire for any wholesome reform, but that they will be given consistently with the policy of the Ultramontane, the Jesuit party, who hold really free institutions to be so antagonistic to their objects and those of the Papacy, that any measure is justifiable for the purpose of uprooting them. This, sir, is the feeling in the United States with respect to this class of politicians. I was conversing with an American gentleman, and I asked him 'are you prepared in the United States to adopt this proposal for female suffrage, which is now agitating this country?' 'No,' he replied; 'I was a strong advocate for the enfranchisement of the coloured population; but as to this agitation for women's rights which would shake the very foundations of society, by disregarding the natural relations between the sexes – no!' said he, and he spoke, sir, very plainly, 'we are not such fools as to do that.' (Hear, hear.) The fact is, that the whole history of this measure and the whole process of reasoning upon which it is founded are unworthy of and degrading to this House. What has the right hon. gentleman the member for Northamptonshire (Mr Ward Hunt) said, in answer to the formidable arguments of the Hon and learned Member for Taunton? The Hon and learned Member for Taunton stated that the female population of this country have not been trained in those higher sciences which are necessary to direct the legislation of this House; that they have not been trained in diplomacy; that they have not been trained in law; that they have not been trained in political economy. The right hon. gentleman replies to this by saying, that there are some small municipal questions – questions, perhaps, touching family business for example; at most small municipal questions upon which women would be qualified to vote; and, therefore, the right hon.

gentleman, setting at naught the united opinion of the majority of the people of England – for I am certain that the majority of the English people are opposed to this measure – setting at naught too the deliberate verdict of the men of the United States, would confuse and confound the constituencies of this country by introducing an element, which has been adopted nowhere unless in Italy. The right hon. gentleman is not, that I am aware of, an advocate of the ballot. And I am not aware either that he is an advocate for voting by delegation. Why, sir, in the United States they have the ballot, and yet the people of the United States have the common sense to resist this proposal. In Italy they have a different system of election. The people vote there by delegation, upon the same system that is adopted in Prussia; and I ask the right hon. gentleman whether that is the principle which he would introduce into the electoral system of this country? If not, the objection of the United States is unanswered. I am unwilling to detain the House, but it does appear to me that the arguments which have been advanced in support of this measure are utterly futile. What was the argument used by the Hon Member for Penrhyn (Mr Eastwick)? He said that because the Spaniards in South America oppressed the Indians, therefore the women of England ought to be enfranchised! Now I would put it to the common sense of the House, is there any analogy between the position of the Indians in South America, and that of women in England! Then the hon. gentleman attempted this further argument in favour of this measure: he would have the House of Commons enfranchise the women of England – why? Because he thinks it would set a good example in Turkey and in China! I have listened to the somewhat chemical analysis of the hon. gentleman the member for the University of Edinburgh: he seemed to me to adopt this kind of argument, that whereas there are the same chemical elements to be found in the composition of men and women, therefore it is plainly just that women should be enfranchised. There may be some differences. I could not help imagining he might have continued, in the physical construction of men and women, and then he would have told us that through some Darwinian process of development these differences would eventually be obliterated. (Hear, and laughter.) I will content myself with again thanking the right hon. gentleman, the member for Kilmarnock, for having so plainly traced the evil source of the mischievous principles from which this measure has sprung, and for having, as he has often done before, effectively defended the dignity of the House, for such I trust will now be the result, from being betrayed into the extreme folly of adopting this gross exaggeration.

Mr JACOB BRIGHT briefly replied. He stated that Arles Dufoure, who was then in London, was of opinion that the best remedy for the unstable condition of things in France, was to give women votes, and said that the one able speech made to-day against the Bill, that of the hon. and learned Member for Taunton, could be demolished with the greatest possible ease, if the rules of the House permitted him to produce some women (who were then listening to the debate) at the bar to state their own case.

The House divided:–

    For the second reading 151

    Against.. 220

        Majority against the Bill 69

The Bill was therefore lost.

Part III
Her sphere

THE READER IS REQUESTED TO NOTE THAT THE FOLLOWING WAS WRITTEN IN 1875. IN 1877 MEDICAL DEGREES OF THE KING'S AND QUEEN'S COLLEGE OF PHYSICIANS IN IRELAND WERE OPENED TO WOMEN. IN 1878 THE DEGREES OF LONDON UNIVERSITY WERE OPENED TO THEM.

'Tis a beautiful thing, a woman's sphere!
I have pondered the question for many a year,
And have reached a conclusion that's pretty clear –
  That it's not the trade that a woman is in,
  The dirt or the weariness, toil or sin
  It is only the money or rank she may' win
    Which will lift her up out of her sphere!

'Tis a beautiful thing, a woman's sphere!
She may trudge through the snow both far and near,
As a teacher for £25 a year.
  But she must not ask a Professor's name,
  To learn in a college she has no claim –
  Much knowledge adds nought to a woman's fame,
    It's but raising her out of her sphere.

'Tis a beautiful thing, a woman's sphere!
She may nurse a sick bed through the small hours drear,
Brave ghastly infection untouched by fear,
  But she mustn't receive a doctor's fee,
  And she mustn't (oh shocking!) be called an MD,
  For if woman were suffered to take a degree,
    She'd be lifted quite out of her sphere!

'Tis a wonderful thing, a woman's sphere!
She may vote for Town Councillors, Schools, or Mayor,
And numberless Boards and bodies – that's fair.
  But one feminine vote would the Commons sink –
  It's presuming, even, in her to think
  That mankind is bound by a mutual link,
   And that woman is man's compeer.

'Tis a marvellous thing, a woman's sphere!
She may starve at her needle with fast falling tear;
She may hammer nails, or sell gin and beer,
  But she shan't be a lawyer, or clerk at most,
  Or take any nice little Government post,
  For the Law and Society'd give up the ghost
   If she stepped so far out of her sphere.

'Tis a terrible thing, a woman's sphere!
She may part with all her sex holds dear,
May bear the curse, the taunt and leer,
  To earn her bread and to fill her cup –
  But when hands are stretched out to keep her up
  Unspotted and free – oh! then we hear
   That a woman must keep to a woman's sphere.

Originally published in the *Englishwoman's Review*, September 1875.

Frances Power Cobbe

Our policy: an address to women concerning the suffrage

THERE is an instructive story, told by Herodotus, of an African nation which went to war with the South Wind. The wind had greatly annoyed these Psyllians by drying up their cisterns, so they organized a campaign and set off to attack the enemy at head-quarters – somewhere, I presume, about the Sahara. The army was admirably equipped with all the military engines of those days – swords and spears, darts and javelins, battering rams and catapults. It happened that the South Wind did not, however, suffer much from these weapons, but got up one fine morning and blew! – The sands of the desert have lain for a great many ages over those unfortunate Psyllians; and, as Herodotus placidly concludes the story, 'The Nasamones possess the territory of those who thus perished.'

It seems to me that we women who have been fighting for the Suffrage with logical arguments – syllogisms, analogies, demonstrations, and reductions-to-the-absurd of our antagonists' position, in short, all the weapons of ratiocinative warfare – have been behaving very much like those poor Psyllians, who imagined that darts, and swords, and catapults would avail against the Simoon. The obvious truth is, that it is Sentiment we have to contend against, not Reason; Feeling and Prepossession, not intellectual Conviction. Had Logic been the only obstacle in our way, we should long ago have been polling our votes for Parliamentary as well as for Municipal and School Board elections. To those who hold that Property is the thing intended to be represented by the Constitution of England, we have shown that we possess such property. To those who say that Tax-paying and Representation should go together, we have pointed to the tax-gatherers' papers, which, alas! lie on our hall-tables wholly irrespective of the touching fact that we belong to the 'protected sex.' Where Intelligence, Education, and freedom from crime are considered enough to confer rights of citizenship, we have remarked that we are quite ready to challenge rivalry in such particulars with those Illiterates for whose exercise of political functions our Senate has taken such exemplary care. Finally, to the ever-recurring charge that we cannot fight, and therefore ought not to vote, we have replied that the logic of the exclusion will be manifest when all the men too weak, too short, or too old for the military standard be likewise disfranchised, and when the actual soldiers of our army are accorded the suffrage.

But, as I began by remarking, it is Sentiment, not Logic, against which we have to struggle; and we shall best do so, I think, by endeavouring to understand and make full allowance for it; and then by steadily working shoulder to shoulder so as to conquer, or rather *win* it over to our side. There is nothing astonishing or blameworthy in the fact that both men and women (women even more than men), when they first hear of the proposal that political action should be shared by both sexes, are startled and shocked. The wonder would be if, after witnessing women's inaction for thousands of years, the set of our brains were *not* to see them for ever 'suckling fools and chronicling small-beer.' The 'hereditary transmission of psychical habits,' which Dr Carpenter talks of, could not fail to leave such an impression; nay, a very short period of seclusion would have sufficed to stamp a prejudice against our ever taking part in public affairs. I had myself the misfortune at one time to consult fourteen eminent surgeons concerning a sprained ankle, and, as a result of that gross imprudence, to pass four of the best years of life as a miserable cripple upon crutches. At the end of that period, when my friends saw me once more walking erect and free, they unanimously exclaimed, 'Oh, do not attempt it! For pity's sake do not go into the street!' One of the tenderest of them even added, almost in tears, 'I cannot *endure* to see you going about without your crutches!' Of course I had much difficulty in persuading these kind people that there was really nothing indecent, or even unladylike, in making use of the limbs wherewith nature had provided me. But I succeeded at last; and so I think women in general will eventually succeed in converting the world to the notion that the faculties bestowed on us by Providence – whether they be great or small – ought all to be used. Humanity might very properly be represented by a man who has all his life used his right hand vigorously, but has kept his left in a sling. Whether the limb were originally weaker than the right, and could not have done as good work, it is not easy to say. It is quite certainly now a poor sinister arm, soft, tender, and without muscular force, and so long accustomed to hang from the neck, that when by chance it is set to work it begins to move in a very nervous and unpractised fashion. Nevertheless, unless any one be prepared to maintain that a man is the better for keeping his left hand tied up, and doing his work with his right alone, it must, I think, be obvious, that this same Humanity will be considerably more happy, and perform its labour more satisfactorily, with two free arms than one.

To win over the public Sentiment now opposed to it, to this great and portentous emancipation of the Left Hand from its sling, very many different sagacious methods will, I am sure, suggest themselves to my readers. I shall venture merely to offer a few hints, which appear to me most important, regarding, 1st, the things which we women ought to *stop doing* and *being*, and, 2ndly, the things we ought to begin to *do* and to *be*.

For the first, we decidedly ought (if we can) to cease to be silly. It is very tempting, I understand, to be silly, when silliness is obviously infinitely more attractive than sense, and when a sweet little piece of utter folly is received as 'so charming' by all who are privileged to hear it. The lady who said (or perhaps did not say) to one of our eminent senators, that 'if she had a vote she would sell it directly to the candidate who would give her a pair of diamond ear-rings' – that sweet young thing (if she ever had existence) was no doubt rewarded by the cordial and gallant approbation of the representative of the masculine gender to whom she confided her elevated views. Nevertheless, her silly speech, and the tens of thousands of speeches in the same vein, made in every ball-room in the kingdom, serve, like so many flakes of snow, to hide the ground. The woman who makes one of them with an ingenious simper, generally has her reward in a rapturous smile; but she has done in that moment of folly all that lay in her power to defer a measure of justice on which hangs, more or less directly, the moral and physical welfare of thousands of women.

Nor is it only, or chiefly, by directly scoffing at the demand for Woman Suffrage that silly women hurt our cause. They hurt us much more by showing themselves unfit for it; by perpetuating the delusion that women are so many kittens – charming to play

93

with, but no more fit to be given political rights than Caligula's horse to be made a Consul. In looking over an American journal devoted to our interests, I have just fallen on three names in succession, which alone seem (very unjustly no doubt) to place the ladies who are willing to bear them through this serious mortal life, rather in the kittenish than the womanly category. Think of gravely demanding political influence, and then signing oneself as Miss 'Mettie' Wauchop, Miss 'Lulu' Wilkinson, or Miss 'Vinnie' Ream! Silly Dress is a subject so portentous, and on which I feel so little competent to speak, that I shall only remark that, while true taste in attire must always add a pleasant prepossession in favour of everything a woman may ask of right or respect, the style which betrays that hours have been devoted to devising it, is absolutely prohibitive of such consideration. The human soul which has been occupied for an entire morning, like one of Pope's sprites, striving –

> Invention to bestow,
> To change a flounce, or add a furbelow.

has, by the hypothesis, neither leisure nor inclination for the graver and nobler pursuits of a rational being.

Another point on which it behoves us women to mend our ways, is the matter of Courage. Men give courage the first place among the virtues, because, without it, there is no guarantee for any other virtue. Assuredly this principle applies no less to women, who, if they be cowards, may be bullied or coerced into every kind of falsehood and baseness, like Ingoldsby's Duchess of Cleves, when her husband pinched her to make her betray her friends –

> His hard iron gauntlet, the flesh went an inch in,
> She didn't mind death, but she couldn't stand pinching.

If we cannot 'stand pinching,' in more ways than one, slaves we are and slaves we must ever be, whether civil and political rights are given to us or not. When I hear a woman say, with a complacent smile, as if she were announcing an ornament of her reputation, 'O, I am *such* a coward!' I always feel inclined to say, 'Indeed? And, may I ask, do you ever go about boasting – "O, I am such a liar?" If you are really a coward you will become a liar any day.' Because we have more sensitive nervous systems than men is no reason why honour, and conscience, and self-respect should not teach us to dominate them. I have no doubt there are some virtues, like Temperance, which cost a man more self-control to exercise than they cost a woman, but we do not hold him exonerated on that account if he fail to exert such self-government. We may pity a woman who cannot stop herself from shrieking if a horse runs away, or a boat tosses on the waves; but assuredly we do not feel she is a person to be trusted with an important charge. On the other hand, the sight of a weak, and perhaps sickly or aged woman, calm, silent, and resolute in the face of peril, is a thing never to be forgotten; and the veriest jackanapes alive who expresses his sublime horror of a 'strong-minded female' will bless his good fortune that it is in her carriage or boat he is sitting, and not in that of the shrieking Angelina.

There are many more things which we ought to refrain from doing if we desire to conquer public Sentiment to our side; but I must hasten to the second part of my subject – the things which we Ought to Do for that end. In the first place, we ought to perform our present share in the world's work – the housekeeping, the house-adorning, the child-educating – so as to prove that, before we go a step further, we can and will at least do *this*. Before Political Economy comes the Economy of the Kitchen, the Larder, and the Coal-cellar; and before the national Budget the household weekly bills. I do not say that the wife, daughter, and sister who manages a house with perfect order and frugality, to the comfort of all the in-dwellers, will thereby convince them of her right to the Suffrage; but I am quite sure, that if she neglect so to manage the house, or live in a despicable muddle of eternal strife with her servants, she will very completely prove her *un*fitness for any higher functions.

Next, we should, as much as possible, seek for employments of the kind for which we are suited, but which have been hitherto monopolized by men; and when we have chanced to obtain one, we should take good care not to lose it by fitful, irregular attendance, slovenly work, or any appeal whatever to special consideration *as women*. Secretaryships, clerkships, telegraph and post-office work, and especially work on the public press (wherein our influence can be direct, as well as indirect), are all objects of concern. I rejoiced much recently to see thirty charming young ladies, the daughters of professional men, at work in the Prudential Insurance Office on Ludgate Hill; and as many more painting porcelain for Messrs Minton at South Kensington. Mr Stansfeld's generous appointment of Mrs Nassau Senior, to report to Government on the condition of pauper girls in London, and that lady's admirable performance of her task, will, I trust, lead ere long to the regular employment, by the State, of Female Inspectors of workhouses, schools, and asylums of all kinds wherein either women or children find refuge. I do not hesitate to say that one woman who does such work as this – even the humblest of those I have named – steadily and thoroughly, does at the same time more for the cause of Woman Suffrage than one who clamours for it most vehemently, but does nothing to prove the fitness of her sex for any public function.

Lastly, we must avail ourselves with the utmost care and conscientiousness of every fragment of Civil Rights which have hitherto been conceded to us. Not the election of a Poor Law Guardian or a parish Churchwarden, still less a municipal election, ought to pass without all the female ratepayers giving their votes, and showing that they do so intelligently, and after due enquiry. If it were possible for us to act in each locality mainly in concert – a committee of the more leisurely obtaining and transmitting the information needed – and everywhere upholding the best candidates, our action would in time come to be felt throughout the country. As to the School Board elections, had they been devised expressly as a prelude and preparation for women's entrance into political life, we could not have had anything better, and we must needs regret that, as yet, they have been very inadequately utilized for such purpose. The ladies who have fought the good fight, and their generous male supporters, deserve from us the heartiest thanks, whether they have or have not proved successful.

The sentiments of men about women must necessarily be formed on the characters of those with whom they associate. If a man's mother be a fool, and his sisters 'Girls of the Period,' and if he select for himself the society of ladies of the *demi-monde*, or of that section of the *grande monde* which emulates the *demi-monde* as closely as it dares, it is quite obvious that when the abstract idea 'Woman' is suggested to him, he will think of a creature in paint, powder, and chignon, whose breath of life is the admiration of men like himself, and who has no more heart, mind, or conscience than a broomstick. He will tell you, and tell you truly, that a woman – such as he knows the creature – loves nobody in earnest, but is ready to pretend to love anybody who will marry her and make her rich; that she is envious of all her female friends, especially the pretty ones; and that she has neither fixed religious nor political opinions, but only pretends ardently to adopt those which she thinks will commend her to the man whom she desires to attract. When I hear a man talk in a mode which implies that this is, at bottom, his idea of a woman, I always make a private memorandum regarding the quarter whence he must have derived his models; just as when I was an *habitué* of the Roman studios I knew precisely from which old beggerman on the steps of the

Trinità one painter had taken his 'Jupiter,' and from which damsel of uncertain morals another had copied his '*Madonna Immacolata*.' Of course I am not afterwards surprised when such a man answers the demand for Woman Suffrage by such laughs as resound through the House of Commons when the subject is broached.

Who would care for a doll, though its ringlets were curled
And its petticoats cut in the fashion?

If women *be* dolls, none but children would play the farce of giving them political rights – in a Baby-house State. The only question is, *Are* they toys? Or is the opinion of the men who find (or make) them so, the one to be acted upon?

On the other hand, if a man's mother be a wise and loving woman, if his sisters be innocent-hearted and intelligent girls, and if he have associated in manhood from preference with good and sensible women, the notion which he forms of the other sex is absolutely the reverse of all I have described. He knows that a woman is capable of love – motherly, conjugal, sisterly – the purest, most distinterested, and most tender. He knows that, so far from being without fixed opinions, she is apt to hold those which she has early acquired with too rigid and narrow a prejudice; and that the ideas of duty and religion occupy commonly a far larger space in her mind than in those of the majority of his male companions. Lastly, by one curious test, his view of woman may always be discriminated from that of the man who has preferred to associate with the *Hetaira* order of female. He will know that, instead of being jealous of her associates, the true woman generally carries her loving admiration for the gifts and graces of her female friends to the verge of exaggeration, and glories in their achievements in educational competitions, in literature, and art, with a generous enthusiasm not often found among masculine rivals. He will take, for example, the letters published in Mrs Somerville's 'Recollections,' which passed between that lady and Mrs Marcet, Miss Edgworth, Miss Berry, and Mrs Joanna Baillie – each expressing her warm delight in the other's gifts and successes – as precisely the most natural outcome of the feelings of women of their class for one another.

To a man trained to think thus of women, the proposal that they should begin to take a part in public affairs, may indeed, at first, seem startling, even offensive; but it will be because he has thought so highly of them, not so lowly. By degrees, perhaps, he will come to learn that the Niche does not make a Saint, and that Idleness is not the root of all good for women, while it is that of all evil for men. Possibly, at last, he will think as the devout Dr Upham said at the close of his life – that, 'since the coming of Christ, no event has promised so much for the virtue and happiness of the human race as the admission of Woman into a share of public duty.'

Thus then, it seems clear, that if the Sentiment of men is to be won over to the claims of women, it must be by compelling them to recognise as the true ideal of womanhood, not a Phryne or a Ninon, but a Zenobia or a Madame Roland.

The great obstacle to the concession of the claims of women does not lie with *men*, for even those most opposed to them might be won over. Still less is it with *busy* women, for it has never happened to me yet to meet a woman who had done much work in the world as a philanthropist, artist, litterateur, or landed proprietor, who did not emphatically endorse the demand for the removal of those political disabilities which she had surely found at one point or another clog her steps. But the great obstacle lies with *idle* women, and nearly exclusively with those for whom nobody dreams of asking for the franchise – for the wives of rich men who have never known a want unsupplied, who have been surrounded by tenderness and homage from their cradles, and have lived all their days like little birds in a downy nest, with nothing to do but to open their beaks and find food dropped into them. It is to the eternal disgrace of such women that, instead of feeling burning shame and indignation at the wrongs and hardships which (as every newspaper shows them) their poorer sisters undergo, they think that, because the world is easy for *them*, it is 'the best of all possible worlds,' and that nothing ought to be changed in it. Like Marie Antoinette, they tell those who want bread to live on buns; and they extol the advantages of the 'chivalry' of men as ample compensation for the lack of every right, without once troubling themselves even to inquire whether the same 'chivalrous' gentleman, who hands them so courteously into a carriage, will not rudely brush past the shabby old governess, or call up the poor work-girl's blushes by his insolent address. When the time comes – perhaps in this approaching Session – when the doors of the Constitution will be opened once more to welcome a new and still lower horde of Illiterates, by the assimilation of the County with the Borough Franchise, we shall, doubtless, again hear the oft-repeated assertion, that our legislators would gladly extend the privilege to women if they believed they really desired it; but that all the ladies whose opinions they have asked, vehemently repudiate the proposal. They might as well offer bread to an alderman at the end of a feast, and, because he declines it, refuse it to a pauper begging at the gate.

But, in spite of the rich and idle wives; and in spite of the men who think the archetypal women was – not a Monkey – but a Doll; in spite of every obstacle, public Sentiment is unquestionably slowly veering round, and it depends on women themselves to bring it altogether to their favour. In this, as in all other things, however, to *be* is a much more important matter than to *do*. The walls of modern Jerichos do not fall down by any trumpeting outside, and the more women shriek for the franchise, or for anything else, the less will men be disposed to open their ears to that extremely unpleasant sound. Let us cease to be silly, and affected, and idle. When we are ignorant, let us cultivate the grace of silence; and when we adorn ourselves, let us do so by the light of the 'Lamps' of Truth and Simplicity. This achieved in the first place, let us become steady, diligent sharers in the world's work, creeping up by degrees as we prove our fitness for one higher task after another; never for a moment asking or wishing to have allowance made for our defects, or over-estimation of our success 'because we are women.' When a sufficient number of us have taken this method of gaining public Sentiment to favour the claims of our sex, the victory will be assured. We may lay by our darts and catapults. The Simoon will blow quite in the opposite direction.

Millicent Garrett Fawcett

*Electoral disabilities of women**

11 March 1871

THE subject of this lecture is one which few are prepared to discuss quite dispassionately. Most people are either enthusiastically in favour of the extension of the suffrage to women, or are violently opposed to it. The former are inclined to think that those who disagree with them must be blinded by prejudice or wilfully opposed to the principles of justice and freedom; the latter look upon a 'woman's rights' woman as the incarnation of all that is repulsive; and a woman's rights man, they think, must be bereft of his senses. I desire to approach the subject of the claims of women to the suffrage in a different spirit to either of these contending parties. I will attempt to state fairly and impartially the main arguments on both sides. If I fail in doing justice to the views of those with whom I differ, I shall not do so wilfully, but through ignorance. I will only add before entering upon the general subject that in my opinion this is not exclusively a woman's question, above all, it is not one in which the interests of men and women are opposed. If the exclusion of women from political power be right and just, women as well as men are interested in maintaining it; if it be unjust and antagonistic to the principles of freedom, then men as well as women are interested in destroying it. 'If one member suffer, all the members suffer

*A lecture delivered at the New Hall, Tavistock.

with it,' is as true as regards national as individual life. Praying your indulgence for many shortcomings, I will at once proceed to give a categorical list of the principal arguments urged against the removal of electoral disabilities of women. You will probably observe that all these arguments could not be used by the same person, as some of them neutralize others. It is, however, better to mention them all, as I am anxious not to omit anything which has been urged in objection to women's suffrage. The objections are: −

1 Women are sufficiently represented already by men, and their interests have always been jealously protected by the legislature.
2 A woman is so easily influenced that if she had a vote it would practically have the same effect as giving two votes to her nearest male relation, or to her favourite clergyman.
3 Women are so obstinate that if they had votes endless family discord would ensue.
4 The ideal of domestic life is a miniature despotism. One supreme head, to whom all the other members of the family are subject. This ideal would be destroyed if the equality of women with men were recognised by extending the suffrage to women.
5 Women are intellectually inferior to men.
6 The family is woman's proper sphere, and if she entered into politics, she would be withdrawn from domestic duties.
7 The line must be drawn somewhere, and if women had votes they would soon be wanting to enter the House of Commons.
8 Women do not want the franchise.
9 Most women are Conservatives, and, therefore their enfranchisement would have a reactionary influence on politics.
10 The indulgence and courtesy with which women are now treated by men would cease, if women exercised all the rights and privileges of citizenship. Women would, therefore, on the whole, be losers if they obtained the franchise.
11 The keen and intense excitement, kindled by political strife, would, if shared by women, deteriorate their physical powers, and would probably lead to the insanity of considerable numbers of them.
12 The exercise of political power by women is repugnant to the feelings and quite at variance with a due sense of propriety.

13 The notion that women have any claim to representation is so monstrous and absurd, that no reasonable being would ever give the subject a moment's serious consideration.

The first of these arguments, viz. that women are sufficiently represented under the present system, is an old friend. Its face must be very familiar to all who took part in or remember the great agitation which preceded the Reform Bill of 1867. Those who were opposed to an extension of the suffrage were never weary of repeating that working men were quite well represented; there was no need to give them votes, for their interests were watched over with the most anxious solicitude by noblemen and gentlemen, who knew far better than the artizans themselves, what was good for the working classes. We all know that this opinion was not shared by working men; they pointed to the inequality of the law relating to masters and servants, and the unjust efforts which legislation had made to suppress trade societies. They said, 'These laws are unequal and unfair, they will not be amended until we have some hand in choosing the law makers.' Besides this, they said, 'We bear a large portion of the taxation of the country; for every pound of tea and sugar we consume we contribute so much to the national revenue, and in common justice we ought to be allowed to exercise a corresponding control over the national expenditure.' For years and years these arguments were repeated in every town in Great Britain; orators like Mr Bright, Mr Ernest Jones, and Mr Cobden devoted immense energy and splendid eloquence in forcing the claims of the working men to representation on the reluctant middle classes. We all know how that struggle terminated; the obstacles were at length surmounted, and the rights of working men to citizenship were fully recognised. Now I appeal to working men and to all who took their side in the great reform agitation, not to cast aside and repudiate the very arguments which they found so useful during that struggle. I would say to them, 'You have reached the top of the wall, don't push down the ladder by which you have ascended.' Apply your arguments to the case of women. Are women sufficiently represented? Are there no laws which press unjustly on them? Is that state of the law equitable which relates to the property of a married woman? Is the law equitable which gives a married woman no legal right to the guardianship of her own children? Perhaps you do not know that 'the married women of this country, when their children are seven years old, have no kind of power to prevent their children from being removed if their husbands choose to remove them!' Would this be the case if women were virtually represented? Finally, using the very same argument which has been so often applied to the working classes – Is it right or just that anyone should be forced to contribute to the revenue of the country, and at the same time be debarred from controlling the national expenditure? Either this argument is good for nothing, or it applies to women as forcibly as it does to men. I think it does apply both to men and women, and that, therefore, it is not accurate to say that women are already sufficiently represented, and that their interests are, under the present system, fully protected.

Now let us turn to the second argument urged against the extension of the suffrage to women, namely, a woman is so easily influenced that if she had a vote it would practically have the same effect as giving two votes to her nearest male relation, or to her favourite clergyman. This is a curious argument; if it were applied indiscriminately to both men and women, very few people indeed would have votes. For instance, it might be said that the *Times* newspaper exercises an extraordinary influence over the political opinions of thousands of people. This is perfectly true; nearly everyone must have noticed how, in ordinary society, the conversation of nine people out of ten echoes the general tone of the leading articles in the day's *Times*. Now it may be said, following out the argument just quoted, the effect of giving all these people votes is only to multiply a million-fold the voting power of the editor of the *Times*, or the writers of the articles in that journal; therefore all people who take their political views from the *Times* ought to be precluded from exercising the franchise. By carrying out the principle, nearly everyone would be disfranchised, except the great leaders of political thought, such as Mr Gladstone, Mr Disraeli, Mr Bright, Mr Mill, Lord Salisbury, and the editors of some of the principal papers. For there are very few indeed whose political opinions are not biased by the views of some of these distinguished and able men. But perhaps this argument, that women's suffrage would only double the voting power of some men, can best be answered by making way for the next argument, namely, that women are so obstinate, that if they had votes, endless family discord would ensue. Now the people who urge this as a reason why women should not be allowed to exercise the franchise, seem to have an erroneous notion of what a vote is. The mere possession of a vote does not confirm or intensify any opinion. If any man here, at present without electoral power, became a voter to-morrow, would the mere possession of a vote effect any change in his political convictions? A vote is not an opinion, but an expression of opinion. Now let us suppose the case of a family in which the husband and wife hold similar political views; their talk is probably often of politics, and I cannot see that it would make any difference to their domestic happiness if the wife could vote as well as her husband. But you say it is all very well for me to illustrate my argument by the case of a husband and wife whose political views are similar; how would it answer for a wife to have a vote if she disagreed with her husband's political opinions? I reply by asking in return – how does the present system answer? In those cases in which the husband and wife hold different political opinions, one of three things happens: either politics are suppressed as a subject of conversation – the husband goes his own way, and the wife never interferes or obtrudes her own views; or the husband and wife are sensible enough to discuss political subjects and defend their respective opinions with energy, and yet without temper; or else, finally, they take no pains to smoothe over or hide their differences. The wife, for instance, fasts every 30 January, in honor of the sacred memory of King Charles the martyr; whilst the husband hangs up the death warrant of that monarch, and treasures it as a glorious memento of British freedom. Now in each of these cases the perfect concord and sympathy which form the ideal of marriage are more or less destroyed. What is it which destroys this concord and sympathy? The answer must be – essential difference of opinion on a subject constantly affecting every-day life. It is the divergence of opinion which destroys the harmony, not the expression of that divergence. Under the present system women cannot be prevented from having political opinions, or from expressing them, and I venture to think that if they had votes there would be more domestic harmony on political subjects than there now is; for then marriages would not so frequently take place between those who hold diametrically opposite political views. Suppose, for instance, that in order to insure conjugal harmony on religious matters, a law were passed to prevent all women going to church. The advocates of such a law might say, 'Suppose an Evangelical married a Roman Catholic, what disagreement it would lead to, if the husband went off to one place of worship and the wife to another.' As a fact such marriages seldom take place; for it is recognised that women have a right to think for themselves on religious subjects, and there is therefore a strong and reasonable feeling against marriages between people of opposite religious opinions. Would not the same feeling come into existence against marriages between people of opposite political parties, if the political independence of women were recognised. If this feeling were prevalent I believe a higher harmony than any yet generally known would gradually pervade domestic life.

Let us now consider the validity of the fourth objection raised against the enfranchisement of women, namely, 'The ideal of domestic life is a miniature despotism, in which there is one supreme head, to whom all other members of the family are subject. This ideal would be destroyed if the equality of women with men were recognised, by extending the suffrage to women.' I am ready at once to concede that if the truth of the premise is granted, the truth of the conclusion must be granted also. Family despotism would receive a deadly blow from the extension of political power to women. But let us enquire how and why men – Englishmen at least – have come to consider despotic national government immoral and then let us see whether despotic family government differs essentially in principle from other despotisms. First let us enquire why despotic national government has been so successfully opposed in this country, and why representative government has been set up in its place. It may be briefly said that despotic government has been got rid of in this country because it has been felt to interfere unwarrantably with individual liberty. The leaders of popular rights from the time of Magna Charta to this day, have always insisted on the importance of preserving individual liberty. Why has the name 'Liberty' always had such a magic spell over men? Why has liberty been valued more than life itself by all those whose names make our history glorious? Why have our greatest poets sung the praises of liberty in words that will never be forgotten as long as our language lasts? Is it not because it has been felt more or less strongly at all times that man's liberty is essential to the observance of man's duty? A contemporary philosopher has thus analysed the right of mankind to liberty. He says 'It may be admitted that human happiness is the Divine Will. We become conscious of happiness through the sensations. How do we receive sensations? Through what are called faculties. It is certain that a man cannot hear without ears. Equally certain that he can experience no impression of any kind unless he is endowed with some power fitted to take in that impression; that is, a faculty. All the mental states, which he calls feelings and ideas, are affections of his consciousness, received through his faculties. There next comes the question – under what circumstances do the faculties yield those sensations of which happiness consists? The reply is – when they are exercised. It is from the activity of most of them that gratification arises. Every faculty in turn affords its special emotion; and the sum of these constitutes happiness; therefore happiness consists in the due exercise of all the faculties. Now if God wills man's happiness, and man's happiness can be obtained only by the exercise of his faculties, then God wills that man should exercise his faculties; that is, it is man's duty to exercise his faculties, for duty means the fulfilment of the Divine Will. As God wills man's happiness, that line of conduct which produces unhappiness is contrary to His Will. Therefore the non-exercise of the faculties is contrary to His Will. Either way then we find the exercise of the faculties to be God's Will and man's duty. But the fulfilment of this duty necessarily supposes freedom of action. Man cannot exercise his faculties without certain scope. He must have liberty to go and come, to see, to feel, to speak, to work, to get food, raiment, shelter, and to provide for all the needs of his nature. He must be free to do everything which is directly or indirectly requisite for the due satisfaction of every mental and bodily want. Without this he cannot fulfil his duty or God's Will. He has Divine authority therefore for claiming this freedom of action. God intended him to have it; that is, he has a right to it. From this conclusion there seems no possibility of escape. Let us repeat the steps by which we arrive at it. God wills man's happiness. Man's happiness can only be produced by the exercise of his faculties. Then God wills that he should exercise his faculties. To exercise his faculties he must have liberty to do all that his faculties naturally impel him to do. Then God wills that he should have that liberty. Therefore he has a *right* to that liberty.' The only limitation to perfect liberty of action is the equal liberty of all. 'Liberty is not the right of one, but of all! All are endowed with faculties. All are bound to fulfil the Divine will by exercising them. All, therefore, must be free to do those things in which the exercise of them consists. That is, all must have rights to liberty of action. Wherefore we arrive at the general proposition that everyone (man or woman) may claim the fullest liberty to exercise his faculties compatible with the possession of like liberty by every other person.' Never has the basis of individual liberty been more clearly explained than in this passage. It proves conclusively that despotism being antagonistic to the principle of 'the perfect freedom of each, limited only by the like freedom of all,' is at variance with the Divine will. How then can the ideal of family life be despotism, when despotism is proved to be antagonistic to the Divine will? If I have dwelt at some length on the importance of recognising the real basis of the rights of man, it is not to prove to you that these rights exist, – all in this room are probably willing to concede that, – but to 'show that the rights of women must stand or fall with those of men;

derived as they are from the same authority; involved in the same axiom; demonstrated by the same argument.' Much more could be said in defence of the assertion that despotic family government is very far removed from the ideal state. If time permitted I think it could be shown that command is blighting to the affections, and that where anything approaching the ideal of domestic happiness at present exists, the subjugation of all members of the family to the husband and father is not enforced. But it is necessary to pass to the consideration of the next objection to the extension of political power to women, namely, that women are intellectually inferior to men. I am not going to enter upon the vexed question whether the mental powers of men and women are equal. It is almost impossible from want of evidence to prove whether they are or not. It may be very interesting as a philosophical discussion, but I maintain that it is quite irrelevant to the present subject, – that is, whether women ought to have political power. Suppose it could be proved beyond the slightest doubt that on the average the intellectual powers of women were inferior to those of men. If this were fully and satisfactorily established, as a fact, it would not furnish the slightest justification for depriving women of electoral power. Suppose it were also proved that the intellectual powers of the inhabitants of the north of England are superior to those of the inhabitants of the south of England. I can assure you I have often heard very accomplished people assert seriously that this is the case. Would you recognise that as a reason why the inhabitants of the south of England should be deprived of electoral power? Would the people of Tavistock be willing to relinquish their right to the franchise if it were proved to demonstration that on an average and taking them altogether they were intellectually inferior to the inhabitants of Edinburgh? It is ridiculous to suggest such a thing, and yet this absurdity is exactly similar to what is really urged against allowing women to exercise the franchise. But the question may be looked at from another point of view. It is said that women on the whole are not the intellectual equals of men. Whether this is true I neither affirm nor deny; but even the most ardent asserters of the inferiority of women have never said that all women are inferior to all men. In the sphere of Government I need only mention Zenobia, Maria Theresa, and Elizabeth to remind you that these women's names stand preeminent. Let us hear what the authority previously quoted has to say on this subject. Granting for the sake of argument, that the intellect of woman is less profound than that of man, he adds 'Let all this be granted, and let us now see what basis such an admission affords to the doctrine that the rights of women are not co-extensive with those of men: –

1 If rights are to be meted out to the two sexes in the ratio of their respective amounts of intelligence, then must the same system be acted upon in the apportionment of rights between man and man.

2 In like manner, it will follow, that as there are here and there women of unquestionably greater ability than the average of men, some women ought to have greater rights than some men.

3 Wherefore, instead of a certain fixed allotment of rights to all males and another to all females, the hypothesis involves an infinite graduation of rights, irrespective of sex entirely, and sends us once more in search of those unattainable desiderata, – a standard by which to measure capacity, and another by which to measure rights. Not only, however, does the theory thus fall to pieces under the mere process of inspection; it is absurd on the very face of it, when freed from the disguise of hackneyed phraseology. For what is it that we mean by rights? Nothing else than freedom to exercise the faculties. And what is the meaning of the assertion that woman is mentally inferior to man? Simply that her faculties are less powerful. What then does the dogma that because woman is mentally inferior to man she has less extensive rights, amount to? Just this – that because woman has weaker faculties than man, she ought not to have like liberty with him to exercise the faculties she has!'

We will now pass to the sixth objection to women's suffrage – that the family is woman's proper sphere, and if she entered into politics she would be withdrawn from her domestic duties. I may mention in passing – it is a fact to which I do not attach any special importance or regret – that there are some million or so of women in this country without families and without domestic affairs to superintend. The number of women is constantly in excess of the number of men, and so there must always be a certain percentage of women unmarried, and who therefore have no families to be withdrawn from. It is all very well to tell a woman that her sphere is to be a wife and a mother, when there must always be a large number of women unmarried, owing to the simple fact that there are more women in the world than men. But let us look at the case of women who are married, and see whether the objection that politics would withdraw them from domestic duties, is valid. I should like to find out exactly how many hours in the year an elector in such a town as this devotes to his political duties. Do you think that on an average, taking one with another, they spend an hour a week, every week in the year, in discharging their electoral duties? I don't know whether they do, but I doubt it. I don't think an elector, unless he is engaged in some particular work, such as superintending the registration, or as secretary of some political society, need devote as much as an hour a week, no, nor half-an-hour a week, to duties which the franchise imposes on him. Then what does this objection, that the right to vote at Parliamentary elections would withdraw women from domestic duties, really come to? Why soon it will be objected that women should not go to church or out for a walk, because so doing withdraws them from their domestic duties. But it may be urged that it is not merely the exercise of the franchise, but all that an interest in political questions involves, – the reading of newspapers, the attending of meetings, and the like – that would have a mischievous influence in withdrawing women from their domestic duties. But surely the wife and mother of a family ought to be something more than a housekeeper or a nurse, – how will she be able to minister to the mental wants of her husband and her children if she makes the care of their physical comforts the only object of her life? I do not say that physical comfort is to be despised, but if there is no moral and intellectual sympathy between a husband and wife, or between a mother and her children, a permanent and life-long injury is inflicted on them all, which no amount of physical comfort can in the slightest degree compensate. It is, however, quite erroneous to suppose that an attention to domestic duties and to intellectual pursuits cannot be combined. There is no reason whatever, why wives and mothers should not cultivate their minds and at the same time give proper attention to their domestic affairs. As far as my experience goes, the notion that a woman, in order to manage her house and family well, must devote her whole time and mind to it and do nothing else, is quite incorrect. If I were asked to name the most orderly, neat, bright, and best managed houses that I am acquainted with, I should name those which are respectively presided over by women whose names are justly celebrated for their achievements in literature and science, or for their activity in promoting educational and social reform. Perhaps my experience is exceptionally favourable, but I do not think I know one distinguished woman whose home does not do credit to her taste, refinement, and love of order. I do not, therefore, think the plea that the franchise would withdrawn women from their domestic duties, is a valid objection to their enfranchisement.

We now come to the seventh objection. That the line must be

drawn somewhere, and if women had votes they would soon be wanting to enter the House of Commons. This objection was some years back considered a conclusive argument against removing the electoral disabilities of working men. At any rate, said the Tories, let us have gentlemen in the House of Commons – fancy sitting next a man who didn't sound his hs. They were also quite certain that working men would be great failures in the House. We all know the reply of the Reformers to such objections as these. They said, 'These are questions for constituencies to decide; they are not likely to select a man to serve them in the House of Commons unless he is capable of devoting sufficient time, trouble, and ability to the discharge of his duties.' The selection of a fit person to serve them in Parliament may safely be left to constituencies. At the present time there is no necessity to pass a law that a man wholly immersed in the conduct of a large business, should not offer himself as a candidate for a seat in Parliament. All these things are settled by candidates and constituencies without any legislative interference. As Mr Mill very justly says – I quote from memory – there is no necessity to pass laws to forbid people doing what they cannot do. There is no Act of Parliament needed to enact that none but strong-armed men should be blacksmiths. And so it would prove if all the electoral disabilities were swept away. The would-be-witty caricatures of sickly women fainting in the House of Commons under the weight of their legislative responsibilities would lose their brilliancy and point in the cold light of stern reality. No constituency would deliberately choose a representative who would be quite incapable of serving it faithfully and well. All questions about who should or who should not have seats in Parliament may safely be left to constituencies.

I now turn to the consideration of the eighth objection to the extension of political power to women – that women do not want votes. Notwithstanding the obvious reply that a considerable number of women do want votes, and are continually petitioning Parliament to remove their electoral disabilities, I must confess that this objection to the enfranchisement of women appears to me more formidable than any other which has ever reached me. Of course it makes no difference at all so far as abstract justice is concerned; but still in practical politics abstract justice does not usually weigh much with statesmen, unless it is accompanied by an urgent and pressing demand for the amelioration of the law. There must always be a certain adaptation between the characters of the people, and the rule under which they live. The existence of the Irish Church Establishment was as much opposed to abstract justice in 1769 as it was in 1869, but disestablishment did not take place until the demand for it was so urgent that it could no longer be disregarded. The demand for the extension of the suffrage to women is daily growing more earnest and more general. The Bill now before Parliament has been supported by petitions from every part of the kingdom, signed by many tens of thousands of men and women. In the presence of such facts it cannot be said that there is no demand on the part of women for the suffrage. There is also this very strong argument, which is sometimes overlooked by those who consider that the suffrage should not be extended to women, because the majority of women do not desire to exercise their electoral rights. None of us who desire the extension of the franchise to women wish women to be compelled to vote. Only those who desire political power need exercise their newly-acquired rights. Any woman who thinks that voting would be unfeminine or injurious to her health, would be quite at liberty to refrain from taking part in elections. But it seems to me very unfair that those who don't wish for political power should be enabled to deprive those who do wish for it, of the right to exercise the franchise. Let us now turn to the next objection, namely, that most women are Conservatives, and that their enfranchisement would consequently have a reactionary influence on politics. I have often heard this argument from the lips of men for whom I have the greatest respect, but I never hear it without astonishment and regret. What is representative government if not government by a national assembly chosen by the people to represent their views, and to produce a corresponding influence on the state of the laws? Do those who object to the enfranchisement of women, on the ground that they are usually Conservatives, think that all Conservatives ought to be disfranchised? Surely representative institutions require that all differences of opinion should have their due and proportionate weight in the legislature. No class of persons should be excluded on account of their political opinions. What would be thought of a Conservative who gravely asserted that he thought all Dissenters should be disfranchised because they are generally Liberals? I am almost afraid even to suggest the hard names which such a misguided person would be called by the very people who oppose women's suffrage, because most women are Conservatives. And yet the two cases are exactly parallel, and equally antagonistic to the fundamental principle of representative government. A representative system which excludes half the community from representation surely is a farce. In my opinion the question ought not even to be asked. 'How would women vote if they had the franchise?' The only question ought to be, 'Is representative government the best form of government that can be devised?' If the answer is in the affirmative the exclusion of women from electoral rights can in no way be justified.

The next objection which I have set down is that the indulgence and courtesy with which women are now treated by men would cease if women exercised all the rights and privileges of citizenship. As I hear this objection the old Bible story forcibly recurs to my mind, of Esau, and how he sold his birthright for a mess of pottage. Let it be granted that women would no longer be treated with exceptional courtesy and indulgence if they exercised the rights and privileges of citizenship. What do this exceptional courtesy and this indulgence really amount to? I am not going to say that they are valueless, but let us analyse them and see of what sort of things they consist. Women are usually assisted in and out of carriages; they also take precedence of men in entering and leaving a room; the door also is frequently opened for them; they are helped first at dinner; and they are always permitted to walk on the inside side of the pavement. Besides these there are more substantial privileges; such as being allowed to monopolise the seats in a room, or in a railway carriage, in those cases where, owing to overcrowding, some of those present are compelled to stand. I hope I do not unduly underate these little amenities of social life; they are very harmless and perhaps even pleasant in their way; but I think it must be confessed that their practical value is small indeed, especially if the price paid for them consists of all the rights and privileges of citizenship. If the courtesy of men to women is bought at this price, it must not be forgotten that the *sale* is compulsory, and can in no case be regarded as a free contract. But now let us consider whether women would really lose all the politeness now shown to them if their right to the franchise were recognised. At elections it is not usually the case that those who have votes are treated with the least consideration; but apart from this, how would the courtesy of every day life be affected by an extension of the suffrage to women? I incline to the belief that some of the mere forms of politeness which have no practical value, such as always giving precedence to a woman in entering and leaving a room, would slowly but gradually fall into disuse if the electoral disabilities of women were removed; but I am quite convinced that true politeness, which is inseparably associated with kindness of heart, would not suffer any decrease from the extension of the suffrage to women. As far as my experience goes, those who are invested with political power of any kind are always treated with more deference and respect than those that are destitute of that valuable commodity. The highest political power in the kingdom is vested in a woman, and what man is inclined on that account to be less courteous to her, or less considerate of her feelings? Have the women who have taken part in late municipal and School Board elections been treated more rudely since they acquired that instalment of political power? In answer to this objection to women's suffrage – that women would lose in the politeness with which they are now treated more than they would gain in political power – I reply in the first place that women are compelled to pay a great deal too dearly for this politeness, if they are forced to sacrifice for it all the rights and privileges of citizens. And secondly, there is no reason to suppose that the acquisition of political power would cause women to be treated with less courtesy and respect, though some of the mere forms of politeness might disappear, if the equality of the rights of men and women were recognized.

The next objection to the enfranchisement of women is one which has probably never occurred to anyone in this room. I certainly should never have thought of it had I not noticed it in a daily paper, the writers of which have shown the greatest inventiveness and originality in their persistent attacks on women's suffrage. Argument after argument they have advanced against it, and as no one took much notice of these attacks, I suppose the editor thought that something quite new must be tried. The following was the result. 'The keen and intense excitement kindled by political strife would, if shared by women, deteriorate their physical powers, and would probably lead to the insanity of considerable numbers of them.' I think if medical men were called upon to reply to such an objective as this, they could easily prove that a great many more people – especially women – suffer in regard to their health, through having nothing to do, and no absorbing interest in life, than through overwork and excitement. If the editor of the journal just quoted would condescend to practical experience, perhaps he will enquire if those women who have lately taken part in the municipal contests and the School Board elections, have since exhibited any alarming symptoms. Such an argument as that just mentioned would be more comprehensible if women were entirely debarred from mixing with the outside world; but as it is, there is nothing to prevent women from sharing the general excitement caused by elections. It is notorious to everyone that they do share it, and I have no hesitation in saying that many of them are a great deal better for it. But suppose it were satisfactorily proved that the health of some women would be injured by the excitement caused by taking part in elections, is that a reason for excluding all women from political power? The health of many men is frequently injured by excessive political work and excitement. Instances of such cases must occur to everyone present. The illness from which Mr Bright is now suffering, and the extreme exhaustion of the Prime Minister, at the end of the session of 1869, were both doubtless produced by the mental strain attendant on too much political work. But such facts furnish no argument against the exercise of political power by these eminent persons. We all hope the only practical result of their maladies may be to make them more solicitous of their own health than they have hitherto been. It may safely be left to the inhabitants of a free country to take the necessary precautions for preserving their own health; and if any woman found that the excitement of elections endangered either her mind or her body, no Act of Parliament would be necessary to induce her to withdraw from political strife. It has almost become a proverb that you cannot make people moral by Act of Parliament. I am sure it is equally true that you cannot make them healthy by Act of Parliament.

The next objection urged against the enfranchisement of women, is one which I am not perhaps wrong in saying is the one which has had the most powerful influence in producing the opposition to women's suffrage. Consciously, or unconsciously, most of us are greatly under the dominion of our feelings, even when they are directly opposed to the dictates of our reason. But let it not be forgotten that reason must be listened to sooner or later, and the feelings must ultimately submit to be modified by the understanding. This objection which I believe to be so potent with most people who oppose women's suffrage is 'that the exercise of political power by women is repugnant to the feelings, and quite at variance with a due sense of propriety.' In Turkey, a woman who walked out with her face uncovered, would be considered to have lost all sense of propriety – her conduct would be highly repugnant to the feelings of the community. In China, a woman who refused to pinch her feet to about a quarter of their natural size, would be looked upon as entirely destitute of female refinement. We censure these customs as ignorant, and the feelings on which they are based as quite devoid of the sanction of reason. It is therefore clear that it is not enough, in order to prove the undesirability of the enfranchisement of women, to say that it is repugnant to the feelings. It must be further enquired to what feelings women's suffrage is repugnant, and whether these feelings are 'necessary and eternal,' or 'being the results of custom, they are changeable and evanescent.' I think these feelings may be shown to belong to the latter class. In the first place a feeling that is necessary and eternal, must be consistent, and the feeling of repugnance towards the exercise of political power by women is not consistent; for no one feels this repugnance towards the exercise of political power by Queen Victoria. In the second place it has been previously shown that the equal freedom of all is a necessary prerequisite of the fulfilment of the Divine Will, and that the equal freedom of a part of the community is destroyed if it is deprived of political power. Now it seems to me in the highest degree blasphemous to assert that the Supreme Being has implanted in man necessary and eternal feelings in opposition to his own will. Again, the state of popular opinion as to what women may, or may not do, is constantly changing in the same country and even in the minds of the same individuals, and the feelings on this subject differ in different classes of the community; it is, therefore, quite impossible to say that these feelings are necessary and eternal. If they are not necessary and eternal they are the result of custom, changeable and evanescent, and are destined to be modified by advancing civilization. It may be that a great deal of the repugnance which undoubtedly exists against women taking part in politics arises from the disturbance and disorder which are too often the disgraceful characteristics of elections in this country. I should like to say a few words on this point. In the first place the adoption of the ballot and the abolition of nominations, which are almost certain to take place before the next dissolution, will, in all probability, cause elections to be conducted with perfect order and tranquility. A distinguished statesman, whose name I could mention, lately told a friend of mine that his last objection to woman's suffrage would be removed by the adoption of the ballot. In the second place I think the danger of women proceeding to polling places under the present system is greatly exaggerated. As the result of my own experience I can testify that during the last election at Brighton, I was walking about from one polling place to another, the whole of the day; the town was in a state of great excitement; the contest was very severe, and party feeling ran high. I walked through an excited crowd just previous to the close of the poll, after having been assured that it was not safe for me to venture, and I never heard one word or saw one gesture which would have caused reasonable annoyance to the most sensitive and refined lady. But I can give another and perhaps more striking example from my own experience. During the general election of 1865, I went round to many of the polling places in Westminster, accompanied only by a young girl. We met with no incident whatever which could have alarmed or annoyed anyone. My experience on this point has always been the same, and it is corroborated by the experience of all ladies with whom I am acquainted, who, like myself, have tested by personal experience, whether it is either unpleasant or unsafe for a woman to go to a polling place. Their unanimous testimony has been that there is nothing to deter a woman from recording her vote. I, for one, have too good an opinion of my countrymen, to believe that they would insult or annoy a well-conducted woman in the discharge of what she believed to be a public duty.

I now pass to the last objection, for by this time I am sure you must be getting weary of me. This objection, that the notion of women's suffrage is monstrous and absurd and deserves only to be treated as a joke, is one which is slowly dying a natural death. You still hear of it in remote country districts, but it has received its death blow from the names of the many very eminent persons who are the warm advocates of women's suffrage. Perhaps I need only mention such names as Mr Mill, Canon Kingsley, Mr Darwin, Professor Huxley, and Professor Maurice, to remind you that women's suffrage is advocated by men occupying the highest ranks in philosophy, science, and literature. Mr Mill and others have shown in their writings, the grounds on which they base their support of the claims of women to representation. It is easy to laugh; but when the leading philosophical thinkers of the day use all their weight and influence, and employ their great genius in striving to produce a recognition of the rights of women, their arguments must be met with arguments; they will never be answered by a sneer. I think I have now made a reply to all the objections previously enumerated against women's suffrage. In doing so I have perhaps sufficiently indicated the grounds on which I advocate it. I have endeavoured to show that men's rights and women's rights must stand or fall together; their maintenance is necessary to the fulfilment of the Divine will – man's happiness. For if God wills man's happiness, and man's happiness depends on his freedom, then God wills man's freedom. 'Equity knows no difference of sex. The law of equal freedom necessarily applies to the whole race – female as well as male. The same reasoning which establishes that law for men may be used with equal cogency on behalf of women.' These are not my words, they are the words of a great philosopher, whose writings will probably mould the opinions of unborn generations. I refer to Mr Spencer, and as I have, perhaps, passed rather too briefly over the objections of those who urge that women's suffrage would destroy the harmony of home, I cannot do better than quote in conclusion what he has said on the effect of the complete enfranchisement of women on domestic happiness. 'Married life under this ultimate state of things will not be characterised by perpetual squabbles but by mutual concessions. Instead of a desire on the part of the husband to assert his claims to the uttermost, regardless of those of his wife, or on the part of the wife to do the like, there will be a watchful desire on both sides not to transgress. Neither will have to stand on the defensive, because each will be solicitous for the rights of the other. Not encroachment but self-sacrifice will be the ruling principle. The struggle will be, not which shall gain the mastery, but which shall give way. Committing a trespass will be the thing feared, and not the being trespassed against. And thus instead of domestic discord will come a higher harmony than any we yet know.'

Lydia E. Becker

*The political disabilities of women**

1 January 1872

THE question of the political disabilities of women, which, long
dormant but never dead, has remained hidden in the hearts of
thoughtful women, to be repressed with a sigh over the
hopelessness of the attempt to gain a hearing, has suddenly sprung
into life and activity, and assumed, in an incredibly short time, an
acknowledged position among the most important social and
political subjects which call for the attention of the nation. This
result could not possibly have been attained unless the principles
involved in the claim had been in harmony with those great ideas
of progress and reform which have taken so deep a hold on the
minds of the people of this country, and which have received so
sudden a development in about the same period of time as that
comprised in the history of our present movement.

Within the last half century there has been a revolution in the
principles which govern the distribution of political power. Shall
the people be governed by rulers claiming to be divinely
appointed, or shall they be ruled by representatives of their own
choosing? Shall the right of the common people culminate in the
claim for good government, or shall it rise to that of self-
government? Is it enough for the populace that their irresponsible
rulers shall govern them according to what they, the rulers,

*Originally published in the *Westminster Review*.

believe to be just and beneficial principles, or have those who must submit to laws and governance a right to be consulted in the election of the governors and the enactment of the laws? Such is the problem which it has been the task of the last fifty years to solve, and which has resulted in the triumph of the principles of popular government by the passing of the Representation of the People Act of 1867. This principle is now accepted by both the great parties in the State. A measure based upon it has become law by common consent. It has therefore changed its position from that of one which had to be recommended and enforced by those who urged the adoption of any measure founded upon it, to that of one which is admitted to be established. Therefore any class in the community which seeks for the removal of political disabilities does so on principles which are now sanctioned by the Legislature as those on which the government of the country shall henceforward be conducted.

We, who make this claim for the enfranchisement of women, do so from the feelings and for the reasons which have led other classes of the community to make the same claim, and we ask that our claim shall be decided by the same principles which have guided the judgment of the Legislature in the case of others. In making this demand we are, however, met at the outset with the allegation that the same principles of justice are not applicable to both sexes – that the claim which is just when made by a man, is unjust when made by a woman – that when men say that the Government has no moral right to hold them responsible to laws enacted without or against their consent, nor to tax the fruits of their labour without giving them a voice in the imposition and disbursement of such taxation, their complaint is just and reasonable, and deserves attention; but that when women say the same thing, their complaint is unjust and absurd, and must be suppressed. Now we say that we can see no reason for this alleged discrepancy, and we challenge those who maintain it to show cause why the same broad principles of justice are not applicable to all human beings. We maintain that women are equally liable with men to suffer from misgovernment – that they have the same interest as men in securing good government – that they have the same intelligence as men in regard to the method of obtaining it, and further, that the only security for good government, either of women or men, is that the governed shall be consulted in electing the rulers and making the laws. We say that the disadvantages and hardships entailed on women by their deprivation of representative government are analogous to those suffered by the lower classes at the hands of the more powerful interests in the country. Women complain of the want of the means of education, want of liberty to engage in honourable or lucrative professions, want of opportunity of earning the means of subsistence, want of security for the possession of their property, their tenure being forfeited by marriage; want of sufficient protection for their persons from the violence of men; these and many other grievances are enough to justify any class of persons in seeking for their removal. Whether the special grievances of women are or are not precisely like those suffered by the common people at the hands of the privileged classes, there can be no doubt that they spring from the same root, political slavery, and their redress must be sought by the same means, political emancipation.

The theory on which the right of voting under the new Reform Act is ostensibly based is that of giving a vote for every household or home. Mr Disraeli stated in the House of Commons that by the Act regulating the franchise, the House gave it, and intended to give it, to every householder rated for the relief of the poor. But when this declaration comes to be practically tested, it is found that about one-seventh of the ratepayers in every borough are adjudged to be out of the pale of representation. This happens though they are taxed to the same extent as the others, and, moreover, have been subjected to the special burdens imposed by the ratepaying clauses of the Representation of the People Act, for which the vote conferred by that Act was confessedly offered as an equivalent. A woman would not only be derided, but punished, who refused to obey a law on the ground that 'man' did not include 'woman,' that 'he' did not mean 'she,' and that therefore she was not personally liable for contravening any Act so worded. Accordingly, though the 'occupiers' and 'owners' who come under the operation of the ratepaying clauses of the Reform Act were referred to throughout by masculine pronouns only, women were made to pay the increased rates thereby imposed. These clauses bore with distressing severity on thousands of poor women, as we gather from police reports which appeared in London and other newspapers. At Hackney in one day more than six thousand persons, mostly women, were summoned for non-compliance with them; and at Lambeth, we are told that several poor women applied to Mr Elliott for his advice how to save their 'things' from being seized by the parish authorities for rates under these clauses. Mr Elliott did not appear to have any power to help them, and the applicants left, lamenting that they were likely to have all their 'things' taken for rates for the right to vote under the new Reform Act. But when women came into court to claim the vote conferred on the occupiers who were fined, they discovered that 'words importing the masculine gender' were held to include women in the clauses imposing burdens, and to exclude them in the clauses conferring privileges, in one and the same Act of Parliament.

One of the excuses alleged for excluding women from the right of voting is a desire to save them from the unpleasantness of contact with a crowd during the conduct of an election. But no one proposes to force women to record their votes, and if they did not like the crowd, they would have full liberty to stay away and exempt themselves from the operation of the vote-giving clauses. But there was no escape from the operation of the ratepaying clauses; and under these, thousands of poor women were dragged from their homes, and haled before the magistrate, for no wrong that they had done, but solely by the operation of an Act from the benefits of which they were excluded under the pretext of exempting them from an unpleasant duty. Men must have a very low idea of the intelligence of women when they endeavour to impose on them by pretences such as these.

The political position of women under the existing law has been compared to that of minors, criminals, lunatics, and idiots. But a little examination will prove that the status of persons of all these classes would be considerably lowered were it reduced to that of women. Minority, if a personal, is merely a temporary disqualification. A householder who is a minor will in time come into the enjoyment of his vote. But adult women are kept throughout their lives in the state of tutelage proper to infancy. They are never allowed to grow up to the rights of citizenship. As Justice Probyn said, 'Infants cannot vote, and women are perpetual infants.' Criminals are also only temporarily disqualified. During the debate on the Bill of 1867, Lord E. Cecil proposed a clause providing that persons who had been sentenced to penal servitude for any offence should be incapable of voting. Mr Gladstone objected to the clause because 'a citizen ought not to bear for life the brand of electoral incapacity.' Another member objected to 'extending a man's punishment to the whole of his life.' The clause was finally negatived. But the brand of life-long electoral incapacity, which was thought too severe for burglars and thieves, is inflicted without scruple on rational and responsible human beings, who have never broken the law, for the sole crime of womanhood. Parliament deems an ex-garotter morally competent to exercise the franchise, whilst it rejects the petition of Florence Nightingale. So much for the moral standard required for the exercise of the suffrage. Let us now see what the law says to lunatics. In a legal text-book we find the following statement: –

Lydia E. Becker

'With regard to a lunatic who, though for the most part he may have lost the sound exercise of his reason, yet sometimes has lucid intervals, it seems that the returning officer has only to decide whether at the moment of voting the elector is sufficiently *compos mentis* to discriminate between the candidates and to answer the questions, and take the oath, if required, in an intelligible manner.'* But the law never allows that a woman can have a lucid interval during which she is sufficiently *compos mentis* to discriminate between the candidates, and to comply with the formalities incident to recording a vote. Thus it places her mentally below lunatics, as it does morally below felons. The courts have a very kindly consideration for the electoral rights of idiots, as a case quoted by Mr Rogers will show. He states that the voter had no idea of the names of the candidates, but he had of the side on which he wished to vote. He seems to have been unable to answer the ordinary questions, and the returning officer rejected the vote of this idiot; but on appeal the decision was reversed, and the vote held to be good. Mr Rogers states that it is difficult to determine, since the decision in the 'Wigan Case,' what degree of drunkenness needs to be shown in order to disqualify an elector. It is a question of fact for the returning officer to decide; and with respect to persons deaf, dumb, and blind, he says, that 'although it is difficult to believe that such persons should have understanding, still if such a person can show by signs or otherwise that he knows the purpose for which he has come to the poll, and can also comprehend the obligation of an oath, and the temporal dangers of perjury, it is conceived that a returning officer would not be justified in refusing his vote.' It will be seen by these extracts that those who compare the political status of women to that of criminals, lunatics, and idiots, give too favourable a view of the facts. The true comparison is that which was used by Mr Justice Byles in the Court of Queen's Bench, when he likened the political condition of women to that of dogs and horses. After indignantly scouting the claims of woman to humanity: 'I will not,' said the Judge, 'allow that woman can be man, unless in a zoological treatise, or until she is reduced to the condition of fossil remains,' he proceeded to level the political rights of woman to those of the domestic animals. He would not even allow her to be 'something better than his dog, a little dearer than his horse,' but assumed the absolute identity of the political rights of all three. The case was that of 1,600 ratepayers, who had been placed on the register by the overseers of Salford, and who

*Rogers, 'On Elections,' 10th edition, p. 153.

122

had been struck off by the revising barrister without inquiry, merely because they bore such names as Mary, Hannah, &c. No objection was raised by any one to these names, though they had been published in the usual way. The mayor, the overseer, and the public generally concurred in the propriety of retaining them, and the representatives of both Liberals and Conservatives in the Revision Court did their best to keep them on the register, but in vain. Though the revising barrister expressed doubts as to whether he had a right to expunge the names, he said he should do so. This decision was appealed against, and the counsel was arguing that the revising barrister had exceeded his jurisdiction in striking off the names of persons not objected to, and the description of whose qualification was good upon the face of it; when he was interrupted by the Judge asking whether he meant to say that if the barrister found the name of a dog or a horse on the register he would not be justified in striking it off. This sudden question rather staggered the learned counsel, who had evidently up to that time not looked upon his clients as exactly on a level with brutes; but he could only follow the Judge's lead, and reply that in case a man happened to be called Ponto or Dobbin, he did not see why he should lose his vote.

In the election petition at Oldham, where a scrutiny was demanded, one set of objections turned on alleged legal incapacity of the voters. These comprised some aliens, some minors, and one woman, who, being upon the register, had recorded her vote. Mr Justice Blackburn decided that the objections to the aliens and minors should have been taken before the revising barrister, and that it was then too late to challenge the votes on the ground of legal incapacity, but a woman was not a man at all, and he should strike off her vote at once. He added, however, that if the vote became of consequence, he should reserve the point for the Court of Common Pleas. We hereby perceive what a mere fetish sex becomes according to the principles of English law. The attributes that distinguish man from the beasts are speech, reason,* moral responsibility, and religious faith. Out of these attributes springs the capacity for political functions, for knowledge and experience, and for the formation of a stable, regular government. Yet in seeking the proper basis of a qualification on which to rest the possession of political power, men deliberately reject as insufficient all those attributes of reason and conscience which raise humanity

---

*We must not be understood as denying that the lower animals reason to a certain extent; but this does not affect the argument, as the distinction between these and mankind is sufficiently marked.

above the brutes, and select one which they have in common with these.

We say that this principle is injurious, because it sets a stamp of inferiority on women. The opinion of a woman is not esteemed so highly as the opinion of a man, because the law does not deem it worthy of being taken into account in reckoning the votes of the people. This lowers women in their own eyes, and in the eyes of men. By making the capacity for feminine functions a disqualification for political functions, the female sex is depressed from its natural position as the one whose preservation is of the most importance in the human economy to that of one which is deemed of secondary consequence, and the welfare of the race suffers accordingly.

The exclusion of women from political power has been defended on diametrically opposite grounds. On one hand it is said that the interests and sentiments of women are identical with those of men, and that therefore women are sufficiently represented by taking the votes of men only in the various classes of society. But if the opinions and interests of women are identical with those of men of a similar social grade, there could be no possible harm in giving them the same means of expressing them as are given to men. On the other hand it is said that women are morally and intellectually distinct from men; that they possess mental attributes not inferior but diverse, and consequently the ideas which they may form on questions of national polity will be of a different character, or based on different principles, from those entertained by men. On this view, however, whether we regard political questions with reference to the interests of the community at large, or of the feminine element in particular, the recognition of the right of women to vote seems absolutely necessary in order to secure that fair representation of all classes of the community, and that impartial consideration of subjects involving the interests of these various classes, which is the final cause of representative government.

In illustration of this necessity we may refer to a speech by the present Attorney-General in the House of Commons during one of the debates on the Bill to render legal marriage with a deceased wife's sister. He is reported to have said: – 'If ever there was a woman's question it was this one, and he asked if it were reasonable or generous to legislate on a matter of marriage against the well understood feeling of one of the sexes who were parties to it.' Now whether Sir John Coleridge was right or wrong in his estimate of the feelings of his countrywomen on this question, there was surely justice in his appeal to the House not to legislate

upon it without taking the sentiments of women into consideration. But under the present law what possible means exist for
gauging the opinions of women on this or on any subject? The
process of carefully eliminating from the electoral body every
person otherwise qualified who belongs to the sex whose views
are especially desired, seems singularly ill-adapted for the purpose
of arriving at a trustworthy estimate of those views. Probably the
opinions of women are divided on this question of the marriage
law as on other topics, but until women are allowed to vote no-
one can possibly determine on which side the majority lies. Every
attempt to do so is mere random guesswork, and until women are
allowed to express their sentiments as freely, as fearlessly, and in
the same manner as men, no man has a right to speak in their
name. Legislation in regard to the interests of women, by an
assembly from which the representation of women is rigidly
excluded, is truly a 'leap in the dark.'

Another question specially affecting women is that of the right
of married women to own property. Strange to say – or is it
strange? – there seems less disposition to acknowledge the justice
of consulting women in regard to this proposed amendment of
the marriage law than on the other. In the debates which took
place in both Houses of Parliament on the Married Women's
Property Bill of 1870, it was throughout assumed that the matter
must be settled according to men's notions of what was just and
expedient for women. Women's ideas on the subject counted for
nothing. The opponents of a change in the law relating to
marriages of affinity appealed passionately on behalf of the
presumed sentiments of women. They arrayed them in opposition
to the measure, and claimed for them the right to be heard. But
the opponents of a change in the law relating to the status of
wives were silent respecting the opinions of women. Either they
did not dare to appeal to them for fear of an adverse verdict, or
they thought that although women might be generally in favour
of the maintenance of the existing law, their opinions were not
worth quoting in its defence.

The law relating to the property of women is an instance of
flagrant wrong inflicted on the unrepresented half of the nation.
What would be said of a law which deprived the majority of adult
men of the right to own property? It would be at once concluded
that such men had no votes, or they would not allow a session to
pass without enforcing a measure to secure their rights. Yet this is
exactly the position of the great majority of adult women under
the common law of England. The act of 1870 does not in any way
interfere with this principle of the common law, but leaves it in

full force. It merely extends to the personal earnings of women, to small amounts of property accruing to them by deed or will, and to certain descriptions of property, on special application, the facilities offered by the Chancery Courts for evading this principle. It would not touch such a case as the following: – A woman selling oranges in the streets of Liverpool related her history to another woman as follows: Her first husband died leaving her in possession of a comfortable inn in Liverpool and one thousand pounds in the bank. She married again. The second husband, after living with her a short time, ran away to Australia, having previously paid a visit to the bank and drawn out the thousand pounds. The wife continued her business, by which she was able to earn a comfortable subsistence for herself and a daughter by the first marriage. After a few years the prodigal husband returned without the thousand pounds, penniless, ragged, and ill. He professed penitence for his past offences and begged of his wife to forgive and receive him. She consented, and took care of him until he recovered. For a time all went well, the husband was kind and attentive, and the wife began to think they might be happy. One day the husband observed that he thought a drive in the country would do his wife good after the care of nursing him through his illness; he would order a carriage for her and her daughter. The wife did not wish to go, but in order to gratify her husband she consented, and she and her daughter departed. On her return she did not see her husband, but found a stranger in the bar. When she asked his business he produced a bill of sale by the husband to him of the house with all it contained and the business. The mother and daughter found themselves turned adrift homeless and penniless on the streets of Liverpool without appeal and without redress. The husband has not since been heard of.

This robbery was committed under the sanction of the marriage law, and the law which sanctions it is still in force.

Sometimes it is urged that since the husband is bound to maintain his wife, it is but just that he should pocket all her property and earnings. But this is a fallacious argument. The claim of a wife to maintenance by her husband is based on the performance by her of the duties of a wife. Her maintenance is an equivalent for services rendered – an equivalent to which she is justly entitled whether she owns property or not. In truth, in the majority of cases, a husband no more 'maintains' his wife than a man does his footman or his cook. To each is given maintenance in requital of services rendered. A cook or footman receives wages in addition to maintenance – a wife usually does not. To claim from a wife in exchange for mere maintenance not only her personal services, which are a full equivalent, but the surrender of all the property she may possess or acquire independently of her husband, is to demand something for which no equivalent is offered.

Under a system of free trade in labour every able-bodied single man or woman is presumably capable of maintaining himself or herself by the exercise of bodily or mental powers. Each such person has two classes of labour to accomplish for this end: 1. Out-door labour – i.e. the earning of the money necessary to procure food, clothing, and shelter. 2. In-door labour – i.e. the application of this money for the personal sustenance and comfort of the individual. It is not enough to earn money to purchase food in order to sustain a man; that food must be prepared and made ready for his use. It is not enough to earn money to pay the rent and furniture of a house; a very considerable amount of daily labour is requisite in order to keep that house habitable and comfortable. Suppose the case of a labouring man working for wages, who had no domestic inmate – who had to light his fire, prepare his own breakfast, and ere he set forth for his day's toil had to make his bed and set his house in order. Then, when he returned for the midday meal, had to go to market to purchase the food, to cook it for himself, to wash up the dishes and arrange his room before he again went forth to his labour, to return at the close to repeat the same process before he could get his supper; and in addition to these daily toils, had the periodical scrubbing of the floor and washing of his clothes, and such mending as is rendered necessary by their wear and tear. It may be safely assumed that a man so circumstanced would not be able to earn more than half the wages which he could earn were he relieved of all these laborious and time-consuming offices. Let us imagine a woman similarly situated, half of whose time was consumed in out-door or money-earning labour, and half in domestic or comfort-earning labour. Let us now suppose that these two marry. In order to perform the domestic duties for the man, and thus set him free to devote his whole time to money-earning labour, the women must give up that portion of her time which she had hitherto devoted to money-earning labour. Because of this, she has an equitable claim to share the money which this sacrifice on her part enables a man to earn. The claim of a wife to maintenance arises from the simple fact that marriage enables a man to earn money by relieving him from the burden of domestic cares, while it disables a woman from earning money by imposing upon her these cares.

The claim of a wife for maintenance we hold to be absolute under these circumstances – i.e. where neither husband nor wife owns property of income other than the earnings of their daily labour. It becomes considerably modified when either possesses a fortune sufficient for maintenance without such labour. Since marriage need not of necessity, and would not, had the Bill introduced in the House of Commons by Mr J. G. Shaw Lefevre, in 1869, become law, have actually dispossessed a woman of her income or in any way disabled her from its possession or enjoyment, and since the possession of independent means of subsistence relieves her from the necessity of maintaining herself by marriage, and renders such an engagement a purely voluntary one on her part – the claim which a woman who gives up her independent means of subsistence in order to marry, has on the man at whose invitation she gives it up, does not exist, and in the case of persons who marry possessed each of independent property, we should be disposed to admit that the claims of husband and wife upon each other for maintenance are mutual and equal.

But this difference in the condition is not recognised by our laws. Whatever obligation the law at present imposes on a man to maintain his wife is totally irrespective of the amount of her possessions: it is the same whether she be a beggar or an heiress. Moreover, this vaunted liability shrinks to the narrowest limits when examined. If a man refuse to supply his wife with food and clothing, she has no means of enforcing her claim upon him. No magistrate could listen to a woman who complained that her husband would not maintain her. All he could do would be to recommend her to apply to the parish, and then if the guardians chose to supply her with pauper's allowance, they could recover the amount from the husband. But if the parish authorities were to find that the husband was in the receipt of good wages, and therefore to decide that they would not relieve the woman, she must starve, for the wife has no direct remedy against the husband for neglect to maintain her. Cases have occurred of women being actually starved to death under the circumstances.

If, instead of bringing his wages home to his wife, to be applied to the maintenance of the family, a man takes them to the public house and spends them all in drink, the wife has no remedy. Yet surely, when the husband has induced the wife to marry him on the faith that he would provide her with a maintenance, he contracted an obligation as binding and as capable of legal definition and enforcement as any other contract for the performance and reimbursement of personal services.

Suppose the common case of a working man paying court to a servant-girl in a good place. She is earning board and lodging of a much better quality than the wives of working men usually enjoy, and from ten to twenty-pounds annually in addition. He asks her to leave all this, to give up all prospect of earning money, to devote herself to his service, to be not only his wife, but his servant – to wait upon him, to cook for him, to wash for him, to clean his house; and to perform all these arduous and multifarious duties, not only while she is well and strong, but through the period when the cares of maternity render them physically oppressive and injurious. In requital, he undertakes to provide her with uncooked food, lodging without attendance, and clothing. Now this is not a very tempting bargain, and commercially it cannot be considered advantageous. But such as it is, the terms ought to be carried out, and the law ought to provide means for enforcing their fulfilment. If the wife does not, at the end of the week, receive a portion of her husband's wages sufficient to provide her with these things, she ought to have as ready a means of redress as the working man would have who, after performing his week's work, should find that his employer neglected to pay him his week's wages.

Were the rights of the wife to her share of the husband's wages recognised as fully as the right of the workman to his share of the profit of his labour, a husband would no more think of defrauding the wife of her due than the employer now thinks of defrauding the workmen of their wages. The knowledge that wages can be recovered, effectually secures punctual payment without the resort to actual process of law, while this power in no way disturbs amicable relations between master and man. The experience that employers are now as a rule in the habit of paying wages punctually, would by no means induce the workmen to forego their legal claims. They would not think it just to be bound to spend their time and strength in working for their masters, and then be compelled to trust to their caprice or favour, or sense of honour alone, for the payment of their wages. Yet we are unable to discover in what way the position of a man earning his livelihood by working for a master who supports him in return for his labour, differs as regards the question of right to maintenance from that of a woman who earns her bread by the performance of household duties for the husband who has undertaken to maintain her in return for her labour. If, when pay-day came round, the master were to inform the men that he had no money for them, as he had spent it all in selfish indulgence, and they would get nothing for that week's labour, the men would consider themselves unjustly treated. What, then, must the wife feel whose husband comes home on the Saturday night with his head full of drink and his pocket empty of cash? But the case of the wife is the harder of the two. The money she has a right to find in her husband's pockets at the end of the week is not hers for her personal use. It is the fund out of which she has to furnish food for her husband, her children, and herself. When that is wasted, their sustenance is gone.

A short time ago a lady was asked by a poor woman for a loan to pay off a debt at a provision shop for food supplied for the use of her family, consisting of her husband, herself, and three children. The husband was earning good wages, which he spent mostly in drink, and he did not give his wife enough even to provide the cost of his own food. The wife was obliged to go out to work, in order to earn money to pay for her own and her children's food, and make up the deficiency in that of her husband. The lady was advised not to lend the money, but to say to the poor woman that her husband was legally liable for the debt incurred at the provision shop, and that the shopkeeper should sue him for it. The reply was, that the husband had threatened to strip the house and sell off every stick of furniture, and that if he were asked to pay the debt he would very probably carry his threat into effect. The furniture had not been provided by the husband; it had been bought with money advanced by the lady who was our informant, and repaid by the wife in weekly instalments out of her earnings. But as this transaction took place before the passing of the Married Women's Property Act of 1870, the husband would now be upheld by the majesty of the law in desolating his wife's home, the fruits of her honest industry.

The clergyman of a parish in Lancashire stated the case of one of his parishioners, the wife of a drunken, truculent collier, who is earning good wages, but who spends all on his own vicious indulgences, and gives his wife nothing for the maintenance of the household. Nevertheless he expects to be provided for at home, and kept 'like a lord,' as the clergyman said. The woman is industrious, clever, orderly, and a good manager. She contrives to earn enough to maintain a comfortable home and provide good meals for her legal master, who makes no scruple of abusing her if things are not served to his mind.

Such cases are very common: but were they as exceptional as they are common, they would afford ground for altering the law which supports and sanctions them.

The franchise is needed as a protection for women in regard of equal law. In every case where the laws determine the relative duties of men and women, the interest and the feelings of the unrepresented half of the nation have been made wholly subservient to that of the class which has political power. In the marriage relation, the wife's separate existence is lost; the husband is the only person recognised by the law. One of the most sacred natural rights, that of a mother to the child she has borne in her bosom, flesh of her flesh, bone of her bone, is set aside; and to the married mother's legal master is given the power to dispose of her offspring, not only during his lifetime but after his death. The law does not recognise a mother, even after her husband's death, as the natural guardian of her children. Her husband can will them away from her, and even if he names no other guardian, the mother does not become such by law. A married woman's children are not her own. Until a very few years ago an unweaned child might be torn from its mother's bosom, and deprived by a father's will of its mother's milk. However unnatural or bad a man might be, the law, without making any inquiries into his character, invested him with irresponsible power to make such a decree, and sanctioned and enforced it effectively. One of the revising barristers who adjudicated on the claims of women to be put on the roll of electors, desiring to say something especially insulting and unpleasant to the claimant who came to plead in his court, stated that he declined to recognise suckling as a qualification for the suffrage. But if womanhood had not been a disqualification for the suffrage, it would have been impossible that for hundreds of years the law should have vested the right to the custody of an unweaned child in that parent who could not nourish it. This glaring anomaly has been partially remedied, but at the cost of an injustice which is almost more cruel than the original one. By Sir Thomas Talfourd's Custody of Infants Bill, passed soon after the accession of her present Majesty, the married mother is as a matter of grace kindly permitted to keep – not her children – oh no! the law does not recognise them as hers – but she is graciously allowed to keep her husband's children until they are seven years old. Why! that she may have all the care, trouble, and anxiety of their helpless infancy, and the – it may be – profligate father be relieved from the same, and the torture and the uprooting of her heart be all the more cruel at the end of the seven years, when the fiat of separation goes forth. What that torture is, none but a mother can know. It is probably the greatest that a human being can suffer. And the law sanctions the infliction of this torture on Englishwomen at the irresponsible will and pleasure of a man who may be a cruel and heartless scoundrel.

The despotic powers of a father are by no means a dead letter.

But a short time ago a scene took place which shows what can be done, and what is done, under the sanction of man-made laws. The account went the round of the newspapers in a paragraph entitled

PAINFUL SCENE IN A COURT OF JUSTICE – In the Irish Court of Queen's Bench, Mr Justice Fitzgerald had a *habeas corpus* application made by the Rev Henry Newenham, to obtain custody of his two children, Adelaide and Edith, who were under the care of their mother, Lady Helena Newenham, and her father, Lord Mountcashel. His lordship ordered that the younger girl, a child of about seven years, should be delivered up to her father; but the other girl, who is nearly sixteen, the age at which she is legally a free agent, having already expressed her unwillingness to comply with her father's wish, was permitted to exercise her choice. A painful scene occurred as an officer came into the court, bearing the younger child, a pretty little girl, with long fair hair, and intelligent beyond her years. She screamed and struggled violently, exclaiming repeatedly, 'Oh, must I, must I? Oh, dear, I won't go to my father.' Mr Justice Fitzgerald took her up and spoke kindly to her, telling her her father would be fond of her, and that her mother would often see her. To this the child only replied again and again, 'Oh, please, do let me do as I like. Don't send me away. Will mamma ever see me again? Grandpa, grandpa, where are you?' Mr Justice Fitzgerald: 'I shall take care of that, my dear. Your mamma will see you as often as she likes.' Child: 'Will it be every day? Tell me – will it be every day?' Mr Justice Fitzgerald: 'Oh, yes, every day.' Lord Mountcashel (who was much moved): 'Knowing what I know, that is impossible. He is a d – l.' Mr Justice Fitzgerald said: 'I am sorry I cannot leave the two sisters together. If I could, I would persuade you to that, Mr Newenham. However, I hope you will allow free communication between the girls; and I must order that the mother be allowed to see her child as often as she wishes.' Mr Purcell: 'Yes, my lord, all reasonable opportunity will be given her.' The child was then handed over to her father, who carried her out.

What a mockery to call the above a court of justice! A mother is to be 'allowed' to see her child as often as she wishes, and a lawyer promises that all 'reasonable opportunity' shall be given her. But suppose that on one of these reasonable opportunities on which the mother is 'allowed to see' her child, she sees that the child is unhappy, or harshly treated, she cannot take it away, and the permission to 'see' it may only add to her agony.

We appeal to every mother in the land to say, Is that mother and is that child justly treated by this country's law? Is it enough for those who are happy to say, 'These laws, though unjust, are a dead letter in my case; therefore I take no care for these things?' As well might those who are warmed and fed allege their own sense of personal comfort as a reason why they should bestow no thought on the sufferings, or care for the relief of the cold, the hungry, and the naked. We ask all women who have happy homes to join us in trying to protect those women who have unhappy homes, or who have no homes. For it is only the happy who have strength to help. The unhappy are helpless entirely.

We thought it necessary before appealing to this condition of the law as an argument for the necessity of the franchise, to ascertain with more precision the state and animus of the law with regard to mothers. From a legal text-book which enters fully into this subject we gather that the fundamental principle of English law is, that the father alone is entitled to the custody and disposal of his children; that this right inheres totally irrespective of his moral character or fitness for the charge; and that it will be confirmed and enforced by the courts, though he be an open and notorious evil liver. That while the law is thus jealous of the natural gifts and parental feelings of the father, those of the mother are utterly disregarded; and that in the rare instances in which the absolute power of the father in regard to the disposal of the children is restrained or modified by the action either of the judges or special application of the law relating to the custody of children under seven years of age, this is done not in consideration of the natural right or parental feelings of the *mother*, but solely out of care for the supposed interest of the *child*. The courts have specially and expressly disclaimed any other intention than that of interfering for the protection of the child, and the claims of the mother have been dismissed as altogether out of the consideration of the Court. Such modified rights to the custody of the babies as are permitted at the discretion of the judges to be conceded to a mother, are wholly forfeited if she has been guilty of adultery, while a father may be living in open adultery, yet may withhold the custody of her children from a virtuous mother. It seems so monstrous and incredible that so unjust a law should prevail, that we think the fact will scarcely be credited on assertion only. We will therefore offer to our readers some cases and decisions quoted by Mr Macpherson, to set forth the state of the law: –

Lydia E. Becker

I

On the petition of a mother and her daughter, a child of about fourteen years of age, praying that the daughter might be placed under the mother's care, or that the mother might be permitted to have access to her daughter at all convenient times, it being stated at the bar that the father was living in habitual adultery, on account of which the mother had obtained a divorce in the Ecclesiastical Courts, Sir Anthony Host, LC, said that the court had nothing to do with the fact of the father's adultery; that some conduct on his part, with reference to the management and education of the child must be shown to warrant an interference with his legal right to the custody of his child. He did not know of any case which would authorise him to make the order sought. If any could be found, he would most gladly adopt it; for in a moral point of view he knew of no act more harsh or cruel than depriving the mother of proper intercourse with her child.

II

The mother of three girls, the eldest aged five and a half years, left the house rented by her husband in which she was living with the infants, and afterwards removed them, and instituted proceedings in the Ecclesiastical Courts for a divorce. On the application of the father a writ of *habeas corpus* was granted to bring the children before Mr Justice Paterson. The judge ordered that the mother should deliver up the children to the husband. In this case it was stated that the father was living in adultery.

III

An Englishwoman married a Frenchman domiciled in England. She separated from her husband on account of ill-treatment, and he by force and stratagem got into the house where she was, and carried away her child, an infant, at the breast. The mother obtained a *habeas corpus* upon affidavit, stating these facts. Lord Ellenborough said, 'The father is the person entitled by law to the custody of his child. If he abuse that right to the detriment of the child, the court will protect the child. But there is no pretence that the child has been injured for want of nurture, or in any other respect.' The child was remanded to the custody of the father.

IV

G. H. Talbot, a Roman Catholic, married a Protestant lady. They had two children, John and Augusta. By a deed of separation between the parents it was agreed that Augusta should remain with her mother till the age of ten. The father died, having by will appointed a Roman Catholic priest to be the guardian of his children. The infants were made wards of court. The mother married Mr Berkeley, a Protestant.

A petition was presented on behalf of the infants, stating that the guardian had removed the boy, aged ten years, from school, and placed him under the care of his uncle, the Earl of Shrewsbury – that Lord Shrewsbury refused to allow him to visit his mother. The petition prayed that Augusta might continue with her mother, and that John might have unrestrained intercourse with his mother, and might reside with her for convenient periods.

The guardian petitioned that Augusta might be delivered to him.

The Lord Chancellor (Lord Cottenham) said that the *mother had no right to interfere with the testamentary guardian*. The Court would exercise a discretion whether an infant should be ordered to be delivered up to such guardian. The female infant was of the age of eight years and seven months, residing in her mother's house, under the care of a Roman Catholic governess, and there was strong evidence showing her to be of delicate constitution, and requiring the care of her mother. There was also a statement of the late father's wishes that she should be left in the care of her mother till the age of ten, and on that circumstance his lordship relied as evidence that she might safely be left with the mother till that period. He therefore left the female infant in the care of her mother. The petition of the guardian was ordered to stand over, no order being made upon it for the present. As to John Talbot, the Lord Chancellor said that it was right that he should live with Lord Shrewsbury. The petition of the infants was dismissed. The only access to her son which the guardian would afford to Mrs Berkeley was at Lord Shrewsbury's house, and in the guardian's presence.

Mrs Berkeley petitioned that her son might be allowed to visit

Lydia E. Becker

her for a month; the petition was accompanied with a medical certificate that she was in ill health owing to her anxiety to have access to her son.

'The Lord Chancellor felt it to be necessary to *look only to the interests of the infant, and to the wishes of the father*, expressed in his appointment of a guardian, and declined to make any order on the petition. 13 June 1840.'

V

A father applied to obtain possession of a child of five years old which the mother kept from him. There was reason to doubt whether the child was his; he had been divorced from the mother soon after its birth. Lord Kenyon had no doubt but that the father was entitled to the custody, as the Court saw no reason to believe that he intended to abuse his right by sacrificing the *child*.

VI

Lord Eldon, on *habeas corpus*, ordered two children of the respective ages of five years and seven months, to be delivered to their father by their mother, who was living apart from him, and who claimed their custody in virtue of a deed which provided for their residing with her in the event of a separation, and of another deed by which a provision was made for her separate maintenance, and an allowance was agreed to be paid her for the maintenance of the infants.

VII

In a modern case, in the Court of Common Pleas, a husband ill-treated his wife; a separation took place. The wife kept her child, which was six years old. The husband cohabited with another woman. The husband sued out a *habeas corpus*. The judge decided that neither the father nor the mother was entitled to the custody of the child, and it was given up to a third person.

The propositions which these cases illustrate are the following: –

The law vests parental rights in the father alone, to the entire exclusion of the mother. The father has power to remove children from their mother, not only during his life; but he may by will appoint a stranger to be guardian after his death, and such guardian may separate mother and child. The power of the father is not forfeited by his immoral conduct. It inheres in him by law, and he cannot be divested of it at the discretion of a judge. The Custody of Infants Act allowed some modified rights to mothers. But these rights are not conferred directly on any mother. They do not inhere in her by virtue of her motherhood; the Act is merely permissive. It declares that it shall be lawful for a judge, upon hearing a petition, *if he see fit*, to make an order that a mother shall be allowed access to her child, and if it is under seven years of age, to order that it be delivered to and remain in the custody of the mother until attaining that age, subject to such regulations as he shall deem convenient and just. Another section of the Act declares that the judge shall have no power to make the order if the mother has been guilty of adultery.

The franchise is needed as a protection for women from the uncontrolled dominion of the savage passions of men. In the less cultivated classes of society these passions rage with terrific violence, and their effects fall chiefly on the unhappy wives whom the law delivers up to the mercy of their legal masters. The existence of this savage element in our population will not be denied. Yet we will call two witnesses whose testimony is well calculated to arouse attention to this commonly acknowledged but commonly neglected fact. At the meeting of the British Association in Liverpool, after a lecture by Sir John Lubbock on 'Savages,' Professor Huxley, in the course of some observations, said: –

> Since I have walked in your great town of Liverpool I have seen fully as many savages, as degraded savages as those in Australia. Nay, worse; in the primitive savage there remains a certain manliness derived from lengthened contact with nature and struggle with it, which is absent in these outcast and degraded children of civilization. The people who form what are called the upper strata of society talk of political questions as if they were questions of Whig or Tory, of Conservative and Heaven knows what, but the man who can see, will, I think, believe that in these times there lies beneath all these questions the great question whether that prodigious misery which dogs the footsteps of modern civilization shall be allowed to exist – whether, in

fact, in the heart of the most polished nations of the present day – of those nations which pride themselves most on being Christians – there shall be this predominant and increasing savagery, of which such abundant instances are in your midst. I believe that this is the great political question of the future.

We agree with the eminent Professor in this belief, and we ask – Have not women the deepest interest in, and is it not their duty to care for, political questions such as this? For women, and notably the women of our own land, are the chief victims of this savagery. There is not, we believe, any class in the world so subjected to brutal personal violence as English wives.

Soon after these remarks of Professor Huxley at Liverpool, Mr Justice Brett held the winter assizes at Manchester. The following are extracts from his charge to the grand jury: –

> The calendar is not long, but I am sorry to say it is serious, and this seems to me to arise principally from a habit of brutal violence, and giving way, without the smallest provocation, to evil passions. There are no fewer than four persons accused of murder, and there are many cases of violence by stabbing and cutting with knives. . . . The first case is No. 1 in the calendar, and it is the case of a man who is accused of the murder of his wife. According to the depositions, by his own confession, he went in without any particular ill-feeling to this woman. The principal evidence against him is his own child. He put a rope round his wife's neck, tied it with a knot under her ear, and dragged her about the room until she was dead. . . .
>
> The next case is No. 6 on the list. It is also that of a man charged with the murder of his wife. In this case no one was present when the blow was struck, but the man was seen going into his house, a scream was heard, and the woman was seen coming out holding her apron to her head, the blood streaming profusely from a severe wound in the head. There was a brush or part of a broom found on the floor, and the woman made a statement in the prisoner's presence that he struck her with the broom. When she was examined by the doctors it was found that her skull was crushed in, and she was seized with paralysis and died. . . .
>
> The next case is No. 27. This, again, is the case of a man who is charged with the murder of a woman with whom he lived as his wife. There is evidence that he struck the woman a blow. . . .

Another case is that of a man who killed his wife; and here, again, the blow was not seen, but the man was seen going into the house, and shortly afterwards the woman was seen bleeding about the head, and several contused wounds were afterwards found on her person. She seems to have died from what the doctors call prostration and weakness from exhaustion; and in presence of the man she said he not only struck her with a poker, but stamped upon her after having knocked her down. . . . How terrible this is! Here are no fewer than four cases in which men are charged with wilful murder, with brutal violence to women with whom they lived as their wives. Some steps must be taken to put an end to such conduct.

Men say that women are not oppressed. But women themselves tell a different tale. From all parts of the country, from suffering and sorrowing women, come voices blessing the efforts that are made and bidding them God speed. Sometimes they come from the ranks of the peerage – sometimes from the well-to-do middle classes – sometimes from the poorest of the poor. From all sorts and conditions of women the cry of distress has gone forth. And the story is ever the same deep and cruel wrong, suffered at the hands of those who in theory are their natural protectors. All have the same hopeless consciousness that for them there is no help and no redress. They are made legally subordinate to men, and their sufferings are held as of no account.

We are persuaded that the sufferings and the wrongs of women will never be considered worthy of attention by the Legislature until they are in possession of the suffrage, and not until they are politically on the same level as men, will their education and their welfare receive equal care from the Government. All those who are interested in the general progress of society in intelligence and virtue should aid in the effort to remove the political disabilities of half the nation. When this shall be accomplished the additional power thereby gained will enable those who are working for measures of social and political reform to carry them on at a rate of progress hitherto undreamed of. At present half the people are excluded from participation in matters of national interest, and of the privileged half a great portion are held back by want of public spirit, of knowledge, and of interest in these matters. This apathy is the natural result of the influence of the huge mass of political ignorance, partly engendered by the exclusion of women from political existence. Remove the cause, and the effect will begin to diminish; enfranchise the whole people, and the whole people will begin to develop political life. In a celebrated Essay on the Education of the World, the writer has personified the human race under the figure of a colossal man, whose infancy, education, and growth represent the development of religious and political civilisation throughout the period of authentic history. If we can imagine this man determining that his right leg alone must have the advantage of exercise, and the left should be regarded as an ornamental appendage, it will not inaptly figure the attempt of humanity to make progress by cultivating only one sex. All who have turned their energies to public affairs feel how lame and imperfect is the advance of opinion on great questions, and in the suppression of intelligent and responsible opinion in women we find the cause of this lethargy.

Anne Isabella Robertson

Women's need of representation *

21 February 1872

At a General Meeting of the Members of the Irish National Society for Women's Suffrage, and others, held at St James's Place, Blackrock, Dublin, on 21 February 1872, the RIGHT HON. LORD TALBOT DE MALAHIDE in the chair, MISS ANNE ISABELLA ROBERTSON, President of the Society, delivered the following Lecture. She said:

ALL who are acquainted with the history of any new and important political movement must be aware of how long it often takes before the public mind can grasp the subject, so as to comprehend it fully in all its bearings; but the rapid progress made by the agitation to procure the suffrage for women-ratepayers has surprised even its warmest and most sanguine promoters. The National Society for Women's Suffrage has now branches in every part of the kingdom. From the first it was set on foot and supported by some of the deepest thinkers and most intellectual men and women of the day, and now a brilliant array of names adorns the lists of the Women's Suffrage societies. Clergymen of different creeds warmly support the cause; practical men of business, heads of great commercial houses, are to be found standing in the ranks of adherents, beside professors and fellows

*A lecture upon the necessity of giving women the parliamentary franchise.

141

of colleges of every university of note in the United Kingdom; while upwards of two hundred members of parliament of different political parties, including Mr Disraeli and Sir John Coleridge, have voted in favour of Women's Suffrage. These facts are in themselves sufficient to make men and women give some reflection to the subject; yet still we find many persons, both men and women, who know very little about the matter, and who consequently feel indifferent as to whether women receive the benefit of representation or not. It is a fact that where the subject is best known, it is most approved of. There are numbers of people who see at once the injustice of excluding women who pay rates and taxes from the suffrage; but still they cannot perceive that the injustice extends a great deal beyond the mere insult and indignity of that exclusion. There are few who think of tracing any of the wrongs that they know women suffer from, to their being denied the power of representation; but eminent political writers have proved clearly, that without the political franchise, no class of people will receive justice or consideration for their interests. Whatever good is to be gained by the British Constitution, would be derived by women from their admission to the franchise, and we cannot dispute this without disputing the advantage of Parliamentary government and the representation of property – in fact, the British system of government altogether. Viewing the subject in a clearly constitutional light, we must admit that if the representation in Parliament of those who are interested in property, is a national benefit conducive to the maintenance of all property interests, and to the increase of our national prosperity, then the disfranchisement of any class of holders of property must have an injurious effect. Women are considered intelligent enough to be allowed to hold property, great or small, and it is a fact that the numbers of independent women are increasing in Great Britain, which renders their admission to the franchise a matter of much practical importance. Women are also considered intelligent enough to understand that they must pay the tax-collector their rates and taxes when he comes knocking at their doors, or, in default of payment, that their furniture may be seized for the amount. There is not the slightest indulgence shown to women by the law in any particular. When they commit offences they are punished quite as heavily as men are, and although denied the privilege and protection of representation, are obliged to obey to the letter all the laws made in a parliament whose members they have no voice in electing. Public opinion is fast coming round to the belief that this state of things, which originated in a false idea of the mental and moral qualities of women, should no longer exist.

One reason, perhaps, why the movement for obtaining the suffrage for women may be in any degree retarded, can be traced to a very simple origin. Many English writers have expatiated upon the great respect which women receive in England, and contrast this so-called respect with the bad treatment of women in other lands. Thus, many persons are under the impression that women in this country have no wrongs to complain of, and therefore, of course, they do not see any necessity to support a movement which is set on foot to redress the wrongs which its advocates believe women labour under, owing to the want of political representation. Men who imagine that England is a free country, and who boast of its liberty, can hardly bring themselves to believe that the women of England are not included within the pale of that constitution which is supposed to be so great a blessing to the nation. If we declare that the representative system of English government is really a blessing to those who enjoy its privileges and protection, then we must acknowledge that women who are denied representation are denied this great blessing. If there are any who imagine that women are excluded from rights and privileges, and the power of political representation, in order to preserve their dignity, and to keep them from rough contact with a rough world, I would recommend them to read something of law, and something of the history of those ancient times when the laws oppressing women were chiefly originated. It is a matter worthy of note that among our warmest supporters in this movement, are many eminent professors of law and of history – men whose large amount of information respecting the political condition of different nations in different ages, has taught them that in the early ages, when many of the laws respecting women were made, the general treatment of women was often cruel and barbarous, and devoid of reason. They were occasionally persecuted, tortured, and calumniated; they were declared to be so innately mean and wicked as to be wholly unfit for any amount of freedom; they were oppressed in hundreds of ways; and when they committed offences, they were often given far more severe punishments than men were awarded for the same crimes. In the writings of Michelet will be found many allusions to the cruel and unjust treatment of women in mediæval times, and the literature of the middle ages speaks itself of the want of reason that characterized the opinions of men respecting women. It is difficult, perhaps, at this time of day to determine whether our ancestors were really as absurd as they seem to us now when reviewing their bygone opinions; whether they really believed that women were mentally and morally inferior to men, or whether they merely said so from policy, to excuse themselves for their oppression of women, and to induce women to despise themselves and each other. But, however it may have been, no one with any large amount of reflection or information could for a moment imagine that the laws respecting women were framed in a spirit of tenderness or indulgence towards them. They bear too strong a resemblance to the laws relating to serfs, to slaves, and to the people of conquered nations, to admit of any such delusion in the minds of the well-informed. No doubt they bear traces of that spirit of oppression that characterized the ages when they were chiefly framed. We may excuse the early framers of those laws because they were narrow-minded and ignorant – believers in witchcraft and other superstitions; but still that does not make their laws any more tolerable to the women of the present day, nor less disgraceful to the age we live in, and which calls itself civilized.

A good deal has been said about the position that Providence has designed for women; but we must acknowledge that their positions are many and various. We see them as reigning queens and as charwomen; we see them as peeresses of the realm in their own right, and as servants of all work; we find them earning their bread in shops, in factories, in public and in private occupations; we find them staying quietly at home, scarcely stirring outside the walls of those homes; and we find them, especially in this country, as emigrants, leaving home and parents and friends, to seek a living in a strange land among strangers thousands of miles away. Millions of women are engaged in the hard struggle of life at present under every possible disadvantage; but many thoughtful people are at work trying to ameliorate their hardships, and to procure for them some redress. Those persons who are earnestly labouring to procure the franchise for women, are not doing so merely to enable a few rate-paying women to vote for Mr Brown or Mr Jones, but to procure for women the protection of representation. The franchise is the best means that has as yet been devised for the protection and representation of the people, and until a better method is discovered, women will be glad to have the benefit of it. It is not merely those women who are self-dependent and self-supporting that suffer from unjust laws, and whose difficulties require to be represented. In that very department of life called the sphere of woman – the family and the home – the deep sufferings of women have often struck those who are obliged to administer the law which bears so cruelly upon mothers with regard to the education, the guardianship, and

the custody of their children. Women are frequently told to ı
politics alone, and to think only of devoting their whole time a
attention to their children. You would naturally suppose, then,
that at least they enjoyed some rights and privileges here; but they
have no more legal rights as to their own children, than the hired
nurse who helps to take charge of them. A child may be taken
from its mother and educated in direct opposition to her wishes;
and even if her husband, at his death, leaves the guardianship of it
to her – which he does not always do – she cannot appoint a
guardian for it at her own death. The law has determined that she
has no rights whatever as a mother; and yet she is taught to
believe that all her hopes, all her affections, all her ambition,
should be centred in the rearing of her children – thus rendering
her misery the greater when those children may be removed from
her care by the caprice or malice of a cruel husband. It has been
well said that, as regards their children, women in this country are
treated legally exactly like the slaves of the United States before
the war of emancipation. Fortunately, it is not often that women's
feelings are harrowed in this way by a separation from their
children; but that is no reason that they should be left altogether
to the mercy of chance. If women in any department of life seem
to be treated in this age and in this country any better than they
were treated in former times, or are now treated in other lands, it
is because men are better educated and more reasoning than they
were formerly, and more civilized here than they are in barbarous
regions. But our laws have not been altered to suit the advance of
the times, as far as women are concerned; and until women
receive the franchise they will probably remain unchanged and
utterly inconsistent with public opinion, yet giving free scope
occasionally for the most cruel wrongs to be inflicted on the sex
which is the weaker.

The idea that women have nothing to do with politics, and
ought to have nothing to do with them is, happily, fast giving
way, and will soon have departed from the minds of all but those
who do not really understand what politics mean. Considering
that politics so frequently affect the minutest particulars of
household life and economy – all that is acknowledged even now
to be within the range of what is called 'woman's sphere' – it
cannot be denied that women should take an interest in such
affairs. The multitude for which a nation legislates is composed of
individuals, and each individual, small or great, may be concerned
in, or affected by, such legislation. Each subject discussed in
parliament, from the debate upon a war in a foreign land to the
tax upon the cheapest article of food, may have its effect equally

upon the men and women of the country for good or for evil. Politics, which simply mean the government of the country, concern common-place men and women and the common affairs of life; and those persons who say that women have nothing to do with such matters, prove either their want of sincerity or their want of reflection.

I am occasionally informed by persons opposed to women's enfranchisement, that the ladies of their acquaintance, intelligent women too, do not care to have votes; and I am even told that some ladies are not merely indifferent, but are actually hostile to the movement for gaining the suffrage for their sex. Now it is precisely to meet cases of this kind that our Society has been organized. If every body of intelligence understood the question, or had comprehended it from the first, we would be spared the trouble and expense of having any society of the kind. Our object is to bring before the notice of people some knowledge of the benefit which would accrue to women from the franchise being conferred upon some members of their sex. The first step, then, to be taken in this movement when seeking for adherents, is to ascertain if the persons spoken to on the subject understand the meaning of the franchise. Do they comprehend the advantages which men gain by possessing it, do they know why men engaged in a life and death struggle rather than lose their constitutional privileges, and the liberty of electing their law makers? If they do not understand that, their opinions cannot have that weight which would attach to the opinions of persons who know exactly what they are talking about. Sometimes I have heard ladies expressing disapproval of women gaining the power of voting; but when I have asked them if they knew what the good of votes was to men, they frankly confessed they did not know. It is no wonder, therefore, that they did not prize the franchise, since they did not understand what it meant. There are several men also who really do not comprehend the matter any better, and who speak against the suffrage for women, not knowing, at the same time, the signification or value of the suffrage to any one, man or woman. These persons evidently do not appreciate the advantages of representative government.

An important point, then, is to impress on persons ignorant of the matter the benefit of the franchise. Men in this country possess the franchise, and they are thereby enabled to watch over their own interests, and to guard them as far as relates to the laws of this country. No woman in this kingdom has got the franchise, and I shall now point out some of the evil consequences which result to women, and some of the hardships with regard to the law, which they suffer from by their not being able to watch over their own interests in Parliament, where the laws are made. I shall proceed, for instance, to illustrate the position, according to law, of a mother with regard to the religion of her children – taking real cases that have actually occurred at quite a late date. I choose these cases because they are so intimately connected with the sphere which is said to belong especially to woman – the sphere of home, where by a popular fallacy she is supposed to reign. We have all, no doubt, heard of the woman's kingdom, and many of us have believed that there really existed such a realm. An opponent of women's claims to the suffrage has observed 'that the mission of women in life is different from that of men – women having reserved for them a higher position, in which the delicacy, the refinement, and grace, which form the charm of the female mind are more important than the pursuits of science. And this mission is the training of a family, which is, after all, the most important education that can be imparted to mankind.' These are very fine words, and some mothers might be greatly pleased to think they were of so much consequence, and that their mission was so extremely exalted. But how vague and misleading are the words when we come to look at plain facts. Does the law recognize that mothers have this higher mission? Does the law treat the mother as if she had delicacy or refinement, or tenderness of feeling, or indeed any feeling at all? Quite the contrary. Perhaps many persons here may not be aware that the law existing in this country at present pays no respect whatever to a mother's feelings, even with respect to so sacred a subject as her child's religion. In some countries, Austria for instance, a mother can by law decide upon the nature of a daughter's religious education – the law there authorizing the father to determine the religion of the sons. But in this country the mother is paid no such respect or consideration. The law never enquires what she thinks about her daughters, or her sons either. Her wishes go for nothing. Now, no one can consider that women, whether Catholic or Protestant, think one religion much the same as another, and do not care what religion their children profess. On the contrary, it is generally believed that women have much stronger religious convictions than men, and certainly the appearances of our places of worship on Sundays, and that of religious meetings on week days – to which women resort in so much greater numbers than men – would lead us to consider this popular belief was not unfounded. Nevertheless, the law of this land treats mothers, whether Catholic or Protestant, as if their children's religious education was nothing whatever to them. I shall here quote the words of the Vice-Chancellor of the Lancaster Court of Chancery, in deciding a question lately as to the creed in which a little girl named Catherine Hawksworth, of Liverpool, was to be brought up. The father was a Catholic, and died when the child was only six months old. Her mother was a Protestant, and the child had lived with her, and been reared by her, and had been in the habit of attending the religious service of the Church of England. However, when the little girl was about eight or nine years old, some of the relations on the father's side desired that the child should be brought up a Catholic, as it had been the religion of the deceased father. The mother was, no doubt, astonished that relatives of her husband, long dead, could presume to have any authority over the child she had nursed, and cherished, and taught for so many years. She appealed to the law, but soon found that the law had no protection or sympathy for her. The Vice-Chancellor was obliged to decide according to the law which he was appointed to administer; but he declared, were he at liberty to follow his own opinion, he would have had no hesitation in yielding to the mother's appeal, and allowing her to retain the training and education of her own child. His words were these: 'To direct that the child should be brought up in the Catholic faith, will be to create a barrier between a widowed mother and her only child – to annul the mother's influence over her daughter on the most important of all subjects on which it can be exercised, with the almost inevitable result of weakening it in all others; to introduce a disturbing element into a union which ought to be as close, as warm, as absolute as any known to man; and lastly, to inflict the most severe pain on both mother and child. But it is clear that no argument which would recognize any right in the widowed mother to bring up her child in a religion different from its father's, can be allowed to weigh with me at all. According to the law of this court the mother has no such right. The duty of the widowed mother is, in general, to bring up the child according to the faith which its father professed, even though she utterly disapproved of it, and feels that to do so will diminish her influence over the child, and cloud the relation between them.' For those reasons his Honor directed that the child should be educated in the Catholic faith. The mother, however, appealed once more to English law, anxious to try a last chance to keep her child, and the case was brought to the Court of Chancery before the Lords Justices of Appeal. The decision was again adverse to the mother. One of the Lords Justices, Lord Justice Mellish, had the grace to say that he could quite conceive a difference of opinion as to the propriety of the rule of law, but that court could not alter the rule of law, which was that unless there existed some strong reason in the interest of the child rendering it undesirable, a child ought to be brought up in the religion of its father. The other Lord Justice, Lord Justice James, gave his decision without any apparent qualms, concluding with these words: 'The mother has had the charge of the child up to the time when her regular religious instruction ought to commence, and the court ought now to direct that she be brought up and educated as a member of the Catholic church.' This decision was given on the 26 April 1871, the mother's appeal being *dismissed with costs*.

Here we perceive only too plainly that the interests and the feelings of a mother are taken into no account whatever by the law. The law recognizes no claim on the mother's part. It appears to forget her existence. This is the result of women not being represented in Parliament. If women had votes to elect members of Parliament, the laws made in Parliament would of necessity be careful to recognize women's claims to justice; their right to fair play and consideration could not be forgotten or be laid aside, if women were permitted to attend to what concerns their sex in the framing of laws.

I shall now mention the case of a Catholic lady married to a Protestant gentleman of the County of Cork. This lady, Mrs Purcell, was left a widow with two little children, a son and a daughter; and she was appointed the guardian of the children by the Court of Chancery, and was allowed five hundred pounds a year for the children's maintenance. Six years after the father's death, a relative of the father caused Mrs Purcell, the mother, to be communicated with touching the religious education of the children. The Catholic mother could not openly resent such interference between her and her children on the part of a relation of her deceased Protestant husband. She knew too well that the law was all against her, and that instead of giving her sympathy, it would decide directly in opposition to her wish, to educate her children in her own religion. She did not therefore appeal to the law at all. And what steps do you think she took? In order that she might be enabled to bring up her son and daughter in the creed she thought best, she fled with them secretly, like a criminal, from her native land, well knowing that she was acting against the laws of her country. Does not this case remind us of the flight of the slave-mother depicted in 'Uncle Tom's Cabin,' when escaping from the United States to Canada, where her little boy was safe from the slave-dealer who wished to separate mother and child?

Mr Beresford Hope, a Member of Parliament, who often gets

up to oppose Women's Suffrage, says that women require sympathy and protection; and no doubt if he were convinced that the possession of the suffrage would afford some safeguard to women where their dearest interests are concerned, he would support the Bill to Remove the Electoral Disabilities of women, instead of opposing it. The case of Mrs Purcell is a practical commentary on the amount of sympathy and protection given to women by the law as at present existing, when they wish to fulfil their high mission of training their children in the mode they think best. The Court of Chancery directed that the yearly allowance for the children's maintenance should not be paid to Mrs Purcell until she obeyed the order directing her to rear her children in the Protestant faith, and to bring them back to Ireland forthwith. Mrs Purcell, actuated by irresistible religious convictions, persisted in living in a foreign land, and in educating her children as members of the Catholic Church. And so this poor anxious mother struggled on for years, a stranger in a strange land, not receiving a shilling from the Court of Chancery of the sum allotted for the children's maintenance. But at the end of eight years Mrs Purcell's daughter died; and then the mother ventured to return to her own country, as her only remaining child, her son, was then nearly fifteen years of age, and was too deeply imbued with the principles of the Catholic religion to have another faith forced upon him.

You see here that it is no question of which is the wiser, the father or mother, or no question of which is the better religion, the Protestant or the Catholic. If it were one particular religion only in which the law of the land required a widowed mother to educate her children, a state religion for instance, we might imagine that a narrow-minded bigotry actuated the framing of such laws on the part of the ruling powers, and we might entertain some kind of respect for sincere though mistaken views; but we see by the two cases I have just mentioned, of the trials severally of a Protestant mother and of a Catholic mother, that it is not a question of religious intolerance, but of an utter forgetfulness of woman's claims to justice or fair dealing, even in her so-called sacred sphere of wife and mother. The question is, which is the religion of the father? and even where daughters are concerned, the religion of the mother is of no account. The law of Austria furnishes an example, as I have observed, of a rough and ready attempt at justice; for while it permits the mother to decide as to the religion of her daughters, it leaves the father to determine the creed of the sons.

But some people may say that in the cases I have mentioned

there was a difference of religion between husband and wife; and that a woman could easily prevent such trials as I have spoken of, by marrying only a person of her own religious creed. It must be remembered, however, that the rule of law which forgets that a mother is interested in her child's religion, must always place the mother merely at the mercy of chance. She has no security by law. Should her husband change his religion, then he can have his daughters as well as his sons educated in the creed he has just newly adopted, and in case of a dispute with his wife on the subject, the law would uphold his wishes, and would not listen for one moment to the wife's appeal to be allowed to direct even the religious training of her daughters.

Permit me to state a case where the husband, a reputed Protestant, changed his religion on his death-bed, making a will about a week before his decease, directing that all his children, three girls and two boys who had all been baptized in the Protestant Church, should be handed over to certain guardians, in order that they might be brought up in a religion different from that professed by their mother. In the newspaper report of the case, it is stated that the dying man in question, Thomas Marson, of Belfast, said that his wife was a Protestant, and that he wished to make arrangements to have his children brought up in the Catholic faith; and he expressed the great unhappiness he felt that they had been baptized Protestants. The reverend gentleman who administered the last sacraments to him said the proper course would be to appoint legal guardians to carry out his wishes. Such indeed is the law! The dying man might take a pen and make a will, without warning to his wife, separating from her every one of her children, boys and girls alike, and the law would support him in this exercise of power.

I may observe that it only serves the more to show the want of thought and feeling which characterises the present law, for persons to tell women to leave politics alone, and that their truest happiness consists in cultivating their domestic affections. It would be better, considering the state of the law, that women had no affections at all, and then they could not have their feelings wounded so cruelly with express legal sanction. It may be said that such cases of hardship occur very seldom. The same can be said of murder; it fortunately occurs very seldom, but we would not feel very safe or comfortable in a country where a murderer was not legally punishable for his crimes, and where we had for our safety and protection, merely to depend upon people being too good-natured, or too well-principled to kill us. When women really understand the law, they may feel somewhat uneasy that it does not surround them with more safeguards for the protection of their dearest interests. Not long ago a report appeared in the newspapers of a case where the mother, Mrs Garnett, was said to have tampered with her child's religion, because, having changed her creed from that of her deceased husband, she taught her child the religion she thought best. Thus, if you see a child saying its prayers at its mother's knee, you cannot know whether she is bringing it up piously and properly, or whether she is unlawfully 'tampering' with its faith, until you know what creed the father professed, even if he be dead for several years. For, according to law, the mother's faith, as I have before said, is of no account; but the father, whether he be Protestant or Catholic, is always of the right religion. Those ladies and gentlemen who write romantically about the 'woman's kingdom,' and woman's powerful influence in the sphere of home, evidently do not know much of the law, which gives to a woman no more rights with reference to her children than with reference to politics. It must be acknowledged that however men have disregarded the feelings of women in making the laws, they have taken pretty good care of themselves, settling everything in a manner highly conducive to their own peace of mind, to the exercise of their own ambition, and to their special interests at home, abroad, and everywhere. A woman must not be allowed to think of entering a profession and earning a good income (especially if she be in the rank of those who determine our social customs and make the laws) because she has to look after her children, and give up her whole time to them; and then she must not expect to have any rights or legal power over these children, because she does not earn anything for their support.

I have drawn especial attention to the religious education of children; but in every other branch of education the mother is equally powerless by law. She may have a good deal of influence, and probably some real power in the family; but this is in accordance with the law of nature, and in spite of the law of the land, and the ladies and gentlemen here assembled are aware that it is the law of the land we wish to improve, as far as concerns the interests of women. Some women think themselves very generous and self-sacrificing in saying that they do not wish for any rights, and are quite willing to give up all privileges in favour of their husbands; but evidently our law-makers did not expect any such generosity on the part of women, for they determined not to leave it in the power of any married woman – gentle or simple – to retain rights or privileges. Without allowing any choice in the matter, the law deprives a woman, as soon as she marries, of almost her legal existence – except in the case of serious crimes, for she can be executed as a separate individual when she commits a murder. It would be too much to expect that the 'husband and wife are one, and that one the husband,' when the scaffold and the hangman are in question; but if a good property falls to the wife, then it is convenient and proper that the husband and wife should be one, and that one the husband.

People sometimes say that to give women the suffrage would take them from their domestic duties. This argument would lead us to infer that the women of this country were very hard-worked indeed; that they were more constantly occupied with domestic drudgery than the busiest lawyers, the busiest doctors, the busiest grocers, the busiest blacksmiths, were occupied with their various callings: for all these last-named individuals are supposed to find time to vote. Other opponents of women's suffrage declare that women ought not to be allowed votes because they do not work at all, and are entirely provided for and protected by men who save them all trouble.

In answer to those romantic people who imagine that women are shielded from the necessity of working for their own support, I may mention that nearly three millions of unmarried women in England alone are gaining their livelihood by their own exertions, and managing their own affairs; while eight hundred thousand married women, with their husbands alive, are engaged in occupations by which they earn money. In the manufacturing parts of the country especially, from whence springs so much of our national wealth, women are employed in large numbers, always, however, receiving less wages than men even for doing the same amount of work as men. Again, it has been said that women are not sufficiently educated to vote; while, at the same time, we know that men who can neither read nor write may now possess the privilege of voting. A highly educated lady, possessing thousands a year and paying a large amount in taxes, besides perhaps contributing to the support of many charitable public institutions of the country, is not considered intelligent or worthy enough to be permitted a vote, while the blacksmith who shoes her horses may be endowed with the privilege.

Many years ago there were three prizes offered for the three best essays on a particular political subject. The competition was open to the entire kingdom: and when the time came for declaring the names of the winners, it was found that the three prize political essays were all written by one and the same person, and that person a lady about twenty-four years old. To think that women could find any difficulty in comprehending political questions is simply ridiculous. The faculties for studying politics are far greater than those for studying any other branch of knowledge. What is so cheap as a daily newspaper? Books upon botany or painting, Berlin wool for executing square featured men and women, and angularly-formed animals, as ornamental covers for ottomans, etc. cost a great deal of money; but our newspapers are a cheap luxury, and there are few households, whether consisting of men or women, where the daily paper is not received as almost a necessary of existence every morning.

It is often said that no-one could object to the franchise being given to women of what are called 'the better classes' of society; but any one who has a knowledge of the industry, the integrity, and good sense so generally displayed by those hard-working women who as heads of families, or as single women, are earning their bread honestly and independently, must acknowledge that the women of each separate class are quite as capable of voting conscientiously as the men of the same class. The franchise is spoken of as a privilege and protection for men, and why not the same for women? Some people profess to think that women would lose rather than gain in dignity by exercising the franchise: but let us take a glance at the male persons who rank politically with women. The law books state that some persons are disqualified for ever from being voters – such as 'women and idiots.'

To some ladies and gentlemen this may, perhaps, appear an extremely dignified and graceful position for women, but I confess I cannot agree with them.

I will briefly allude to another argument occasionally made use of by opponents of women's suffrage, who seem to have arrived at their wits' ends in trying to discover something to say in opposition – namely, the argument that as women are not called upon to defend the country as soldiers, they should not expect to be politically represented. One answer to this argument is, that British soldiers themselves cannot exercise the franchise, because they are not ratepayers or householders; while clergymen, who certainly are not expected to undertake military duty, and men utterly incapacitated by age or infirmity from entering warlike service, are, nevertheless, permitted to exercise the privilege of electors, when they pay the requisite amount of rates as householders. Women are strictly keeping within the bounds of the British constitution when they ask for the suffrage as householders and ratepayers.

To point out the many hardships suffered by women from not being represented in the councils of the nation, would take up far more time than can now be spared; but I shall mention one or two cases more. Mr Mill, in his memorable speech made in favour of women's suffrage in the House of Commons in May 1867, mentioned that Christ's Hospital in London, generally called the Bluecoat School, and which had been founded originally for boys and girls alike, was then supporting and educating eleven hundred boys, destined for gentlemanly professions and callings, and only twenty-six girls, who were being trained for domestic servants. That was the just way the girls were treated; nearly all the money of the endowment was monopolized for the advantage of the boys. With regard to education generally, the interests of women have been almost entirely neglected by the State. There was formerly a vague idea prevalent, no doubt, that if women were educated highly they might not be contented to be such constant drudges as it was wished they should be, or would not believe so implicitly all that was imposed upon them to keep them contented with holding an inferior position. The scientific institutions of the country have displayed great injustice to women. The Royal Astronomical Society refused to give its gold medal to Miss Caroline Herschel, for her discovery of five comets, because she was a woman – frankly declaring that if the discoverer had been a man, he should have been awarded it. Mrs Somerville, whose scientific works are so well known, and who is now upwards of eighty years old, only received about a year ago a tardy recognition of some work she accomplished twenty or thirty years before, by being given a medal for it; and this was owing to the representation of some of those persons engaged in the present movement for obtaining justice and fair play for women.

While thus discouraging women in every pursuit of high knowledge, by excluding them from scientific societies, and by refusing them marks of distinction and honours, when, in spite of obstacles, they happen to make important scientific discoveries; opponents say that women have no taste, and in fact, no brains for science, or for any pursuit that requires deep thought. They first deny them the means of cultivating their intellect, and then they declare they have no intellect to cultivate.

It has been said that Members of Parliament chosen altogether by male voters might remedy all the legal injustices under which women labour; but what guarantee would they possess that succeeding law-makers might not bring back the old state of oppression? Until women gain the suffrage themselves, they never can be thoroughly protected against the caprice of the ruling powers. In the history of the world it will be found that privileges have been sometimes granted to women, and have been sometimes taken from them again, and have oftener been withheld from them altogether for no palpable reason. In some countries women can reign, whether as despotic rulers or as constitutional sovereigns, and in others they are excluded from the throne. But no-one has ever proved that the nations where only male monarchs were permitted were uniformly better governed or more prosperous than where women as well as men were allowed to reign. Hanover would not permit Queen Victoria to ascend the throne of that kingdom. Her Majesty might do well enough to be the sovereign of the British Empire, but she was not thought good enough for Hanover. Now, however, Hanover has lost its king, and the conqueror reigns in his stead. In France no woman could ascend the throne, yet royalty there is in no higher favour for all that; and according to the present law there, every man in that country, however uneducated, possesses the privilege of the franchise; while no woman in France, however gifted, has any political rights whatever. These arrangements, whereby women are excluded from legitimately exercising political power, have not been productive of such beneficial effects as to make France serve as a brilliant example to other lands, of a method in which a country may provide stability and security, combined with liberty, progress, and happiness. Apparent caprice and inconsistency towards women may also be pointed out as instanced by France, which would not have a female sovereign, granting now medical degrees to women; whereas in England, where a lady at present sits upon the throne, no woman, notwithstanding, can attain at present the dignity of doctor of medicine. To point out further inconsistency in the treatment of women, it may be observed that in the matter of public distinction, women may enjoy it in some particulars, consistently with receiving the highest possible respect; while, nevertheless, there is a vague idea that it is feminine and graceful to like retirement, and to shrink from public notice. For instance, some people think it would be unfeminine for a young lady to have her name published as having won a prize in any solid branch of learning; but they do not think it unfeminine for her to have her dress minutely described in the public papers when she attends either the drawing-room or state balls in London, or the Viceregal court in Dublin. When they read in their morning papers that Miss Angelina Blank, of 260 Fitzwilliam Square, wore a train of the richest *poult de soie*, trimmed with *bouffants of tulle*, and *jupe* of magnificent lace, and corsage ornamented tastefully, they think this publicity is quite right for Miss Angelina Blank; but they would not think it so nice to see her name in the papers as having won a prize in history or mathematics; though I think we must all agree that the young lady who is thus tacitly taught to feel ashamed of intellectual attainments, and proud of wearing the richest lace, will naturally think attending to her dress more important than cultivating her mind. A lady may also make a speech to a regiment of soldiers, before an assembled multitude, on the occasion of presenting new colours to the corps; or she may give the name to a ship, likewise in presence of thousands; or lay the foundation stone of some public building before all eyes. But nobody thinks her unfeminine for doing these things. On the contrary, it is a proof of the respect in which she is held that she is asked to do them. She feels it as a compliment, and so do her whole family, that she has been selected for such distinction. Moreover, there are various public positions now filled by women in this country, and neither Government nor society in general object to them. For instance, a woman may sit all day at a street corner, winter and summer, selling fruit at a stall under the shelter of a dilapidated umbrella; she may let lodgings and be liable to the intrusion of any one who sees her bill on her window-pane; and no one will say that these employments are unfeminine. The Government has been careful to exclude women from all high, well-paid appointments; but it permits them to engage in almost any low occupation that poverty may drive them to, thus proving that it is quite a delusion to imagine women are debarred from political or other privileges, in order to preserve their refinement.

With reference to public notice, I may observe, that it is the most refined ladies in the country who have their movements chronicled in the newspapers for all the world to read in the 'Fashionable Intelligence.' It is precisely the ladies of greatest distinction that we know most about, whom we are expected to respect the most; and if women see, as they do, the photographs of princesses in shop windows, and can ascertain from the public press the hour at which the royal ladies attended divine service on Sunday, and where they drove on Monday, and whom they visited on Tuesday, and so on through all the days of the week, surely no-one could expect women with any reasoning powers whatever to believe the public notice is in itself so objectionable, that women, sooner than run the risk of appearing before the public, had better give up all idea of voting at elections, and securing for their sex the advantage of being able to look after their own interests concerning the laws of the country.

At the same time, no compliment can be greater than that paid to women by many opponents of women's suffrage, who are so satisfied with ladies as they are at present that they do not think there is any room for improvement: who fear that if women become in any way different, it must be alteration for the worse, as it would be impossible for them to imagine that women could be any better than they are now. In answer I may say that as political power does not make polished gentlemen unmannerly, nor make rough men rougher than they were before they attained such power, so I trust that refinement and courtesy may not disappear when other women in this country besides her Majesty, the Queen, are admitted to political privileges.

The efforts to procure the suffrage for women ratepayers have already done much for the advancement of their whole sex. Wrongs have been pointed out that remained unnoticed, except by the silent sufferers, for centuries; and men in high places are awakening to a sense of the deep injustices endured so long by the women of the nation. I myself heard Mr Gladstone say in the House of Commons that the laws had done much less than justice to women; but he was induced to consider the subject by the fact that Mr Jacob Bright's Bill for removing the electoral disabilities of women was then being discussed in the House. At the present time the difference between those who can guard their interests and those who are thrown defencelessly upon the mercy of others, is the political franchise. I would earnestly impress upon all those who are interested in the elevation of women – whether as regards their higher education, or their admission to any profitable employments now shut out from them – to do what they can to further the movement in favour of women's suffrage. When women are granted the franchise they can no longer be refused any just or reasonable privileges; but as long as they remain without it, their wishes and requirements will be liable to meet with slights and neglect from government. Those who are working in this great cause, giving time, and thought, and money for its promotion, and who have brought it to its present state of prosperity, believe that the wrongs of women – both social and political – arise from their exclusion from the franchise, and that all schemes for advancing their position will utterly fail unless built upon the solid foundation of constitutional rights.

Let none, therefore, who have women's welfare really at heart, refuse a helping hand in this movement, that a successful termination to it may not be delayed.

Rhoda Garrett

*Electoral disabilities of women**

3 April 1872

IN speaking on the subject of the Electoral Disabilities of Women, it is no longer necessary to preface one's remarks by an elaborate explanation of what is meant by this demand that we are now making for admission to Electoral Representation. The subject has of late been too widely discussed to allow of any very great ignorance as to the matter to be dealt with in a lecture upon Woman's Suffrage; still I do not for a moment venture to hope that this discussion has caused even one-hundredth part of the excitement created by the Tichborne case, for example, though it involves a great political reform affecting not one family alone, but all classes of Her Majesty's subjects. In what manner it thus affects the interests of the entire nation, it will be my endeavour to point out in the course of my lecture to-night.

In order to bring my subject within as narrow a compass as possible, I will divide it into three parts –

1 The education of women;
2 Their economic position;
3 The existing laws especially affecting the interests of women.

I dare say that at first sight you will be unable to see how the

---

*A lecture in the Corn Exchange, Cheltenham.

possession of the Suffrage by women would improve their position either educationally, economically, or legally; but by the time I have concluded my paper I am bold enough to hope that I may have convinced those who need convincing, that the Suffrage is, as Mr John Stuart Mill says, the turning-point in women's cause, and that with it, they cannot long be denied any just right, or excluded from any fair advantage.

Let us first of all consider the present state of education among women, from the time when they are first capable of receiving any education at all, until they arrive at that happy climax, when they are pronounced by their parents and guardians 'finished.' In the training of very young children there is, of course, comparatively little difference between the actual teaching given to boys and girls, but in their moral and physical training, the difference is even then apparent. Boys are taught from the earliest period of life to be self-dependent and self-reliant; while girls are taught, on the contrary, to be yielding, self-sacrificing, and reliant on anyone rather than upon themselves. A boy is encouraged to develop his physical powers by out-door sports of all kinds, and to interest himself in a variety of pursuits, which cultivate habits of observation, and often lay the foundation for a love of natural science which in after life proves most valuable. A girl generally receives a training of a very opposite character. If she shows a disposition to join in her brothers' games and amusements she is probably told that such conduct is 'unladylike,' that little girls should not be 'tom-boys,' and that, instead of running and jumping and climbing she should get to her sewing and knitting and 'keep quiet.' I believe it is a generally received axiom that men are more selfish than women, and it is easy to trace the growth of this selfishness in men to that spirit of excessive self-sacrifice in women which, even as boys, they have been taught to look upon as natural, and to regard as a right.

Passing from the home life, let us see how boys and girls are respectively prepared for the work of life by the education given to them at school. Everyone knows how immensely superior the educational advantages open to boys are, to those which are offered to girls. A boy is sent, or at any rate may be sent, to one of the great public schools and afterwards to one of the Universities. In each case his education will be conducted by men of the highest ability and learning. Contrast with this the education his sister is likely to receive at the small private school which is open to her. The teachers here, when they are women, have seldom been trained to teach, and have in nearly every case undertaken the profession from necessity, and not from choice;

consequently they are only able to impart to their pupils the smatterings of knowledge that it has been in their own power to acquire. The most important subjects for female education are generally considered to be accomplishments so-called – a little bad French and music, and worse drawing, with a great deal of fancy needlework. If anyone doubts the truth of my statements let him read the School Commissioner's report which lately enquired into the state of education in girls', as well as in boys' schools. Here the evidence is so united and voluminous that my difficulty, in selecting any one part as especially illustrating the poverty and worthlessness of the education now offered to girls, has been to choose, out of so great a choice, not to find suitable matter. Before I read the quotation I should like to draw the attention of those present, who take an interest in the education of girls, to a book which has been compiled by Miss Beale, of Cheltenham, from the reports issued by the Schools' Inquiry Commission; it is most valuable as containing in one small volume all the evidence, and the reports, which were received by the Commission on Girls' Schools. After describing the teaching given in a girls' day school, one of the assistant commissioners says 'The boarding school, (assuming it, as one may do, to belong to the same class), follows (in all probability), the same vicious system as the day school; and the only difference that it makes to the girl is to take away some of the primitive roughness or simplicity of her manner, and give it an air of affectation and restraint. Then at sixteen she goes home "for good." She displays the two or three pieces of ornamental needlework, each of which has occupied her three months, and some drawings, copies from the flat, of figures and landscapes, whose high finish betrays the drawing master's hand. A neighbour drops in, conversation turns upon Jane's return from school, and the mother bids her play one of the pieces she learnt there. For two or three weeks this exhibition of skill is repeated at intervals, and then it ceases, the piano is no more touched, the dates of inventions, the relationship of the heathen gods, the number of houses burnt in the fire of London, and other interesting facts contained in Mangnall are soon forgotten, and the girl is as though she had never been to school at all. There are few books on her father's shelves, perhaps two or three green or yellow novels, some back numbers of the Family Herald, Mr Tupper's *Proverbial Philosophy*, Cowper's poems, with gilt edges, dusted more often than opened, Enquire within upon Everything, and one or two religious biographies. It is not this want of material, however, that quenches her taste for reading, for school gave her no such taste; her life henceforth, till marriage, is listless and purposeless, some of it spent in petty occupation, more of it in pettier gossip; and when at last she is called upon to manage a household she finds that her education has neither taught her anything that can be of practical service, nor made her any fitter than nature made her at first to educate and govern her children. In point of knowledge and refinement, she is just where her mother was, and her sons and daughters suffer for it.'

I must here say a few words on the question of endowments as affecting educational establishments. It is a well known fact that all the enormous sums set apart for purposes of education are almost entirely devoted to the teaching of boys. The trustees of public educational charities have generally managed to employ the funds exclusively for boys, and Parliament, in voting money for education, has very often forgotten the existence of girls. Where funds have been left for education without distinction of sex, girls have often been unfairly dealt with; as in the case of Christ's Hospital (the Bluecoat School) which was originally established for the purpose of maintaining a certain number of boys and girls. The funds of this school now amount to £42,000 a year; out of these funds one thousand two hundred boys are fed and clothed, and educated in such a manner as to fit them to proceed to the Universities, and nineteen girls are trained as domestic servants.

It must be remembered, moreover, that it is not alone to boys whose parents are rich that all those advantages are open. To every large public school there are attached scholarships open for competition to all the pupils, and therefore any boy of fair ability and perseverance may, by gaining one of them, obtain a sufficient yearly sum to enable him to pay, at any rate, a considerable part of his college expenses; and, when once the doors of the University are open to him, it is surely his own fault if he does not win for himself both honour and emolument.

Where now shall we look for similar advantages for the sisters of these fortunate boys? Referring to this subject, the report of the Schools' Inquiry Commission before mentioned says: 'Examinations and endowments afford, at the present time, the best practical method of improving female education. We can only improve the education of the classes below by beginning at the top and improving the higher education, especially that of the teachers. Here scholarships would be most useful.'

Of course it is impossible to me to point out, in the brief space of time at my disposal, all the evils that must arise from such a one-sided system of education as this – in the one case, we educate entirely for life in the world, in the other, for life at home. We well know that men neither can, nor do, live entirely in, and for, the world; nor can women live entirely in, and for, the home. Both are impossible as both are undesirable.

Let us now trace the connection between the education of women and their electoral disabilities. It will be readily admitted that the scope of education is to fit the child for his, or her, future place in the world; and here, as elsewhere, as we sow, so also shall we reap. If, therefore, we give to girls such an education as that I have just described, is it unlikely that when they grow up they will be both physically and mentally weak, ignorant, dependent and frivolous, unfit, as they are often declared to be, to be entrusted with civil and political rights?

But think you these evils will be best remedied by insisting upon their remaining in this state of dependence, or by admitting them to a broader and a freer life; by giving them responsibility as an educational power? Is not this what was done for working men in the passing of the last Reform Bill? Was it not argued that none but working men could tell what the needs of their own class were, and that, through their representatives, they had a right to express their opinions in Parliament? Is the same argument less forcible when applied to women? Would they consent to be excluded from a fair share in educational advantages if they could, in like manner, make their voices heard in the Legislature of the country? Would not their claim to be educated as solidly, and in the same branches of knowledge as men, be argued with a far greater chance of success, if they possessed the power of urging its justice before that tribunal where men are able to lay their grievances, and enforce their redress?

Having now given a brief sketch of the early life and training of a woman, let us see how she is likely to fare when she is ready to take her part in the real work of life. In other words, let us examine the economic condition of women. Most people will tell us that a woman has no need to take part at all in the world's work; that if she is all she ought to be, attractive, young, and with an adequate knowledge of cookery and shirt-buttons, some man will certainly wish to marry her, and then she will have no need to trouble her head about politics and the like, with which she has no concern. This is no doubt very plausible, and the majority of women will probably always choose to marry, if a suitable opportunity presents itself; but granting that the greater part of the female population is thus comfortably provided for, there still remains an enormous proportion of unmarried women, most of whom must support themselves by their own earnings. Now custom usually attaches a kind of stigma to what is called an 'old-maid,' that is to say, a woman who, either from necessity or choice, is still unmarried when she has passed her early youth. But possibly custom might be a little more lenient to her misfortunes, if it were universally known that, in consequence of the great excess of the female over the male population in this country, there are two millions and a half of British women without husbands, many of whom are obliged to work for their own subsistence. As, therefore, a great many women are, willing or unwilling, compelled, by the law of this land that a man shall have only one wife at a time, to remain in single blessedness, it will be for the advantage, both of themselves, and of the community at large, that they should not only be self-supporting, but productive labourers.

I will not here enter particularly into the many difficulties and disadvantages of women of the so-called working classes, simply remarking, as I pass, that the universally low rate of wages amongst them, as compared with those of men of their own class, is accounted for principally by the fact that women rarely receive a proper training for the work they undertake to perform; consequently, their work is unskilled, and therefore inferior. Even where a woman is able to perform the same work equally well with a man, her labour is not remunerated in the same degree in consequence of the custom I have just alluded to. If a man engages in the trade of a mason or carpenter, or even a tailor or cook, he receives a proper training, and serves a regular apprenticeship; but it is not thought necessary to give these advantages to a woman; at any rate not on the same thorough and distinct understanding. I will give one or two illustrations of what I mean in regard to this subject, and then pass on.

Let us take as one example, out of the many that might be advanced, that of a cook in a wealthy family. If this same cook is a man, he has exactly similar work to perform as a woman would have in the same position – neither more nor less – but he has, in all probability, served a proper and recognised apprenticeship to his trade, and he can, therefore, always command a high price for his labour. A woman may have exactly the same amount of knowledge; may be quite as competent to prepare those marvels of cookery that aristocratic palates delight in, but she has no credentials from Soyer or Francatelli to assure her employers of her capability; she has, moreover the precedent of custom against her, and therefore, for the same work, performed in an equally satisfactory manner, she is paid half, or at any rate, one third, less than a man would be. Again. A large hairdresser in London has lately (to his credit be it spoken) adopted the sensible custom of employing young women in his establishment to cut and dress the hair of his lady customers. One of the girls employed in this business told me the other day that the women were always paid less than the men. Now this is obviously unfair. The girls do their work most satisfactorily; and their department is certainly more difficult and requires more skill than that of the men, for they have not only to cut a lady's hair, but also to construct upon her head one of those marvellous erections with which too many English girls in these days disfigure themselves, and which I am sure it would puzzle their male competitors to fabricate.

These two instances alone will show you how unfairly even the skilled labour of women is remunerated. But I grieve to say there are thousands of women, who through deficient training, have not the same skilled labour to offer, and must suffer accordingly. We do not ask for these that competent, or incompetent, they should receive the same wages as men. What we *do* ask is that women should no longer be placed at a disadvantage; we ask that they should have as good an education, and as many opportunities as men for fitting themselves for their work; which, with the removal of trade monopolies, will at least give them a fair chance; and then, and then only, can it be justly said that it is their own fault if they do not make their way in the world as men now have it in their power to do.

But, bad as the economic condition of women of the working classes is, it cannot be regarded as so difficult to improve as that of the more educated middle-class women, who, in addition to a training which tends absolutely to unfit them for work, have to contend with a mass of prejudice against their working at all, which is all the more formidable inasmuch as it is unreasonable, and therefore *unconvinceable*. The economic condition of such women, their exclusion from nearly all lucrative and honourable employments – their consequent dependence upon men for their support – are evils which increase with the growth of the population, and which the State is no longer justified in ignoring. For an educated woman there is no middle path. Either she must be Queen of England – the head of the State – or she must be shut out from nearly all the advantages of a citizen in a country over which a woman rules. To begin with the offices under Government. The numerous servants employed thereby (some of whom earn, or, to speak more precisely, *receive* several thousands a-year) are exclusively male subjects of her Majesty; except in the telegraph offices where, through the exertions of Mr Scudamore, women have been admitted. But even here, they are admitted, as Mr Scudamore himself told me, only in the lower grades, where, after years of faithful work, they might eventually earn £200 a-year. The office of superintendent, which women are quite as competent to fill as men, is denied to them, solely because they are women, *not* because they are in any way incapable of fulfilling its duties. There are many other civil offices quite as suitable to women as telegraphy, though requiring a higher education, for which hundreds of British gentlewomen would gladly fit themselves, the greatest proportion of whom, even the most delicate, would have physical strength enough to read the *Times* daily from ten to four.

The influence thus exercised by the Government in declaring women ineligible to hold office under it permeates through society and countenances their exclusion from the three learned professions – from the Church, where, as teachers of morality their influence and example would be as valuable as that of men; from medicine, though it is often said that it is a woman's special province to minister to the sick; and from the law, where – well, perhaps, some more of that tenderness of conscience, which men tell us is one of the peculiar characteristics of woman, might not be injurious to the higher interests of that learned profession.

Let us now note the difficulties a woman is likely to encounter, if she seeks to enter trade. Here there are no charters, it is true, as in the professions, to prevent her entrance at the very threshold. But there are lions in the way quite as formidable; blind prejudice, on the one hand; and a fear of injuring established interests on the other. You must not think I am drawing a fancy picture – that no woman would wish to engage in trade. I know women who have tried to do so, and whose difficulties lay, not in their want of power to acquire the requisite knowledge, but in the almost over-whelming prejudice of those already in possession of the vantage ground which stops them at every turn. It is often urged against admitting women to a share in the real work of life that they are neither physically nor mentally strong enough to compete with men; but no amount of hard work, with the hope of success at the end, would break down a woman's health in comparison with the struggle with anxiety, disappointment and contempt, which she now has so often to endure, and which truly makes 'the whole head sick, the whole heart faint.' I do not believe that men mean deliberately to be unjust to women; but they think *they* are the best judges of what nature intended women to be, and to do, and it must be confessed that, to a certain degree, women have hitherto endorsed this opinion, by accepting with more apparent than real content, the rôle of dependence and frivolity prescribed for them. The only qualities expected, nay, insisted upon, in women by men, are but too often those declared by Sir Charles

Sedley to be the sole characteristics of the female mind:

> All that in woman is adored
> In thy fair self I find,
> For the whole sex can but afford
> The handsome and the kind.

But here let me point out that the prejudice middle-class parents, almost without exception, have against their daughters working, possesses a power which in very few other cases prejudice is able to wield. There is no trade which can be entered into without capital, whether a shop of the humblest dimensions be opened, or a brewery established. Years before a boy has left school the prudent father is casting about in his own mind what trade or profession shall be adorned by presence of his cherished young hero. Every taste that he has given the slightest indication of is considered; and even, in some cases, the merits of his personal appearance and manners receive due weight. But the trade fixed upon, the next question which the father propounds to himself is, 'How can I provide the capital, first to article my boy to a respectable firm in the trade he has chosen, and afterwards to establish him in a business of his own?' But though parents thus recognise the necessity of providing capital for their sons, it never seems to enter their heads that the same thing should be, at any rate, *offered* to their daughters. Girls never have any capital; they hardly know what it means; yet without it the very first move is impossible; they may *enter* a shop, but they cannot *own* one. A boy is considered almost a miracle of goodness if, his premium paid, and his living expenses provided for, he lives morally and respectably, keeps out of debt, and applies himself with a moderate amount of intelligence to learn his business. To a girl, who, without any of these encouragements, plods on her way, eagerly learning the drudgery of some trade in which she can scarcely ever hope to be a master hand, such a meed of praise and encouragement is rarely offered. The excuse which parents generally give for making such a distinction between their boys and girls, is that if the girl married at the end of her apprenticeship, the money paid for her premium would be lost.

In answer to this several counter arguments may be used. In the first place it may be urged, that even if she did marry before she had regained in trade the sum expended upon her training, the business habits acquired during her apprenticeship, and the knowledge of how to expend her money to the best advantage would ensure her becoming the satisfactory steward of her husband's domestic expenditure, instead of (as is now too often the case) the thoughtless and extravagant agent, who is, during the first few months of her marriage '*chaffed*' for her ignorance in money matters; next, angrily expostulated with, and finally deprived of any power over the expenditure whatever. In the next place the advantage may be pointed out, that the girl who has a trade at her fingers' ends, would not be likely to accept the first man who offered himself for her hand, whether she loved him or not. In other words, marriage would not be (as it too often is now) the only profession into which women can enter, and the one position in which society will recognise their right to lead free and individual lives. For, as the *Times* observes, 'At present the language held by society to women is "marry, teach, die, or do worse." ' I do not for one moment believe, and, if I did, I should never succeed in persuading you, that boys and girls will leave off falling in love and marrying. I am sure that few men are so modest as to believe that they are likely to find really formidable rivals in dusty ledgers, hard office stools, or even in full cash boxes. So far from this I would contend that the wives they would gain would become their wives voluntarily and joyfully, and the more joyfully because voluntarily. Whatever business they were engaged in would either be disposed of, or perhaps carried on for the advantage of the family. Women now but too often feel that in marrying they are submitting themselves as it were to a fate which they suppose is inevitable; for as Mr Mill says, marriage must be regarded as Hobson's choice – that or none – so long as its only alternative is a dull, lonely life, embittered by the thought of the wasted energies or mis-used talents that, under other circumstances, might have been turned by the despised old-maid, to her own welfare, and to the advantage of the world.

Is there any difficulty now in seeing how the general position of women hinges on their exclusion from the suffrage? Has not Representation been the point for which all classes, who have had wrongs real or imaginary, have struggled? Is it necessary to explain what an advantage it would be to many women, now forced to work with competitors, who, at every turn, receive privileges and encouragement which are denied to them, to be placed in this respect, at least, on an equal footing with men? And lastly, is it necessary for me to point out how the responsibility of possessing a share in the government of the country (and a vote does give that share) would awaken from their lethargy those women who are now leading selfish – wickedly selfish – lives of indolence and gaiety; would force them to think out questions to which they now persistently shut their eyes, because they are painful or disagreeable, and would teach them that the souls and lives of their poorer sisters, whom a helping hand might save from despair, or guard from temptation, will be required of them. Thousands of women need only this awakening to be capable of doing noble deeds. 'Women often take meaner things because meaner things only are within their reach.'

Having now considered, as fully as time permits, the position of women educationally and economically, we come to the last point that remains for me to examine. What is the legal position of women in this country? I will speak, in the first place, of the laws relating to married women; and, in exposing their injustice and partiality, I hope all the husbands here present will not think I am having a sly hit at them individually and collectively; at the same time, if, in any case, the cap should fit, they have my free permission to put it on. Of course we all know that laws are not framed for those who do well; and it is a merciful thing that the majority of husbands have not the disposition to put in force all the power of tyranny and cruelty that our English laws place in their hands. As marriage is the only, or almost the only, career appointed by society for a woman; the one for which she is educated and taught that it is her highest duty to prepare herself; it might naturally be supposed that everything would have been done to make this condition as eligible and attractive as possible, so that she might never be tempted to desire any other. But surely, if women carefully considered what the laws of marriage really are, they would be more likely than when they are absolutely ignorant of these laws, to remain single, and to believe, with St Paul, that 'they are happier if they so abide!' Wives in England are, in all respects, as to property, person, and children, in the legal condition of slaves. When a man takes a wife he swears to endow her with all his worldly goods; then the law steps in and helps him to keep his vow by at once handing over the entire property of the wife to the husband, and declaring her incapable of holding property. Speaking on this point reminds me of the amusing description of the marriage service given by Sir John Bowring. 'Look at the marriage ceremony,' he said, 'it is wicked from beginning to end. "With this ring I thee wed" – that's sorcery; "With my body I thee worship" – that's idolatry; "With all my worldly goods I thee endow" – that's – that's a lie!' It is true that the richer classes in this country are able, by the costly means of settlements, to set aside the law, and to withdraw the whole, or a part of the wife's property from the control of her husband. But even then they are not able to give it into her own keeping – it must be held for her by trustees, and hedged round by numerous perplexing and irritating provisions.

In the Session of 1870 an Act was passed entitled, the Married Women's Property Bill. This Act was supposed to do for poor women what settlements do for rich ones. It was intended to prevent the personal property of a woman, her wages, her savings, and her earnings, being at the absolute mercy of her husband or his creditors. I have not time to enter into all the provisions of the Act, which is certainly a step in the right direction, but unfortunately a very short step; for it does not in any way recognise the only just principle of all legislation, namely, the perfect equality of all before the law. One illustration will be enough to demonstrate to you the kind of justice meted out to women under the new Act, and you shall judge for yourselves whether it is unreasonable for women to ask for something a little better. The case was recently tried in the law courts, and the account of it which I am about to read to you was taken from the *Pall Mall Gazette*, a paper which, as a rule, certainly never errs on the side of over-justice to women. 'It is to be hoped,' remarks the *Pall Mall Gazette*, 'that women will not read the case of Shillitoe v Shillitoe, which has just come before Vice-Chancellor Wickens, for it will give them a real grievance with which to make themselves and others uncomfortable, instead of those imaginary grievances that occupy so much of their time and attention. It seems that no settlement was executed on the marriage of Mr and Mrs Shillitoe. At the time of her marriage, Mrs Shillitoe had a sum of £500 at the Selby Bank in her maiden name. Soon after the marriage, at her husband's request, she drew the sum out of the bank on a cheque of her own and brought it home in order to pay rent and other specific sums with it. Two days after Mr Shillitoe died. No rent was paid, and Mrs Shillitoe for the first time ascertained that her husband was indebted to his father and his brother and to other persons, and was so when they married. The estate was being administered, and she was called upon to account for the £500 as part of her husband's property, without which sum the assets would be insufficient to pay the creditors. She declined to account for, or to pay over the money, and claimed it as her own by right of survivorship. It was insisted, on behalf of the creditors, that there had been a good reduction into possession of the £500 in the lifetime of Mr Shillitoe, and that his widow could not retain it. On the other hand, Mrs Shillitoe's counsel urged that the bank had paid the money to that lady as hers, and would not otherwise have paid the money at all; that it was in equity hers, for if she had known her husband's actual position at the time of the marriage, she would have insisted upon a settlement of the money, and could have done so at any moment if he had refused. If this fund were taken from her she would have only £4 10s. a-year to live upon. The Vice-Chancellor decided that there had been a perfectly good reduction of the money into the possession of Mr Shillitoe, and that the widow must hand it over to the executors. The case was no doubt a hard one for her, but the law – and a most important one it was – was too clear upon the subject.'

Well! this is how the law protects an Englishwoman's property. Now let us see what protection it affords to her person. A wife is regarded by the law as part of the husband's goods and chattels; and, in olden times, women were absolutely *sold* by their fathers to the husband. Even in these days there are some (of course very ignorant persons) who believe that the law sanctions such a proceeding. Only the other day I saw a case in the newspapers of a man who sold his wife to another man for half-a-crown. Again, how many cases of the brutal personal violence of men towards their wives, may be read of every day in the columns of our newspapers, and the very inadequate punishment frequently accorded to them, by the magistrates, for the offence. Many a man, I really believe, conscientiously holds with the old proverb:

> A wife, a dog, and a walnut tree,
> The more you beat 'em the better they be.

Again, if a woman is cruelly treated by her husband, she cannot leave him, or, if she does so, she can be compelled to return to him by law or by physical force. It is only legal separation by a court of justice, which can entitle her to live apart from him; and this legal separation is most difficult to obtain, and is only granted in cases of desertion and extreme cruelty.

Now what is the power of a woman over her own children, who are, at least, as much hers as her husband's? They are by law *his* children. He only has legal power over them; she can only act towards them by delegation from him; after he is dead she is not their legal guardian, unless he by will has made her so; he could constitute any stranger their legal guardian, and deprive their own mother of any power whatever over them. After seven years of age, the custody of a woman's children belongs exclusively to her husband; after that age she has not the right even to see them, unless by special legal decree.

'My brethren, these things ought not so to be!' But there are laws affecting both married and unmarried women, worse even than these; more degrading, more cruel, more unjust, more barbarous; laws, which if Englishmen once thoroughly understood, and reflected upon, would not, I venture to say, disgrace much longer the statute books of our country. And if women had the power of showing by their votes at an election, that they approved or disapproved of laws which have so much to do with the happiness and well-being of their whole lives – if they had this power, would they not, I ask you, do their share in helping to abolish such legislation as this?

It is constantly said that women's interests are so carefully guarded by men that it is unnecessary to give them any voice in the matter. Did working men think that their well-being was so completely safe in the hands of the richer classes, that it was unnecessary to pass the Representation of the People's Bill? We women demand, as men have demanded before us, the right to protect ourselves; and we believe, as they believed, that this end will only be gained by our obtaining a voice in the framing of those laws which we are called upon to obey.

At the commencement of my lecture I expressed a hope that before I had finished speaking I might have convinced some of those who differed from me on this subject, that politics have, after all, a great deal to do with women; that as they cannot live in the world without bearing a part in its business, responsibilities, and sufferings, they therefore do well to strive for a share of the power to work with men, for the general well-being and prosperity of their common country. In order to do this, I have pointed out, that they demand the removal of their electoral disabilities, believing that until this is done they can have no efficient weapon with which to fight their battles. We are constantly told, in tones of scorn, that the women who desire the suffrage are a mere handful of female fanatics. As compared with the entire female population we *may* be only a handful, but we are an ever-increasing handful of very obstinate people; and, if a wilful man must have his way, a wilful woman is likely to be quite as invincible:

> If she will, she will, you may depend on't;
> And if she won't, she won't, and there's an end on't.

Every year a larger number of petitions are presented to Parliament in favour of this measure, and last year these petitions were signed by 187,000 persons. One hundred and eighty-seven thousand persons is, at any rate, a considerable handful, especially if they are all, as they have been declared to be, violent fanatics.

Before I conclude I must make it clearly understood what the measure really is to which you will be asked to assent in the Resolution which will be put to this meeting. There is apt to arise a little obscurity on this point, I know. At a meeting in one of the large towns in the North, a short time ago, the Mayor, who was to preside, came up to me just before the meeting began, and said, in an excited manner, 'Now promise me that you will not advocate the suffrage for *married* women.' I have no doubt that my worthy chairman had visions of his wife rushing to the polling-booth to record her vote in favour of the wrong candidate; and, worse still, of being kept waiting for his dinner! However, I assured him, as I now assure you, that we are not seeking in any way to change the present basis of the suffrage. We only ask that women who fulfil the same conditions as men – who are householders, who pay taxes, and are rated to the relief of the poor, shall be admitted to the franchise. More than this we do not ask – at present.

I have not attempted, this evening, to answer many of the objections that are commonly urged against giving women the suffrage. So much has already been said and written on the subject that those who wish to read the arguments on either side can easily obtain pamphlets by application to the secretaries of the Association.

In conclusion I will quote from one, whose name in the cause of freedom is of world-wide fame, and whose words, taken in their widest meaning, will need no comment of mine. What he – a man – pleaded for men, I – a woman – would plead for women. Mr John Bright, in upholding the claims of working men to the suffrage, said: – 'England has long been famous for the enjoyment of personal freedom by her people. They are free to think, they are free to speak, they are free to write; and England has been famed of late years, and is famed now the world over, for the freedom of her industry, and the freedom of her commerce. I want to know, then, why it is that her people are not free to vote? Who is there that will meet me on this platform, or will stand upon any platform, and will dare to say, in the hearing of an open meeting of his countrymen, that these millions for whom I am now pleading, are too degraded, too vicious, and too destructive to be entrusted with the elective franchise? I, at least, will never thus slander my countrymen. I claim for them the right of admission, through their representatives, into the most ancient and the most venerable Parliament which exists among men; and when they are admitted, and not till then, it may be truly said that England, the august mother of free nations, herself is free!'

E. M. Sturge

*Women's suffrage**

6 December 1872

I HAVE much pleasure in supporting this resolution as I should have in supporting any resolution that tended to the removal of unnatural restrictions upon life and liberty. But I sometimes find that the words I design for support, damage the cause I desire to serve. I know many ladies think this was the case, when I set a low value upon the surface forms of politeness which we are supposed to receive in lieu of a vote. If these surface forms of politeness represent a reality of kind-hearted self-denying consideration for others, they are *good* – but they are only a *symbol*, and if a symbol comes to be mistaken for a reality – it is at once a snare and a delusion. I meet plenty of gentlemen carrying ladies' umbrellas, the ladies as a rule are perfectly well able to carry them themselves – therefore this is only a symbol. I wish I could think these same gentlemen were equally ready to help the little child in the streets with her heavy burden, or the weary woman with her barrow of coals. One day when I was passing through one of our busiest thoroughfares, I met a little girl with a basket of boots – they were evidently too heavy for the child, and I turned to help her. There were plenty of passers by. If any gentleman had offered to carry those boots, I should have thought him really polite, because it might have been at the sacrifice both of time and

*Speech delivered in the Town Hall, Birmingham.

174

appearances – but I believe it would have been useless – that little child in her short life had seen far more reasons to distrust appearances than I have ever had – I do not believe she would have allowed a man to touch her boots – she would have expected him to disappear with them. If our English politeness is distrusted by a little child in the streets, I am afraid it is a sad proof that the counterfeit is more common than the reality. I am told that I receive certain social attentions and distinctions because I am a woman – if I find that the seamstress and the kitchenmaid are not also receiving them – this must be a mistake for they are equally women. I think I really place more reliance upon the courtesy and consideration of my countrymen, than some ladies do who think I am prepared to ignore both. I know that I can go and return from public meetings alone at night without experiencing the slightest difficulty or annoyance. I firmly believe that wherever ladies choose to go, men will see that it is proper, fit, and suitable that they should go. It is said that the presence of ladies at dinner parties is a check upon the excessive use of wine and improper language. If ladies really hold this control for good over men they ought to carry it everywhere and into everything. Surely God never gives any capacity for good without requiring its widest and fullest exercise. As a Liberal, I naturally feel grieved that the Liberal Association seem to care so little for Women's Suffrage. This is said to be because they think women will be Conservatives. But how can the Liberals expect women to be other than Conservatives so long as the Liberals are Conservatives towards them. It would seem as if they trained women up in the way they should not go, and then expected them to depart from it. How can anyone expect to reap what they have not sown? Another explanation that has reached me is, that women do not subscribe to Liberal Associations. This must be a mistake, for if it means anything, it would mean that Liberal Associations only give justice to those who can afford to pay for it. I think the gentleman who made the suggestion could hardly be aware of the monetary disadvantages to which women are subjected. In well-to-do families, when a son comes of age his father either finds him an income, or the means of obtaining one. His sister meanwhile, is only allowed enough to adorn herself with – she poor girl is not trusted, therefore she has no chance of becoming trustworthy. There is no intentional injustice in this; probably an equivalent amount of money to that given to her brother is set aside as a premium for a husband.

If the girl thinks that she has capacity to excel and be useful in some profession in life – the father will say that he cannot spare the money – the mother that she cannot spare her daughter. But if a husband should appear he can take girl and gold to the Antipodes – the father will find out that he can spare the money – the mother that she can spare her daughter. It would almost seem as if a girl had no right to her own life. Do not mistake me! I am not undervaluing the beauty and holiness of a life of unselfish devotedness to the interests of others – but an act to be unselfish must be perfectly voluntary – so long as services are exacted from women as if they were obligations, they have no power to be unselfish.

I sometimes take up a Liberal paper, one which never has a good word to say for Women's Suffrage, but in it I find week after week, and day after day, articles complaining of the extravagance, the frivolity, and the mischievous match-making propensities of women. Probably it is all lamentably true, but I wonder the writer does not see it to be the natural fruit of the system he upholds. When will mankind learn, that if they will not allow room for the virtues of independence, they must be content with the vices of dependence? If there is an evil under the sun which affects men injuriously, you dig for the cause and drag it out by the roots; but if it affects women *only*, you are content to despise the fruit and throw stones at the branches.

The *Spectator*, Henry Holbeach and other authorities, think they have discovered a philosophical objection to Women's Suffrage. They say it is dangerous to dissociate physical force and political power. This may be a sort of philosopher's stone – it was buried so long ago – buried in the fact that policemen and soldiers do not have votes. Mr Bouverie and Mr James represent the Parliamentary objections to Women's Suffrage. They both talk about a woman on a pedestal, I have never met with her and never expect to do so, unless it is in the pages of *Punch*. I do not understand what they mean by it. Sometimes when a Bank breaks, or a financial company comes to an end because a man has carried off the money – women unaccustomed to work are reduced to poverty. If Mr Bouverie and Mr James would then come forward and find the means for these ladies to remain upon their pedestals I might understand and respect the views they hold. Mr Bouverie has said that 'work political or otherwise would degrade a woman.' I should say that idleness political or otherwise would degrade her. I have a friend, a young governess – she says she hates 'Women's rights,' but she wanted to know how to earn her living if she gave up teaching, and after reading a good deal on the question, she thought, as Mr James understood 'Woman's Sphere,' she would write and ask him. She received a polite reply – Mr James was very sorry that he had 'no practical suggestion to offer.' I am afraid Mr Bouverie and Mr James are not practical men. Mr Bouverie has said that Parliament would willingly pass any measure to put boys and girls on an equality so far as education is concerned. I have thought of presenting him with a case of present inequality. Government appears to give all its premiums to things in which men are likely to excel. Why should not a woman be able to take a certificate for competence in cooking or sewing just as much as for drawing or science? Are not cooking and clothing of as much value to the world as drawing and science? But we must have women inspectors to look after these. I was in the North the other day and a lady told me of the visit of the Government Inspector at a girls' school, he examined the sewing and wished to make some appropriate remark, so he said it was not so good as his pocket-handkerchief – to their amusement the ladies saw that his handkerchief was machine made.

Men say, 'women don't know; they can't see plainly; they don't understand.' Very likely they do not see plainly, because men will stand between them and the light, and this is just as injurious to the men as to the women for they get dazzled with the sense of their own superiority, and as long as women bow down before this assumed superiority, our women will be dolls and our men will be idols. It is bad to be a doll – it is worse to be an idol – worse because it is more profane. There can be only two grounds on which men refuse the Suffrage to women duly qualified to receive it, either because women have no souls, or because men are infallible. Men will not allow infallibility to the Pope, therefore they cannot consider themselves infallible. It has been said in old times that women had no souls but I do not think anyone tonight is prepared to reiterate it. You may say we have liberty of conscience; liberty of conscience without liberty of action is a mockery. I have no desire that women should be a law unto men, any more than men unto women. I long that they may both seek after a higher law, and in this unity of purpose there will be harmony. Restrictions have too long stunted intellectual and spiritual growth.

> Yet now and then,
> A beacon blazeth out below
> Which startles men!
> A sudden tingle at the springs
> Of noble feeling,
> The spirit-power for valiant things

E. M. Sturge

> Clearly revealing,
> Alas! the grasp upon the heel
> Holds back the soul,
> And Eden's curse doth deal
> Its daily dole!

The grasp upon the heel is doubtless a necessity of our earthly condition, but to mind and soul is given the power largely to overcome it, if you will remove the unnatural grasp upon them that they stand free and untrammelled. With careful consideration I think you will not long refuse what we ask.

Frances Power Cobbe

Why women desire the franchise

1874

POLITICIANS consider that a subject enters an important phase when it becomes publicly recognised as a 'Question.' During the last five years the proposal to give votes to women has very distinctly grown into the 'Question of Female Suffrage.' Few of the most sanguine advocates of the cause would have ventured, in 1865, to hope that by the close of 1872, it should stand where it now obviously does in public opinion, or that 355,801 persons should have petitioned in its behalf.

The last Reform Bill, by lowering the franchise for men, has affected the claims of women in several indirect ways. In the first place, by admitting to the exercise of political judgment a class whose education is confessedly of the narrowest, and whose leisure to study politics extremely small, it has virtually silenced for all future time the two favourite arguments against the claims of women; that their understandings are weak, and their time too fully occupied by domestic cares. The most strenuous asserter of the mental and moral inferiority of women cannot urge that the majority of the new voters have more power to understand, or more leisure to attend to, public affairs than even the inferior class of female householders; not to speak of such women as Miss Nightingale and Mrs Somerville, Miss Martineau and Lady Coutts. Rather, on the contrary, may it be maintained that the picked class of women who would be admitted by Mr Bright's

Bill to the franchise are needed to restore the just balance in favour of an educated constituency against the weight of the illiterate male voters now entrusted with the suffrage.

Again, by the introduction of the ballot the threat of a supposed practical difficulty to be found in the recording of female votes has been permanently set at rest; while the triumphant success of female candidates at the School Board elections has demonstrated how warmly the general feeling of the nation welcomes the accession of women to a share in the guidance of important public affairs.

Lastly, by identifying the duty of ratepaying with the right of voting in the case of men, the Reform Bill has made more glaring than before the inconsistency of enforcing rates upon women while refusing to them the avowedly corresponding right.

At the present moment our proper course appears to be this: to form committees in every town in England for the purpose of directing attention to the subject, and affording information and aid to all friends of the cause. Local petitions, as numerous as possible, will afford the best machinery for carrying on such a plan; not because of their direct influence on the Legislature, (which is notoriously incommensurate with the labour of their preparation), but from their convenience as tangible methods of enrolling allies and interesting new associates. Already, in this last session, some 843 petitions, with the signatures of 355,801 men and women, were presented. The parable of the unjust Judge will probably not be found inapplicable to a masculine Legislature, when 'poor widows' (and also rich ones, and other single women), by their 'continual coming,' become wearisome. Women are not prepared to break any pailings, material or metaphorical, albeit they have been taunted with the indifference they thus betray for their rights; but it is just possible that keeping the peace and signing petitions to Parliament may eventually be thought almost as well to prove their fitness for a voice in the Legislature of their country.

Women are often asked, Why they desire the franchise? Have they not everything already which they can possibly desire: personal liberty, the right to hold property, and an amount of courtesy and chivalrous regard which (it is broadly hinted) they would bitterly regret were they to exchange them for equality of political rights? Why should those epicurean gods, who dwell in the serene empyrean of drawing-rooms descend to meddle with the sordid affairs of humanity? What a pity and a loss it would be to the toiling world could it never look up and behold afar such a spectacle of repose as a true lady now presents! We can easily dispense with more legislators; but what is the world to do without those mild Belgravian mothers, those innocent young 'Girls of the Period,' those magnificent *grandes dames* who are the glory of our social life?

Let us briefly answer these questions, once for all. We do not believe that one particle of womanly gentleness and dignity, nay, not even the finest flavour of high-bred grace, will be lost when women are permitted to record their votes for representatives in Parliament. We consider the fear that it might be so among the idlest of chimeras. What *will* be lost, we are persuaded, will be a little of the frivolity, a little of the habit of expressing opinions without having conscientiously weighed them, a little of the practice of underhand and unworthy persuasion, which have been hitherto faults fostered in women by their position. Women can lose nothing, and have much to gain by entering a field of nobler interests than has hitherto been open to them. It was deemed well said of the old Roman, that nothing human was alien to him. It will be well when all women learn to feel that none of the wrongs and sins and sufferings of other women can be alien to *them*. The condition of women of the lower orders is beset with hardships; and it is for the very reason that a lady is freed from those heavy trials, that she should exert every power she possesses or can acquire, first to understand, and then, if possible, to remedy them. How these evils are to be lightened; how the burdens of the poor toilers are to be made less intolerable; how wives are to be protected from brutal husbands; how, above all, the ruin of the hapless thousands of lost ones is to be stopped: – how these things are to be done, may need more wisdom than all the men and women in England together may possess. But it is quite certain that if women had heretofore been represented in Parliament, such evils and wrongs would never have reached, unchecked, their present height, and that whenever women are at last represented, some more earnest efforts will be made to arrest them.

But it is not only for the sake of women of the suffering classes that we seek for female influence on politics; nor for that of happier women whose sphere of usefulness might thereby be enlarged, and their lives supplied with nobler interests. We believe that the recognition of the political rights of women, as it will be a signal act of justice on the part of men, so it will also prove an act beneficial to them no less than to us; and that when a generation has passed after the change, it will be said, by all alike, 'What did our fathers mean by forbidding women to have a voice in politics? If it were nothing more, their influence must always be the safest ballast to keep steady the Ship of State.'

Finally, to sum up our meaning in the most concise terms we can find, we desire that the political franchise be extended to women of full age, possessed of the requisite property qualification, for the following eight reasons: –

1 Because the possession of property and the payment of rates being the admitted bases of political rights in England, it is unjust that persons who possess such property, and pay such rates, should be excluded from those rights, unless from the clearest and gravest reasons of public interest. Such interest, however, we believe, requires, not the exclusion, but the admission of women into the franchise.

2 Because the denial of the franchise to qualified women entails on the community a serious loss; namely, that of the legislative influence of a numerous class, whose moral sense is commonly high developed, and whose physical defencelessness attaches them peculiarly to the cause of justice and public order.

3 Because, under a representative Government, the interests of any non-represented class are confessedly liable to be misunderstood and neglected; and nothing but evidence that the interests of women are carefully weighed and faithfully guarded by the Legislature would nullify the presumptive injustice of denying them representation. Such evidence, however, is not forthcoming; but, on the contrary, experience demonstrates that the gravest interests of women are continually postponed by Parliament to the consideration of trifling questions concerning male electors, and, when introduced into debates, are treated by half the House rather as jests than as measures of serious importance.

4 Because, while the natural and artificial disabilities of women demand in their behalf the special aid and protection of the State, no proposal has ever been made to deal with their perils and difficulties; nor even to relieve them of the smallest portion of the burden of taxation, which they are compelled to bear without sharing the privileges attached thereto.

5 Because women, by the denial to them of the franchise, are placed at a serious disadvantage in competition for numerous offices and employments; especially women of the middle class, whose inability to vote tends extensively to deter landlords interested in politics from accepting them as tenants, even in cases where they have long conducted for their deceased male relatives the business of the farms,

shops, &c. to whose tenure they seek to succeed.

6 Because the denial to women of the direct exercise of political judgment in the typical act of citizenship, has a generally injurious influence on the minds of men as regards women, leading them to undervalue their opinions on all the grave matters of life, and to treat offences against them with levity, as committed against beings possessed only of inferior rights.

7 Because the denial of the direct exercise of their judgment has a doubly injurious effect upon the minds of women, inclining them to adopt, without conscientious inquiry the opinions which, they are warned, must be always practically inoperative; and beguiling them to exert, through tortuous and ignoble channels, the influence whose open and honest exercise has been refused.

8 Finally, we desire the franchise for women, because, while believing that men and women have different work to do in life, we still hold that, in the choice of political representatives, they have the same task to accomplish; namely, the joint election of a Senate which shall guard with equal care the rights of both sexes, and which shall embody in its laws that true Justice which shall approve itself not only to the strong, but also the weak.

L.S.

*The citizenship of women socially considered**

July 1874

WHAT is the position of women in England at this day? It has, doubtless, risen with advancing civilization at war with old traditions; it has been improved by very slowly improving education; it is ornamented and disguised by masculine compliments; and it is surrounded, in drawing-rooms, by chivalrous homage, meaning thereby politeness, as well as by an abundance of outward comfort and luxuries. Yet – legally, and therefore, more or less, socially – it is merely a modification of ancient barbarism, ordered on barbarian principles, mitigated in their working but still barbarian. The progress made in other directions, the changes other institutions have undergone, make this fact still more conspicuous, the position of women still more exceptional.

In the early ages of the human race advantage was taken of woman's physical weakness to make her literally a slave; she is now – in civilized nations, that is – merely in 'subjection.' In old times – and not such very old times either – she was reviled and despised for the defects fostered in her by slavery; she is now more gently branded by the law as an inferior, in company with 'criminals, lunatics, and idiots;' and complacently told by men – seriously, with the most complimentary intentions it may be, and with full conviction – that this legal inferiority, this positive

*Originally published in the *Westminster Review*.

subjection, imply and result in a social superiority, first formulated by 'chivalry' (only women of the drawing-room class being
recognised under this theory) and form the safeguard of that
higher moral excellence she is credited with along side of a lower
mental capacity.

But this legal position of woman does, I think, tell on herself
and on society in general, in quite a different way, whilst at the
same time the unconscious, or half-conscious, efforts she has
herself made hitherto, according to her more or less of education
to resist these evil influences, produce the strangest incongruities.
It has fostered grievous private and individual wrongs; and, worse
still, it helps yet, as the principle on which it was founded has
helped for ages, to lower the tone of that society it is supposed to
benefit. Many thinking men and women, in continually increasing
numbers, have begun to perceive this; and a good many others
have been from time to time aware that there was something a
little wrong in matters of detail – something here and there that
might be amended. To these latter, and, we believe, to English
legislators in general, it has always seemed easier to modify the
evil workings of a vicious principle than to abolish it altogether.
Such minds do not even seek to distinguish the authority of old-
established prejudice from the sanction of nature and reason. It
seems to them more natural to grant privileges than justice,
indulgence than liberty. It has not occurred to them to ask
themselves whether, after all, woman may not be allowed a voice,
or at least the fraction of a voice, in the ordering of her own
position in the world, of her own dearest interests and liberties.

It would be useless, most unjust, most unphilosophical, to
bring a railing accusation against men on this account – especially
unphilosophical because such, or such like, has been the course of
action of all irresponsibly dominant classes since the world began,
until the eyes of both ruler and ruled have been at last opened to a
sense of its injustice. And, further, it would be most ungrateful to
those noble and generous minds amongst them whose hearty
sympathy and active efforts to obtain justice for women – that is,
in fact, justice to all society – deserve the most ample
acknowledgment. It requires – and this is true of every one of us,
man or woman – much imagination, much sympathy, much
reflection in the first instance, to shake off the influence of ancient
prejudice instilled into us from birth and inherited from ages.
Many minds are wholly incapable of this effort. How many
unconscious and even benevolent oppressors throughout the long
history of class and race-dominations, down to the modern slaveholder (for there have been kindhearted slave-holders, we doubt

not), have been able to comprehend, or to how many has it even occurred, that traditional acquiescence on the part of the subjected does not necessarily constitute a natural or religious sanction; that a time may come when it is actually not enough to tell the subject-class that they have everything they want or ought to want, that they ought to be thankful to be taken care of, for they cannot take care of themselves, that they are by nature inferior? There comes a time when irresponsible power appears in a different light to those on whom it is exercised from that in which it is seen by those exercising it. It is long, indeed, before both parties become equally aware that *both* are injured by it; that justice, in such cases as these, 'blesses both him that gives and him that takes,' much in the moment of giving, more in its after results.

This domination of one sex over the other – that is, of one half the mature human race over the other half – has lasted longer than most others, because the physical force is permanently on the side of the first. And this, indeed, is sometimes itself considered as a decisive reason why women should not plead right and justice: they cannot enforce them; therefore nature means that they should not have them any further than man finds it convenient to allow. But to refuse justice because it cannot be enforced is not in other relations of life reckoned the highest morality.

To many men, conscious in their hearts of nothing but kindness, indulgence, and generosity to the women they associate with; to many who see, or think they see, fairly happy marriages all round them; who see how often women 'get their own way,' as it is called, by the good nature of their own particular rulers, by cajolery, by unconscionable teasing, by temper, by the obstinancy of their prejudices – those prejudices that men have fostered in women as 'so feminine' – or even by superior good sense; to those who have perceived that society, even as it is, can produce noble-minded women, and have possibly worshipped such in their hearts, or who ask for nothing better than to be allowed tenderly to protect some tender creature whom they love – to these it may seem exaggerated, unreal, and ridiculous to talk of the domination of men over women – at least in England and in most civilized countries. I think, with all deference to the feelings of such men, it is because the evils it has produced and is still producing are so deep-seated and complex, and extend so far beyond their own especial social surroundings, that they have escaped their notice; their very position of legal superiority, of which they are scarcely conscious, so habituated are they to it, having blinded their eyes.

And so are many, many women's eyes blinded; many who,

happy in their own circumstances, have never dreamed, any more than their masters, of questioning the authority of old tradition; have never connected the vices of the society around them, or their own shortcomings, in any way, however indirect, with the position women hold in it. These will generally seem unconscious that their contentment with their own condition, their ignorance how far even it might be higher or more useful, do not necessarily constitute an argument for other women in other circumstances. They will perhaps protest, when female suffrage is spoken of, against women 'stepping out of their right place.' The question, however, is, what, after all, *is* woman's right place, the precise line beyond which it is profanation for her to step? Is it necessarily, precisely, and only the line pointed out by men – the point fixed by them in different ages, countries, and even classes, being different? Obediently as such women have adopted the traditional teaching of men, yet the question will arise, is it not just possible that men too have a little stepped out of *their* place in imposing these limits on women? It is allowed that they have done so, in more barbarous times, are they not doing so still?

Others again – multitudes – married and single, and of all classes, are conscious of something wrong in their own and others' lots, are pained by a vague uneasiness or suppressed bitterness, whilst without the culture needed to guide them clearly to *one* source of the evils – we say *one*, for we are of course aware that the countless inequalities and iniquities growing up with a complicated civilization, and pressing so hardly even on many men, must have many sources. The evils however from which women suffer are especially aggravated by their legal position being essentially unchanged, whilst all things are changed around them.

In arguing for the principle of female citizenship, I must observe that the suffrage has no inherent magical or divine property in it to remove as by a charm all the evils of which we complain; yet, under our present institutions, the extension of it to women is the only way of expressing that principle, and is, I believe, an absolutely necessary balance to the increasing number of men now admitted. I am not, however, anxious to dwell much in this essay on the directly political aspect of the question, nor yet on the terrible wrongs and miseries of women under its legal aspects, but rather to call the attention of candid minds to various social considerations deeply affected by their political and legal position. For all these, I maintain, are interdependent, acting and reacting on each other.

In carrying out this view, I may seem sometimes to be

wandering rather far afield; but I hope that some few, both of men and women, will perceive that these apparent wanderings do in fact all lead up very directly to the point at which I am aiming.

Before going further in this direction, however, I will just notice the chief objections that have been raised to the emancipation of women, objections mostly of detail, raised by those who, unable to grasp a large general idea, instinctively fix their eyes successively on the supposed difficulties in carrying it out. Some of these objections – most of them, in fact – serve to display the curious ingenuity of the human mind imagining hindrances to any alteration of an established order of things, the first feeling being always, not, how can we see our way to grant this? but, how shall we discover a sufficient number of objections to justify our refusal?

The objections in question have been answered over and over again; and it is a curious fact that in this discussion masculine opponents to the emancipation of women seem to have changed their traditional parts with women. Women urge a principle, men stumble at the details. Or they do acknowledge the principle, but decline to carry it to its legitimate results. Women ask for justice, men offer privileges; women advance reasons, men answer with their own feelings and instincts; women meet assertions with evidence in disproof, men re-assert them without attempting further proof.

Here, however, is the first, perhaps only, objection which really deserves attention, that the majority of women do not desire the suffrage.

I answer, that the minority which does desire it is a constantly increasing one (not adequately represented even by the increasing number of signatures to petitions). I must further point out that a large portion of the majority, which does not desire it, has simply not been educated to think about it, and has passed a great part of life without the subject having been brought before it at all; whilst the minority, that does desire it, includes very many women of the highest intellect and cultivation, who have thought deeply on the subject, and many who, feeling for themselves and their neighbours the need of better protection than masculine legislation has hitherto allowed them, gladly welcome the faintest hope of emancipation. Next, as to those who desire the suffrage without signing petitions for it, few men can realize, without some effort of the imagination, the pressure put upon women in all cases where their views differ from those of the masculine public. There is, to begin with, their own tenderness for the prejudices of those with whom they live, not to say positive prohibition by fathers and husbands – such arbitrary interference with the independence of mature minds being so sanctioned by law and custom that it is hard, even for those who suffer from it, to resist it. Next, we must take into account that intense shrinking from masculine sarcasm and mockery which has been so carefully fostered in women that they have justly been said to 'live under a gospel of ridicule.' And it is part of the argument that this moral coercion *has* been lavishly employed to supplement the legal subjection of women, much of their boasted acquiescence in what *we* consider a faulty state of things having been thus produced. Few can realize, I repeat, without some reflection, some sympathetic insight, how much silent revolt goes on in subjected classes before they openly rebel. In men this silent revolt is generally held to be dangerous, and worth inquiring into; in women, for obvious reasons, it is not. And with women it will be longest maintained, and with more corroding bitterness in proportion, in spite of the persuasions, half contemptuous, half flattering, which now, more frequently than before, alternate with sneers.

Others again – thinking and conscientious women – are still undecided to put their names to the movement, deterred by an overstrained sense of their responsibility; but these may at any moment conclude in its favour, and cannot be reckoned in the majority against it.

I am ready to allow that there are women – and doubtless even some thinking and cultivated ones amongst them – (oftenest, however, such as profess no knowledge and reason on the subject, only 'instincts' and 'feelings') who deprecate female suffrage altogether; many more who are absolutely indifferent, and all of these are apt to conceive that their own individual dislike or indifference is argument enough against extending the suffrage to those who do desire it, reason enough for withholding even their sympathy. Of all such women I would speak with respect and indulgence; yet may I not point out to them, and to the men who appeal to their authority, that it is scarcely reasonable that numbers of the thinking, the cultivated, the sensible, the practical, the suffering and oppressed amongst women should be denied their desire in deference to the 'feelings and instincts,' the individual disinclination, or indifference of the others? Many, too, of these others are precisely those whom the present demand for the female franchise would not affect personally. I hold, nevertheless, that even these, the indifferent – all in fact – would be directly or indirectly benefited in time by the change. Those who do not want the franchise need not exercise it – that is their own affair, as it is of men, who in like manner may decline to vote, though we hold that the choice ought to be given to them nevertheless. I doubt, however, whether these very female dissentients will not be glad, when the time comes, to use their own votes after seeing how easily and quietly other women have used theirs before them. And what is more, I suspect the masculine objectors will be equally glad to profit by these votes.

Finally, the argument that women do not want the franchise and would be better without it, is in spirit the same as that by which slaveholders have always justified slavery. We do not hold that the negro's ignorance of the moral evils of his position was an argument for keeping him in it.

Of the other objections it may almost be said, that to state them is to refute them. First of these we will take men's 'instincts and feelings.' To us it does not seem more fair to decide the question of justice by the 'instincts and feelings' of men than, as we have said, by the 'instincts and feelings' of some women, as against the reason and practical needs of the others. And these 'instincts and feelings' have been cited as authoritatively in sanction of restrictions which would *now* be thought barbarian, as of those still enforced and not yet thought barbarian.

Again, it is said that women are unfit for the vote, because they are women. It is true that the training enforced upon women, directly and indirectly, for ages, by men, whereby their characters and minds are in some sort the artificial creation of men, has seemingly had for its object to make them unfit for the powers men exercise. Women have, in consequence, for ages made no combined effort for emancipation; but exactly as they become aware of the real nature of this traditional training, does this supposed unfitness lessen, and the best way at this moment completely to fit them to exercise those powers is to grant them.

What mental or moral 'fitness' is sought for as a qualification for the masculine voter, except by that rough sort of classification which does not exclude the drunkard, the wife beater, the illiterate, the liberated convict, and the semi-idiot? And when you place beside these Harriet Martineau, Florence Nightingale, George Eliot, and many more whose names we all know, as well as the numbers of women who show every kind of practical fitness in common life – to say that *these* are unfit because they are women, and *those* are fit because they are men, is very like begging the question.

But there are special unfitnesses urged against women. I cannot condescend to dwell on the argument that they are incapable of giving their vote for want of physical strength, or that the chronic state of 'blushing and fear' prescribed for them by Mr Bouverie would make it improper and impossible for even a middle-aged woman to face the bustle of polling-places, otherwise than by observing that if it were wished to grant women votes, means might easily be found for making it possible to deliver them. But I will mention one other (I think the only special) unfitness alleged against them (except indeed their want of training in political and official life, which they share with a large number of franchise-holding men). This special unfitness resides in their greater 'impulsiveness,' 'excitability,' and 'sympathy,' which are supposed to include and imply 'unreasonableness' and 'injustice.' Till, however, it is argued that Ireland, for example, is naturally disqualified for the suffrage because the Celt is more 'excitable,' 'impulsive,' and 'sympathetic' than the Saxon – or indeed till, as I must repeat, moral or intellectual qualifications are made a *sine quâ non* in any class of masculine voters whatever, this objection can hardly stand. I will, therefore, only suggest that the co-operation of impulse and sympathy with the more solid and matter-of-fact element in legislation may not be wholly without its political advantages.[1]

Next, it has been alleged that already too many *men* have the suffrage, as a reason for withholding it from women. Even granting the fact, it is not just to say that, because A has had too much given him of a good thing, therefore B shall have none at all, especially when B even requires it as a protection against A. At all events, the extended suffrage has been granted, and cannot now be withdrawn – one reason the more, as I have implied, why women should desire it in their turn, since they now see the drunkard, the wife-beater, the illiterate called, in much larger numbers than before, to legislate indirectly for their dearest and the most delicate domestic concerns, those alike of the most refined and cultivated as of the most helpless and uneducated of their sex.

Here, naturally, comes the assertion that 'women are virtually represented by men.' Indeed, on every proposed extension of political rights, it has been usual for the classes who thought their interests opposed to it to urge that *they* virtually represented the others. This assertion is disproved by the whole course of class legislation in all ages and everywhere; and the harshness of masculine legislation for women certainly forms no exception to the rule.[2]

If I am reminded that some classes of men are still unrepresented, I answer (putting aside the possibly near approach of universal household suffrage), that *all* women of *all* classes are unrepresented, are all declared to labour under an irremediable birth-disqualification. Individual *men* of the unenfranchised classes can rise to acquire a vote: a woman never can. And women only ask for the vote on the same conditions as those on which it is conferred upon men.

Let us consider here the confessed difficulty of protecting wives in certain classes against the violence of their husbands, as bearing on the plea of 'virtual representation.' I would not brand any class of our countrymen with hard names, least of all those who have so long suffered, in common with women, such grievous legislative wrongs, such cruel deprivation of education, and are even now struggling to emancipate themselves, scarcely conscious yet that the women's cause rests on the same ground as theirs. But it is too sadly notorious to be denied that, in these working and labouring classes, public opinion and the growth of education have not yet banished drunken habits and consequent brutality, and that the difficulties in the way of adequate legal interposition are almost insuperable. Compare the penalties inflicted in these cases with those in which a wife has assaulted a husband, or one man another man. *Here* there is no difficulty in carrying out the full severity of the law. I do not assert that those who administer it do not *wish* to enforce it in behalf of women, though judges and juries do sometimes give us cause to suspect them of considering an assault by the inferior on the superior, by the weaker on the stronger, as more heinous than one with the conditions reversed.

The wife is, in these classes, so helplessly in her husband's power, so trained to feel the violence of her master as a part of his conjugal superiority, that she very often dares not, perhaps actually does not, resent his brutality. It seems to us that at least one approach towards remedying this state of things would be to surround her social status with every equal right and dignity the law can give her. Law should not aim at rendering her *more* helpless, *more* dependent than inferior strength would naturally make her. The same barbarian prejudice which excludes all women from every political right also subjects the wife to a law which has been called 'the most barbarous in Europe.' It has naturally taken its full effect on the uneducated classes, that is, it has degraded both man and woman together. That almost superstitious, dog-like patience and loyalty which lead a wife to submit to a beating without complaint, and which some men tenderly praise as the *ne plus ultra* of wife-like excellence, might, I think, be exchanged for a nobler form of devotion by making her her husband's legal and social equal; and one indirect step towards this will be giving women some share in making the laws which concern themselves.[3]

A favourite objection is, that the exercise of the suffrage will interfere with women's duties. It cannot be seriously meant by this that the taking up of a few hours every few years in delivering a vote will hinder a woman – even the most hard-working – in her daily duties more than it would a hard-working man. Indeed, in the present case, it is only asked for unmarried women and widows, many of them possessed of ample leisure and sufficient means. But is it meant that the possession of this franchise would so much more excite and unsettle their minds, and throw them so much more violently into political agitation in the quiet intervening years, than men, as to unfit them for those duties which we are assumed it is their nature to perform, and which they find their chief happiness in? This argument rests on the following assumptions: – That it is the business of the Legislature to provide more rigorously for the performance of women's private duties than men's; that their good sense and conscience will be found less trustworthy in proportion as they have liberty to exercise them; that whilst we legislate to prevent the race in general from following blindly its natural instincts, we must also legislate to prevent women from *forsaking* theirs at the first opportunity; and, finally, that women (unlike men) have no rights, only duties. Assuredly to a noble soul the word 'duties' has a higher inspiration than the word 'rights;' only some of the highest duties cannot be so well performed without rights. The circle of a slave's duties is very small, and that of a woman's – though she is no longer in England a slave – has been restricted to a point that future generations will view with wonder.

Again, some who do not so much object to the admission (taken by itself) of the unmarried possessing the legal qualifications, cannot see their way to the admission of wives, and consider that objection conclusive against the admission of any, as this would be granting privileges to the recognised 'failures' of society while they are withheld from their recognised superiors. I can but say, that if to grant the suffrage be an act of justice, you ought not to refuse it to some because you cannot yet see your way to extending it to all. This theory of the inferiority of women in general to men, and the special inferiority to be enforced by legal subjection on the married amongst them, who are yet declared to be the superiors of the single, involves some curious contradictions.

And further, these objectors fear that if you grant the suffrage to the single having the proper qualification, wives will by-and-by demand it as well – either by a change in the qualification for a vote, or in the marriage law. I answer, let that question be discussed when the time comes. It is neither just nor generous to refuse a rightful concession for fear other concessions may be asked for. Meanwhile the supposed moral difficulty of granting the suffrage to wives still rests mainly on the old assumption that women only wait the opportunity to discard their natural duties and affections; that men can be safely trusted with absolute authority over their families, but women not even with the exercise of an independent opinion; that wives at present neither have, nor in fact ought to have, any difference of opinion from their husbands (except on trivial points), but certainly would, if they were once permitted to act on their opinions; and that they will necessarily seize the vote as an occasion for quarrel; also on the assumption that it is the business of the State to provide against these little domestic difficulties in married life (but only, of course, by laying restrictions on the wife). I can scarcely suppose, however, that any man blessed with an affectionate wife seriously anticipates that, once possessed of a vote, she would make it her business to thwart and oppose him. If his wife is not an affectionate one, I fear the Legislature cannot help him, and I am very sure it is not its business to do so. I think this fancied difficulty would be best met in the case of a wife not quarrelsomely disposed, but having an independent mind, by her husband's good humouredly reconciling himself to her possible difference of opinion in politics as he often has to do in matters of theology. But if such differences of opinion do so seriously affect the happiness of married life, let them be more carefully considered before marriage.

There is also the contradictory assumption that the wife's vote will be merely a double of her husband's, thus giving him two votes instead of one. Between these last two assumptions of perverse opposition on the one hand, and undue submission on the other, we may fairly strike a balance, and hope the State will fare none the worse in the end for the female married vote, should it be granted.

To be serious, I do not believe the harmony and dignity of married life – not even the dignity of the husband – can be best promoted by legislation to prevent quarrels; or by the theory that, as has been said, husband and wife are one, that the husband is *the* one, and that the two ought to have only one opinion in politics between them – viz. the husband's. If we are accused of overlooking the practical difficulties which might arise in adjusting the votes of husband and wife, we answer that we may leave these to the moment when it is actually proposed to extend the franchise so far: if the principle is once conceded, a way will be found of carrying it out; for the rest, husbands and expectant husbands may defend their rights hereafter when they are attacked.

Having said thus much, I must add my own distinct opinion that the sooner this notion of marriage in any way disqualifying women for the exercise of personal rights or responsibility to the State is got rid of, the better for all parties. And I believe, moreover, that, when once the vote is granted to single women, married men will themselves begin to perceive this, and will desire that dignity for their wives which has been attained to by others.

The same answer will apply to the objection that women, when once admitted to the vote, will (logically) be eligible to a seat in Parliament. I think we may confidently leave this question also to be decided on its own merits by some future generation, and by the constituencies concerned.

Lastly, there is the objection – the most formidable of all to some minds – that all female aspirants to the suffrage are 'strong-minded women,' and that 'strong-minded women are very disagreeable.' If by 'strong-minded women' is meant women of masculine character and idiosyncrasies, I believe as many of these might be found on one side as on the other, if it were worth while to inquire. If 'strong-minded' means having a highly enlightened understanding, large ideas, and an ardent desire for the improvement of other women, I may suggest that these objectors would often be surprised to find how very charming such persons can make themselves. I dare say that the agitators for the abolition of slavery made themselves very disagreeable when urging their engrossing topic in season and out of season. People engaged in a great struggle will not always pause to consult the conventional rules of good taste, yet the cause may be a good one nevertheless. But I cannot gravely discuss this objection any further.

And now come two more serious reproaches addressed to women. 'They have done so much mischief.' 'They are agitating from a love of power.'

The accusation of 'doing mischief' means, I imagine, only that women are not infallible in their judgment, any more than men (why is a human liability to mistake *more* disqualifying to women than to men?), or that there are points on which the objectors differ from some women, or that there always will be points on which some men will differ from some women, it being assumed, of course, that women will always be in the wrong. If the objectors mean that women, having power given them by the Legislature to do mischief, will do a great deal more than men in the same position have ever done, that is in fact begging the whole question. No past experience can be appealed to as decisive, since women have never been placed in the position supposed; although the absolute denial of all direct legitimate exercise of power sometimes drives intense and ardent natures into exercising it by methods less wholesome than a recognised responsibility would employ. But even granting this – alas! have men never done mischief, terrible mischief, during the long ages of masculine domination? Take, as one instance, the legislation for Ireland up to this century, and more recent times still; could any female legislation be more blind, unjust, inhuman, and – mischievous?

Is the world, as governed by men, a thing even now to congratulate ourselves upon? and may not women think that even a slight co-operation of their own with the other sex in the councils of the nation – we are not now speaking of admission to Parliament – might have prevented, might still prevent, some of this mischief?

The reproach that 'women are agitating from love of power,' does not come with quite a good grace from that sex which has hitherto monopolized all power, exercised, as we think, with such grievous injustice to the other. But, in fact, the reproach is undeserved. Those who make it show such a misunderstanding of the deeply conscientious feelings and convictions on which this new movement is founded, as almost disqualifies them from discussing this question with us at all. Power to protect themselves from injustice women may be allowed to desire. But a still stronger motive is the belief that the welfare of society requires a different position for their whole sex.

Finally, recurring from all these details to the broad principle with which we started, that justice to women is morally the same as justice to man, I will only add, let this be acknowledged in the full meaning of the word, and all the ingeniously devised objections founded on woman's assumed inferiority to man fall at once to the ground. In the original fallacy, other false principles are involved, as that absolute perfection, moral and mental, is more needful in female than in male electors, and that to guard against possible inconvenience to men is a more pressing obligation than to remove an actual wrong to women.

I now come to those selfish inducements held out to woman herself to acquiesce in her present subjection, first glancing, however, at the half-triumphant warning that, with the privileges of citizenship, she must accept its burdens. That special burden which, I believe, the true Briton regards as the weightiest, that of taxation, she bears already, without the very privilege attached to it by divine right, as understood in Britain – to wit, the electoral franchise. This, though a flagrant departure from a cherished principle, I do not complain of as her hardest practical grievance; because in this case men, in fighting their own battle, must necessarily also fight that of women, and in some sort, therefore, do really represent them.

I must also advert to that appeal to women themselves on which men seem most triumphantly to rely. They say, that, if they are obliged to grant women equal social and legislative rights, i.e. justice, they will no longer receive from men that so-called 'chivalrous homage' which they regard apparently as sufficient compensation for every disadvantage and every humilia-tion attending the whole sex, in and out of drawing-rooms, and which they think women cannot reasonably look for except as a tribute to their legal inferiority and helplessness – that, in short, every virtue of which we can imagine women possessed, every gift of grace, beauty, and intelligence, joined, too, as they must *still* inevitably be, to inferiority of physical strength, will fail to secure for her man's respect and tenderness, unless she will accept him as her master and irresponsible political ruler. How is this? Is the spirit of 'chivalry' a spirit of bargain? and a very one-sided bargain? Or, putting aside the idea of deliberate bargain, is this a faithful picture of man's nature – at least of Englishmen's, which is our chief present concern? Is it contrary to his nature, for instance, to yield kindly aid to inferior strength unless it will meekly confess to mental inferiority and will promise obedience? Is it contrary to his nature to be just and generous at the same time? We believe that men do themselves injustice in affirming this.

As for those outward symbols of 'chivalrous homage' with which we are all familiar in drawing-rooms and such-like scenes, it is certainly, at first sight, hard to connect the forfeiture of these with the elevation of some women, or all women, to citizenship. But though it might be quite possible to do without these little privileges for so great an object, yet, truth to speak, the force of custom in regard to social etiquettes, even those generally felt to be burdensome and absurd, is so great that probably such harmless ones as these will long survive. I incline to think it will be long before all gentlemen remember to press out of drawing-rooms before their lady-acquaintances, to help themselves first at table, to stand by whilst the objects of their former homage step out of their carriages, or into boats, without offering a hand, or in railway travel to remember not to be charmed by the looks or conversation of a lady fellow-passenger till they have satisfied themselves that she has not a vote. Seriously, I incline to think that men will observe all this innocent little ceremonial – which is partly a civilized regulation to secure orderliness in social intercourse, partly an assumption of a difference in physical strength, which, false or true, will not be affected by the possession of a vote – till women forfeit men's respect by forfeiting their own, a result not certain to follow from their acquiring a sense of higher responsibility to the State. These things will last probably till all society is placed on a different, perhaps simpler and nobler footing, by other concurrent changes in civilization and education still far distant. But what is best in our social humanity need never disappear – mutual courtesy, kindness, such consideration between the sexes, and such help and sympathy from each to each, as are surely no more to be grudged from men to women, in any case, than from the younger and stronger man to the old, and infirm, and respected of his own sex, however his equal in political rights and political intelligence.

On the other hand, there is surely something more real, more trustworthy in manly heroism, manly devotion to duty, than even in that 'chivalrous homage' so admired as the most perfect compensation for female subjection, the most satisfactory modification possible of barbaric female slavery, and which generally expects in return some natural little gratification to its own self-love or vanity. I am not going to quarrel with it for thus seeking its reward – only it must not boast itself too much. We may be sure, too, that the spectacle of any brave, honest work, whether of the hand or the brain, done for love or duty, kindles the heart and imagination of the true woman, and exalts her respect for her partner, far more than that other spectacle of man making or upholding laws to secure to himself his wife's obedience, the possession of her property; and his own undivided control over his and her children, far more than his assurance that he classes her politically with idiots, lunatics, and criminals, in order to increase his own respect for her, and because she likes it – or, at least, ought to do so.

If these 'chivalrous' opponents have the faith they profess in woman's native grace and refinement; if they do not believe these qualities to be entirely the creation of certain artificial restrictions on her liberty of action, which no education of thought and reason can supply the place of; if they do not believe she is dignified and refined solely by accessories and surroundings, having *within herself* under no circumstances the power to dignity and refine *them*; if they do not hold this strangely 'unchivalrous' and dishonouring doctrine of woman's nature, then how is it that they suppose all these precious attributes can be got rid of so very easily? They can scarcely believe she will lose them by learning to take an interest in the concerns of her country, and to express that interest every few years by a conscientious vote, in the delivering of which she may be as well protected as in witnessing the procession of a royal bride, a race, a play, or an opera. If there should appear, in any woman's ardour on these subjects, anything ungraceful or exaggerated, there is probably some such defect in her natural organization manifesting itself alike in all her doings. On the whole, a woman will be in politics pretty much what she is – by her natural temperament – in all other spheres.

But in fact such objectors, however 'chivalrous,' however kind-hearted – as many of them truly are – *have no faith* in woman, no faith in the goddess they worship with flattery, incense, and gay pageantry; and it would be well if they would frankly confess this. Then we should know exactly where to meet them. In the meanwhile, till man can acquire this faith, this generous trust, society will make small moral progress – and need we remind the shallowest student of human nature that to make human beings trustworthy, you must take courage to trust them?

That women's tender interest in those they love would be deadened by these enlarged views of political and social life, that they would thus grow somehow more selfish and less useful to men in consequence, is a prejudice such as has been held to justify even harsher restrictions, and one I think unworthy to influence for a moment a generous mind. That the blind idolatry with which they have often injured, sometimes ruined, their idols, will be exchanged for a feeling more elevated and elevating, is very likely; but we need not regret *this* transformation.

There is a refined and tender side, as I shall again and again admit, to these remonstrances. The ideal of graceful, clinging weakness, the 'smiling domestic goddess'-ship (divorced indeed both from intellect and good sense), so admired by Thackeray, the sacred pedestal-worship of poetic theories, have such a charm for some manly imaginations, that the suggested introduction of some newer type is as terrifying to them as the threat of a new railway or row of houses to the inhabitants of a rural paradise. I predict, however, that amongst the many varieties of the female type we hope to see developed, whatever is really good and beautiful in their own favourite one is likely still to 'abound;' what is not so good and beautiful will be less easily rooted out than we could wish, and many a 'fair defect' will long remain to rejoice their hearts and fancies. Such will be as the childish element in the race, and, as such, worthy of all indulgence and tenderness.

But I must also remind the 'chivalrous' that their ideal is, and always has been, the monopoly of a small privileged class. For 'chivalrous homage' has nothing to say to the poor, hard-working wives and mothers outside that, nor to the thousands of courageous single women who are too strenuously fighting the battle of life – often for others as well as for themselves – to have time to cultivate graceful clingingness, or to stand on pedestals. It would be hard, truly, to withhold citizenship, and whatever dignity and support it may confer from these 'lonely, unadmired heroines,' for the sake of keeping up a special feminine ideal as the monopoly of a special class.[4]

We see, indeed, where this long subjection of women, most favourably exhibited in the placing of some of them on a fancied pinnacle, has landed us at last. It finds us confronted by a glaring discrepancy between profession and performance, which must make the very word 'chivalry,' if they even heard it, seem a cruel mockery to the rest.

Some theorists, we know, will say, 'True, all is not right as it now is; but there is a remedy. She is now *too* independent, she has got *one* hand free; bind *both* again, bind her hand and foot – put her more completely in men's power; but educate men and women better, so that man may be less likely to abuse his power, and woman may know her proper place; protect her exactly as you would a child, by stringent legislation, leaving her no discretion, no option, and then trust the rest to man's generosity, and the perfect dignity this perfect subjection and perfect powerlessness will give her.' But women have a right to a voice before this theory of a dominant sex can be forced on them.

Moreover, let me remind the upholders *par excellence* of 'feminine delicacy and refinement' how very different are and have been the ideas attached to these words in other ages and other countries, and maintained with obstinate persistence, and confidence that they rest on the immutable sanction of nature and religion. Ask the respectable Turkish father of a family what will happen to society when the harem doors are unlocked, and the women allowed to go forth unveiled – nay, ask the respectable Turk's ladylike wife and daughter – and their answer will be the same. Go back to the days, not so very long ago, when in all countries, Christian and pagan, a woman was married without her consent being asked; when worthy fathers of families would have been shocked at the indelicacy of a girl presuming to have a choice, or even a veto on her parents' choice. Nay, when the bold idea was first started of teaching women to read, 'Fancy,' can we not see it said in some popular journals of those mythical days?

'fancy a woman forsaking the spindle and frying-pan, her own peculiar sciences, to plunge into the unfeminine mysteries of the alphabet!' Not to mention some *very* civilized European countries where, even in the present day, if a girl (of the drawing-room class, I mean) were known to have once walked out in town unattended, it would destroy her chance of marriage, and where it is with difficulty believed that such liberty in England is not abused.

Why, then, is it so certain that we here, in England and now, have reached that exact point of feminine freedom beyond which we cannot go without contradicting nature – that exact type of refinement which admits of no further modification? Let us remember that with every fresh instalment of liberty and independence granted to women by advancing civilization, every step forward from her primitive condition of slavery to her present position of legal subjection, she has received not less, but more, kindness and respect from men, and the masculine ideal has not ruinously suffered thereby. Women have attained to far more self-reliance and liberty of movements in the United States of America than in England; but no-one has asserted that they are as a consequence of less importance to men, or treated with less deference. To say that their manners are not to the taste of those Englishmen who know them only by hearsay is beside the argument, nor is this distaste generally shared by Englishmen who know them by personal acquaintance.

Why, then, should we fear that one step further in the same path of independence would do all that the others have failed to do – at once revolutionize all the natural relations of the sexes, and transform, as we are so often told, women into men?

The truth is, social circumstances in all civilized communities, and notably in this, have outgrown the old theory of women's proper place in the world. The increased difficulty of living, felt in all classes, the 800,000 women in excess of men, the exclusion of women from all but one or two modes of gaining a precarious livelihood, the increased importance of education with so small an increase of the facilities offered to women, making it impossible for them to cope with men in the struggle for actual existence, and all these causes rendering marriage for women at once more necessary and too often more impossible, such realities have reduced to a mere figment the theory of universal protection, dependence, and homage.

The men of the past did what seemed the best in those days; the men of the present are not to blame for the altered conditions which have made it the worst. But they will be to blame if they persist in upholding it and in regarding attempted reforms as attempts to 'remove the landmarks of society;' if, in a word, they endeavour to force the life of successive generations of women into the old Chinese shoe of subjection and restraint, fancying that if they just make it a little easier, all will be right. The shoe must be made to fit perfectly, and women themselves must decide whether it does so.

And now comes the question of the influence actually exercised by women, in the cultivated and comfortable classes that is, for no other female influence over men is generally spoken of as of any importance. Gentlemen, when they speak of women, mean 'ladies.' And as 'ladies' are the wives, mothers, and sisters of the class which at present governs us, their influence *should* be important, fearfully important; though this is no reason for casting aside so much as, in common parlance, we are too wont to do, the interests of women in the sphere beneath that recognised by 'chivalry,' and the influence which they too *ought* to be able to exercise.

But let us see what this influence of 'ladies' is. We are told that it is very great, and those who say so are apt to go further, and fling all responsibility for social vices on the women of society. Let women humbly acknowledge to themselves their own shortcomings; they could not do much, but some of them, perhaps, might have done more. Capable, it may be, of better things, too many have been led ignobly astray by vanity and frivolity, too many by precept and example have done harm where they might have done good, thus, and in a thousand other ways, under a thousand disguises, rendering back to man the ill that the long domination of masculine ideas has wrought upon them. But while it is safe to be severe on themselves individually, it is not so safe to be blind to the faults of the social system under which they live. The fact remains that the influence of women for good, is very small, compared with what it is said to be, and might be, if men so willed it. No good influence, worth naming such, can be exercised but by an independent mind, and such independence is made tenfold more difficult to women at the present day, not only by men's prejudices, but by the difficulty of marriage resulting from the conditions before alluded to. This, an evil over which neither men nor women have any immediate control, is no doubt in great part the secret of the humble attitude which women are apt to take towards men, and the triumphant scorn of the sex so frequently displayed by popular journals. But once conscious of these facts, the efforts of society to counteract their mischievous results should be unremitting.

This dependence, then, acknowledged, for men to lay the blame of their own weaknesses on their so-called 'weaker' sisters, to seek to silence their remonstrances by assuring them that *they* are the guilty party, or at least equally guilty with their masters, of these social corruptions we all cannot but see around us, is an unconscious baseness which even good men sometimes fall into when judging of the other sex.

In order that woman may really exercise that wholesome and purifying influence ascribed to her as her natural attribute, she should herself be left free and unbiassed by fear or favour. If she is to inspire men with a refinement and morality a little deeper than drawing-room decorum, she must not herself have first to learn by rote from him the lesson she is to teach him again; she must not be cheated into taking all the rules of life unquestioning on man's traditional authority, and mistaking the dread of his reproach and ridicule for the voice of innate womanly conscience. She must not be coaxed, from earliest girlhood, by ball-room admirers, and even the gravest philosophers, into preferring her own (so-called) 'feminine instincts,' that is, prejudices, to the dictates of reason, sense, and duty, to find in later life 'feminine unreasonableness' a bye-word in men's mouths, to find herself exposed to the good-humoured contempt of the placid husband and the scolding of the irritable one, and to hear – no longer as the delighted tribute to youthful charms, but as a grave disqualification – that women have 'no sense of justice.' She must not be taught that narrow views of religion are especially becoming to women, and the only safeguard to their virtue in the eyes of the laxer sex. She must not, as the mother of a family, have always that warning voice in her ear that 'men hate learned women,' or that 'men don't want intellect in their wives' (which indeed is not so surprising in those who themselves have neither intellect nor learning) till her very schoolboy sons catch up the cry. She must not be brought up utterly to ignore all great social and national interests, all enlightened views of politics; she must not be taught that the one great object of woman's life is marriage, when every day the social obstacles in the way of marriage are increasing; and, above all, she must not be forced or hoodwinked into accepting from masculine dictation two distinct moral codes – one for men and the other for women.

Where these teachings have not been perfectly enforced, as of course will often be the case, either from partial enlightenment in the teacher or instinctive revolt in the taught, they will be found to have caused in simple and noble minds more mental and moral suffering than actual moral deterioration. But what society has lost, still loses, by the waste of such good material, it has not yet attempted to reckon up. A movement has now been set on foot, and is slowly gaining strength, to repudiate these teachings, which have, as we have said, found rebels scattered here and there at all times; yet while legislation, man's legislation for woman, still represents the ideas embodied in them, still ignores the incongruity between the theory and the facts of woman's position in the world, so long will it be, not the elevating and purifying influence of woman upon man (the theory of 'chivalrous' moralists), but the depressing and deteriorating influence of man upon woman, that regulates society. Let men, even philosophers, repeat as they will that 'women have everything in their own power, that it is their own fault if men are not better than they are.' I affirm that the more we look below the surface, the more we shall be convinced that whilst man remains the irresponsible legislator for women, these things will be as I have said.

The social phenomena developed by man's domination in women's education, ideas and character are so numerous and complex as almost to defy classification. I am far from classing the women, even of the sphere which we have taken for our text, 'all in one,' but this seems evident, that the general result has been a most disheartening mediocrity. We have hopes, it is true, that the efforts now being made by those social benefactresses, who are so earnestly fighting the educational battle for their sisters, powerfully aided by like-minded and generous men, will greatly mitigate this state of things for a fortunate part of the younger generation. But, for the present, though 'the softening influence of domestic life,' 'the purity of English homes' are pretty phrases, yet all the same, men and women are doing their best to degrade each other to a pitiful mediocrity. Not all the prettiness of blooming girlhood (and a pretty English girl *is* a charming object, whether one is in a moralizing mood or not), not all the brightness, activity and kind-heartedness of narrowly-educated women, however 'clever' they may be, can hide this sad truth from our eyes.

Let us begin – working upwards from seeming trifles – with one time-honoured social institution, through which the wholesome and refining influence of one sex over the other is supposed to make itself felt. I tremble as I approach this sacred field, and find myself compelled in sober sadness to drop disrespectful words on the privileged flirtations of the young. I would not be severe either on those who encourage or those who practise this favourite diversion. Yet, after all, in spite of the glamour thrown by youthful excitement and inexperience, by the regretful and sympathetic retrospect of age, and by the imagination of poets and painters over the ball, the croquet, the picnic, and all the other playgrounds of 'society,' it must be owned that the prospect is not encouraging to our hopes of the young. The 'flirtation' which reigns here between the two sexes, encouraged by all social customs, provided for at the cost of time, money, health and mental improvement, has in it mischief which lies deeper than at first appears. It is more than 'matter for a flying smile.' Many will agree with me so far, but will strenuously resist the application of radical remedies to the whole position of society. Palliatives, not prevention, not cure, have ever been the favourite study of English philanthropy.

It is at this point of transitory, counterfeit courtship (in itself damaging to the freshness of youthful affections) that we first trace the effect of that low standard of excellence required from women. Man in general requires little from the woman he loves, still less from the woman he flirts with: we all know that a pretty face, a pretty dress and a few 'womanly' coquetries generally suffice for him in either case, and he takes his chance of finding other qualities behind these when it is too late to make a fresh choice; while woman, dwarfed to meet these small requirements, requires little from him in return. And so the taste is formed, so marriages are made, and so society and the race are deteriorated.

The last thing I would wish to disparage is the natural, light-hearted, innocent enjoyment of each other's society, in the young of the two sexes. I wish it were far more easily come by and begun earlier too, and were freed from that uneasy self-consciousness which is so often and so needlessly substituted for the frank courage of innocence. From that morbidly-watchful egotism, which, under the name of 'propriety,' used to be so much enjoined, and which would be ill-exchanged for the 'fastness' of which, in certain circles, one hears so much, we turn with relief to that artless enjoyment of life and society which characterizes unspoiled girlhood, accompanied by a really strong interest in some pursuit. It finds its salvation in those genuine tastes which carry us out of ourselves (not necessarily 'learned' or 'intellectual') – it may be gardening, or music, or painting, or some kindred art – only, for Heaven's sake, let it be *real*, let it be good of its kind, let it be honestly followed; and the more of such the better.

On such common ground of genuine tastes and pursuits, young men and women may healthfully meet each other and prepare for the closer partnership and co-operation of after-life; and much, very much, I trust, will this common ground be enlarged by wider education. But what has this happy, true-hearted sympathy, which one longs to see prevail everywhere, purged more and more from vanity and *arrière-pensée*, to do with the artificial sentimentalities, the unmeaning personalities, and empty rattle of flirtation, either between two equally trifling beings, or a so-called sensible man and a poor girl taught that to be admired she must 'flirt' prettily, and dress prettily, and need not be well-informed? *These* have nothing in common but the common interest of vanity; and whether such a flirtation end in marriage or not, they who pursue it are equally injuring their own tastes and characters, and unfitting themselves for true marriage.

Sometimes indeed, as we all know, great misery follows from this playing with fire – especially in the woman, where an untrained, unoccupied mind is joined to a warm heart or vivid imagination. But how much of this suffering might be saved to either party if a frankness, now thought impossible between men and women, could be cultivated! Were this united to a more trained judgment and more engrossing occupations for women, we might less often see the sensational coquette followed by trains of admirers, her heart ever half-touched, and only half-satisfied, her frivolous vanity never satiated; we might less often see truer and more passionate hearts racked by the ignoble indecision or still more ignoble insincerity and heartlessness of a counterfeit lover. Women would then oftener see through the unworthiness of such a nature before it was too late, and the irretrievable waste of many a precious year of life be averted. The coquette, too, and even the much-abused 'fast girl,' would find better fields for their love of power (as natural to some women as to some men), as well as for the restless animal spirits and healthy untrained energies which are perhaps chiefly answerable for those vagaries to which the world is so severe.

And what must the marriages be to which this style of social intercourse leads up – putting aside for the moment moral questions of a more tragic significance? Will not this account partly for the falling off of youthful love and all the poetry of life which is thought almost inevitable in marriage? And may not much of the ignobleness of society, of class selfishness, national selfishness, have something to do with these commonplace impulses by which marriages are brought about and families are formed?

In this discouraging view, it must be observed, that we are speaking of what are considered the better kind of average marriages – that is, those which are more or less of choice (perhaps they might just as well be called of chance); not of the many which are in great measure dictated by motives of interest or convenience, which latter, on the woman's side, is too often the supposed desperate necessity of being married at all. And this too is the result of our social arrangements!

It seems wonderful how that prevalent taste among men for female mediocrity is shared even by such as appear fit for better things. Negatives seem to attract, as if woman were to be admired rather for what she is without than what she has; the absence of some power or intellectual gift being constantly mentioned as a positive quality, not to say merit, rather than as a deficiency – a mode of estimation never used with men. And the qualities which do attract are too often superficial attributes, often those semi-childish prejudices and conventionalities, the result of a narrow education for generations, which are generally called 'feminine instincts,' and considered charming. This is partly the result of a prevalent idea that tenderness of feeling and good household management can seldom be found apart from these, and that the clinging subjection to man which is thought the natural position, the crowning grace of woman, is incompatible with a cultivated mind and original views. As often as not, however, his fancy invests with this poetic charm some nature below even the low standard he prefers; since whenever we limit our aspirations after excellence, we are liable to fall short even of that limit. Even these limited ideals vary, however; some profess to be content with the ideal of the intelligent cook and housekeeper, and hold that a woman cannot and ought not to have time for anything else.

Yet do not those men of sense and intellect who seek for attractive mediocrity, if they think about it at all, expect their sons to inherit their own masculine superiority, and their daughters to renew the maternal type? But there is no natural law forbidding – what in fact we so frequently see – the descent of intellectual gifts to the daughters, and the more commonplace attributes to the sons. These sons will probably marry their likes; the daughters, not finding their natural mates, and not able to seek for them, as probably as not remain unmarried.

Fortunately there are various types between the extremes we have mentioned, some, if rare, yet beautiful – tender, sympathetic, refined female natures, incapable of initiative, but appreciative and reverent of true superiority, by associating with which they gradually educate themselves, and in whose society a man tender and refined enough to appreciate their charm, may well feel himself blest. Yet even such beloved and tender beings feel too often a vague, painful sense of incompleteness and inferiority never quite absent – the greater because of its instinctive admiration of what is excellent. These, too, suffer practically from that deficiency in the masculine ideal of women, which originally stunted their education.

One can understand and respect the man of uncultivated intellect who has the manly humility to acknowledge that a highly educated woman would not be a fit mate for him, and that tenderness, simplicity, and purity of heart, without even the perfecting grace of intellect, are enough for his needs. But what does fill us with regretful wonder is, that this incapacity to appreciate the best and completest should be ever made a boast by men, and expressed with the evident feeling that men's preference for the mediocre is a crushing sentence against the woman of trained intellect. Our most popular novelist, whilst sneering at the 'heroic female character,' bids us regard as the standard to which women should most aspire, the having 'all the men in a cluster round her chair, all the young fellows battling to dance with her.' According to this judgment, this special court of appeal to which the loftiest-minded woman must bow – her wisest policy, her most womanly grace, will be to disguise, at least, if she cannot extinguish, her superiority.

No woman of real refinement and right sympathies can wish to disparage *true* grace, beauty, and sweetness. They form together a power worthy of respectful homage. But they can hardly exist – at least, hardly last – without a certain strength and elevation of character. True sweetness means strength, not servility, not undiscriminating devotion (beautiful and commendable in a dog we allow, but not quite an adequate expression of womanly affection), not characterless good nature, not the mere liveliness of youth, nor silliness; true grace implies a harmonizing artistic faculty and a moral balance which can scarcely belong to a commonplace nature, guided only by conventional laws. As for true beauty, how little do we yet realize what glorious types of form and feature are in store for the world, when strength of body and mind, health, courage, and freedom have been developed by generations of enlightened culture – what radiance and fulness of life, what new intelligence and ardour of expression, what splendour of frame, such as we should now look on as fitter for another planet! These are dreams as yet, but they have a practical value if they preserve us from seeking our ideal in a direction contrary to true progress.

But to descend from these poetic heights – at least since the young, pretty, and lively have an influence over men's acts and wishes at present quite out of proportion to their power to use it well, they should be trained, if only with a view to the welfare of their own households, to a more enlightened sense of their responsibilities than men can at present appreciate. If any modest man is alarmed at the prospect of an era of learned and splendid women, let him be assured that it will be long, very long before it comes, and that when it does, by the necessity of the case, men will have risen too. There will long be a supply of the women whom men emphatically call 'feminine' – a word which has been for ages the engine of women's oppression. Its meanings have varied, but having been all imposed, directly or indirectly, by man, they are all so many badges of female subjection, both material and moral. Here we know we shall be contradicted by most men and by many women. Men will confidently appeal to the 'instincts' of some female friend – perhaps some pretty young girl – and be confirmed by her positiveness, or her flippancy, or her timid acquiescence, in his belief that all true womanhood is on his side. It is much as if a slaveholder should appeal to some faithful, ignorant slave, born on his estate, as to the divinely-appointed necessity of slavery, and the virtues proper to his condition, and be quite satisfied with his 'Yes, massa,' in reply. It is quite possible that the slave does believe in the divine origin of slavery; it will not be the fault of his master's theological teachings if he does not. Women have been taught to do more than this – not merely to acquiesce, but to glory in their subjection.

One feature of this subjection is, as has been somewhere pointed out, that a double code of laws has been imposed on woman – one supposed to be common to all humanity, the other containing special regulations for herself – not merely supplementary of, but sometimes even contradicting, the other. These seem devised to keep up an enfeebling self-consciousness, and to turn the simple government of a healthy conscience into a sort of Lord Chamberlain's office of etiquettes. But there is, or ought to be, only one law for men and women; and such a 'codification' will be, we trust, the great moral work of our age. One conscience, one education, one virtue, one liberty, one citizenship for men and women alike. It will not force them to do the same work, but it will enable them freely to choose their work. It will not make them the same, but it will help to make them perfect of their kind, and the world twice as great, and twice as happy.

Would it not, to begin with, be well first to instruct girls that weakness, or cowardice, and ignorance cannot constitute at once the perfection of womankind and the imperfection of mankind – to cease, in short, to impress upon her the lesson epitomized in Mr Charles Reed's short dialogue –

L.S.

She I feel all my sex's weakness,
He And therein you are invincible.

May they not be led to cultivate grace, refinement, taste and beauty, because these things are good in themselves and make the world brighter and happier; not because men admire this, that, and the other in women, and are disgusted at its absence, and that therefore this, that, and the other are feminine attributes, and will get them partners at a ball, and perhaps for life. The original motive to this cultivation of grace and charm colours the whole of the after-life and character. On this depends whether she is to be a truthful free woman, the equal, sympathetic, and ennobling partner of man, or a sort of attractive slave, as man so often likes to picture her, to coax him by her personal charms into tenderness and morality without any trouble of his own.

'Female instincts,' a favourite idea of unphilosophical minds, are called 'feelings' as opposed to 'reason;' and some mysterious moral advantage is supposed to accrue to the more 'rational' sex from the presumed incapacity of their partners in life to look beyond personal and family interests, to draw rational inferences from facts, and to be just as well as generous. The 'sacred nonsense' of mothers' talk to the child at their knee, recalled in Parliamentary utterances as one blessing to be destroyed by female suffrage, is a good illustration of this theme.

A good many sensible men, whilst unprepared to grant women equal rights and citizenship with themselves, will advocate a better education for them generally, will by no means confess to admiring ignorance and prejudice, and will even enjoy the conversation of a clever woman, if she be not *too* clever, and too much in earnest. But these notwithstanding, the view of woman's supposed defects, which I have stated before, defects either charming or provoking as you choose to take them, or as the subject of them is fifteen or fifty years old, is what has met and thwarted enlightened women at every turn.

Now, as regards 'feeling' and 'instinct,' held, as they often are, as preferable respectively to 'reason' and 'judgment,' let us compare that untrained, unenlightened maternal instinct which leads the mother to indulge her child to its own future injury, with that instinct trained and enlightened, which leads her for its future good not to shrink from its present suffering. Compare 'feeling' which, in the shape of ignorance and prejudice, leads to narrow views of religion and to intolerance of some of the noblest and wisest of human thoughts and sentiments, with that 'feeling,' founded on knowledge and reason which leads to enthusiasm for what is noblest and wisest, whilst yet it can be kindly indulgent to that very ignorance which despises knowledge. The obstruction to social progress, caused by the fostering of these theological prejudices in women through the indulgence of even those husbands and fathers who have them not themselves, can only be glanced at here. It is not a question of reason against feeling, but of allying the two, instead of keeping them apart by an irreligious divorce. To some minds the voice of reason is as the voice of conscience, and such, once awake to their responsibilities, can no more disobey the one voice than the other. These seem absolute truisms, yet how few there are, even of those who cannot contradict them, who will accord them practical recognition!

'Good Heavens! a young lady reason!' was once the exclamation of an educated Roman Catholic when mildly argued with by one of the angelic sex. Of course, as we were told in Parliament, 'women's minds are absolutely closed to logic,' – this said in the face of an ever-increasing number of women who can reason, and reason well, and whom men have not yet been able to answer. And why should it be 'unfeminine' and 'ungraceful,' and all the rest of it, to appreciate the æsthetic beauty of a well-woven chain of reasoning? Partly, perhaps, because women have not the monopoly of reasoning ill. It is the superficially dexterous arguers, possibly, rather than deep and sincere thinkers amongst men who find a charm in female perverseness and irrationality in religion, politics, and subjects of thought generally. I can no more regard the power of right reasoning as a mental luxury, a privilege to be kept for the enjoyment of one sex, than I can regard correct drawing or correct intonation in music as perfections necessary in professionals, but merely unpleasing pedantry in amateurs.

Yes, surely the ardour of reason, so nearly akin to the passion for justice, is as proper for a woman as any other ardour looked upon as feminine *par excellence*. And there is an earnest vein in women which, as far as we have been able to observe, is opposed to the sophistications of the *merely* logical intellect, the cold-hearted amusement of arguing an important question without any real convictions. Such conscientious sincerity, even from a man's point of view, cannot be unwomanly.

'Unfeminine' – Alas, how much of good and great has that word blighted at its birth! On women's sensibilities, artificially fostered to an intense tenderness to the lightest sting, it does fall like the cut of a lash. But, after all, the government of the lash can only make slaves. As woman takes larger and loftier views of duty, she will learn to dread the stings of her conscience more than the lash of man's ridicule. She will look at the sun itself with undazzled eyes, not through the smoke-dimmed glass man has handed her for her special use. As it is, this fear, inculcated through ages, haunts women from the cradle (and men cannot realize the effort it costs, even those who seem bravest, to shake it off), this fear which holds them back from expressing their real opinions, hinders woman herself, as much as it hinders man, from knowing what she really is.

It is too true that a very large number of the women of one class, the comfortable drawing-room class, have ranged themselves with well-meaning docility in the ranks of this social police, have been the unconscious agents of a social terrorism, which man himself exercises almost unconsciously, while they innocently repeat the warning words of 'feminine delicacy' and 'ladylike propriety' which men have put into their mouths, and which they believe are the utterances of nature and religion, and the immutable conditions of civilized life.

Let us think how much we need a counteracting influence against those base motives of personal and class-selfishness which now honeycomb and almost threaten to destroy society, and how little women's 'instincts' and 'feelings' have done to supply this. I do not forget that, in all ages, at times of temporary excitement, there have been women found to sustain a man in the sacrifice of those whom he loves to duty, even when she and her children are to be the sacrificed; but one longs to see something of this spirit in everyday life and in peaceful times. The same woman who will cheerfully destroy her own health in nursing one she loves, who will uncomplainingly share with him his involuntary poverty, or even deserved disgrace, would on the other hand discourage him with all her powers of persuasion from risking his worldly fortune or bringing on himself the world's reproach, at some call of conscience with which she has not been taught to sympathize. Again, a husband should blush before his wife for a mean public action, a vote given through self-interest, or class-interest, or faction, as he would for cheating his neighbour, for official falsification as he would for perjury in a court of justice, for conniving at the bribery of an elector as he would for receiving stolen goods, for taking an unfair advantage in trade as he would for picking a pocket. But we hear nothing of the desirableness of feminine influence in such matters as these.

I turn now to the married state as affected in England by the marriage law, 'the most barbarous,' it has lately been said, 'in Europe.' 'A woman,' as has also lately been said, 'loses when she marries, her name, her freedom, her individuality, her property, her vote' (municipal and other). A man takes from the woman he marries everything she has, yet is not bound to maintain her while she lives with him,[5] can use the forms of law to force back a reluctant wife in spite of her aversion to live with him, and finally can take her children from her and give them to the care of some other woman if he pleases. This law, of which these are some of the most striking features – though, more or less, of course, a dead letter in affectionate marriages, but an easy instrument of iniquity in the hands of the unscrupulous – would almost seem indeed to be maintained for the special use of the bad. This law which, however modified in its practical workings by individual character, cannot but lower the whole conception of marriage for all but the exceptional few, even good men will tell us somehow helps to secure the happiness of married life generally! In its remote origin it was doubtless a valuable modification of worse evils, and in the days when no personal freedom was allowed to any woman, married or unmarried, when marriage was therefore merely an exchange of one servitude for another, there was at least no glaring incongruity in the theory of a wife's subjection. But now, when she is supposed, once arrived at the years of discretion, to be a free agent, and to have a free choice in marriage, the position has become an antiquated anomaly. It would seem still to be upheld on the principle that because woman is weak, she should therefore be made helpless – because man is strong, he shall have additional protection against the weak. In the classes where this law is most abused, because there education has done least to counteract its brutalizing effect on public opinion, there has been found a tendency in women (notably in manufacturing towns), to prefer unmarried unions to legitimate ones, for the sake of the greater protection of their self-earned contributions to the household, and the greater willingness of their partners to contribute their share, instead of spending all on themselves. Here, at least, is one natural result of a degrading and tyrannical law of marriage on those who suffer from it most helplessly. Before this new form of union tends universally to supplant the other, it might be better instead of vaguely deploring the immorality of the 'lower classes,' or contriving such piecemeal mitigations as have lately been enacted – to see if a radical reform of the old institution be not worth considering.

The truth is, our ideas are still perverted by the old fetish worship of husbands, so ludicrously expressed in the literature of past generations – that curious religion which made it a wife's highest virtue to pay the obedience of a slave to a master, however cruel, capricious, or irrational he was, however noble and wise she might be – in short, the greater his mental and moral inferiority to her, the greater the merit of her absolute submission. This doctrine, which turned him into a monstrous idol to be propitiated by an abject ceremonial – this ideal of wifehood, maintained by men with astonishing complacency, was carried to its highest perfection in the legend of 'Patient Griselda,' in which many men, we believe, still see a kind of pathetic beauty. It really exhibits the most repulsive perversion of moral feeling on both sides to which such a grotesque theory of marriage is capable of leading. This fetishism continues in a modified shape to be represented by the law of the land, and it colours more or less the ordinary ideal of marriage. There is, to be sure, a sort of humility in insisting on this right divine of husbands, since no more than the divine right of kings does it require any inherent superiority in the individual possessing it. But this kind of humility has in neither case proved beneficial to the governing or governed. Mr Herbert Spencer has observed in the 'Social Studies' that even as we 'loathe' the custom which in savage nations forbids women to eat in company with men, so shall we come to loathe the civilized theories of the wife's subjection to her husband. The wonder is that any man can endure it.

Till absolute social and legal equality is the basis of the sacred partnership of marriage (the division of labours and duties in the family, by free agreement, implying no sort of inequality), till no superiority is recognised on either side but that of individual character and capacity, till marriage is no longer legally surrounded with penalties on the woman who enters into it as though she were a criminal – till then the truest love, the truest sympathy, the truest happiness in it, will be the exception rather than the rule, and the real value of this relation, domestic and social, will be fatally missed. People may get on pretty well together, and be fairly fond of each other, without their married life presenting a spectacle particularly worthy of admiration, or suggesting a very excellent development of human nature. Of course, in numberless cases, a wife will find it her best wisdom as well as comfort in the conduct of life (especially as society is now constituted) to yield to the judgment of a husband who may probably be her superior in age, experience of life, and knowledge of the world; but this accidental part of marriage, if I may call it so, has nothing to do with the theory of divine right on the one side, and indelible inferiority on the other.

Connected with this faulty view of the marriage relations, is that other difficulty with which woman has been burdened by immemorial prejudice, grievously overweighted as she is already without it – I mean the stigma of conventional humiliation, attached to those women who pass their lives unmarried. It is, no doubt, like the fetish-worship of husbands, a relic of barbarism, but it is still strongly felt, and has been impressed by men on women themselves to their great detriment. It is not simply the opinion that, as a general rule, women are happier married than single; but that the unmarried woman, when she has ceased to be young, is an object not merely for pity, but more or less for contempt, though it is not always held good taste to express it, and some men are too sensible and manly to feel it. Apparently this notion rests on three assumptions, all of barbaric origin – namely, that a woman's highest glory and merit is to please men, that if she has not married she has failed to please men, and that her whole *raison d'être* is wifehood and motherhood. A *man* who has not become a husband and father may feel himself an honoured and important member of society; and till it is universally understood that a woman who from choice or chance is not a wife and mother, may fill an equally honoured and important position, true respect will not be paid to woman in any capacity, whether married or single. For the rest, the fact – not, I hope, without a possible good result on her general position as time goes on – of the eight hundred thousand women in excess of men in England, who must of necessity remain unmarried (and the disproportion continues, we believe, to increase) justifies us still further in protesting against this old world prejudice.

But the spectral difficulty it has raised is already diminishing. Women have done much for themselves towards that result, and if they will persevere it will be removed from their path altogether. The dignity and independence of womanhood must be maintained by an upright scrupulousness of choice in the first instance, to help which a much larger variety of occupation should be opened to women; and by faith in themselves, whether married or single. But in fighting this battle, as in so many others, she has been too often hindered rather than encouraged by the stronger sex.

'It is nonsense,' Hawthorne remarks in the *Blithesdale Romance*, 'and a miserable wrong – the result, like so many others, of masculine egotism – that the success or failure of a woman's existence should be made to depend wholly on the affections, and one one species of affection, while man has such a multitude of other chances, that this seems but an incident. For its own sake, if it will do no more, the world should throw open all its avenues to the passport of a woman's bleeding heart.'

Before quitting the subject of the married relations, we must say a few words on the typical and most painful exemplification of the different moral codes imposed on men and women – one having a most important bearing on these relations and the family and social influences which spring from them. We allude to the prevalent assumption that man is not bound by the same rule of moral purity as woman. An obvious development of the primitive barbaric notion of woman as the natural property of man, it is still held as a moral axiom, we believe, by the large majority of men. Unacknowledged in so many words by good men, abhorred, I doubt not, by many, denounced by the religion in whose dogmas the vicious still generally profess belief, it receives practical and almost universal recognition in the most civilized countries. Virtuous women, even, are perverted by conventional custom, persuaded, or tricked by their carefully-maintained ignorance, into assenting to it – and legislation is based upon it, as witness, amongst other examples, the law of divorce. Yet what does this distinction mean – unless it be wholly *un*-meaning and self-contradictory – except that *some* women are bound to lead purer lives than men, but *not all*? – That is, by man's traditional doctrine, the women of his own family, the women of the class he intends to marry into, are bound to be of unblemished purity, whilst the degradation in his behalf of less privileged classes is to be acquiesced in, nay, almost desired, as a social necessity. And is it at *this* price we purchase the boasted purity of English homes, with all its graceful accompaniments of chivalrous homage – by the maintenance, in a sort of pretended secrecy, of an unparalleled humiliation and slavery of woman, in a so-called free country, by those who profess to honour her the most?

Even good men, with consciences individually clear as to this matter, will shake their heads and say it *must* be – that this evil cannot be expelled from society; – indeed some say it ought not to be expelled, lest a greater evil take its place. And the good, by their silence, their acquiescence, play into the hands of the majority. But those women who think for themselves on this terrible subject, indignantly ask – By what right does any society exist on such a foundation? What right have certain classes of women to enjoy, safe and untempted, an aristocracy of virtue at the expense of the poor, the ignorant, the young, orphaned, helpless and thoughtless, the desolate and deserted, yearly, daily bribed, entrapped, tempted, goaded, and betrayed into a Hell upon earth – that men may go on talking about the 'purity of English homes' – the beautiful result of high civilization and feminine subjection? Upon the seething surface of this infernal region men build their own happy households, content if no sound from below rises up to shock the ears of unconscious wives and daughters! The denizens of that region are not waiting at leisure till it shall please them to forsake their evil lives, and become the happy and honoured heads of families: that crowning reward is reserved for the men who have profited by, and shared in, their degradation, whose easy repentance is gloried in as one more tribute to the moralizing influence of women, and in whose persons the sacred names of husband and father are thus daily and triumphantly profaned. For when they are weary of base dissipation, there is always some ignorant girl ready to confer these names upon them, to learn, probably, by degrees, that men are not bound to be as pure as women, to resign herself to her sons leading the same lives as their father before them, and to her daughters marrying men who lead the same lives as their brothers. But if this is what is meant by the 'purity of English homes,' are we so very sure that even this one-sided purity will always be maintained? Is it certain that no moral contamination from men's earlier associations ever enters there? Are we sure that the house built on such a foundation will always stand firm?

This brand upon society, this blight on every effort at true reform in any direction, will not be removed by sentimentalism, by costly subscriptions to churches, refuges, and reformatories, nor any other of the palliatives society seems to prefer to prevention, and which so often tend to maintain the original evil – no, nor by efforts to keep the women of one class ignorant of the degradation of women in another. The jealous trades-unionism of men which meets women at every turn in the struggle for existence, does not close the avenues of *this* trade to her. All the restrictions on her honest industry which well-meaning masculine philanthropy can devise, on the theory that she is a grown-up child, do not debar her from *this* calling. The romantic homage of the chivalrous does not shield her from *this* dishonour.

Many influences, no doubt, not directly traceable to masculine domination, tend to swell this evil. Against these the two forces of the human race should be brought to bear in combination, as they have never yet been brought. The single government of man has proved unequal to the task. Till woman has an equal or something more like an equal share in the councils of humanity, till she ceases to be the submissive subject of man, the two will not be brought to agree together on one standard of moral purity for both; and till then, man will not learn to reverence and desire purity, not in the women of one class only, but in all women – and not in woman only, but in himself as well.

In what I have just said I shall have, I am sure, some sort of sympathy and agreement from any who can in noways go along with me as to the proposed radical treatment of social mischiefs. Some of these have set before them a never yet realized and unrealizable ideal, in which I must once again acknowledge, with all sincerity and respect, a certain refinement, tenderness, and artificial beauty, nay, a kind of generosity gone astray. Such I oppose with regret. These would fain crystallize for all time the whole system of sentimental and sublimated injustice embodied in the chivalry theory. For them woman is always to be a glorified, but well-educated invalid, who is to influence man for his good by her physical imperfections, as much as by her ethereal and intuitive morality and docile affections. She is to guard this physical incapacity as well as her supposed incapability of sharing in the highest national concerns, and her unfitness for any social business beyond the precincts of home, as sacred treasures, because man, it is said, requires this contrast to himself as a moralizing element in his life. In his own particular walk of life, which is apparently to be kept as separate from hers as possible, it would almost seem he may be hard and coarse with a safe conscience because the woman he leaves at home remains soft and delicate.

And so on. To me the whole theory seems a morbid one. One longs to take off these golden chains, open the hothouse doors, and turn the ethereal prisoner into free fresh air, to develop her moral and intellectual muscle and stature at her will. The proposed arrangement consistently carried out, as we know it never has been, and I believe never can be, seems to us much as if we mortals should invite an angel from heaven to cast in his lot with us, to purify our morals and affections by his example and sympathy, to educate our children, and housekeep for us, on condition of strictly acknowledging our absolute authority and his own unalterably subordinate position, renouncing as unangelic all independent action and opinion, all share in deciding those earthly laws under which he is to live amongst us, and promising to *stay at home*, we on our side engaging to pay the obedient angel semi-divine honours, and in general to treat him with every indulgence and consideration. But then, if the angel should not like the bargain, he would at least be free to stay in heaven – whilst woman is here, and has no neutral ground to retire to, pending the negotiation. It seems scarcely fair to take advantage of her necessary presence amongst us, to impose on her conditions more stringent than with absolutely free choice, and full comprehension of the state of the case, she would care to accept.

No, let her have as free play for her natural capacities as man; not necessarily, as I have said before, to do always the same things as man, but to try fairly what she can do, and possibly thus greatly widen the sphere and vary the details of what she ought to do. If *then* she is willing to forego all the new, natural, healthful and legitimate ambitions and aspirations (as I hold them to be), growing up within her, and lightening even that burden of glorified invalidhood, thought to be her divinely appointed portion (except indeed in the working classes); if, after full and intelligent consideration, she decides she is not fit to share any of the higher responsibilities of citizenship with man; if, after trying what liberty of thought, conscience and action means; if after enjoying a free field for those gifts and faculties which are as various, and as imperatively cry out for exercise in women as in men; if, after learning to look on marriage as the happy alternative to other happy and satisfying occupations – not a social necessity; if after finding her voice in all that concerns the morals and welfare of society, deserving of, and listened to, with as much respect as man's; if after feeling herself a part of the state, not a servant submitting by compulsion to the will of the men in it, whether or no her judgment concurs in theirs; if after experiencing the blessing of having some little control over the laws by which the most sacred concerns of her life are to be governed; if, in one word, after being grown up, and after enjoying the privileges of a free woman, she is willing to become a child once more, and to fall back again into absolute subjection to an irresponsible sex – well and good. But the fair opportunity of choice – of understanding even the nature of the choice – has not yet been given her. If her instincts and characteristics are really as indelible as the 'metaphysical' chivalry-theory makes them, then, with all freedom of choice possible, she will of course renounce the new life opening upon her. But we shall see.

For myself I fervently believe that generations of a nobler and freer culture will ennoble and liberate her very bodily frame (as I have before said) into a health, strength and beauty hitherto undreamt of; not transform her into man – why was such a senseless misrepresentation ever dragged in to degrade a serious discussion into burlesque – but into glorified womanhood. This change, alone, would in time revolutionize the whole race, and man himself would grow to a greatness he denies himself whilst he ignorantly insists on stunting woman. Hitherto nature has always been brought into court as a hostile witness whenever it has been a question of elevating her condition in any one direction. We shall see whether nature, allowed to speak freely, is not *the* irresistibly conclusive witness on woman's side.

I must now add a remark the truth of which is, indeed, obtaining general recognition – viz. that men themselves are often, as might be expected, the victims of the faulty social system of which we complain, and are as unconscious as the majority of women are of the causes and possible remedy of its evils. Certainly many a hard-worked father who wears out health and spirits in an irksome profession that his daughters may enjoy amusements and luxuries in which he has little share, and to the earning of which they contribute nothing, might well be confounded at finding himself classed amongst the oppressors of women, and the women of his family as victims. Assuredly, it is not these latter whom we pity, except for that melancholy conventionality fostered by false views of woman's position in society which has so long sanctioned such contented idleness in young ladies' lives, and for the possibly bitter regrets of after years. Women, too, have their own class-privileges over other women; they, too, have to be constantly on their guard against a consequent blindness to the claims of others. There are class-abuses, class-difficulties, which it will take the whole united strength of society to sweep away. But of all class-reforms in store for the future we can still conceive of none so vitally important to the whole human race as the emancipation of woman. It will be the beginning of a new world-era, a new revelation, a new religion to man.

Yet one word more. I have still to thank with heart and soul, and in the name of all women who have the same aspirations as myself, those men who for us represent whatever is most truly wise and most truly just in the other sex, who for us, that is, represent man as he will be in the new era. It is they who by their faith in us strengthen all our efforts to deserve it; whose noble sympathy, and patience with the mistakes which women, as well as men, must needs fall into when entering on an untried course, may most worthily be repaid by care to appreciate what is best even in those who as yet oppose our dearest wishes, and, as we think, our highest destinies. Those men whose self-respect and dignity of nature forbid them to fear loss or injury to themselves from the elevation of others so long held to be their inferiors, should, by their willingness to abdicate their old conventional supremacy, inspire a corresponding generosity and a true humility in ourselves.

I will conclude my whole subject with a quotation from the American writer, who having made a successful practical protest, during the late war, against the theory of indelible race-inferiority by the training of a negro regiment, has since generously taken up the case of sex-domination. He thus writes: –

'Thus far my whole argument has been defensive and explanatory. I have shown that woman's inferiority in special achievements, so far as it exists, is a fact of small importance, because it is merely a corollary from her historic position of degradation. She has not excelled because she has had no fair chance to excel. Man, placing his foot on her shoulder, has taunted her with not rising. But the ulterior question remains behind – How came she into this attitude originally? Explain this explanation, the logician fairly demands. Granted that woman is weak, because she has been systematically degraded; but why was she so degraded? This is a far deeper question – one to be met only by a profounder philosophy and a positive solution. We are coming on ground almost wholly untrod, and must do the best we can.

'I venture to assert, then, that woman's social inferiority in the past has been to a great extent a legitimate thing. To all appearance history would have been impossible without it, just as it would have been impossible without an epoch of war and slavery. It is simply a matter of social progress – a part of the succession of civilizations. The past has been inevitably a period of ignorance of engrossing physical necessities, and of brute force – not of freedom, of philanthropy, and of culture. During that lower epoch, woman was necessarily an inferior, degraded by abject labour even in time of peace – degraded uniformly by war, chivalry to the contrary, notwithstanding. . . . The truth simply was, that her time had not come. Physical strength must rule for a time, and she was the weaker . . . and the degradation of woman was simply a part of a system which has indeed had its day, but has bequeathed its associations. . . . The reason, then, for the long subjection of woman has been simply that humanity was passing through its first epoch, and her full career was to be reserved for the second. . . . Woman's appointed era, like that of the Teutonic races, was delayed but not omitted. It is not merely true that the empire of the past has belonged to man, for it was an empire of the muscles, enlisting, at best, but the lower parts of the understanding. There can be no question that the present epoch is initiating an empire of the higher reason, of arts, affections, aspirations; and for that epoch the genius of woman has been reserved. Till the fulness of time came, woman was necessarily kept a slave to the spinning-wheel and the needle; now higher work is ready; peace has brought invention to her aid, and the mechanical means for her emancipation are ready also.'[6]

NOTES

1 It has been argued that the supposed excitability of women will drive them downright mad, if they are allowed to vote. Mrs Anderson has met this droll suggestion by affirming, from her own professional experience, the good effect, more interesting occupations, more important objects in life have on women's health, bodily and mental. If a woman finds her interest in politics bringing her to the brink of insanity, she will perhaps, under proper medical advice, be able to refrain; but that is her own affair. We do not legislate to prevent *men* from going mad if they choose.

2 Take, as one instance, the laws of the custody and guardianship of children, whereby the married (only the *married*) mothers, they whose sex's special and highest function is said to be the maternal, are denied any legal right over their own offspring past the first few years of infancy, as against the will of the father, whatever or whoever he may be, living or dead.

3 This is the more needful since legislation for women, whether so called protective or other, is more and more taking the shape of restrictions on their personal liberty.

4 The number of women supporting themselves by manual labour, alone, is stated at three millions.

5 He *is* supposed to be bound to keep her off the rates, no more; but this practically means merely that she will be refused relief, if her husband is known to be able to support her.

6 *Ought Women to learn the Alphabet?*, T. W. Higginson.

Lydia E. Becker

*Liberty, Equality, Fraternity**

1874

THE above words, which have hitherto been the motto of those
who sought to establish the principles they affirm, have lately
been adopted by an eminent man as the title of a book, the
professed object of which is to oppose the development of the
ideas they represent. The particular application of the principles
implied by the words, which Mr Fitzjames Stephen has set
himself to controvert, is embodied in the writings of Mr John
Stuart Mill; and three books, the Essay on Liberty, the Subjection
of Women, and the work on Utilitarianism, are selected as
exemplifications of each of the three ideas from which Mr Stephen
feels himself impelled to express his 'dissent in the strongest way.'

We are not here concerned with the first and last of these
subjects, although it appears to us that Mr Stephen has not
represented his opponent quite fairly, and has drawn inferences
from the position he attributes to Mr Mill which are not deducible
from Mr Mill's own language. We have never understood
'Liberty' to mean – 'the removal of all restraint on human
conduct;' nor do we believe that Mr Mill, or any disciple of what
Mr Stephen calls 'The Religion of Humanity,' interprets it in that
sense. We think, also, that the method adopted by Mr Stephen of
drawing out a set of propositions in his own words, which he says

*Originally published in the *Women's Suffrage Journal*.

are deducible from the work under consideration, and then setting himself to refute, not the original statements of his opponent, but his own version of them, which to other eyes often appears strangely distorted, transcends the limits of fair controversy.

In reading Mr Stephen's book one would think that he regarded liberty as a curse, and that he looked to restraint and coercion as the most effectual means of promoting the good of mankind. How such a faith is reconcilable with the profession of 'Liberal' politics we leave to the next constituency which Mr Stephen may canvass on such grounds to discover and determine. But there was a time when the trumpet gave forth a different sound. In 1862 the English law courts were called upon to decide a momentous issue in the cause of religious liberty. Dr Williams, in the exercise of the freedom secured to the ministers of the Established Church, published an essay containing opinions then unpopular, and supposed by many to be contrary to law. He was prosecuted; and the penalty would have been deprivation of his living and his status as a beneficed clergyman. He was fortunate in an advocate who knew how to pierce the clouds of popular prejudice which had obscured the true issue, and to bring out the grand and fundamental principles on which the question hinged. Mr Fitzjames Stephen's defence of Dr Williams was subsequently published in a volume, and it doubtless formed an epoch in the mental history of all thoughtful persons into whose hands it fell, and who were previously unaware of the legal and historical facts on which the argument is based. Even at this distance of time, and when the immediate interest of the controversy has passed away, we turn to the book with renewed admiration for the noble thoughts and noble language in which it abounds. Freedom is its watchword. 'Do not assume the functions of a legislator, and that for the sake of restraining, and not enlarging liberty.' And he speaks of the cause he is defending as 'a cause which might dignify the greatest genius that ever wore these robes, which might enlist the warmest sympathies of the human heart, for it is the cause of learning, of freedom, and of reason.' We do not believe that the advocate will command these sympathies in an equal degree, when the cause he is defending is that of restraint, coercion, and force.

The portion of Mr Stephen's later work with which we are most directly concerned is that in which he maintains the expediency of the legal subordination of one sex to the other. We advert to this, not because there is any novelty in the views advanced by Mr Stephen, but because the grounds on which he bases his opinion are simply the old common-places; and it is instructive to find that so accomplished an advocate can neither discover any fresh arguments nor dress up the old ones in a logical manner. He says, – 'The first point is to consider whether it (i.e. the law) ought to treat them (i.e. men and women) as equals, although, as I have shown, they are not equals.' Now, it appears to us that a fallacy underlies these words. The assumption implied in the question is that the law ought to treat as equals those only who are equals in moral, physical, and intellectual vigour. If this be so the law ought not to treat all men as equals, since there are among men all gradations of physical and intellectual vigour. But if the personal rights of all men are equal in all things that concern their individuality as men, notwithstanding all differences of personal strength and power, logic seems to demand that the personal rights of women and men shall be equal in all that concerns their individuality as human beings, notwithstanding any difference which may exist between them in physical strength. Another false assumption is that the recognition of equality before the law implies that the law is supposed to secure equality of condition among men, or as between men and women. But the equality for which we contend is aimed at no such conclusion. It is the equality which may be fairly demanded by those who are started on the race of life. It is the duty of the umpire in a race to see that all the competitors start on a footing of equality. It is no part of his duty to provide that they shall reach the goal in equal line.

Mr Stephen has mentioned the inequality of age as one which is and which ought to be recognised by the law in bestowing unequal rights on persons of unequal age, and he places the inequality of sex on the same footing. But the inequality of rights between young and adult persons does not extend to all personal rights; there are certain rights secured to the youngest infant – to the unconscious babe – which the law protects as jealously as the rights of the strongest man. The law allows and secures property rights to the unborn child. The law protects with the highest sanction known to it the life of the new-born babe, equally with that of the full-grown man. It is clear, therefore, that there are certain personal rights with which society and the law invest men at an age when they are utterly unable to assert or even comprehend them. If it were thought expedient to invest women with equal property rights with men, and with the electoral franchise, the law would be as competent to secure these rights to women – notwithstanding any inferiority in physical power – as it is to secure the property rights of infants, who are infinitely weaker than women, but who are in this respect treated by the law as the equals of the strongest men.

The legal disabilities, founded on inequality of age, differ so essentially from those founded on inequality of sex, that no argument can be drawn from expediency in one case as to expediency in the other. The same essentially inherent personal rights are recognised in men of all ages – but during the period when their faculties are immature they are disabled from the exercise of functions which require a certain degree of maturity of powers for their due performance. An infant cannot divest himself of property, or bind himself by contract; these disabilities are imposed for his own protection. An infant cannot exercise the franchise; this disability is imposed for the benefit of the State, which rightly requires, as a qualification for the suffrage, a presumed age of discretion for its exercise. No inference can be drawn from the fact that 'perhaps a third or more of the average duration of human life – and that the portion of it in which the strongest, the most durable, and beyond all comparison the most important impressions are made on human beings, the period when character is formed – must be passed by every one in a state of submission, dependence, and obedience to orders;' to the conclusion that half of the human race should remain throughout their whole lives in a condition of subjection. The influence exercised by this state of tutelage and obedience on the mind of an individual who knows that it is but the preparation for a period of his life when he shall become independent, and even be called upon to assume towards others the attitude of commander or guardian, will be widely different from that exercised on the mind of one who is brought up in the faith that it is a natural and permanent condition. There may be differences of opinion as to the duties and responsibilities which ought to be imposed by the State on men and women, just as there may be with regard to different classes of men; but there is an essential diversity of principle between those who would class women, as to personal rights, with children, who are necessarily in a state of tutelage, and those who would class them with men, who are dealt with as competent to direct their own actions and affairs. The question at issue between Mr Mill and Mr Stephen in this controversy is simply whether women are human beings with the full rights and responsibilities of humanity, or whether they are a superior kind of inferior beings, whose personal rights and duties must be regarded as subordinate to those of men. Whether, in fact, the ludicrous misapplication which is so commonly made, both in jest and earnest, of the phrase 'lords of the creation,' by using it with reference to the male sex instead of to the human race, is to be the rule on which the relative political and social position of the two sexes of humanity is to be based.

Mr Stephen says 'If society and Government ought to recognise the inequality of age as the foundation of an inequality of rights of that importance,' – (i.e. that of command and obedience) – 'it appears to me at least equally clear that they ought to recognise the inequality of sex for the same purpose, if it is a real inequality.' We deny the proposition on which Mr Stephen bases his inference, and we deny the justness of the inference drawn. The relations of command and obedience which are admitted between parents and children are not based on mere inequality of age. They depend on the fulfilment of the conditions and performance of the duties of parentage. A child owes obedience to his own parents, or to those who stand towards him in the place of parents; but he owes no obedience towards other men merely because there is an inequality of age between him and them. The ground of the relation is the dependence of the child, who from weakness is unable to support and govern himself, on the sustenance and authority of the parent for maintenance and guidance. As soon as the child has gathered strength to depend on itself the 'inequality of age' is not recognised in this country as furnishing the basis of a claim to obedience, although in some countries the filial relation is or was so recognised.

The sole reason for the subjection of infants to their parents and guardians is the fact that infants are unable to maintain and govern themselves. The subjection is not for the benefit of or for the sake of the parents, but for the sake of the maintenance and education of the children. It is temporary in its duration, and tends to train children by habit of obedience into the capacity for command. The subjection of women to men is different in its reason, in its character, and in its duration. Women are capable of maintaining themselves and of governing themselves, without other assistance from men than that which men render to each other in the ordinary relations of business and society. There are vast numbers of women who maintain themselves by their own exertions, who owe nothing to the personal protection of individual men; nay, who may have helpless or incapable men dependent on them. Mr Gladstone stated in the House of Commons that 'the number of self-depending women is increasing from year to year, especially in our great towns.' We say with Mr Gladstone that 'this is a very serious fact;' and we may adopt Mr Stephen's style of argument and say if it be true that there is a progressive increase in the number of self-dependent women the law ought to recognise that fact.

The subjection of women to men is different in character from that of children to their parents, inasmuch as it is maintained avowedly for the sake of securing to men the services of women as wives, toys, housekeepers, or domestic servants. Men who oppose the enfranchisement of women are not afraid or ashamed to imply that if women were free they would not consent to hold these relations to men, and therefore that it is necessary to hold them in legal subjection in order to secure the permanence of domestic relations. The subjection of children to their parents is never advocated for the sake of the value of the children's labour to the parents, nor for reasons analogous to what has been called the 'cold mutton and buttons argument,' which is still so popular with certain classes of men, neither do parents claim that vested right to the services of their children which some men claim in virtue of their sex to the domestic services of women.

The subjection of women to men is different from that of children to their parents, in that the one is temporary and disciplinary, the other permanent and lifelong. The temporary subjection of the infant to the parent is an accidental relation of two persons having inherently equal personal rights. The permanent subjection of women is affirmed to be a relation which pre-supposes inherently *unequal* personal rights. Therefore any inference from the expediency of maintaining the subjection of infants to their own parents to the expediency of maintaining the subjection of all women to all men is faulty as to fact and reasoning.

Mr Stephen's proposition is that society and Government ought to recognise inequality of sex as the foundation of inequality of rights. He illustrates this proposition by stating that if we were engaged in a great war it might be necessary to have a conscription both for land and sea service. He asks, 'ought men and women to be subject to it indiscriminately?' and he implies that an answer in the negative should be taken as a confirmation of his proposition. But the question cannot be reduced to such a narrow issue. In case of a conscription men would not be subject to it *indiscriminately*, the maimed, the blind, the halt, and the aged would be exempt, at least, until all the able-bodied had been called out. Yet no-one proposes to recognise a difference in the personal rights of able-bodied and infirm men, based on their liability to compulsory military service. In the next place a conscription could only take place in a great national emergency, and, in such a crisis, women equally with men would be called upon to devote themselves to the service of their country, both by contributing the sinews of war, and by personal exertion and risk of some kind. There are more kinds of service, even of military service, than actual bearing of arms, and more kinds of force, even in warfare, than material force. When Nelson joined the fleet at Trafalgar he added one to its numerical strength, yet the frail one-armed man brought moral force so great, that it was said that every ship was doubly manned from that instant. When France lay prostrate at the feet of England's king, a woman brought force enough to an army and a nation to enable them to repel the invader; and though this be the age and France the land of pilgrimages to the scene of supernatural revelations said to have been vouchsafed to women, we may be pardoned for believing that the spirit which inspired the Maid of Orleans was the womanly spirit of courage, patriotism, and self-devotion, that this spirit is of no particular age or country; and that in any great crisis touching the life of the nation the daughters of England, as well as her sons, would bear an equal if not a similar part in the services and the sacrifices which the nation as a whole was called upon to render. It would be as reasonable to say that because men do not hazard their lives in the duties of maternity they ought to be deprived of political rights, as to say that because women are not called upon to run the risk of being shot in the service of the country they are therefore not to be counted as citizens. As a matter of fact, we understand that the percentage of women who lose their lives in the dangers incident to them in the profession of marriage exceeds the percentage of soldiers killed in battle. Why should the risk of life be thought so honourable and heroic in the one sex as to form the basis for claiming a monopoly of a voice in the government, and so little worthy of honour in the other that the mere liability to be called upon to enter the condition of life which demands it is to be held as a permanent disqualification for the exercise of political rights?

Mr Stephen has adduced military service as a subject on which inequality of treatment, founded on a radical inequality of the two sexes, is admitted. He claims education as another subject on which the same question presents itself. He says, 'Are boys and girls to be educated indiscriminately, and to be instructed in the same things? Are boys to learn to sew, to keep house, and to cook; and are girls to play cricket, to row, and to be drilled like boys? I cannot argue with a person who says "Yes." A person who says "No" admits an inequality of the sexes on which education must be founded, and which it must therefore perpetuate and perhaps increase.'

We may here remark that Mr Stephen's professed inability to argue with a person who maintains a given proposition does not necessarily prove the proposition to be false. Plato held the doctrine that boys and girls ought to be educated indiscriminately and taught the same things. Were the philosopher to re-appear and maintain this doctrine, Mr Stephen would dismiss him with the remark, 'I cannot argue with Plato.' But something more than this would be needed in order to prove that Plato was in the wrong. There are many doctrines, in themselves erroneous, which are believed by people who are sufficiently reasonable to be capable of being convinced by an opponent who has the ability to argue and to prove that they are unsound. There is no proposition so false and absurd that its falseness and absurdity cannot be demonstrated by argument. This does not imply the assertion that everybody can be convinced by the argument, because there are some persons who are unable to follow a chain of reasoning, or to judge adequately of the value of evidence. If an astronomer were to say, 'I cannot argue with a man who maintains that the earth is flat,' such a declaration would go no way towards proving that the earth was round. The proposition that the earth is round was established by men who knew how to argue with those who believed that it was flat; and the principles which are to serve as the basis for just legislation must be established by the same methods as have served for the discovery and recognition of the laws of nature.

In the passage we have quoted Mr Stephen appears to play fast and loose with the word 'education' in a manner which is more convenient for his purpose than conducive to the elucidation of a sound principle. It is remarkable that the things which he selects as appropriate respectively to boys and girls lie altogether out of the province of 'education' in the proper sense of the word. The subjects he selects for girls are matters of purely technical or industrial instruction. Those for boys refer to physical education. There are some persons who think that boys would be no worse for being trained to use their fingers in some occupation which might beguile their leisure hours and produce some useful results. There are more who believe that the bodily training afforded to girls is miserably insufficient, and that they would be mentally and physically benefited by the introduction into their schools of athletic exercises similar in spirit and purpose, if not exactly identical in kind, with those practised by boys. But setting aside these considerations, we can afford to make Mr Stephen a present of the admission that every girl should be taught to sew, to keep house, and to cook, and every boy be taught to row, to play cricket, and be drilled, without prejudice to the proposition that boys and girls ought to be educated alike, and to be instructed in the same things. We object to the use Mr Stephen makes of the word 'indiscriminately,' for we suppose he would not allow that all boys should be educated *indiscriminately*, and instructed in the same things. Since the whole field of human knowledge is too vast to be mastered by any one mind, there must be discrimination in selecting the particular subjects of instruction for each youth with reference to individual tastes, capacities, and circumstances in life. But the main purposes of education are the same whatever be the differences in its method and appliances. These are, the acquisition of information, the cultivation of habits of observation and reasoning, and the application of the knowledge and reasoning so acquired to the general purposes of life. There is no difference between boys and girls as to the manner in which they must severally acquire the mastery over any special subject of study. As there is no royal road, so there is no female road to learning distinct from that which must be traversed by men. We do not understand whether Mr Stephen means to affirm that there are some branches of a liberal education which women have no right to cultivate. But it would seem that he does mean this when he 'admits an inequality between the sexes on which education must be founded, and which it must therefore perpetuate and perhaps increase.'

Now we think Mr Stephen should not have left matters in this undefined state. If only in compassion to those women, if such there be, who are content to accept his limitation of their mental sphere, as one beyond which no woman ought to pass, he should have condescended to explain somewhat more clearly what are the subjects of study to which he considers women have unequal rights with men. The old-fashioned notion was that boys should be taught classics and mathematics, and girls modern languages and accomplishments. The rule has become so far modified that it is no longer deemed unfeminine for a woman to understand Latin, or effeminate for a boy to know French. The old landmarks are removed, and the oracle sets up no new ones in their place. We should like to know also whether supposing the field of education is to be partitioned between boys and girls, whether male trespassers on the feminine portion are to be warned off as inexorably as girls who may show a desire to wander in the forbidden masculine ground? We are persuaded that could such a separation be effected between the education afforded to boys and girls respectively, that the consequences would be disastrous in the extreme to the mental culture of both; that there is no foundation for the assumption that the law ought to recognise an inequality between the sexes as to the right to education, that the existing inequality with regard to educational endowments and appliances is unjust and injurious in the highest degree, not only to the girls themselves, but to the community of which they will hereafter become the mothers; and further, that no human being has a right to prescribe to another human being the limit which must not be passed in the cultivation of the mental powers either as to direction or extent. Equal opportunities should be afforded to all children, without distinction of sex, for acquiring such education as may be within reach of their means, and no differences as to general culture should exist between the men and the women who associate together in the same rank of life. Individual inequalities of the widest kind there always will and must be, but there should exist no general inequality between the intellectual culture of men and women founded on difference of sex.

Mr Stephen says, 'Follow the matter a step further to the vital point of the whole question – marriage. All that I need consider in reference to the present purpose is whether the laws and moral rules should regard it as a contract between equals or as a contract between a stronger and a weaker person involving subordination for certain purposes on the part of the weaker to the stronger.' Now, we say that the special relations of man and woman in marriage are *not* the vital point of the whole question as to the political and personal rights of women. Women are women before they are wives, and have rights independent of and antecedent to the latter relation. If it is just to place the wife in the status of legal subjection, to whom does the unmarried woman owe obedience? We say that the personal and political rights of unmarried women ought to be equal and similar to those of unmarried men, and that the conditions of the marriage contract ought to be determined by the free consent of both the sexes who are parties to it, and not arbitrarily imposed by one sex on the other by physical force. But Mr Stephen says, 'If the parties to a contract of marriage are treated as equals it is impossible to avoid the inference that marriage, like other partnerships, may be dissolved at pleasure.' To us it appears that instead of being impossible to avoid, it is impossible to draw such an inference from such premises. It would be equally easy, and equally untrue to say – if marriage is regarded as a contract between a stronger and a weaker person, involving subordination on the part of the weaker, it is impossible to avoid the inference that marriage might be dissolved at the pleasure of the stronger party. The fact is the permanence of the marriage contract does not depend upon the strength or the pleasure of either of the parties to it, but upon the law of the land; and the law would be equally powerful to enforce its permanence, whether it were regarded as a contract between equals or as a contract between persons of unequal antecedent rights. The law secures the permanency of the marriage tie by refusing its sanction to other engagements contracted by one party during the lifetime of the other, and by enforcing on appeal the compulsory 'restitution of conjugal rights.' This sanction could be maintained quite as well whether marriage was considered as a contract between equals or unequals in personal rights.

Mr Stephen is good enough to allow that 'No one contends that a man ought to have power to order his wife about like a slave, and beat her if she disobeys him.' We are very much obliged to him for the concession, but we do not see how it is to be defended on his own principles. We are afraid that as a matter of fact a great many men do order their wives about like slaves, and beat them if they disobey, sometimes even if they do not disobey. What answer would Mr Stephen make to a man who treated his wife in this manner, and who turned his own arguments on him? If physical force is the foundation of personal rights, the man who beats his wife establishes his right to do so by that which Mr Stephen considers the foundation of all law. Put a case in which a man orders his wife to do something which she considers that he has no right to command. Here the issue is a difference of opinion, and a conflict of will, between husband and wife. Granted that the wife ought to obey her husband and give way. But suppose she will not, what has the husband a right to do in such a case? After exhausting all peaceable means of persuasion, he may either beat his wife till she obeys, or he may, on finding all persuasion useless, give way to her rather than resort to physical force. Is the first course justifiable? and if not, why not, on Mr Stephen's principles, when the man has no alternative between submitting to his wife's will, or coercing her by physical force? Suppose that it is a case in which even Mr Stephen would admit that the wife was in the right and the husband in the wrong, as in the instance he adduces of the captain giving an order to the lieutenant which the latter, who is the better seaman, knows to be wrong. There is no doubt that the captain in such a case would be justified legally and morally in the employment of any degree of physical force necessary to enforce obedience in case of contumacy on the part of the lieutenant. He would betray his trust if on being satisfied that his own judgment was right, he were to refrain from putting his subordinate in irons, or even proceeding to stronger measures in a case of emergency. But is there any corresponding right in a husband to enforce his commands by similar means? Mr Stephen says 'no;' but what would he say to a man who addressed his wife, stick in hand, in the following words quoted from 'Liberty, Equality, Fraternity' – 'It is impossible to lay down principles of legislation at all, unless you are prepared to say I am right and you are wrong, and your view shall give way to mine, quietly, gradually, and peaceably, but one of us two must rule and the other must obey, and I mean to rule' – and who applied this reasoning practically by means of the stick?

It may be said that this is an extreme case, but the soundness of a principle can only be tested by applying to an extreme case. If it breaks down when pushed to its legitimate conclusion it cannot be a right one.

There are two principles on which the subjection of women to men in marriage can be maintained. The one considers the parties to it as having antecedently unequal personal rights; divides the people into two classes according to sex, and decrees that the one class shall be subject to the other irrespective of the personal relations of contract between individual men and women. The other considers that all human beings, whether male or female, have the same inherent personal rights. As the principle is more directly expressed by a reviewer of Mr Stephen's book in the *Quarterly Review*, 'That women have an equal right with men to recognition as persons, and to every civil right following on that recognition, is no longer likely to be disputed in any quarter.' In passing we may be allowed to express our surprise that such an assertion should be made in reviewing a book, one of the main objects of which is to dispute the proposition that women have equal civil rights with men. The recognition of equal antecedent rights between men and women is perfectly compatible with the recognition of subordination for special purposes of women to men in the marriage relation, just as the recognition of the equal personal rights of all men is compatible with the recognition of subordination for special purposes of some men to others in the relations of commanding and subordinate officers and men, and masters and servants. There is nothing degrading in such a relation, nothing humiliating in the obedience so rendered. It is a case of voluntary association for a special purpose, which can only be carried out by allowing legal authority to rest somewhere, and the obedience is limited to matters which concern the business of the partnership. The rights of masters and servants are unequal in the affairs of the household; they are equal in matters outside this domain. A man may lawfully order his coachman to drive him in a given direction, but if the coachman be an elector the master may not lawfully order him to vote for a particular candidate. A husband may lawfully order his wife to do certain things; he may not lawfully order her to go to a particular church, or profess any particular creed, against her own convictions. A man whose wife is a physician, or a member of a School Board has no authority over her with respect to the treatment of her patients, or the administration of the Education Act. It is perfectly possible to maintain the expediency of the subjection of wives to husbands for the special purposes of family government, along with the recognition of the equal rights of men and women who do not hold these relations to one another, and of husbands and wives in matters unconnected with family affairs. The *Quarterly* reviewer, to whom we have previously alluded, says, very justly, that there are two questions about women's rights which have been a good deal confused – the reviewer says by Mr Mill and his friends – we say by Mr Stephen. The first – which the reviewer says should never have been a question at all – is whether the legal nullity of women under the old Roman and under the feudal law, should be the legal doctrine of days of more advanced civilisation; the second is whether marriage involves or does not involve a subjection of woman to man which is natural and necessary, and not legal and artificial in its origin. Mr Stephen's arguments are addressed mainly to the latter question, and when he has, as he believes, proved his case, he says he has established the general proposition that men and women are not equals, and that the laws which affect their relations ought to recognise that fact.

Mr Stephen appears to base his argument on the general proposition that the law or the Legislature ought to take a survey of all sorts and conditions of men, to observe whether there is any actual inequality in their relations or conditions, and whenever it finds any existing inequality it should 'recognise that fact,' by legislation based on the inequality, and designed to perpetuate it. We do not know whether Mr Stephen is or was an advocate of negro slavery, but the arguments he advances for the maintenance of the subjection of women would have applied equally well to the maintenance of slavery in the United States. He might have harangued the Abolitionists in the style he uses about Mr Mill's claim for equal rights for women. 'Ingenious people may argue about anything, but all the talk in the world will never shake the proposition that [white men] are stronger than [negroes] in every shape. They have greater muscular and nervous force, greater intellectual force, and greater vigour of character. This general truth has led to a division of labour between [white men] and [negroes] the general outline of which is as familiar as the general outline of the differences between them. These are the facts, and the question is whether the law and justice of man ought to recognise this difference.'

Mr Stephen grossly misrepresents Mr Mill's doctrine by the gloss which he intrudes into it. He speaks of 'Mr Mill's doctrine that the law of the strongest, *or the law of force*, has been abandoned in these days.' The words in italics are an interpolation which alter the meaning of the doctrine. Mr Mill's words are – 'We now live in a state in which the law of the strongest seems to be entirely abandoned as the regulating principle of the world's affairs' – a very different proposition from that which Mr Stephen combats. We understand Mr Mill to mean that the state of society in which the law of the supremacy of the will of the strongest individuals over the lives and the wills of the weaker members has given place to a state of society in which the force of law is supreme alike over the strong and the weak. The maintenance of personal rights no longer depends on personal strength, but on the force of the law. Mr Mill maintains that the subjection of women is the relic of a condition of things in which law, or the collective force of society, was weak, and individuals were strong, and that it is unsuited to a state of society in which the law has irresistible force, and the individual is powerless before the law. In days of old a powerful noble or an audacious bandit not unfrequently openly and successfully defied the power of the law and the Government. In these days there is no safety for the law breaker, save in concealment or flight. The illustrations Mr Stephen has given by way of confuting the doctrine he foists on Mr Mill do in fact so admirably confirm that on which he really founds his claim for the enfranchisement of women that we give them here. He illustrates the state of society, which Mr Mill calls 'the law of the strongest,' by the condition of Scotland in the fourteenth century, as portrayed in Scott's novel *The Fair Maid of Perth*. 'My name,' says one of the characters, 'is the Devil's Dick, of Hellgarth, well-known in Annandale for a gentle Johnstone. I follow the stout Laird of Wamphray, who rides with his kinsman the redoubted Lord of Johnstone, who is banded with the doughty of Earl Douglas, and the earl, and the lord, and the laird and I, the esquire, fly our hawks where we find our game, and ask no man whose ground we ride over.' Mr Stephen says that the first impression on comparing this spirited picture with the Scotland we all know is that the fourteenth century was entirely subject to the *law of force*, and that Scotland in the nineteenth century had ceased to be the theatre of force at all. We say that the impression, from Mr Mill's point of view, would be that in the fourteenth century Scotland was subject to the *law of the strongest*, 'the good old rule, the simple plan, that those should take who had the power, and those should keep who can,' and that in the nineteenth century, the reign of the strongest had given place to the reign of law. Under the first rule women could not have assured to them equal rights with men, because they have not equal personal strength to maintain them. Under the second rule women can have equal rights secured to them with men, because the maintenance of rights assured by law does not depend in any way on personal strength. Mr Stephen says, 'Look a little deeper, and this impression' (i.e. the impression that Scotland in the fourteenth century was subject to the law of force, and that Scotland in the nineteenth century has ceased to be the theatre of force at all) 'is as false, not to say childish, as the supposition that a clumsy row-boat, manned by a quarrelsome crew who can neither keep time with their oars nor resist the temptation to fight among themselves, displays force, and that an ocean steamer which will carry a townful of people to the end of the earth at the rate of three hundred miles a day so smoothly that, during the greater part of the time, they are unconscious of any motion or effort whatever, displays none.' The fact that a supposition is childish ought to be a guarantee even to Mr Stephen that a reasoner like Mr Mill never could have made it. The simile is another apt illustration of the doctrine really maintained by Mr Mill. While the motive power of the ship of the State was vested in individual rowers, and the direction of the voyage determined by the greatest number of the strongest arms, without reference to law or reason, it is evident that women, however deeply interested in the result of the venture, could have exercised no effective control over the guidance of the craft. But in the case of the ocean steamer owned, say, by a company of shareholders of both sexes, whose voice in the direction of the voyage is determined, not by the degree of physical strength, but by the amount of the shares they hold, women shareholders could exercise power on exactly the same terms, and at neither greater nor less disadvantage, than men.

Mr Stephen says, 'The force which goes to govern the Scotland of these days is to the force employed for the same purpose in the fourteenth century what the force of a line-of-battle ship is to the force of an individual prize-fighter. The reason why it works so quietly is that no one doubts either its existence or its crushing superiority to any individual resistance which could be offered to it.' We recognise this fact with gladness, for it is the basis of the possibility of the recognition of the equal rights of women and men before the law. Let the collective moral and physical force of the whole community of men and women be organised in support of laws which declare equal personal rights to all human beings, and the laws so supported will prove adequate to assure and protect in the exercise of these rights even the weakest man, woman, or child in the community, and to repress the usurpation of lawless power by the strongest baron who might awake out of a Rip Van Winkle's sleep in the belief that he still lived in the good old times.

There are many passages in Mr Stephen's book which convey the impression that he thinks the change that has taken place in society since the days of the 'gentle Johnstone' a matter for regret. Apparently he does not think political power worth having unless a man can grab a large share of it, and use it in his own way. Speaking of the recent extension of the suffrage he says, 'we have succeeded in cutting political power into very little bits, which with our usual hymns of triumph we are continually mincing, till it seems not unlikely that many people will come to think that a single man's share of it is not worth having at all.' He says again, 'Political power has changed its shape, but not its nature. The result of cutting it up into little bits is simply that the man who can sweep the greatest number of them into one heap will govern the rest. The strongest man in some form or other will always rule.' We may admit this last proposition while giving an emphatic denial to the first. Granted that under any form of representative government the strongest man will always rule, there is an essential difference in the nature of the political power exercised by a representative and a despotic ruler. The difference is occasioned by that same sweeping process which Mr Stephen dismisses so unceremoniously. When political power is distributed in very little bits over a large number of persons, the bits cannot be swept into a heap by force, even by the strongest ruler. He must give or offer some advantage to the possessors of them, or must persuade them that he is the fittest man to rule, before they will cast their bits within the sweep of his brush. And if he disappoints their expectations they can disperse the heap as readily as it was swept together, and his power dissolves like summer snow. The wide distribution of political power renders its possession by the people more secure. It may be easy to rob one man of five pounds – it would be impracticable to rob a thousand men of one penny each.

The 'mincing' process by which political power has been sub-divided and spread over so wide an area, and so many classes and interests, both facilitates and necessitates the distribution of a share to women. It facilitates it, because under the conditions on which it is dispensed it is easy to give to women an equality of political rights, without giving them such an actual share in the

Government as would seriously interfere with the existing order of things, or have the effect of superseding the general conduct of the affairs of government by men. Even under universal suffrage it is probable that the greatest amount of actual political work would continue to be done by men, at least for a long time to come. Under household suffrage, where the men voters so greatly outnumber the women, there would not be the slightest probability of the disturbance of the present method of government. The extension can therefore be made without inconvenience and without risk.

The general distribution of political power necessitates the giving of a share to women, because every extension of the franchise to classes hitherto excluded lowers and weakens the status of the classes which remain out of the pale. Agricultural labourers in counties, and women householders everywhere, are now excluded from influence over the Government. They possess none of those 'little bits' of political power which those who would govern the country need to sweep into a heap by means of persuasion, and offers of just measures and legislative protection. The larger the body of unrepresented persons in the country, the stronger is that body. If the unrepresented body consists of two distinct classes having interests not always in common, and sometimes apparently antagonistic, as in the classes of employers and employed, it is evident that if one class is admitted to the safeguards of representation the one left out is in a worse position than before. It has obtained another master in place of a fellow-sufferer, and its interests will have less chance than ever of being considered, as they will have to withstand the rivalship of those belonging to the class just admitted to a share of these magical and all-potent 'bits' of political power.

It is because each 'bit' is so small that it is safe to assign a bit even to the uneducated and indifferent elector. No man or woman, however stupid or silly, could do much mischief with the infinitesimal share of power comprised in his or her particular 'bit.' It is perhaps for this reason that so many intelligent women and men are slow to appreciate the value of a vote. Because the mere possession and occasional exercise of a vote seems a small thing in itself, is actually an infinitesimal factor in the sum of most persons' experience, they imagine that it is an equally unimportant matter to the interests of a class. One drop is an infinitesimal item in a shower, yet it would not be safe to say that the shower is unimportant because each drop composing it is a very small thing. It matters little or nothing personally to any individual woman whether she has a vote or not. It is of vital consequence to the interests of women as a class that they should have representative government.

We have limited our remarks on Mr Stephen's book to those portions having especial reference to the enfranchisement of women. But it is not only liberty for women which Mr Stephen deprecates; he seems also averse to the application of the principle of liberty to men. In commenting on 'the opinion that laws which recognise any sort of inequality between human beings are mere vestiges of the past, against which as such there lies the strongest of all presumptions' he takes exception to 'the assumption that the progress of society is from bad to good; that the changes of the last few centuries in our own, and in other leading nations of Western Europe, have been changes for the better,' and while not altogether denying it, he says he cannot assent to it. 'Even if the inequality between men and women is a vestige of the past, and likely to be destroyed by the same process that has destroyed so many other things, that is no reason for helping it on. The proper reflection may be "the more the pity." ' 'The waters are out, and no human force can turn them back, but I do not see why, as we go with the stream, we need sing Halelujah to the river god.' 'It is useless to lament, or even to blame, the inevitable.' We gather from these and similar utterances scattered through the book, first that Mr Stephen considers the movement for the enfranchisement of women to be a part of the general movement of society towards the abolition of class distinctions and legal inequalities, next, that he regards, not simply the enfranchisement of women, but the stream of modern progress of which it forms a part, with dislike and distrust, and, lastly, that he believes the change to be inevitable, and the result of forces which no human power can withstand.

Helen Bright Clark

Speech at a meeting held in support of the bill to remove the electoral disabilities of women, at the Victoria Rooms, Clifton, Bristol

9 March 1876

THE Bill to enfranchise women householders introduced by Mr Forsyth, is a very simple and moderate measure, so moderate, indeed, that some people who don't understand it wonder why it should call forth any enthusiasm; and it is not only a moderate Bill, it is an honest Bill, it means exactly what it says and no more. But when we urge this simplicity and modesty of our aim, we are sometimes met by the statement that we are trying to get something further. Well, in one sense we are. We are not seeking the franchise for women merely that they may have the amusement of handing in a ballot paper once in three or four years; we are seeking it for precisely the same reasons that working men and middle-class men desired and sought it, and with, I venture to think, as much reason. Some of us were not unmoved spectators of the last great struggle for Parliamentary Reform. We saw there the whole force of powerful sections of the community opposed for years to the enfranchisement of the working class; we saw the advocates of Reform denounced as mischievous agitators, and subjected to every kind of misrepresentation and abuse, but we did not see those men give up the work to which they had put their hands. They were confident of the justice of their cause and they persevered. Some of them were men who were not themselves excluded, to whom fortune had not been hard; but they had a great sympathy with their less fortunate fellow-countrymen, and they were ready to give years to the cause of their enfranchisement. Well, that cause is gained so far as the boroughs go, and what is the position of working men now? Do we not see a vastly increased attention to the needs and the feelings and the opinions of working men? Was not almost the first result of that measure a bill for the general education of their children, and does not every borough election show that even the very men who year after year opposed their admission to the franchise with all the influence they possessed, are now most eager to exhibit themselves, if possible, in the guise of true friends of the working class? Well, such lessons are not lost on us. The arguments that were convincing ten years ago are not less so now, and as for the various hobgoblins that are trotted out to frighten timid people, they are not new to us: most of them are very much the same as made their appearance during the last Reform agitation, and forty or fifty years ago, when the middle classes of this country were striving for something like fair representation, they played a still more conspicuous part. If you will look back to the speeches and debates of that day, you will find that the first Reform Bill, which I suppose most people now look upon as almost the foundation of our present electoral system, that that measure was regarded with the utmost alarm by the upper classes of this country. They predicted that it would produce the most disastrous consequences. It was to destroy the throne, the church, the constitution, and liberty itself, altogether. Well, we know that these things did not happen, and that, on the contrary, that measure brought peace and prosperity to this country. There are some people who are always afraid. I don't suppose that any measure of conspicuous justice was ever passed without frightening somebody. I remember reading in that charming and instructive book, *The Life of Sir Samuel Romilly*, that when he was endeavouring to remove from our statute book some of those barbarous laws which disgraced it fifty or sixty years ago, particularly when he had charge of the Bill to repeal the law that condemned to death anyone who stole from a shop to the value of five shillings, he met with the determined opposition of the Cabinet of that day, and of the bench of bishops. They said it was a daring innovation, and that innovations in our criminal law were to be deprecated! and Lord Ellenborough, who was considered a great authority, said he should like to know what would happen next? Well we all know that a good deal had to happen next, and surely the name of Romilly is beloved and revered – it should be especially so in this city of Bristol – when the names of those cruel bishops and Cabinet Ministers are almost forgotten. Now, our cause is in some respects even stronger than that of the working men, for though they were no doubt as a body excluded from representation, yet there were exceptions, and there was always the chance that a working man, by thrift or good fortune, or both might attain to a position of greater affluence, and thus secure a vote. But it is not so with women. The line is fixed and they are absolutely excluded, and no wealth or special interest, or knowledge of politics, can avail to put any woman on a footing of equality in this matter with the meanest male elector, and observe that this exclusion tells more forcibly now than it used to do. It is natural that women should begin to resent their exclusion more now that almost every other great class is enfranchised than they did when it was the exception to vote, and when exclusion was therefore much less marked. Women are often told that they are already sufficiently represented by their male relations. I can only say that that is not an arrangement that would be considered satisfactory by men amongst themselves, and I know no reason why it should be more so for women; and certainly, men who, while desiring and valuing the franchise for themselves, can yet see no reason why women should desire it, are clearly unfit and unable to represent us in this way, since it is evident that they apply a totally different set of rules to themselves and to us. During the last Reform agitation we heard a good deal of the educating effect of the franchise. It was admitted that a good many working men neither knew nor cared much about politics; but it was said that the best way to increase their self-respect and thoughtfulness was to give them a sense of responsibility, and to admit them to some share in the representation. Now I want to know why women are to be deprived of this great educational influence? If you teach girls and boys grammar and arithmetic, you teach them out of the same books and by the same methods. I never heard that there was one way for girls and another for boys if the end to be attained was the same, and why don't you teach them to be public-spirited in the same way? Is it not because some of you don't desire that women should be educated at all in this direction? But I ask, is it fair, is it just, that your wishes and your prejudices should be the measure of other people's rights? Some of you I dare say are liberal enough to allow art, and literature, and even science to women – but is it not 'Thus far shalt thou go and no farther.' Now I think this policy of exclusion with regard to women is a narrow and selfish one, for delightful and valuable as art and literature and science are in education, is there not something that comes even before these? We know that these things may thrive for a time at least under a corrupt government, but public virtue, an enlightened public opinion, these are the surest and indeed the only safeguards of good government. And I ask you now, even supposing you do not care that your daughters should receive this sort of training, how can you expect your sons to grow up high-minded and self-sacrificing in public matters, if you allow those who have so often the greatest influence in forming their early principles to be shut out from all sense of duty and responsibility in political matters? And now I should like to say a few words to those women – I dare say there are some here to-night, who have what may be called in this matter unbelieving husbands. Don't try to drive them; but try by all means to persuade them, only let it be by the most reasonable and judicious persuasion. Sometimes in a family even silence may be persuasive. I can quite sympathize with a man who is always under the apprehension that whatever subject is started, conversation will always come round in the end to women's suffrage. It does not appear so interesting and important to him as it does to you and me; and you must bear this in mind. I am sure that women need to use great tact and patience in this matter, and that for want of this tact and this consideration harm has sometimes been done to our cause. Now you know that one great fear that men have in connection with our movement is, lest an interest in politics and the admission of women householders to express that interest through their votes should draw women away from their domestic duties. It is a curious fear. They seem to forget that men have also domestic duties, and that amongst them is the grave and often very arduous one of providing for their families, and that the conscientious performance of these duties does not prevent a man from being an intelligent citizen and giving an intelligent vote – that is, if he has any intelligence in him to begin with. However, since this fear does undoubtedly beset many people's minds, let me urge on women to be especially careful that their lives should give no sort of colour to this idea. Do you try to make your homes more attractive, not less so because you have begun to think in a somewhat wider circle. And don't let the men with whom you are connected have any reason to think that politics will make women hard. Rather let them see, if possible, that your gentle sympathies, if, as I hope, you have these gentler sympathies they sometimes speak of, may tend to soften politics, and may perhaps do something to make a contest one of principles rather than personalities. If you take an interest in and study those subjects in which your fathers and brothers happen to be specially interested, depend upon it they will find it agreeable, and they will perhaps end in finding that your subjects are interesting to them. But we have not, and we do not wish to have, only a special class of interests. Wherever we look, whether in the country districts, we see the agricultural labourer living on very small wages – as much as one-sixth or one-seventh of those meagre wages too often paid him in cider; his children almost uneducated, himself landless, and sometimes almost homeless, in a country of wealthy men and large landed estates, and where the laws favour that accumulation of land; or whether we live among the crowded population of towns, with their many temptations, and their besetting sin of drunkenness; or whether we look to our enormous and still increasing military expenditure, with all its train of demoralisation and vice, and I am but just touching on two or three of the great dangers that threaten us, surely, wherever we turn our eyes, we cannot fail to see that the fields are white unto harvest, and that the labourers are too few. And it seems to me, if I may venture to say so, that the Lord of the harvest is in these days speaking in the ears of women and demanding from them a wider sympathy and a more earnest life. That they should no longer be content to shut themselves within narrow walls, but that they should venture to look forth on the evils that surround them, and ask themselves the causes of those evils, and whether it is not possible by joint effort to do something towards their removal. And do not give heed to those who would tell you that these dark blots on our civilisation are necessary evils – and do not be led away by the notion, which some may be ready to present to your mind, that your personal purity may be dimmed, or your real influence lessened, because in the strength of your increased love for your fellow creatures you venture to look deeper than you have hitherto done into the causes of human suffering. There are many kind and tender hearts among women, I know, that are pained by the suffering they see. They have long recognised it to be their duty to help and comfort the sufferer, but they have, perhaps, not been accustomed to look to human laws for some, I don't, of course, say all, of the causes of crime and poverty. We are sometimes told that we cannot make people sober and moral by Act of Parliament, and in a sense this is true. But it is not difficult to degrade and demoralize by law. It is easy to give the sanction of law to what could never have that of justice, and if people do what is in accordance with the spirit of the law they are generally satisfied. They are apt to make the law their standard of action, and hence it is of the greatest importance that the law should set forth a just and true standard. So long, for instance, as the law of England says that, when a man dies without a will, his landed property shall all go to the eldest son, even if it leaves the other children almost penniless, so long will average Englishmen think themselves justified in such an unnatural distribution; and so long as the law of divorce is unequal between men and women, will the sanction of the law be given to the idea that there is one standard of morality for men and another for women. Now, if the importance of laws is at all understood, I cannot see how anyone can suppose women to be less affected by them than men. As a matter of fact, they are more deeply concerned since they are subject not only to the laws made for people in general, but also to a number of special laws, made for them alone, made by men alone, and a good many of which it is obvious could never have been passed, if women had had any share in the representation. I think that, on the whole, we have had a great deal of kind help and fair dealing from men in this suffrage work. The various committees are deeply indebted to the thorough-hearted help they have received from the gentlemen belonging to them. I know it is specially the case on this committee, and I believe it to be so elsewhere. We are not afraid of those timid members of the House of Commons who have banded themselves together to defend nature, and revelation, and the British Constitution, against the women householders of this country. We mean to go straight on, and if some who have borne the burden and heat of many an earlier conflict are now resting from their labours, if some of them do not see their way to join us, well we must not expect too much. It is not, perhaps, given to any one to see all truth. We may each see a portion of the truth, and at any rate we may each, in our humble way, strive to extend those principles of justice which have had in the past, and I trust will ever continue to have, pure-minded and unflinching advocates.

John Bright, MP

Speech on the women's disabilities removal bill

26 April 1876

Amendment proposed, to leave out the word 'now,' and at the end of the Question to add the words 'upon this day six months,' – (*Viscount Folkestone.*)
After long debate, Question put, 'That the word "now" stand part of the Question:' – The House *divided*; Ayes 152, Noes 239; Majority 87.
Division List, Ayes and Noes
Words *added*: – Main Question, as amended, put, and *agreed to*: – Second Reading *put off* for six months.

SIR, I need hardly tell you that it is with extreme reluctance that I take part in this debate; but I am somewhat peculiarly circumstanced with regard to this question, and duty compels me, to make some observations. In the year 1867, when Mr Stuart Mill first made a proposition like that contained in this Bill to the House, I was one of those who went with him into the Lobby. In his autobiography he refers to this fact, and he says that I was one of those who were opposed to the proposition being submitted to the House, but that the weight of argument in its favour was so great that I was obliged to go with him into the Lobby. I can very honestly say that he was entirely mistaken in that statement. Though I did vote with him I voted under extreme doubt, and far more from sympathy with him – for whom in many respects, and

247

on many grounds, I had so great an admiration – than from sympathy with the proposition with which he was then identified, and at that time advocating. But if I had doubts then, I may say that those doubts have been only confirmed by the further consideration I have been able to give to this question. The Bill seems to be based on a proposition which is untenable, and which, I think, is contradicted by universal experience. In fact, it is a Bill based on an assumed hostility between the sexes. Now, I do not believe that any Hon Member in this House who is going to support this Bill entertains that view; but if Hon Members have been accustomed to read the speeches of the principal promoters of this Bill out-of-doors, and if they have had an opportunity, as I have had, on many occasions, of entering into friendly and familiar conversation on this question with those who support it I think they will be forced to the admission, that the Bill, as it is offered to us, and by those by whom and for whom it is offered to us, is a Bill based upon an assumed constant and irreconcilable hostility between the sexes. The men are represented as seeking to rule, even to the length of tyranny; and the women are represented as suffering injustice, even to the length or depth of slavery. These are words which are constantly made use of, both in the speeches and in the conversation of the women who are the chief promoters of this Bill. And this is not said of savage nations, or of savages – and there are some in civilized nations – but it is said of men in general, of men in this civilized and Christian country in which we live. What if we look over this country and its population would strike us more than anything else? It is this that at this moment there are millions of men at work sacrificing, giving up their leisure, their health, sustaining hardship, confronting it in every shape for the sake of the sustenance, the comfort, and the happiness of women and children. Yet it is of these men, of these millions, that language such as I have described is constantly made use, and made use of eminently by the chief promoters of this Bill. The object of the Bill is not the mere extension of the suffrage to three hundred or four hundred thousand persons; its avowed object is to enable women in this country to defend themselves against the tyranny of a Parliament of men, and the facts that are brought forward are of the flimsiest character. There is the question of the property of married women. There may be injustice with regard to the laws that affect the property of married women; but is there no injustice in the laws which affect the property of men? Have younger sons no right to complain just as much as married women? If a man dies in the street worth £100,000 in land, and he leaves no will, what does the fiat of this House say? It says that the £100,000 in land shall all go to the eldest boy, because he happened to come first into the world, and that the rest of the family of the man shall be left to seek their fortunes as they like. Is there any greater injustice than that? But that is an injustice which Parliament inflicts upon men as well as women; and the fact of there being some special or particular injustice of which women may or have a right to complain – I am not asserting or denying it – is no argument, no sufficient argument, for the proposition which is now before the House. I have observed when the question of the property of married women has been before Parliament – I think it was brought forward by the right hon. and learned Gentleman the Member for Southampton (Mr Russell Gurney) – that he was supported by several hon. and learned Gentlemen, lawyers of eminence in the House; and, so far as my recollection goes, the matter was discussed with great fairness, great good temper, great liberality, and changes were made which, to some extent, met the view of those who had proposed them. There can be no doubt then – I think no Member of the House on either side will doubt, or allow it to be said without contradicting it – that this House is not as fairly disposed to judge of all questions of that kind which affect women as it is qualified and willing to judge all questions of a similar or analogous character which affect men. If married women are wronged in any matter of this kind, surely we all know that many of our customs and laws in regard to property come down from ancient times, and from times when power was law, and when women had little power, and the possession and the defence of property was vested, and necessarily vested, almost altogether in men. But there is another side to this question. It seems almost unnecessary to quote it, but I would recommend some of those very people who blame Parliament in this matter to look at how much there is in favour of women in other directions. Take the question of punishment. There can be no doubt whatever that as regards that question there is much greater moderation, and I might say mercy, held out to women than there is to men. Take the greatest of all punishments for the greatest of all crimes. Since I have been in Parliament I think I could specify more than a score of instances in which the lives of women have been spared in cases where the lives of men would have been taken. It is a horror to me to have to speak in a civilized and Christian Assembly of the possibility of the lives of women being taken by the law, but the law orders it, and it is sometimes done; but whether it be from mercy in the Judge, or from mercy in the jury, or mercy in the Home Secretary, there can be no doubt whatsoever that the highest punishment known to the law is much more rarely inflicted upon women, and has been for the last thirty or forty years, than upon men. Also in all cases of punishment, I say the Judges and juries are always more lenient in disposition to women than they are to men. I might also point out to some of those ladies who are very excited in this matter that in cases of breach of promise of marriage, the advantage on their side seems to be enormous. As far as I can judge from the reports of the cases in the papers, they almost always get a verdict, and very often, I am satisfied, where they ought not to get it. Beyond that, the penalty inflicted is very often, so far as I can judge, greatly in excess of what the case demands. Take the small case now of taxation. We know that the advocates of this measure deal with very little questions, showing for instance how badly women are treated by Parliament. Take the case of domestic women-servants, who are numerous; they are not taxed, men are. That is an advantage to the women as against the men. I do not say that it is any reason why you should not pass this Bill; but I am only saying that these little differences exist, and will exist; they exist in every country, and under every form of government, and in point of fact have nothing whatever to do with the real and great question before us. The argument which tells with many persons who sign the Petitions to this House is the argument of equal rights. They say, if a man lives in a house and votes, and a woman lives in another house, why should not she vote also? That is a very fair and a very plain question, and one not always quite easy to answer. It is said, there can be no harm to the country that women should vote, and I believe that is a thing which many of us, even those who oppose this Bill, may admit. It is not a question which depends upon a proposition of that kind. As to the actual right, I would say nothing about it. I suppose, however, the country has a right to determine how it will be governed – whether by one man, whether by few, or whether by many. The intelligence and the experience and the opinion of the country must decide where the power must rest, and upon whom the suffrage shall be conferred. The hon. and learned Gentleman opposite (Mr Forsyth) told us that unless this Bill passed there would be a class injured and discontented, and reference has been made to the condition of the agricultural labourer. But I think there is no comparison between the two cases. If the landowners could only vote, the tenants would have a right to complain; and if the landowners and the tenants only voted, the labourer would have a right to complain. The landlord, no doubt, has interests different in many respects from the tenant, and the tenant and landlord different from the labourers; and if a whole class like the agricultural labourers, or like the agricultural tenants, were shut out, they would have a right to be discontended and to complain of the injustice or unwisdom of Parliament. So with regard to merchants, manufacturers, and their workpeople. But the great mistake is in arguing that women are a class. Why, the hon. and learned Gentleman the Member for Marylebone, who, being a lawyer of eminence and a great scholar, ought to be able to define rather more accurately, spoke more than once in the course of his speech as women as a class. Nothing can be more monstrous or absurd than such an appellation for women. Why, Sir, women, so to speak, are everywhere. Not in a class as agricultural labourers, or factory-workers. They are in your highest, your middle, your humblest ranks. They are our mothers, our wives, our sisters, and our daughters. They are as ourselves. We care as much for them sitting in this House as Members of Parliament and as legislators for the country as for ourselves, and they are as near our hearts here as in our homes and our families. I venture to say that it is a scandalous and an odious libel to say that women are a class, and that, therefore, they are excluded from our sympathy, and that Parliament can do no justice, or rather would do any injustice, in regard to them. If there be any fact which seems at any time to contradict this, I am sure it can arise only from the ignorance of Parliament; and that fair discussion such as we bring to bear upon all questions, will at no remote period, but at an early period, do all the justice which it is in the power of Parliament to do. So much' then with regard to these political wrongs. I do not believe that the women of England suffer in the least from not having what is called direct representation in this House. Politically, I believe it would be no advantage if they were so represented. I dismiss altogether the question of what may be called political wrongs, and come to consider whether this Bill has in it more than that which you read in its clauses. Some one has said in the course of the debate that there would be about 380,000 or 400,000 voters added by its passing to the present constituencies – about 13 percent. But the Bill, unfortunately for those who argue about political wrongs, excludes by far the greatest portion of women, and excludes those specially who, if there be any special qualification required for an elector, may be said to be especially qualified – that is the married women. They are older; they are, on the whole, generally more informed; they have greater interests at stake, and yet they are excluded. But, then, it is said by those outside, not by their Friends here – the right hon. Gentleman the Member for Halifax (Mr Stansfeld) went so far as to deny what I am about to say altogether, in which I think he was inaccurate and very injudicious – it is said outside that this Bill is an instalment only, that it is but one step in the path of the redemption of woman. Now, if that be so, it is very odd that those most concerned in the Bill do not appear to be aware of it, because I find that last year, or the year before, there was a general dispute on this matter. The hon. and learned Member for Marylebone himself will acknowledge that he knows that he has only very partially the confidence of his clients. They go with him, or he goes with them, in a certain direction, and they know that at the next milestone, or at some point to be approached by this Bill, they are to part company, and instead of having to listen to half-an-hour's or three-quarters-of-an-hour's pleasant speech on behalf of his present clients, we shall have no doubt to listen to a speech of equal length to show that he has gone so far that nothing could be more perilous than an attempt to go any further. But last year I recollect reading in a newspaper which is supposed to represent the opinions in some degree of a Member of this House who warmly sympathizes with the cause of those who promote this Bill a letter which I will read, because it does not say much more than is generally held by the warmest supporters of the Bill. It says –

> Married women cannot claim to vote as householders, but why should not they, as well as men, vote as lodgers? Since the law recognizes none but a direct payment for lodgings as conferring the franchise, why should not a married woman who desires it, and who possesses money independent of her husband, pay him for her lodging? Married women devoid of means could not make such an arrangement. But let us say, for argument's sake – suppose a wife's position is by English law established, the most abject possible for a human being short of absolute slavery; that she is a servant, differing from, and better than a slave, only inasmuch as her servitude is voluntarily assumed at her will, still, by the law, she retains the right to appraise her services, and to stipulate for her remuneration before she accepts a master, and that remuneration might enable her to constitute herself a lodger.

The lady who writes this – if it be a lady – then says –

> If the money value falls short of the requirements of the franchise, it is just that she, like men similarly poor, should not possess a vote.

That is signed, 'A Married Claimant to the Franchise;' and I believe, though in broader terms, that it expresses very much the kind of extravagant desire there is – I admit on the part of a few women – that this Bill should pass, and that other Bills naturally and logically following it, should at some future time pass. Now, in discussing this question, I am much more anxious to lay before the House the doubts and difficulties that I feel, than to say anything very strong either against the measure or against those who propose it. But I should like to ask two or three questions. How, for example, if this Bill passes, you will contend against further claims? When I was accustomed, and Friends with me, to ask the House to extend the franchise to the householders to any point below the then existing franchise, there were those who argued in this way – 'Well, but this will not settle the question; you will want more. Very likely you will go on to universal suffrage, or what is called manhood suffrage.' But if we did go on to that, we introduced no new principle; we understood what votes were, and that the alteration effected no great change or social revolution of any kind. But when you come to this question of giving votes to women, although the claim may become irresistible at some time, although it may be wrong or right – I am not going to set my opinion against those who differ from me – Parliament ought to have the sense to try and understand where it is going, and what it is intending to do. If this Bill passes, what will be the question asked of this House by some Hon Members whom I need not name. They will say, very reasonably – 'Shall marriage be a political disqualification? You have given a vote to all young women who are unmarried who occupy a house and have property, and to all old women who are widows who occupy a house and have property, what do you say to those who compose, it may be, nine-tenths of the whole, or a very large proportion, what do you say to them? They have votes until they marry, but the moment they come out of church or chapel, though they may bring fortunes to their husbands' – and the supporters of this Bill are very anxious that the property should be separate – 'yet the moment the marriage takes place the lady's vote merges, and the husband becomes the elector.' Having first granted this, that women shall vote, how can you answer any man who says – 'Shall marriage disqualify, and if the unmarried vote, shall the married be disfranchised?' It seems to me that if you pass this Bill, and you go no further, what Mr Mill called the subjection of women will be established, and you must agree upon every Bill which is intended to enfranchise them. Then I would ask another question. If all men, being electors and householders, have a right to be elected, if the constituency choose to elect them, upon what principle is it that women should not have a right to be elected? These are reasonable questions, and we who are asked to pass this Bill, but who oppose it and doubt its wisdom, have a right to ask these questions and to have answers to them. If we are to travel this path, let us know how far we are going, and to what it leads. I have always had a great sympathy with a wide suffrage, and have now, but still I want to know, if we are embarking on an entirely new career, what sort of weather we are to have, and what is the haven to which we are about to steer, if we grant that every woman, whether married or unmarried, shall have a vote? The Hon Member for Mid-Lincolnshire (Mr Chaplin) referred to what would happen if this Bill were passed – namely, that in every house there would be a double vote. If the parties were agreed, it would make no difference at an election. If they were not agreed, it had been suggested that you might introduce discord into every family, if not between man and wife, certainly between the parents and children, the brothers, as had been said, taking the part of their mother, and the sisters that of their father. In any case, you would have discord in the house, and an amount of social evil which surely the friends of this measure do not contemplate, and which cannot arise under the present system. Now, we in this House have one peculiar knowledge – that is, of the penalties which we pay for our constitutional freedom. There are many hon. Gentlemen in this House who cannot look back upon their electioneering experience without feelings of regret, and I am afraid there are some who must look back with feelings of humiliation. Now, I should like to ask the House whether it is desirable to introduce our mothers, and wives, and sisters, and daughters into the excitement, and the turmoil, and it may be into the very humiliation which seems in every country so far to attend a system of Parliamentary representation, whether it be in the United States, where so many systems are tried, or whether in this country, or in France, of which we recently have had an example, we see there how much there is that candidates can scarcely avoid, yet must greatly deplore, and we are asked to introduce the women of England into a system like this from which we can hardly extract ourselves without taint of pollution, which we look back upon even with shame and disgust. I will not say that women would be more likely to be more tainted in this manner than we are; but I believe there have been some experiences even since the Municipal Act gave them votes. I know one place in my own neighbourhood where scenes of the most shocking character took place; and in another borough not far from where I live, whose Member or Members vote for this Bill, at a recent municipal contest women were served, with what certainty was not wholesome or good for them, during the morning and forenoon, until they had been polled. I know at another borough in Lancashire at the last General Election there were women by hundreds, I am told, but at any rate in great numbers, drunk and disgraced under the temptations that were offered in the fierceness and unscrupulousness of a political contest. The Hon Member for North Warwickshire (Mr Newdegate) referred to the Catholic question – to the influence that might be exercised by the Catholic priest. I will not go into that further than to say that every man in this House must be sensible, and those who are in favour of this Bill have never to men ventured to deny, that the influence of priest, parson, and minister would be greatly increased if this Bill and other measures of a similar character were passed. I recollect last year discussing this Bill with a gentleman who was a Member of a former Parliament and a Member for an Irish constituency – I rather think he supported this Bill, but I am not quite sure – and he said – 'One thing you may rely upon, that in Catholic Ireland every woman's vote may be taken to be the priest's vote.' Hon Members who come from Ireland may contradict this, and they are much better authorities on the subject than I am. But I do not give it on my own authority. I give it on the authority of one of their own Members in a previous Parliament, and a man equal to any Members for Irish constituencies or English either, as a gentleman of knowledge and veracity in a matter of this kind. All these risks and all this great change we are asked to make – for what? To arm the women of this country against the men of this country. To arm them, that they may defend themselves against their fathers, their husbands, their brothers, and their sons. To me the idea has something in it strange and monstrous, and I think a more baseless case, that is on the ground of any suffered injustice, was never submitted to this House. I believe that if everybody voted, if all women and all men voted, the general result must be the same; for, by an unalterable law, strength is stronger than weakness, and in the end, as a matter of absolute necessity, men must prevail. My sympathies have always been in favour of a wide suffrage. They are so at this moment, and I grieve very much that a measure should be submitted to this House in favour of the extension of the suffrage to which I cannot give my support. But I confess I am unwilling for the sake of women themselves to introduce them into the contest of our Parliamentary system, to bring them under the necessity of canvassing themselves or being canvassed by others. I think they would lose much of that, or some of that, which is best that they now possess, and that they would gain no good of any kind from being mingled or mixed with Parliamentary contests and the polling-booth. I should vote for this measure, if I were voting solely in the interests of the men; I shall vote against it, I believe with perfect honesty, believing in doing so that I am serving the interests of women themselves. I recollect that an Hon Member who voted for this Bill last year, in conversation with me next day, said he had very great doubts upon the matter, because he believed that the best women were against it. Well, I find, wherever I go, that all the best women seem to be against this Bill. If the House believes that it cannot vote justly for our mothers, our sisters, our wives, and our daughters, the House may abdicate and pass this Bill; but I believe that Parliament cannot be otherwise – unless it be in ignorance – cannot be otherwise than just to the women of this country, with whom we are so intimately allied. Believing that, and having these doubts – doubts which are stronger even than I have been able to express, and doubts which have come upon me stronger and stronger, the more I have considered this question I am obliged, differing from many of those whom I care for, and whom I love, to give my vote in opposition to this measure.

A Lady in 'The Gallery'

A letter to the Rt Hon John Bright, MP

May 1876

SIR,

I listened to your Speech in the Women's Suffrage debate with painful interest.

If I had any personal feeling with regard to your public opposition to a reform which you once supported, and for which your nearest relatives have given years of labour, this feeling was second to another. My chief regret lay in my belief that history would have to record that your long and useful career had been stained at its close by an ungenerous act to your countrywomen.

I felt 'the pity of it' when you rose with pale face and laid a trembling hand on the table before you for support, whilst, with hesitating accents, you repeated against us the worn out arguments you have so often, and so mercilessly, exposed when uttered by your opponents.

The bench on which you sit has often, as you know, done its utmost to obstruct the cause of the Representation of the People. If it is to play that part again, should it not be represented by some other voice than yours?

I watched you, and I watched the faces on our side of the House. If you looked ill at ease in your novel *rôle*, the liberal benches contained anxious and constrained countenances. They reminded me of those we used to see on the other side of the House when Mr Disraeli was engaged in the process of 'educating' the conservatives to 'Household Suffrage.' You are now submitting the Liberal Party to an opposite species of training, and this is the doctrine you wish to enforce: – that it would be a most dangerous thing for the Constitution and social life if Household Suffrage should become a reality.

If it were less pathetic, there would be something irresistibly comic in these two pictures of the education of the conflicting parties of the State by their respective leaders in principles radically opposed to those they commonly profess. On the one hand we have a great conservative statesman diligently educating his party to liberalism; on the other we have a great liberal statesman industriously training his followers in the traditions of toryism. All that is wanted to complete the parallel is that Mr Disraeli should rise and retort on you the taunts you have so often hurled at him for poaching on other people's manors.

I wish to address you with the greatest respect, for the women who are now working for the right of representation owe you much.

You have been in the past the true expounder and defender of political justice; you have fearlessly assailed power in high places which oppressed the weak; you have contended against privilege on behalf of the people; you have denounced class legislation, and you have destroyed the theory of 'virtual representation;' you have made the English people care for, and understand the meaning and use of representative institutions.

Who ever thought to see John Bright plead for privilege? Who ever thought to hear him praising indirect or 'virtual representation!' or saying that people 'did not suffer in the least from not having what was called direct representation in that House,' and expounding to his astonished audience that it is 'no advantage' to the governed to be able to select their governors!

You say that our 'Bill is based on an assumed constant and irreconcileable hostility between the sexes.' It is, on the contrary, based on the belief in the constant and trustful sympathy between the sexes. We believe that it is entirely owing to this sympathy, and to the necessary mutual dependence of men and women that the present unjust legal position of women does not make *every* home wretched.

We are assured that men are willing to do us justice; we

are equally assured that they don't know how. You, who came forward as the defender of family peace and male justice, are still obliged to confess that men fail in justice, sometimes through ignorance. That confession is all we require. Is it possible you can believe that men alone ought to have the prerogative of declaring what is just and what is unjust in legal relations of the sexes, or in the laws which govern women? If men were to carry out such a theory in our houses, what would become of us? Why, all the life and joy and heart of the household would die out if women had no voice in its interests, but were in fact – what they are in law – the dull slaves of their master.

Our Bill is based, then, on faith in men, not on hostility to them. Do we assert hostility when we affirm that we are likely to be better judges of our own feelings, and views, and interests, and grievances than anybody else can be? And do not millions of women love men and care for their interests, and work day and night for them, as much and more than men do for women? Yet would you think a demand for the entire exclusion of men from political representation on the ground of this devotion reasonable?

Our Bill is based on the belief inspired by your own words, 'no class can legislate for another class.' You say women are not a class. Let us not quarrel about words. If a woman believes she has a right to something, and the law allows a man to take it from her by force, it will take a great deal to persuade her that she does not belong to a class widely separated from the robber, even though he should bear the name of 'husband.'

Women are more than half the nation, and when they tell you in gentle and dignified language that they are treated as a class, that they are legislated for as a class, that the delicate instincts and feelings you are so anxious to shield are daily outraged by the Acts of a Parliament of which you were a Member, and of a Government in which you held high office; when they can say that, though thus deeply responsible and holding your own female relatives so 'near to your heart,' you have, yet, during eight years, never raised your voice in protest, nor lifted a finger in this matter on behalf of the miserable daughters of the people, how can you ask them to believe that the House of Commons, as at present constituted, is better able than yourself to represent the honour and safety of their countrywomen?

You say the House is disposed to judge fairly on all

questions affecting the property of married women. It is true that the 'Married Women's Property Bill,' which professed to give women equal rights of property and contract with men, passed a second reading in 1873, and was voted into Committee, where it remained entombed till the close of the Session. Why? There was a large majority in its favour, and the only reason I can find is, that every time it came up for discussion not forty Members could be got to take the trouble to keep a House and vote it through Committee. It was counted out six times in that Session. Do you think if it had been a 'Married Men's Property Bill' this would have happened? Yet the Members of the last House were as well supplied with mothers and wives and daughters and sisters as the Members of the present House. The conclusion we are driven to is in strict accordance with the principles you have always preached, and which you now appear shocked to find that we have learned by heart. Human nature is a curious study. Some months ago a man murdered his wife in a savage manner. When asked his motive for the crime, he said, because he *'loved her so much!'* It is obvious from this, that even love requires sometimes to be controlled and directed in the particular mode of its manifestation. It is true, however, that the tenderest and kindest feelings may exist in the hearts of men towards women, and yet that men may act in a way distinctly prejudicial to women's interests. It is the moving force of direct political responsibility to women that is required in the House of Commons. Effusive tenderness is seen to most advantage at home, where it never need be hurt by any signs of incredulity.

Now I have no intention of detailing our grievances to you, because you evidently consider it 'monstrous' that we should have anything to complain of, and – if I may judge from the tone of your speech – still more monstrous that we should think fit to make our complaints public. You also deny that if cause for complaint existed, it would be a 'sufficient argument for asking for a vote.' I will only remark that it is one of the main grounds upon which men have hitherto asked for votes, and it is the reason which you have always deemed unanswerable when demanding the enfranchisement of your own sex.

Your main argument against our plea appears in the form of an indignant question why we should not be able to trust ourselves absolutely in the hands of our male relatives. Well, I may say in answer that you yourself consider these male relatives so 'fierce and unscrupulous' that you are unwilling even to allow us once in five years to be canvassed by them, lest the 'taint' of their social and political corruption should infect us. Do I speak too strongly? I only use your own words, 'humiliation,' 'shame,' 'disgust,' 'taint and pollution.' If these words are rightly applied to the political doings of our husbands and fathers and sons, we are sorry for them; but we don't understand why, under the circumstances, we should be called upon to give them, unhesitatingly, absolute control over the greatest interests and over the most secret actions of our lives. You cannot, I think, in consistency, tell us that men who would be willing to degrade us in order to obtain our votes, are yet sure to act towards us like chivalrous gentlemen in the House of Commons.

Another inconsistency strikes me – but your speech is so full of them that if it had been spoken by a woman it would have been used by our opponents as a perpetual peg on which to hang the charge of the logical incapacity of the sex – you give us your theory, that the interests of men and women are identical, and yet you say you 'would vote for the measure if you were voting solely in the interests of men.' Surely this throws up the case, for it distinctly implies that men have interests, not only separate from, but antagonistic to those of women.

Although I shall not detail our grievances, I will take one case – the case of the law of primogeniture, because as you have a deep rooted hatred to that system, it will serve as an illustration to bring to your mind the added indignity which women suffer, as women, in connection with it. You ask, 'What can be more unjust than that?' And I answer, the position of women in relation to that law is more unjust than the position of the younger sons. In the first place, men have it in their power to alter this law whenever it pleases them so to do; in the second, not all the sons are disinherited, though only one succeeds to the property. There is always a chance for each. But although a woman is the first-born she may never inherit the patrimony. She is ignominiously thrust on one side in favour of her younger brother, or sometimes of the more distant male relation. 'What can be more unjust than that?'

You allude to the greater mercy shown to women criminals than to men; but in the cases you have mentioned it is not the law (for women are tried under the same laws in these cases as men), but the administrators of the law who are what you call 'merciful.' To avoid a difficulty, however, let us grant that the English law – though, as Judge Coleridge says, 'a disgrace to a civilized country' when it deals with the poor toiling mothers of the nation – is soft and lenient to women murderers and other criminals. You shall have all you can get out of that argument. Still I find it a little hard that because your sex is too weak to deal impartially with criminals who are women, that this should be given as a reason for refusing the small measure of justice we ask for your wives, your sisters, your mothers, and your daughters. Is it not truly astounding that husbands and brothers and fathers and sons should be so terribly afraid of giving votes to duly qualified relatives so 'near to their hearts and sympathies?'

But who are the women who are asking this boon? It appears that an Hon Member has told you that 'wherever he goes all the best women seem to be against this measure.' Did you inform him that your own daughter, Helen Bright Clark, is working and speaking before large audiences on behalf of the enfranchisement of her sex? – or that your own sisters, Mrs McLaren, wife of the Member for Edinburgh, and Mrs Lucas, have given it their constant and hearty support? – or that the daughter of your old friend, Charles Sturge, is a strenuous advocate of this measure. If there are any better women than these, they have not happened to cross my path.

You might have told that Hon Member that there is hardly a woman engaged in any work for the good of her sex or mankind, from Frances Power Cobbe and Mary Carpenter to Josephine Butler, who does not believe that this measure is necessary. It has received also the warm approval of such women as Harriet Martineau, Mrs Somerville, Mrs Grote, and Florence Nightingale. Who and where are the 'best women' who oppose it?

You say 'the country has a right to decide how it will be governed.' How is it deciding? I appeal to public opinion out of doors shown by the yearly increased mass of petitions in favour of the 'Bill to Remove the Electoral Disabilities of Women.' I appeal to the hundreds of crowded meetings that have been held in every part of the country, which have passed resolutions affirming the equal electoral rights of men and women, on grounds even of political expediency. I appeal to the Reform Union Conference lately held in

Manchester, which had adopted an Equal Suffrage as a part of its platform. This Union, I believe, represents over seventy towns. I appeal, lastly, to the decision – the unanimous decision – of the 'Council of Four Hundred' at Birmingham – your own constituency – which you do not represent in this matter, as it has repeatedly, in public meeting, pronounced its verdict in favour of our cause.

Do not say that we wish 'to arm the women of this country to defend themselves against their husbands, their brothers, and their sons.' Rather say, We wish to send true men, armed through the ballot box, with power and right to speak authoritatively in our behalf to the House of Commons, and so to put an end to the unseemly differences of Members, who, judging each by the gossip of his own little coterie, presume now to speak in our name without having received our authority.

In conclusion, here is the criticism of a Birmingham paper on your doctrine of physical force: –

> Mr Bright says, 'If all men and women voted, the general result must be the same, for by an unalterable natural law strength was stronger than weakness, and in the end, by an absolute necessity, men must prevail.' Here is the open and undisguised advocacy of the law of force as opposed to the law of right. It is not a new argument, but one which has been used as long as we have had any political history. The only new feature is the promulgation of the worst principles of Toryism in the name of Liberalism. It would, however, be unfair to call such a principle Toryism – it is barbarism. The vital principle of civilised life is the admission of right irrespective of power.

I am, Sir,

A lady in the gallery of the House of Commons on the 26 April, and a devoted adherent of the principles for which you have suffered and toiled for forty years.

Frances Power Cobbe

Speech at the women's suffrage meeting, St George's Hall

13 May 1876

I HAD no intention of taking part this year in the proceedings of my friends on this platform, having other special interests on hand. I expected that the debate would go on as usual; that we should hear calm, and well-delivered, and (as they seem to us) unanswerable arguments from our advocates, and receive from our opponents in reply that playful shower of remarks wholly beside the question, of solemn platitudes and rather offensive jokes (the brickbats and rotten eggs of controversy) which a few gentlemen in the House of Commons seem to consider proper for the use of masculine senators. We could afford to leave these 'Chartered Libertines of Debate,' as the *Morning Post* elegantly styles one of them, to enliven Parliament as to them seemed fit. But the case is changed when our cause is gravely condemned by a great and generous-hearted statesman – a man whom those who differ from him politically as widely as I do, yet regard with unfeigned admiration and warm personal sympathy and respect. It is because *such* a man as John Bright can misunderstand our case so astoundingly as his speech proves him to do, that I feel bound to come forward and say, 'No! things are *not* all smooth and right with women. No! their interests are *not* always consulted or provided for by men. No! there is no justice in describing their demand for a share in the constitution of their country in the odious light of an hostility between the sexes, or of pitting women against their fathers, brothers, and husbands.' With all my soul, I believe that the interests of women are really the interests of men; that (as Tennyson says) the 'Woman's cause is Man's;' and that it is no more the interest of men that women should be wronged, than it is for the good of my right hand that my left should be maimed, or held in a sling. But does not the same truth hold as regards every limb of the social body? Is not the interest of the sovereign that of the subject? – of the nobles, that of the people? – of employers, that of the employed? – of the capitalist, that of the labourer? Can one member suffer without other members sooner or later suffering with it? Surely not. And yet we have a huge system of political balances and safeguards, and endless laws destined to prevent the trespass of each one on every other! Why is this? For the familiar reason that these deep underlying *common* interests are for ever forgotten in the shortsighted selfishness of the struggle of life. I have yet to learn that, as between men and women, this same shortsighted selfishness has not at least an equal place. Mr Bright says that it is a '*scandalous and odious libel to say that Women are a class,*' or that they '*suffer the least from not having direct representation.*' I am prepared to maintain that they form, on the contrary, *the* class of all others which needs the protection of direct representation, seeing that *their* special interests not only concern money and land but things tenfold dearer; personal rights and rights over children.

Mr Chairman,* the aspect of the Woman Question to my eyes is this: On one side I see some eight or ten or twenty thousand women, lapped in every comfort which the hands of loving parents and husbands can provide – the winds of Heaven never visit their cheeks too roughly. Some few of these women are amongst the most unselfish and excellent of human beings, and live as truly for God in their palaces as ever a nun lived in her cell. But the greater number of them are spoiled by the indulgences which their vanity, their luxuriousness, their selfishness, receive every hour of the day, while all their nobler faculties lie dormant, and the rough but wholesome realities of life never come near them. Thus we have 'Girls of the Period,' who have become a proverb already, and 'Matrons of the Period,' who will be likewise proverbial very soon. I do not say these women are wicked, I say they are silly, idle, heartless – leading the lives of butterflies in a world of toil. They are like the gods of Epicurus, too 'bright and blooming in their own blue skies' (or shall we say drawing-rooms, with blue plates crawling up to the ceiling?) to

*Right Hon Russell Gurney.

heed the groans of their sisters in the sordid streets below. These exquisite ladies pass over the miry places of mortal life like Queen Elizabeth treading on Raleigh's cloak. And then they sweetly assure Members of Parliament, at their own splendid dinner tables, that Women have *everything* they want, that this is the *meilleur des mondes possible* for women, and that they desire nothing to be changed in it. As for the demand for the Suffrage, they regard it with horror – as something between a Joke and a Sin, that worst kind of sin in all the modern Decalogue, a sin against the great god Taste.

And on the other side, Mr Chairman, I see – not ten or twenty thousand, but – several hundred thousand women struggling sorrowfully, painfully, often failing under pressure of want of employment, of underpaid, unhealthful, unhopeful employment, or of grinding oppression and cruelty from those whose duty it is to protect and cherish them. With all the burdens and fetters physical and mental of womanhood, they have to fight a far harder battle than ever falls to the lot of a man. When I look in the faces of these women and see the peculiar expression they so often bear, of hopeless, patient, acceptance of toil and misery and oppression, I say unhesitatingly that there is wrong, grievous wrong, *somewhere*, I say that the state of things is bad for rich women and bad for the poor; and it is bad for men because it is bad for women. I do not know or believe that the Suffrage will cure all these evils, either at once or even eventually, but I believe it will tend more than any other measure which human ingenuity can devise to do so. I believe it will make the rich women at least a shade less frivolous, and give the better ones amongst them an intelligent interest in graver things than blue plates and the last new opera. And I feel assured that it will relieve many of the burdens of the poor, both indirectly and by obtaining speedily legislation upon all matters affecting them. *Indirectly*, it will give even brutal men somewhat more of respect for them, and we shall have no more the cry of one recent murderer, 'Do you think they would hang a man for killing an old woman?' And, *directly*, I believe that from the hour we possess the power to press our wants on legislators we shall never again hear of the House being counted out when our questions come before it, six times running, as it was when the Married Women's Property Bill was under debate a year or two ago.

I must not occupy your time with many remarks, either concerning those feminine privileges which have been cited in this controversy as balancing our loss of the rights of citizenship, or the grievances which that loss causes to remain unredressed. The two most splendid privileges which Mr Bright cites seem to be, first, that maidservants are not taxed like footmen and grooms (a benefit, I should think, much on a par with that which ponies under thirteen hands high enjoyed till last year over larger horses, more felt by the master than the servant) and, secondly, that in trials for breach of promise of marriage women obtain iniquitously favourable verdicts. This last privilege, I must confess, is real. Masculine judges and juries are cold enough when a women loses her property, her limbs, or even her life. But when she loses a MAN their sympathy and sense of indignation at her wrong is to the last degree affecting and instructive! To these great privileges, I observe, the *Times* adds that of telling lies with impunity, or (as it delicately expresses it) 'surviving the broken word which brands the man with ignominy.' I confess I am rather interested to know the gentleman who writes these high-handed articles against us, and who thus honestly avows that *he*, at all events, thinks it a privilege to be allowed to speak falsehoods without peril of being kicked.

As to our grievances, I will not recite the list of them; our educational disadvantages (ninety-five percent of the public endowments being devoted to boys), or the various injustices under which we suffer as regards property. I will only touch on one matter in conclusion, which I think sufficiently proves the position we take up, as against Mr Bright, namely, that Women *have* wrongs, and *do* 'suffer from not having direct representation.'

There is one interest in a woman's life (when God gives it to her) supreme and above all others – the love of her Mother when she is a child, the love of her Child when she is a mother. I need not dilate on the dearness and the holiness of this tie, the image here upon earth of God's own love. Even in the poor brutes we honour the maternal devotion which gives courage to the timid bird or sheep; and there are few human hearts, I hope, which would not burn with indignation at putting such love to the test, like that eminent physiologist who cut to pieces a dog nursing her young, and then in her uttermost agony brought her puppies to her to see what she would do with them. The dying beast, it appears, licked and fondled her little ones – and so 'Science' acquired the fact that mothers love their offspring! Well, in human parents' hearts this love is of course ennobled, sanctified, and made immortal by all the higher elements of our moral nature. No one dreams of questioning its sacredness or its importance; nay, women are sometimes told that they are born for nothing else than for this crown of life. How, then, do the laws of England – the old laws which have come down to us from stern old heathen Rome; but which are but little changed to this day on our statute book – how do they treat this one supreme interest of women? They tell each English mother (you will correct me, Mr Recorder; if I err) that her child is *not* hers, but her husband's; that he may take it from her arms while he lives; and that it is to be wrenched from her when he dies by his heirs; if there be even a *presumption* that he desired it to be educated in a different faith from her own. Of late years some exceptions and mitigations of these laws have been made in cases where so great a personage as the Lord Chancellor may see fit to intervene; but the *principle* of the law, and its deadly educational action – making men deem a human mother's rights no greater than those of the poor cow, whose calf they may sever from her at will – *this* has never been changed. That it *would* be changed during the first Session after the passing of Mr Forsyth's Bill, when *widows* would have votes for Members of Parliament, I have very little doubt indeed; nor that with such change would begin a worthier estimate and a deeper reverence for motherhood and womanhood together.

I advocate Women's Suffrage as the natural and needful constitutional means of protection for the rights of the weaker half of the nation. I do this, as you have heard, as a woman pleading for women. But I do it also, and none the less confidently, as a citizen and for the sake of the whole community, because it is my conviction that such a measure is no less expedient for men than just for women, and that it will redound in coming years ever more and more to the happiness, the virtue, and the honour of our country.

Julia Wedgwood

The political claims of women

THE attempt to remove the political disabilities of women has now reached a stage through which every measure of national reform has to pass, and beyond which progress is extremely difficult. The grounds on which this removal is urged have been stated, enforced, and illustrated, again and again, till they have acquired a familiarity which deadens the attention and tends to mislead the judgment. But nothing is more certain than that words which we have learnt to associate with weariness often convey important truth. There are times when those who speak must reiterate, and those who hear must have patience with, statements of principle and of fact which, being obvious to all who think and observe, have been often made before. Indeed, it is the strong point of our case that they have been often made before. Our opponents have been so busy answering arguments which are not used, that they have not attempted to answer the arguments which are. They have thus imposed upon us a two-fold task. We have to say both what we do want and what we do not want, and the attempt at justifying actual claims which the arguments of our own side have made familiar is complicated by the necessity of disavowing possible claims which the attack of the opposite side have made conspicuous. Yet our demand is a very simple one.

We demand that the test imposed as a qualification for

exercising the full rights of a citizen shall be applicable to every English subject; that those who do not vote shall be such as either abstain voluntarily or have not satisfied the conditions of the law. We claim that such of us as do a man's work shall do it with a man's advantages, so far as these can be secured by Acts of Parliament, and urge that if Parliament cannot confer the strong arm and the powerful frame, so much the more is it bound to shelter those who have to compete with the strong-armed in the difficult struggle for life from the shade of inferiority which attaches to all whom the State refuses to recognize as citizens. We want theories on this subject to be verified, like theories on any other, by the experience of life. Our demands rest not on any theory, but on the facts that a class of unrepresented workers has not the same advantages as one which is represented, and that more than three million women are ill-educated and ill-paid workers. These women have to support themselves, and those dependent on them; the workhouse is not more agreeable to them than to men, and their means of avoiding it are fewer. They are excluded from some trades and professions by the jealousy of men, from others by their want of physical strength, a requisite in many kinds of business where its necessity is not obvious; while the very fact of their not having a vote makes it difficult for them to keep a farm or a shop in their own hands. The persons who, in the face of all these difficulties, satisfy a certain money-test must possess rather more thrift and industry than the persons who satisfy that test without any of these difficulties; and we urge that this test should not be prevented from working where it would work most efficaciously. The class from which we, the opponents of Women's Political Disabilities, seek to remove the slur which such disabilities cast on mature human beings, is not one which we have done anything to create. We have not decided that one woman out of every three should remain unmarried, and that a majority of these women should have to earn their bread. These are facts, not opinions. The question whether the sheltered home or the busy world is a woman's ideal sphere has no bearing upon them. If there ever was a time when you might have regarded women as exceptional creatures, relieved by men from the burdens of life, and surrendering to them its graver responsibilities and some of its liberty, you cannot do so now, when more than a tenth of the nation have these burdens forced upon them. We urge that you should not force any set of persons to unite the disadvantages of both sexes.

Certain difficulties felt by thoughtful men to stand in the way of the proposed change are no doubt worthy of serious attention.

They urge that important as is the welfare of half the human race, the welfare of the whole is yet more so, and they fear this might be imperilled by giving political power to persons so little instructed as most women. They fear that members might be returned to Parliament, for instance, hampered with some pledge extorted by women which men would never submit to see carried out. Our reasonable opponents know, too, that a part of the office of Parliament is imperial, and consider that, however much may be said for the influence of women on the domestic affairs of a nation, there is something questionable in allowing those to have any voice in the career of a nation, who, in a national crisis, can give no physical help. These grounds for hesitation are valid against some demands which we do not make. We are not asking that women should be represented *as women*. There has been much vague talk as if this were the case, but the truth is that the very arguments which prove that you ought not to *dis*franchise a ratepayer because she is a woman, prove also that you ought not to *en*franchise any person because she is a woman; if privilege and responsibility cannot be withheld upon the ground of sex, neither can they be demanded on that ground. If the day ever comes when such a claim is made, the future opponents of Women's Suffrage will find no answer so convincing as the arguments of the present advocates of Women's Suffrage. They can then reply, in the words of the supporter of the Bill of 1872, that, 'There is not a male and female rate of taxation. Parliament does not give votes either to men or women, it applies a certain test, and gives votes to all who can submit to that test.' It is a strange confusion to suppose that any application of the principle which these words embody can ever pass into the principle which they oppose. What possible extensions of the demand that all taxpayers should be represented can include the further demand that persons who are not taxpayers should be represented? In Mr Bright's first speech on introducing his Bill, he gave some specimens (founded on the tests of women admitted to the municipal vote) of the proportions of male and female electors if his Bill became law. From these it appears that at Bath, which is the high water-mark of female ascendancy, they would vote in the proportion of one to three (1 woman to 3.8 men); while at Walsall, the opposite end of the scale, the proportion would be one woman to twenty-two men. Thirteen percent is said to be the probable increase on the whole. Even if we suppose this addition to add to the electorate a compact homogeneous body, its influence need not surely alarm the most timid. We cannot concede that this would be true; women are not of one mind any more than men are; but, even supposing it true, it would not be dangerous.

Not on the present conditions of voting, it is conceded, but we are told that the present electoral test is a mere temporary stage in a rapid downward journey, the ultimate goal of which is universal suffrage. It is true that any movement in the suffrage will be downwards, and equally true that women form the majority of the nation; and in combining these two facts some thoughtful and liberal men feel a natural anxiety at the prospect of the balance of power lying with the sex physically unfitted to wield it. But surely this kind of anticipatory policy is not accepted in any region where men are really interested. To consider the burdens which we leave posterity no choice about bearing is our bounden duty, but it seems a futile precaution to abstain from any measure because our descendants may carry out the principle to inconvenient lengths. They will only extend the franchise at their own will. The electoral area is not expanded by any irresistible law; its extension no doubt is the tendency of our time; but this is the result not of any physical necessity, but simply of the wishes and expectations of human beings. Anything which changes those wishes and expectations will change the result. 'Is it to be said,' asked Sir Henry James, 'that the man who sets the stone rolling at the hill-top is not to look to its effects in the valley?' To render this question pertinent, you must suppose the hill-side to be made up of ledges from which the stone can only be set rolling afresh by human agency, in which case surely the only thing to consider is whether the stone is wanted on the ledge below us. If the time ever comes when it will be proposed to include the adult male population in the electorate, the question is not at all settled beforehand by us, that the whole adult female population shall be included also. We do not decide for our descendants or for our future selves, that any set of persons should be admitted to the poll irrespectively of all tests whatever. We only say, when a certain test has been set up, do not cut off from its operation those to whom its fulfilment is the greatest testimony.

The whole view on which this anxiety is based is that women are much more alike than men are. There would be nothing to dread in their influence if it were supposed to be subject to the same variety of conditions that men's is, but it is considered that there is a certain feminine view of things which is dangerous, apart from its being erroneous, because it is inevitably one-sided. And no doubt this is true, so far that women seem to men more alike than men do to each other. But, then, so do men seem more alike to women than women do to each other. Each sex knows the other from a particular point of view, and members of each sex are apt to confuse the identity of their point of view with some monotony in its objects. Women seem more alike than men *to men*, for the same reason that Frenchmen seem more alike than Englishmen *to Englishmen*. The spectator from without will always discern more resemblance than one from within. No doubt the weak have common fears, and any admission of female influence would embody this element. But this is not what men are afraid of. The most contemptuous of our opponents would surely be glad to ascertain, and at least consider, all claim for protection that might be made by women. This, we admit, would be a common element in the addition to the electorate we are seeking to make. But we urge that any supposed common element beyond this is an imagination which those who point out must justify by argument. Sir Henry James, whose speech against the change demanded was considered the strongest, in 1875, said 'The effect of this Bill would be to drive women to consider subjects connected, I will not say with sentiment, but, at all events, not always with good government. Were female franchise introduced into France the question affecting the elections in every department of the country would be whether there should be war with Italy to restore the temporal power of the pope.' If the line of argument here suggested, in a somewhat elliptical form, and not quite consistent with its context, may be followed out, Sir Henry James appears to have meant that the influence of women would be injurious in enforcing some measure which would be for England what the re-establishment of the temporal power of the pope would be to France. Such an argument can only be met with the assertion of individual experience, not worth much, certainly, but worth more than an assertion which has nothing whatever to do with experience. Take the disestablishment of the Church as the nearest English parallel to Sir Henry James's instance, and consider the opinion bearing on it of those whom this Bill would enfranchise. If a single experience, neither short, nor peculiar, nor narrow of women's views may be regarded as a specimen of an average experience, it may be said that the women endowed with votes by this Bill would be just as keen on one side as on the other. A few would be very keen on both sides. A great many would be perfectly indifferent. Those who are not indifferent would be, perhaps, more keen, blinder to collateral issues, more bitter against compromise, than men would be, but all this just as much on one side as the other. The fear which influences those who would feel no other objection to female suffrage – that of largely increasing the power of the clergy – is the result rather of considering typical women and typical clergy in the abstract, than of experiencing among women as they are, at all events, of such women as would be enfranchised by admitting all those who satisfy the present electoral test.

No doubt clergymen have certain interests in common with women which no other men have, and perhaps there is as a result a certain feminine element in their characters, when much affected by their profession, which there is not in other men. But it argues a strange ignorance of human nature to think that this similarity gives influence. Women are as little under the influence of feminine men as men are under the influence of masculine women. If you can make a rule as to circumstances and characters so various, you may say that in both cases human beings are attracted by contrast.

A truer answer would be given by the mere computation of the female householders in a single acquaintance who would take any important step under clerical influence, if it were remembered that ladies would form an insignificant proportion of this class. Women who work are very much more like men who work than people fancy who know women, as most gentlemen do know them, as social equals. It is from considering only these kinds of women, we suspect, that so much is thought about the influence of the clergy, or that such fears are expressed as that the influence of female voters would be absolutely hostile to the real interests of women in such cases as the Married Women's Property Bill. The influence of ladies possibly might be so. But lower down in the social scale you would find a very different kind of view of the subject from that taken in drawing-rooms.

People are apt, in making up their minds on any subject of social interest, not to think of the men and women they know, whom there is always a curious but explicable tendency to classify as exceptions, but of some abstract type of the character supposed, and fiction is a large source of this kind of general opinion. The intriguing priest and the beneficent pastor are stock characters, and few people take the trouble to ask themselves how often they have seen them realized. When a type of this kind has become current, it acquires an authority of its own, the trouble of investigating its correspondence with fact seems superfluous, and the result of such investigation paradoxical, although, in truth, such types become prevalent through their vividness simply, and not through any faithfulness to the world of reality. But no one should let his opinions be moulded on them; he should consider, not whether women as they are painted in fiction or defined in treatises are under the influence of the clergy, but whether the actual women he knows – the shopkeeper, the schoolmistress, the lodging-house keeper, the writer in magazines, the painter of second-rate pictures – all the commonplace women of his acquaintance who earn their bread, are so. It will be an exceptional experience in which these elements compose a constituency in which clerical influence is an important element.

There is in this matter another source of confusion: people think of a clergyman's influence on the poor and on women together. On the needy classes (who, in London, hardly vote at all) a clergyman has a very definite influence, no doubt. He is the channel through which material help reaches them, and it would be easy for him to use his influence, made up in indistinguishable proportions of gratitude and interest, to get their actual or possible pensioners to vote for Mr A. or Mr B., if it were worth while, and if he chose to take the enormous trouble and run the considerable risk. But with this matter we have nothing to do; it is one where men would be concerned much more than women.

The objections felt by thoughtful men to our demand occupy a curiously small proportion in the whole bulk of argument against the measure we advocate. We find it said, as a ground for rejecting the demand of a quarter of a million persons, that women do not want the suffrage, that it will be a burden to them, that it would take them out of their sphere, that they have enough to do and to think of already. If it is asked what they have to do and to think of we are told their vocation is 'to make life endurable.' A measure justified on the ground that a large body of persons have to struggle for their own livelihood is opposed on the ground that these persons have enough to do in adorning the lives of others. Of course, in saying this Mr Scourfield was thinking exclusively of the women who belong to his own class. The view is not universal even with regard to that class, but when a theory is irrelevant, it is waste of time to inquire whether it is true. It is about as good an argument against the proposed change to assert that it will make the position of rich women less comfortable as it would have been against the last Reform Bill to pretend that it would make the profession of barrister or physician less profitable. It is not an excusable fallacy when one to whom the nation has delegated the office of law-making talks as if the world were made up of ladies and gentlemen, and the shallowest and most frivolous of speakers would not venture to do so when the interests of men were at stake. A statesman ought to be able to see clearly and say boldly that, in considering a Bill which concerns a seventh of the nation, he may leave that small portion of it which belongs to good society out of account. If all women were in the position of the women whose supposed duty it is to 'make life endurable,' Parliament would not have heard of any Bill for doing away with woman's disabilities. It is waste of time to argue whether even those women would not be the better for being made citizens of. Our whole case rests on the fact that a great many women have to work for their living, and that these women have the greatest difficulty, first, in getting an education that will enable them to do any work, and, secondly, in finding work from which they are not practically excluded by men. 'I scarcely ever see,' said the Prime Minister, in the debate of 1871, 'I scarcely ever see in the hands of a woman an employment that ought more naturally to be in the hands of a man; but I constantly see in the hands of a man employment which might be more beneficially and economically in the hands of a woman.' Take another illustration of the truth here stated. There were, in 1861, about twenty-two thousand female farmers in England and Wales, being one eleventh part of the whole number. Now, that farming is a business for which women have no inherent disqualification is evident to any one who will consider how much of a farmer's duty consists in that careful inspection of details which is considered a woman's strong point, and is abundantly illustrated by experience. Almost every one who knows much of country life has some instance of a farm well-managed by a woman to bring forward. A single instance of the case, given in Mr Bright's speech, 1873, may be given here; it is contained in the following extract from the pages of a journal not devoted to women's rights, the *Field*: – 'It may be said, What business have women with farming? In answer to this query the report of the competition for the one hundred guineas prize for the best-managed farm in the central districts of England, offered by the Royal Agricultural Society, may be referred to. Twenty-one farms competed for the honour. It was awarded to the tenant of Ash Grove Farm, near Ardley, Bicester, as showing the best example of good general management, productiveness, suitability of live stock, and general cultivation, with a view to profit. The farm is one of 890 acres, one thousand sheep and seventy cattle are wintered annually. The judges said the farm was an exceedingly good example of a well-managed farm,' and accordingly granted the one-hundred guinea prize, but the society which gave it refused to accede to the tenant thus honourably distinguished the important advantages of membership, for the simple fact that this person was a woman. This is not the only instance that might be quoted of the disadvantages of women that have to earn their bread. The obstruction placed in the way of women in the watchmaking trade, for instance, would afford an example of a kind of difficulty which affects a larger number of individuals. But the case of farmers ought specially to be considered in this connection, because here the want of a vote has a directly injurious influence on the person concerned. In *all* cases it is an indirect disadvantage to a worker not also to be a citizen, but in the case of farmers it is actually a menace to the continued existence of their livelihood. It will hardly be said that a landowner to whom political influence is either indifferent or inaccessible is a common spectacle. No matter whether it ought to be so, the question is as to what *is*, and while it remains an object with the landholder that his tenant should have a vote, and a woman has none, so long one of the trades in which women are best fitted to excel will be closed to them. It is facts like these which contain the justification of our demand. Is it not childish to answer a claim thus supported by the assertion that 'woman is the silver lining which gilds the cloud of man's existence?' (Mr Knatchbull-Hugessen, 1872.)

But we are told that in seeking to escape the shadow of inferiority, thrown by political disability, we are really imperilling the shelter of acknowledged weakness. 'The extension of the franchise to self-dependent women,' said Mr Beresford-Hope, in the debate of 1871, 'might seriously endanger their hard-earned competence by forcing them into the area of political excitement, where they would be exposed to the animosities, the bickerings, and the resentments which are so unhappily inherent in the tough work of electioneering.' Now, no-one has ever justified the refusal of the franchise on the ground that it would be an injury to the claimant, when the claimant was a man. And no obvious difference of man and woman explains this different method of meeting their claims. If an election riot were the ideal condition of a new member taking his seat, indeed, there might be something to say for it, but even then we should say, let us take our share of the blows if we choose to do so. We do not care to argue the question as to the advantage of our claim to ourselves. This is our own concern. It is not for one set of mature human beings to decide what is or is not for the advantage of another. If we are often mistaken about our own vocation we are still more often mistaken about other people's, and whatever may be the right place for women, that is a subject on which women are less likely to be wrong than men.

But women do take this view of their vocation, it is said. The anxiety of the *Times*, that women shall not be dragged 'from their drawing-rooms' to the polling-booths, is echoed by the whole acquaintance of more than one Member of Parliament, and one of ᵗhe speakers read, in 1871, a letter from a lady friend who was 'strongly opposed to the extension of the franchise to women,' and who considered herself 'exactly in a position to express opinions which might be regarded as the exponent of those of her countrywomen.' That is, we should suppose, this lady had mingled with classes below her own; she knew the desires of the poor on the subject, and of that intermediate class which is more difficult to get at than the poor? Not at all. Extraordinary as it seems, this lady, who 'has an immense circle of acquaintance,' and is intimate with Members of Parliament, supposes herself to be a type of the class we seek to enfranchise. The delusion need not be dwelt on after what has been said; certainly the writer of that letter was the type of a class which would not have the smallest difficulty in defending itself from the importunity of candidates. However, to take a parallel case, what would have been thought, in 1829, of an opponent of the Bill for removing Catholic Disabilities, who read out a letter from a Roman Catholic, asserting that, considering the gain to the spiritual life of shelter from the temptations of worldly ambition, he regarded the proposed change in the law as a burden against which he protested? Would such an argument have been thought worthy of any more arduous refutation, than the assertion that it would be hard to force an important body of men to remain unrepresented because among them were some who wanted sense?

A Member of Parliament may continue for a long time to ask the lady he takes down to dinner whether she wants the franchise before he gets an affirmative answer. The class in whose interest we demand it is as much out of the reach of men of position as if each party belonged to a different nation. No Member of Parliament would allow his daughter to marry without settlements. It is one of the many advantages of money that it can obtain security for money. The classes who have wealth can get their wealth secured to son or daughter. But those to whom such money as they possess is far more necessary have no means of making the possession of this money by their weaker members sure. The efforts hitherto made have failed in securing immunity to anything but the earnings of married women; a magistrate consulted by a poor woman as to the possibility of keeping a little furniture belonging to her out of the hands of her drunken husband had no better advice to give her than to leave him secretly and carry it off. And is it considered that the women to whom these things happen are indifferent to them? To suppose that any one can gauge the opinion of those who have experience of the ills needing legislative interference at a dinner party is foolish. If the persons whose wishes were concerned were men, any one would be ashamed of bringing the views of good society into the discussion. The evidence of women's wishes on this question must not be looked for in drawing-rooms. But surely no evidence which would be deemed sufficient to prove that any other class wanted the franchise is wanting in the case of women. Petitions have been presented, signed by about 400,000 persons, one or two of the signatures implying a great deal more than the wish of an individual. These signatures, it is said, have been obtained by 'systematic agitation.' But systematic agitation is not an entity. It is only a short and somewhat contemptuous way of saying that a few persons have cared very much about an object. Now, we consider that so moderate a demand as that persons otherwise qualified to vote should not be prevented from doing so on account of sex needs the minimum of justification. If voting were to be made obligatory it would be right, before any extension of the franchise, to ascertain the proportions of those who wished to have it, and those who wished to be without it; but there is no such necessity when these latter persons have the remedy in their own hands, and at the utmost their inconvenience will consist in the necessity of giving a decided negative. We are asking for permission to do something which no-one will be forced to do. And as for the graces and refinements of life, we believe that they will survive when the women who lose the shelter accorded to weakness cease to be debarred from the independence conceded to strength. But supposing that we are mistaken in this; supposing that we must purchase the greater good by the lesser, we should say – let these things go. It would be a pity that ladies should lead less graceful lives in drawing-rooms, but it would be worth while, if it led to other women leading less miserable lives elsewhere.

The tone of opposition to our demand has sensibly changed during the nine years that have elapsed since it found its first spokesman in John Mill. The quotations made above are mainly taken from the earlier debates in Parliament, and those very words would not now, perhaps, be used in argument against our claim. But, though we mark this change with satisfaction, it is as true of the last debate as of the first, that in order to have made them relevant the question before the House ought to have been, not should a certain class be enfranchised, but should it exist. Almost everything true that has been said on the side we oppose is an argument not against women having votes, but against women having to earn their bread. Sir Henry James, for instance, dwelt emphatically on the physical weakness of women. He quoted

Shakespeare's tamed shrew, in the speech where she rebukes one who by many will be thought to hold more rational theory of a wife's duty, with the query –

> Why are our bodies soft and weak and smooth,
> *Unapt to toil and trouble in the world,*
> But that our soft condition and our hearts
> Should well agree with our external parts?

and the quotation was met with cheers, as if submission to kindly protection were the alternative of those women on whose behalf we make our claim! These women are all *obliged* to 'take the position of men.' They are not asking for independence, they have that already. They have no choice about being independent. I wish it were possible to make one of those gentlemen whose words are quoted here realize the position of a widow left ill off. She bitterly realizes the truth of *Katharine*'s words, she knows well that her body is 'unapt to toil and trouble in the world,' but she finds the difficulties and hindrances which nature has set in her way suddenly increased by others which till then, perhaps, she had not realized. She finds that a change has come over the feelings with which her claims are met by all but the generous. A promise to her means something less than it did. She can no longer expect that inconvenient engagements will be kept to her, tradespeople and inferiors generally look upon her as some one to be taken advantage of, and she finds every arrangement, every effort she has to make, rendered more arduous by the difference there is between the sense of justice that men have to men and to women. Parliament cannot at once change this, but it can refuse to sanction the different estimate which the vulgar take of the struggling woman and the struggling man. It can declare that in the eye of the Legislature no inferiority shall be recognized within the circle of those who fulfil the requirements it makes a test of citizenship.

In doing this Parliament commits itself to no further principle. If it is an exceptional thing that women have to earn their bread, then, speaking broadly, we may say that the withdrawal of women's disabilities would only emancipate exceptional women, for the heiresses and widows whom this measure would include are in number insignificant. We should naturally expect that if sex were not allowed to form a reason for disfranchisement, neither would marriage, and that the true theory of this subject – that the property test should be carried out without any exceptions, but those of lunacy and crime – would be ultimately embodied in legislation. But as in normal cases a wife is by the necessities of nature cut off from those exertions of which the vote is in a rough way the symbol, she would be cut off from a vote in the same manner. Property is a rough and meagre test, no doubt, of the qualifications we desire in a voter, but no better has yet been devised, and on the whole it would be a little less rough and meagre in the case of women than men.

Some of the fears which stand in our way can only be regarded as an extravagant compliment to their object. It was said, for instance, that if women were admitted to vote, they must be admitted to sit in Parliament, as if all that was wanted to create female members of Parliament was an Act of Parliament rendering women eligible! Surely, if any one realized that all that an Act of Parliament could do was to confer on men the right to choose a woman to represent them, he would see that such a fear was a most extravagant compliment to women. No advocate of woman's cause would venture on so arrogant an anticipation of ascendancy.

Most of us have no anticipation of any approach to such a result. The desire for Female Franchise is compatible with every variety of opinion about the intellectual superiority of men. In the days when it was possible, by any stretch of imagination, to regard the Electorate as the intellectual aristocracy of England, the admission of the least instructed, and, possibly the least intelligent, part of the community might have been a questionable step. 1832 and 1867 have made that view impossible, and an elaborate arrangement for enabling persons to record their votes who cannot sign their names has made it absurd. Political ascendancy has now gone over to the ignorant, and one-half the people can no longer be excluded from representation on the ground of their ignorance. In urging their admission, we disavow all enthusiastic hopes. Indeed, the only fear with which we regard the proposed measure is that its effect should be at first imperceptible. If it be asked how, with this avowal, we can still urge it, we reply that in doing so we make an appeal to those who can look into the future. We are convinced that all other measures for the benefit of women would find a new atmosphere and a new soil to grow in when once women were made citizens, and that till that time comes all such measures will form part of a mere patchwork. While men deal with the question as one of affording *protection* to women, the protection they concede will be at once inadequate and enfeebling. It is not till they learn to see that what we demand is *justice*, that they will satisfy those claims which, even from their own point of view, they would allow to be the appropriate demands of the weak.

Arabella Shore

The present aspect of women's suffrage considered[*]

14 May 1877

[The following paper was delivered as a Lecture at a meeting convened by the London National Society for Women's Suffrage on 14 May in St Matthew's School, Great Peter Street, Westminster, when Mr Roebuck, MP, was in the chair.]

IN opening the subject of Women's Suffrage, my first wish is to present it in such a light that it shall not at once awaken prejudices against it; and I should wish to approach it not as a novelty advocated by a distinct and necessarily aggressive party, not as at first blush it may be considered as merely an agitation, a battle maintained by a class whose view of their due position in the world is different from that which the world has hitherto been disposed to take, and who, therefore, can expect for a long time little save uncompromising opposition, contempt, or at least utter indifference.

I hope we have passed that stage; but I wish the question not to be regarded simply as one of Women's Rights – an unlucky phrase fostering bitterness. It is a question of men's and women's rights, the rights of both to the fullest good that our social and political system can yield. It is the complement of other advances – a part of an inevitable movement, of which there can be no more doubt

[*]Originally published in the *Englishwoman's Review*.

than of the lapse of ages or of the movement of the heavens, or of the growth of the human individual. Carrying on the idea, I may say this claim for women is only one outgrowth in a general and manifold development which resembles a tree budding forth in all directions. We find it linked with almost all that is good and useful in public effort and in social renovation, with consciousness of women's needs, social, material, and moral, and of the needs of the community in general. This advance cannot be stayed; it springs from a law of nature more real and fixed than that which draws a hard and fast immoveable line between the spheres of the two sexes according to theories and usages of earlier and very different ages. This law that I speak of is that duties and spheres will change, expand, and modify according to the other changing conditions of human communities. In this case the recognition of this law coincides with the full operation of an established principle. What we now ask is, that the constitutional system may be fully and fairly carried out – that the freedom and justice it is supposed to secure to all classes and individuals may not by legislative enactment be confined to about half the nation – that anomalies caused by artificial restrictions, not inherent in, not contemplated by, the original system, may be removed; the anomaly, for instance, of a large amount of the landed property of the country being in the hands of persons without political rights; we ask that men and women may not oppose but co-operate with each other in all great and wide objects for the national good.

I trust in all that I shall now say I shall appear to be speaking, as I feel, in a friendly and reasonable spirit. How, indeed, can I feel otherwise when I know how many good and wise men are helping us now; when I believe that we shall finally win our cause, and that it will be through the good will of *men* that we shall win it, of those men who compose the House of Commons – and moreover, when I see a most distinguished member of that House kindly consenting to do us the service of presiding at a meeting for the furtherance of our object.

I may as well just say what it is that we ask for – what we mean by Women's Suffrage. We mean simply Women-householder's Suffrage. That is, we ask it only for those women who have the same qualifications as give men a right to vote; for those who are householders and ratepayers – nothing more. But we are argued against as though we were demanding the suffrage for *all* women; that would be Womanhood or Universal Woman's Suffrage. This would be to demand a complete change in the whole constitutional system; and an absurd change, for it would give women the vote in cases where men would not have it. Some who perfectly understand us complain that the term, thus constitutionally limited, is misleading – False Women's Suffrage, they are pleased to call it. This seems to me rather unnecessary quibbling; the words are in fact as correct as the converse term of Women's Disabilities. But to men who reproach us with inconsistency because this definition excludes married women (all but a most minute fraction) we can only say that the laws which necessitate this exclusion by depriving wives of their property are not of our making. As to those very few who *are* householders independent of their husbands, I should myself think it just and desirable that they should have the franchise; but to ask this would be to raise quite a different question. The claim must be based on other than constitutional grounds, and would involve all manner of issues that I cannot dwell on now. As it is, the principle that we are contending for – that sex should cease to be in itself a disqualification, will be once for all secured; and no line can really be drawn between the rights and interests of such interchanging sets of persons as the married and the single. In fine, we ask for what we can get, not for what we cannot; and we know, and those who reproach us know very well too, that to ask for more than this would simply be to ensure the total defeat of the whole Bill under a storm of opposition.

To return to our general subject. This claim of the franchise has been objected to as a novelty – which no doubt it is, and as an innovation – which I shall hope to show that it is not. Every beneficial change was at first a novelty; even an innovation would be matter of alarm only till it ceased to be an innovation; and a political measure in particular becomes an accepted fact in a year or so. This fact in especial will have nothing politically revolutionary in it. It is not, as one might judge from the language of its opponents, a new nation living apart, with laws, language, and ideas of their own, that it will admit within the pale of the Constitution; it will only increase the number of voters within the classes already enfranchised, and in those mainly of the more educated section, that by circumstances most orderly and law-abiding. A small additional number three hundred thousand or four hundred thousand – that is, less than a seventh of the whole electoral body – will share with men the privilege of having a voice in the nomination of the men who are to represent us in Parliament. This will not affect the action of the Constitution or the organisation of Government; the same system of men and measures will prevail, subject as now to the approval of the bulk of the electors.

But this proposal, though denounced as a departure from the

usage of time immemorial, is in truth *no* constitutional innovation. It is against no early custom, was till 1832 against no existing
statute, and is in fact rather a usage let drop than a claim to be
newly conceded.

'Time immemorial,' we know, does not protest against women
having a vote, since the Parliamentary system has not existed
above six hundred years. Still less has 'time immemorial'
protested against women having a share, a good large share, in
government, since from the earliest ages we have seen women-
sovereigns, sometimes with absolute power.

In our own England we have, as the earliest form of a ruling
council under the Sovereign, the Witenagemot, or *assembly of the
wise*, which definition happily did not exclude women, as kings'
wives, and mothers, and abbesses sat by prescriptive right in it.
There was also local government, shire, borough, and parish
courts, the basis of the later system of representation; and in these
women had a vote, as since in our similar modern institutions.
And when Parliamentary representation was established no limit
of sex seems to have been thought of; freeholders simply are
named as entitled to the franchise, and freeholds, we know, might
be held by women. It was a principle expressed then by our kings
that 'what concerned all should be approved by all.' Whether the
right was much used we cannot tell, as no registries of electors
were kept in those days, but probably in times when political
liberty was so imperfectly comprehended women thought no
more of their vote than men did of theirs. In Henry VIs reign
occurred the first limitation of the franchise to 40s. freeholders;
the word used here to designate the voters is 'people.' In James Is
reign, which was about the time when first the idea of civil liberty
began to be associated with representation, we find on two
occasions, when women's votes had been recorded, that the
question was brought before the Courts in Westminster Hall,
where it was decided that 'a *femme sole*, if a freeholder, might vote
for a Parliament man.' And in the Record Office are to be found
the names of several women-electors; women even figure as
returning officers.

In William IIIs time Parliamentary representation first began to
be a matter of party organisation, and the system fell into the
hands of political cliques, of the great nobility, of the wealthy
landowners. As whole classes and masses of men acquiesced in
their exclusion from the suffrage, it was scarcely to be supposed
that women would make any stir for *their* rights. Their claim,
then, may be said to have been simply ignored. But before the
question *was* agitated, the emancipation of women (on the

supposition that a right long unexercised did not exist) was first demanded in 1826 by a meeting of working men! and some thinking men and enlightened women were already raising the question in other circles. So far was the question from being settled that a lady still living with whom I am acquainted, then a young married woman, but of the family of a burgess, once gave her vote in a borough election with no further formula than the being caused to make affidavit before the mayor that she did it under no compulsion from her husband. But when the first Reform Bill, that of 1832, was passed, there was no claim for women made in the House; and those eligible for the suffrage were in the Bill qualified as male persons. In 1850 Lord Romilly's Act declared that all phrases betokening the masculine gender should be taken to include women unless the contrary were expressly provided. And certainly in various Acts at the time the term 'men' was used for both sexes alike, so that when in the second Reform Bill, that of 1867, the word 'male persons' in the superseded Bill was changed to 'men,' it was resolved to put the question fairly to the test.

In the elections that followed a number of women applied to be put on the register and several recorded their votes. The case of those who had been refused registration was tried at the Court of Common Pleas and their cause was argued by several distinguished lawyers, among them the present Lord Coleridge, who held that the 'women's vote was an ancient Constitutional right that had never been rescinded.' And even the *Times* stated that should the plea be rejected 'the nation would be distinctly committing itself through a judicial tribunal to the dangerous doctrine that representation *need* not accompany taxation.' It did so however; it was decided that the word 'men' used in different clauses of the same Act should include women for purposes of taxation, but should exclude them where a right and privilege was concerned. Thus legally foiled, the cause had to be fought out constitutionally.

This movement had already begun, though still in its infancy, when in 1866 a petition was presented to Parliament in its favour, and in 1867 it was nobly inaugurated in the House itself by that great and good man Mr John Stuart Mill. He took advantage of the new Reform Bill then introduced to propose the striking out the words supposed to signify male suffrage only. It is said that at that time Mr Mill was the only man who could have brought forward this claim in the House without exciting general laughter, and even he expected to find scarcely a single supporter. But to his surprise, and thanks to his splendid advocacy, seventy-three members followed him into the lobby. Since then the number of parliamentary supporters has been steadily though slowly rising. Through six successive sessions (from 1870 to 1876, omitting only 1874) the Bill has been regularly presented to Parliament by our faithful and able champions Mr Jacob Bright and Mr Forsyth. In 1875 the majority against it had diminished in a house of 339 members from sixty-seven to thirty-five.

It is true that in the two last sessions the Bill was defeated, in 1876 by a larger majority than usual, and this year not by votes, but simply by a noise, the majority refusing to hear arguments on the other side, and thus literally roaring the question out. But in neither case did the House represent any change of opinion outside; the result must be attributed to special circumstances within – a very strong whip of a party which has lately proved itself exceedingly violent in its opposition to all Liberal views. But the number of its Liberal supporters had not diminished; and I believe Mr Forsyth was right in saying that whatever the chances in this Parliament, in a new House the result could scarcely be doubtful. We shall see how public opinion has been growing if we look back the ten years of this movement. The only notice the public press at first took of it was to denounce it as the work of a few restless noisy agitators; though, as Miss Becker has well remarked in answer, in all great movements for the common good, it has invariably been the few who were restless and dissatisfied with a wrong state of things who first essayed to put it right. In private society there was at first a strong prejudice against it as there always is against anything quite new, and not well understood, a prejudice felt by women as well as by men. But there has been an active and rapid progress since, especially in women's minds, which I think every one who mixes at all in society of any kind or class can testify to, and of which the tangible signs are the increasing number of signatures to petitions in its favour. In 1874 and 1875 there were upwards of four hundred thousand of which about half were women's, about four times the amount of three years before; the two next years somewhat less, only because much less time was given to collect them, but as it is, we have had this year 235,832 signatures. Four thousand women signed a memorial to the Prime Minister in its favour, and numbers of women are coming forward to work for it in every way. These years of effort have meanwhile done us much good; they have made us fitter for the suffrage by teaching us to understand it better. We are thankful for the ridicule, even for the occasional abuse, that has been dealt out to us, it has braced us up to prove it unjust and unwise, it has given ardour to the championship of a well abused cause. I don't mean that the persecution has been very cruel, but some amount of scorn, even of sneers and personalities, must be expected by those who come forward to maintain whatever runs counter to public prejudices. All we ask of favour is to be listened to, not shelved and ignored. We are thankful then for the bracing opposition – and still more thankful for the help which prevents this question from any longer being regarded as one of women *versus* men, the view with which it was first encountered. For men, many men, legal-minded and statesmanlike men, of all parties, from the sincere Conservative to the fervent Radical, have joined our camp and accepted the charge of carrying our banner. Has it ever been known that a cause so begun, so seconded, so long and steadily and earnestly maintained by a growing number of good and able men and of the women best qualified to form a judgment, has failed of final success?

I attribute the increase of favour which this movement has met with, not only to its being better known and more talked of, but also to the increased and increasing need of it. The condition of women in England has been gradually but greatly changing with all the changes – social, political, commercial, material – of the last forty years. In this period of transition, as we may trust it is, the traditional state of dependence and protection for women is becoming less and less the rule, while freedom, power to act and the means of self support have not increased in like measure. The fact that there are nearly a million more women than men, and that fully three millions (that is nearly half of the adult women) are obliged to earn their bread, alone presents a case to which the old theory of 'women's sphere' ceases to apply. The political enfranchisement bestowed by successive Reform Bills, joined with legislation promoting commerce and private enterprise, have very much benefited the men of various classes in this country, have given them laws enabling them to protect their rights, obtain better education and higher wages, laid open to them more extensive and profitable fields of labour, and raised them in dignity and importance in the political scale. Of course, as wives and daughters, women share more or less in the improved material condition of the men, yet legislation keeps them in the same state of thraldom and hopelessness which so often counteracts those benefits; while, as women having to support themselves, few of these advantages are shared by them. The opening of new spheres of employment to men leaves an immense number of women still to starve at shirt making for two-pence farthing the shirt, or at other almost equally unremunerative drudgery, while the higher and more honoured callings are still shut from them. And in such work as they do in common with men, even with equal qualifications and equal skill and sometimes with harder labour, they are almost invariably paid much smaller wages. Too often they are kept down by the ill-grounded fears and jealousies of those very men who force their masters to give the women the most laborious and the worst paid part, or drive them from the business altogether, thus using their trades-unionism both to secure their own rights and deprive women of theirs.[1] Moreover the facilities for education have not been extended to women in anything approaching to like measure with men; and to crown all, that enlargement of Parliamentary representation which has so much helped to raise the position of all classes of men, leaves women the same political cyphers as before.

I do not suppose the strongest upholder of 'things as they are,' could point out a way in which keeping women out of citizenship will remedy such grievances as I have enumerated. But if I am asked what effect political emancipation would have on them, I answer in general terms that in the first place, we believe the social status of women will be raised by the legislative acknowledgement of their complete equality with men. For – explain it as you will, the not having a vote, that is, the belonging to a class not considered fit to judge of or help to decide even its own affairs, is a slur and a brand which must affect the general estimation of women, joined as it is with legislation that in many points expressly affirms their inferiority. Justice to any class or individual implies, in my thought, liberty to make the most of their life, to develop all their faculties, be socially useful and personally independent. Legislation, political or social, that hinders this, is not in my opinion justice. We are not asking for legislation to favour women over men, or to force social regulations to their advantage; we only ask that it may not help to obstruct what, given free play, women may hope to do for themselves.

It is very true that a beginning *has* been made; some steps have been gained, thanks in great measure to the terrible force of necessity, and to the resolute purpose of women themselves in qualifying themselves for wider spheres, and their usefulness in some branches of public work begins to be acknowledged. But all this progress has been hampered by difficulties and opposition at every step, and I contend that the political inferiority of women renders their work much slower and more imperfect than it need be. I ask for a reform on principle to put an end to this curious, inconsistent state of things, a great advance in feeling and knowledge mingled with barbarous survivals that deny on one hand what is inevitably yielded on the other.

In two ways the exclusion from the franchise tells directly against women who have to work for their livelihood; their value as tenants is less to their landlords from their not having a vote, and cases are frequent in which they have not been able to carry on a business which had been their source of maintenance after a husband's or father's death. They have been turned out of a farm, or a shop, or a public house, of which perhaps they had been the real and successful managers; and this may often be a terrible hardship, amounting sometimes to ruin. Again, there is a growing tendency to legislate for women in restriction of their personal liberty, whether supposedly for their benefit or not, without any consulting of their wishes. One of these measures is intended as protective; women's working hours in factories and workshops have been shortened by law. For as the *Spectator* itself says of those natural rulers and protectors under whose reign of chivalry women are supposed to be so safe and happy, 'experience shows that men will always make women work harder than they ought, harder than they do themselves.' The consequences are that women's wages have been reduced, and workwomen often dismissed to be replaced by men. Men, not being meddled with by legislation, have been able to get their hours reduced and their wages not diminished.

The value of the political franchise for men has been so thoroughly recognised that every change has been in the direction of extending it, and the last Reform Bill admitted to it a great proportion of the working classes. By the advocates of 'things as they are,' the very same arguments were brought against this extension as are now urged against the women's franchise. It was said they did not want it; they were not educated enough for it; they would make a bad use of it; it was a revolutionary measure and would subvert the Constitution. But these fears have not been realised, the nation has not been revolutionised, the same class of men is returned as before, and the result is, more equitable legislation, more attention in the law-makers to the needs and education of the people.

This just and simple principle, that all classes should join in choosing the men to make the laws which control them all as classes and as individuals, that some share in regulating the State should be possessed by all who help to maintain it, who bear its burdens and obey its decrees – this principle is now being applied to the only class of men still excluded – the agricultural labourers,

– by the proposal to assimilate the county to the borough franchise. The result of this measure, which will assuredly ere long be passed, will be that the government will consist of nearly all the men, the governed only of the women. I believe the extension of the franchise to be just and constitutional; I do not deprecate it, but I confess that unless this vertical extension is accompanied by a lateral one, I look forward to it with alarm. I think that the necessarily large masses of wholly uneducated electors that it will bring in require counter-balancing by the introduction of a class that will include more of education, responsibility, and cultivated morality; and I cannot but feel that the entrusting of the dearest, most delicate and most domestic interests of this latter class to those which include so many much less fit than themselves to judge of them, is a very serious prospect for women.[2]

It is commonly said that the interests of women are sufficiently represented in those of men. On many points no doubt they are so – but there are points on which the interests of men and women are, or seem to be, in conflict, and these have been hitherto decided in favour of men. Their interests do not really conflict; but when the laws that regulate the relations of two parties are made by one of them only, they will be found to embody the views of only that party, and much that is, in practice, harsh and inequitable, will be the result. 'The laws of England,' Mr Gladstone remarked, 'have in many points been uniformly unfair to women.' Though this unfairness is shown chiefly in the laws respecting wives and mothers, there are laws, as those of inheritance, which are unfavourable to all women, postponing the succession of daughters to that of all the sons and their descendants. But I do not think, though hardships often result from this, that women are given to complaint about it. They are not ambitious to be the richest of their family, but all the more they ask not to be obstructed in honourably gaining their livelihood, and to have a wider field for independent exertion allowed them.

The strongest of these points are the laws affecting wives and mothers. Our marriage-law, which has been called, by one who is no friend to our cause, 'the most barbarous in Europe' hands over the woman in person and property absolutely to her husband's power. By common law the wife possesses nothing of her own. This monstrous injustice dates from the reign of Henry VIII. It was made possible, however, in some measure to evade this law by the help of the Court of Chancery which invented for the use of the richer classes a contrivance called 'settlements,' whereby through special arrangements made before marriage the use of her own property could be secured to the wife, and the capital of such property was put out of the power of herself or her husband to dispose of by the institution of trustees. But wherever these special arrangements had not been made, the wife was helplessly dependent as before, and as the object of the Court was not at all to guard woman's rights but to protect the interests of property, the unjust and barbarous principle remained the law of the land. With great difficulty, and after long resistance, some further modifications have been obtained in a state of things generally acknowledged to be monstrous and unjust, by the Married Women's Property Act of 1870, which secured to wives the control of their own earnings, and the right to property inherited from an intestate. But this law, mutilated as it was by its opponents, is so imperfect and unintelligible, that on the whole, women are little better off than before; and the unsatisfactory device of 'settlements' is still nearly all that they can resort to, expensive and troublesome as it is, often unknown to women whose ignorance of technical law is not surprising, but is a real hindrance to self-defence, and, as I said before, available only for especially privileged classes.

A husband is not liable for his wife's support while she is living with him beyond a plain bare maintenance, that is just so far as to keep her off the parish; but this law is hard to enforce, he can evade it by a petty fine, and parish relief is generally refused when it is known that the husband *can* maintain her; so that the wife may, and sometimes does, starve for want of necessaries under her husband's roof. And this law of maintenance has been made equally binding on the wife if he has squandered his means and she has either property or earnings of her own. That, in spite of the theory that the husband maintains the wife, which I have seen alleged against women's rights,[3] very large numbers of men live in idleness on their wives' earnings, is but too well known to those whose experience lies among the working classes.

Again, a man may, if he chooses, leave all his property away from his wife; she has no rights that can avail against his testamentary dispositions. If he dies intestate, the widow has but a half or a third, even though the whole property may have come originally from her, and the mass of it goes to the next of kin, perhaps an entire stranger.

Next, as to control over the wife's person. By the theory of the common law it is absolute, though of course some checks are provided against the abuse of it. But the husband can compel her to live with him, however bad his conduct, however wretched the place he would confine her to. He can reclaim her by force if she has left him; nay, even if he has deserted her for twenty years, leaving her all that time to maintain herself and her children.[4] In all these cases she is wholly in his power, unless she can prove that his violence causes her to go in fear of her life.[5] As for those terrible cases which we now alas! so repeatedly see in the public papers of savage cruelty towards weak and helpless women, of murder by brutal husbands upon wives, I am unwilling to dwell upon them, shocked as our eyes and hearts daily are by their miserable details. But have not the laws encouraged such unmanly violence and tyranny by teaching men that their wives are their property? Do not these laws, that good men would abhor to make use of, seem meant as a warrant to bad men for ill-doing; and is the punishment inflicted by law anything like adequate to the offence? And has not the tone of conversation, of the public press, of the House of Legislature itself, been too often unfavourable to a serious consideration of the matter? Has it not been regarded as rather a funny subject than otherwise? Has not literature forgotten itself into a defence of the men who kick, pound, mangle, and massacre their wives? And when some good-hearted man brings forward in the House a motion for strengthening the inadequate legal protection for women, is he not sure to be met with jocularity, and the subject dropped as something too unimportant to proceed with?[6]

But perhaps the wrong that women feel most is the state of the law with respect to their children. The child is by law the father's alone; the mother has no legal right to it. He may take it from her and give it to the care of any one he will; the comparative fitness of the respective parties for the charge makes no difference. A late modification of the law (passed in 1873) enables the mother by an expensive and troublesome process – a suit in the Court of Chancery – to obtain the care of the child *if the Court see fit to award it*; but the principle of the father's paramount rights remains the same.[7] In a late terrible case in Scotland where a bad father took from the mother an infant a few months old no redress could be had by Scotch law, and the Lord-Advocate opposed in Parliament any change in that law, on the ground that it was in principle the same as that of England.

Again, the mother is not by law the natural guardian of her child; the father can, living or by will, appoint any guardian he chooses; she, under no circumstances, can appoint one. We all know how this tells in cases where the parents are of different religions; if the father dies first, he can by will decide what religion the child is to be brought up in; nay, if he leaves no such directions the law still presumes the child is to be of the father's creed, and the relations may train it accordingly in spite of the mother's wishes. Can we wonder that mothers have been known to fly the country and hide themselves that their children may remain their own?

Now, in suffering this state of things to stand, I do not accuse men of wanton injustice; they have accepted the time-honoured institutions they have found, and, in true British character, are in no hurry to alter them – that is all. But to those who aver that women's interests are sufficiently cared for in a Legislature of men, nay better than they could be by women themselves, I must needs point out that this state of the law is more or less acknowledged as wrong by almost every one, and that some few just-minded and resolute men have, year after year, brought forward Bills to remedy it; and that, year after year, the House is counted out, or the order of the day voted, or the Bill thrown out, or so altered as to be spoilt and ineffective. The Act of 1870 for amending the law as to married women's property, imperfect as it is, took thirty years to get passed, and an attempt to enlarge and simplify it, by putting the law on a basis of equal injustice, has just been rejected in the House of Lords.[8] 'There is no reason,' says Mr Goldwin Smith, 'why Parliament should not do justice in any practical question as to women's rights that may be brought before them.' There *is* no reason, but that women's practical interests are not always the same as men's, and in the cases where they are not, of course the represented portion of the nation will be more attended to than the unrepresented. This is quite natural; it is, and has always been thus, in like cases. We all know how the unrepresented classes are apt to be legislated for. Such considerations are the very staple of the argument for enfranchising working men. In fact from the pressure of other business deemed more immediately important it is most unlikely that members will even make themselves acquainted with the claims and wants of women. 'Wrongs will be redressed,' says Mr Bright, 'when our legislators know of them;' but it is part of our complaint that they do not know of them.

Against members in general, as I have said, I wish to bring no charge. But with respect to those opponents who most vehemently rebut our plea for equal rights, it is a strong point on our side that none of these have, as far as I am aware, ever attempted to remedy any even of admitted abuses, nor shown a sign of sympathy with the sufferers, nor have, in short, ever come forward in any matter in which women are concerned, except to resist their appeal, and sometimes even with scorn and contumely.

The very contrary is the case with those true Liberals and sound-hearted Conservatives who are helping us now.

Having thus stated the nature of our claim and some of the grievances that we desire to see remedied, I must now inquire what are the objections brought against it. Waiving those that I think have been answered in my previous statements, most of them may be summed up in what I may call the *ad fœminam* argument, as thus: – 'All that you say as to unenfranchised classes and Constitutional rights would apply to men, but not to women, on account of their sex.' If you ask why, you are generally told that women are not fit to vote. To this perhaps a few words furnish a conclusive answer – women are held fit to possess property, and the possession of property is the only fitness required for the vote. But if we press for particulars, we are met by the great Nature-argument; we are told of the peculiarities of our nature, our conditions, our duties, and our character; that is, in other words, our physical and mental inferiority, our home sphere, and our political tendencies. I will endeavour to encounter each of these arguments in turn.

Now I do not, of course, deny the natural differences between men and women. I do not deny that certain works, especially those of which the sole, or chief qualification is physical strength, will best belong to men. That is so obvious, that there is no fear of such works being transferred to women, and we need not legislate to keep them in men's hands. I humbly think that Nature, so fondly referred to by our antagonists, has marked, and will always keep marked, certain broad general distinctions, and we shall realise much better what *are* the natural limits, when artificial restrictions are removed. Nor am I arguing that women can do all that men do; but I ask that what no-one denies that they can do, they should not by law be hindered from doing.

But one would like to know when it is so glibly said that Nature is opposed to this or that, what is meant by Nature. Is it ancient usage or established convention, the law or custom of our country, training, social position, the speaker's own particular fancy or prejudice, or what? And when Nature has been defined, one would like to have defined what particular actions are, or are not, against that aforesaid Nature. It seems that for a woman to manage property, carry on large businesses, be a farmer, a merchant, a parish-overseer, a clerk in various capacities, a municipal elector, or member of a School Board, or even a Sovereign, is not against Nature, but to give a vote for a Member of Parliament is. I once heard that great, comprehensive, tremendous statement, uttered loudly and emphatically at a great public meeting by a worthy gentleman – I cite him only as typical – that 'the female suffrage was against the laws of God and Nature.' But if it be not against the laws of God and Nature for a woman to exercise the direct, simple, sometimes absolute power given by a seat on the throne as she has done 'from time immemorial,' to use the favourite phrase of one of our opponents, can it be impious and unnatural for a woman to have an infinitesimal share in regulating the machinery of the State which controls us all? She will not make laws, she will merely help to choose the men who will help to make laws for us. Our opponents say that this is a demand for women to govern men, but as this Bill would only add to the electoral body by less than a seventh, they must know very well that there is no possibility of that.

'I hate women who meddle with politics,' said Napoleon to a witty French lady. Napoleon, we know, strongly maintained that nature forbade women to have anything to do with politics. 'Ah, General,' she replied, 'you men sometimes have a fancy for cutting off our heads, and we women would like to know what it is for.' She might well have said, too, that women might have something to say to State Councils that sent thousands and thousands of those they loved best to be massacred. Ours is not so extreme a case, but we feel that politics means legislation, and that legislation enters into questions in which we have a right and a necessity to be interested. We cannot separate domestic politics from social conditions of life. If then we are told that we have nothing to do with politics, we can but answer that politics have a great deal to do with us.

As for that mental inferiority imputed to our sex – the mind hopelessly closed to logic, the incapability of taking large views, the want of a sense of justice, are these considered an inherent peculiarity belonging to sex or not? If they are, it would be idle to suppose that any woman ever did, or could do, political work, or any large general work, at all; the point is settled irrevocably, in spite of all historical and present examples to the contrary; and all the women who have shone in various departments of thought, science, and action, must be dismissed as monstrosities. But if it only means that by general experience there are more men found qualified for such work than women, then it is but a question of more or less, and as there is not a logical, nor any kind of intellectual, franchise for men, we may dismiss this argument as irrelevant. And it will also be open to question whether this supposed inferiority of ours, as difficult to prove as it is easy to affirm, is not the fruit of present, long-continued, but removable conditions. *We* ask that legislation may cease, by positive restrictions, to make it impossible for us to judge of or to modify, those conditions.

The second argument drawn from our sex is that well-known one called by Mr Jacob Bright, the 'spherical argument.' He reasoned excellently that we could not practically draw a hard and fast line between men's and women's spheres, they intermingle in the business of life, there is much occupation, many interests, much work necessarily in common. This phrase of 'women's sphere' is the most indefinite of phrases, often the most inconsistent with facts. It varies with every age and every country. In India, for instance, we see it carried out with the most rigorous exactitude according to the men's notion, and the result is, that in the working classes women have all the toil and drudgery; in the upper classes they have the home-sphere in perfection – that is, utter confinement and seclusion.

With respect to the home as the woman's natural sphere, there is a semblance of truth in it which the fact belies. At least, that sphere is by no means her domain, for as wife and mother she has, as we have seen, no legal power, hardly any legal rights. Nor am I aware that our 'women's sphere' friends mean anything more than that she is to be the chief working subordinate, by no means even an equal authority in it. So that this distinction seems to result in man's keeping the supremacy in every sphere to himself. But granting this 'home' to be our sphere – as to many a woman it is a safe and happy one – our antagonists have failed to show how the giving of a vote every four or five years, or even taking an interest in politics as much, let us say, as men commonly do, would take a woman out of her sphere, or prevent her fulfilling its duties. Moreover, since to a large and increasing number of women this sphere is denied, the restriction amounts for them to the exclusion from any. Mr Goldwin Smith says that our business is now to distinguish between men's and women's spheres. Surely, this process has been going on with more or less rigour since the world began; in the face of the fact I have mentioned, and many others, it might perhaps now be useful to ascertain what is their common ground. No doubt, the home duties must be, and always will be, performed, but it is a misfortune, not a glory, if a woman finds it necessary to bound all her thoughts and cares to it; that is, to a very narrow range of personal interests. But every argument founded on the home importance of woman, as the educator of men, and her moral and social influence as man's companion, points to the necessity of her having a sense of wider responsibilities. She cannot educate men who are to be citizens without some knowledge of what citizenship is, or some feeling of citizenship herself.

I come now to the third class of alleged disqualifications of woman, her moral character, and her political tendencies. I have sometimes sat to hear Bills of Indictment drawn against women, to which it is almost a sufficient answer to say that a political dogma that rests on the depreciation of half the human race stands self-convicted of fallacy. And besides, our opponents contradict themselves, accusing woman alike of too much imagination and a want of it, of tenacity and fickleness, of cheese-paring economy and reckless expenditure, of selfishness, and unreasoning sympathy. Between all these I think we may strike a balance and conclude that her faults and virtues are those of human nature in general. But granting the favourite charge that she is more emotional and impulsive than man, what then? Can the more or less of qualities common to the race make the one half of a nation fit to be represented, the other not? Is the Irishman disqualified for a vote, because he is more impulsive than the Englishman? And may not this variety in the proportion of qualities be an advantage rather than otherwise? May there not be a danger from the exclusive preponderance of a certain set of tendencies, and may not the infusion of a new moral element sometimes strengthen the higher considerations which might be in danger of being postponed to merely commercial, or other self-regarding interests? Women have no sense of justice, it is said, and will vote according to their feelings; is that worse than voting according to the sense of drink or to sensibility to a bribe? Will an occasional triumph of sentiment, as a moral feeling is generally called, in the region of politics be more fatal than the triumph of self-interest of the lowest kind?

But then there are the political tendencies of women, and here again our antagonists contradict each other; for some allege our political apathy and want of public spirit, and others our furious reactionary fanaticism. The metaphysicians have, in fact, stepped forward with certain philosophical theories, evolved, I think, from their own inner consciousness, and proving chiefly the desire to justify a foregone conclusion. The language of these theorists implies that man is, properly speaking, all human nature, with all his faculties perfectly balanced, and woman an imperfect anomalous accessory, a bundle of instincts always foolish, and mostly mischievous. I need not say that the opposite theory regards the two sexes with their, not contrary tendencies, but different proportions of the same, as making up human nature, and presenting such a unity in diversity as, co-operating in the world's work, must produce the finest results. But let us see to what conclusions the first mentioned theory, boldly pushed to its extremes in the hands of one of these philosophers, leads him. According to him *all* women are as *one* woman with no variety in thought, feeling, or opinion, and all – I am quoting his admired words – 'by a deep and permanent cause, the sentiment inherent in the female temperament,' at once Tory and reactionary, and also revolutionary and anarchic, and disposed to loosen the marriage ties. This abstract woman, who is like no concrete woman that I ever saw or heard of, has, it seems 'no love of liberty or law,' desiring only the personal government which her weakness needs; therefore, all women will, as soon as the vote is granted them, band together to oppose those personal governors, and against *their* will and in defiance of *them* troop to the poll to 'demolish free institutions,' and 'put an end to all franchises whatever.'[9]

I imagine we shall, most of us, be a little startled at finding ourselves all classed together as one Conservative, priest-ridden, idiotic animal, who, if a modicum of power be granted it, will rise up an insane firebrand to 'overturn the institutions on which the hopes of the world rest.' But I venture to think that even if the mass of female voters were to be so incredibly silly as he gloomily pictures them, men would manage to outvote them. Ours is not a nation in which rampant folly on vital political questions is allowed to have it all its own way. However that may be, I think the general common sense will dismiss the whole grand rhetorical hypothesis as founded on an enormous assumption which no facts have yet justified. I believe, and I think most women, and men who are really acquainted with women, will agree with me, that women vary as men vary, that they are moulded and modified by the same diversified influences as affect men, birth, education, family-belongings, social atmosphere; and that, these variations apart, Englishwomen are of the same race as Englishmen, and partake of the same strong national character. So that, on the whole, Magna Charta is not likely to be repealed by the female descendants of those who won it for us.[10]

Finally, what these metaphysicians and rhetoricians seem to forget is that to the large majority of women voters the claims of practical life will be much more present than political visions and abstract principles; that their votes will represent not only a sex, but members of classes with the interests belonging thereto, landowners, farmers, traders, shopwomen, and handworkers, persons who are likely to be quite content with the general institutions of their land when they do not press too hardly and directly on their own moral and material well-being, which free institutions are much less likely to do than arbitrary ones.

Others of our opponents, as I have said, dwell on our incapability of sympathising with great causes, our natural apathy about politics, and, at the same time, our stagnant Toryism. This, one might say, is adding insult to injury. We are excluded from all practical share in politics, we are taught that they are not our concern, our 'sphere' as it is called, we are brought up in perfect ignorance of them, and then we are reproached for our indifference to them! I might rather wonder that we care as much for politics as we do. It needs but for an intelligent man to be in the habit of talking in his family on such matters, for the simplest and most unassuming women to take an interest in them. But – want of sympathy with great national causes! Have there then been no patriotic women in England's history? Do not our hearts beat for our country, for its welfare and its greatness, for its defenders, for their sufferings, their perils, and their glory, just as strongly as any man's? I do not think many men who have themselves great causes at heart will echo such a complaint.

As for the indictment of universal Toryism, if it be true that there are more Conservatives among women than among men, this cannot to the true Liberal be a just reason for their exclusion. What business have we to make or maintain laws to exclude the political party whose views we dislike? Try and educate them rather to a better view of things is what we should say about an excluded class of men; and if our Bill pass, I dare say my liberal friends will look to this in future in their own families.[11] But it is no part of my argument to decry this phase of political opinion or this habit of political thought. It may well have its tender, its generous, its useful side. What I am concerned with is to show that it is with women, as with men, a phase dependent on their social and intellectual conditions, not on the 'inherent temperament of sex.' It would be more fair to say that in politics women ordinarily adopt the opinion of the men around them than that all women have but one opinion amongst them. If this leads generally to Toryism, we can only say that on constitutional principles the party that has a majority in the nation has a right to a majority in the House. But conversation, books, journals, joined to all the quickening influences of varied society, are rapidly giving women the power of forming their own opinions; and it is a certain fact that for the most part the highly-gifted and enlightened women who, in their own spheres, lead public opinion, are thorough Liberals.

Even should a Conservative Government, in giving a vote to

women, temporarily strengthen their own cause, we shall not be alarmed, believing, as we do, in those general permanent laws, which necessitate progress, yet restrain political excess, maintain, with us, in the long run, a due balance of forces, and have always rendered it impossible for even the most extreme partisans, when in the ascendant, to introduce a real and lasting reaction.

There is one more argument that I must notice which has been rather in favour with literary journals. It is this – that the basis of government is physical force, that is, personal strength, and therefore women being physically the weaker are unfitted for the franchise. This is alarming, for physical weakness, combined with legal inequality, seems to ensure not so much protection as oppression. But what is meant by physical force being the basis of government? I have always thought that government was designed to *supersede* physical force, that civilization meant the reign of law instead of that of brute-strength. Public opinion, moral restrictions, mental power and organisation, make up now the forces on which government rests, compared to which bodily force is simply nothing. This would be going back to savagedom, indeed. Doubtless, before communities were formed, the man who could knock the other down would have most power. But, as soon as people began to live in an orderly way together, it was the strongest headed, not the strongest handed, man who became chief of the tribe. The titles of our first rulers, the eorls and ealdormen, imply not that they were the most muscular, but the oldest, and, therefore, the wisest, and our Witenagemot ('assembly of wise men') was formed on the same principle. Physical force is one of the instruments kept in reserve by government, and the government may be that of a woman or a weak old man, and be none the less secure. Our Cabinet ministers are not chosen from the men who can knock each other down. Depend upon it, it is something more than muscle that keeps society together, or we are living on the brink of a convulsion. If all the muscle of the nation were pitted against the brain, no doubt the women would go down, but so too would all the men of intellect. But I do not fear any such divorce between brain and muscle. The classes who most represent the latter have quite enough of the former to know that the law is still stronger than they; and they respect it accordingly.

And, after all, what connexion has this theory of physical force with Women's Suffrage? with the vote given by a small fraction of them, legally and constitutionally, in an orderly and settled state of things? Does it mean only that none are to be represented but those who can take by force what they want, or defend by

301

force what others attack? This would exclude from the suffrage all sickly men, and most men above sixty. But the embodiment of physical force, soldiers, sailors, and police, have no vote. It would be just as fair to say that women ought not to have property, because, if men wanted to take it from them, they could not defend it by force.

But the philosophers have invented some curious imaginary cases to support this theory. They say that, if women have the vote, they will be sure to attempt to pass some absurd law. That they will force candidates to pledge themselves to it, the House of Commons to pass it, the Ministry to sanction it. That the physical force of the nation will rise in revolt to overturn the Government, and thus all Government will be rendered impossible. This prediction of skill in political organisation and combination beyond that of men, to be shown by the sex asserted to be least interested in and most incompetent for politics, and the assumption that, if half the nation are lunatics the other half must be imbeciles, I think, we may dismiss, in Miss Fenwick Miller's words, as 'speculation run mad.'

Perhaps I ought to take some notice of the speech made against us last year by our most distinguished opponent, Mr John Bright. It will not require much notice, for I cannot think that he was speaking his best, or that his arguments would have much effect, except on minds previously biassed. He dismissed, however, the political objections, which he considered groundless, and rested his case on the 'sentimental' argument. He dwelt on doubts and uncertainties as to what might follow from such a beginning. Surely, this is not the way in which he would regard concessions made to men. If the concessions are, in themselves, just and reasonable, he would trust to the same sense of justice and reason which caused them to be granted to prevent concessions which should be neither just nor reasonable.

In fact, the only two distinct objections that Mr Bright brought forward were – first, that this demand is based on hostility to men, and will cause still more hostility; secondly, that electioneering is too vile a business for women to have anything to do with. As to the charge of hostility, it amazes me. We ask that we may help in the choice of men to maintain a masculine Government. We are not demanding the vote that we may elect women instead of, and in opposition to, men. Hostility! Why, all we ask is to be gained from and through men, and men are helping us now – husbands and wives are working side by side. Is not the hostility shown rather more in the refusal than in the demand?

But Mr Bright thinks that, as soon as men have shown their

generosity, their justice, in raising women to a level with themselves, the women will be armed against the men, and there will be discord and enmity everywhere. To paint this discord in sufficiently alarming colours, he has to travel far beyond the four corners of the Bill. He pictures a household with the father and mother voting different ways, and the brothers and sisters quarrelling in consequence. Does he really mean that we are to legislate to prevent there being a difference of opinion between the men and women in one family, or, rather, to prevent women from expressing a different opinion from the men? At present, assuredly, the men and women in a household can differ about politics, and about things which interest them far more deeply than politics – religion, for instance – without quarrelling. What, then, is there in this vote – given at an interval of years, and done with – to change human nature so entirely? Love depends on the thousand daily incidents of life, not on the abstract opinions of people who, in nine cases out of ten, have no strong interest in such matters. If a man is a kind and just husband, he need not fear his wife's estrangement because he votes Whig and she votes, or would, if she had the power, vote Tory. Mr Bright thinks the fact of our legislators having mothers, wives and daughters must prevent their ever being unfair to women. Yet, he will not allow that women's having fathers, brothers and sons will prevent their arming themselves against men.

But Mr Bright's second objection – that against women having anything to do with the processes of choosing a member – raises more serious considerations. If such grossness, violence, and corruption are, as he says, inherent in the present political system, it becomes a question whether Representative Government is a thing that ought to continue, or whether *men* are fit to conduct it? I need not say that *I* do not admit either alternative at all; but, in taking for granted that the whole thing is necessarily so bad that even a man must feel shame in having had anything to do with it, Mr Bright makes the most damaging admission I ever heard from the lips of a Liberal. But have we not found, to the credit both of men and women, that, on social occasions, whether of business or pleasure, the presence and participation of women have helped to soften, purify, regulate. Will it not be the case here? It is allowed that, since the ballot, the election day no longer presents the objectionable scenes that it once did. May we not hope that the previous process *need* not be such as it will disgrace a woman to have to do with? Let us never, no, not for a moment, acquiesce tranquilly in the necessity of evil accompanying the performance of any work, public or private. Let the desire and effort that women should concur in this work be a pledge of efforts equally strong to lift it above all that can tarnish or debase it.

The other speeches against us in the debate of 1876 do not call for much notice. The arguments were not new nor very profound, and were mostly such as, I think, have been sufficiently answered in the foregoing pages. One of these speakers, indeed, said that, when the majority of women wished for the vote it could not be refused them. But how are honourable gentlemen to discover that majority? The almost impossible task is set before women of *letting it be known* that the vote is wished for, without *showing* that they wish for it. No such paradoxical test was applied to *men* when it was decided that it was fit and just that the great majority of them should have the suffrage, whether they wish for it or no. But, in our case, petitions are scouted as no test; all agitation is regarded as the work of a few restless women, meetings and speeches are ridiculed; the many women of culture, thought, and feeling, of social energy and devoted benevolence, who desire it, are passed over as unknown, or put aside as exceptional, or branded as masculine. This last assertion has not, I believe, been made by any men whom we have reason to respect, nor will it, I hope, deter us. The causes that move us in this matter lie deeper than such men's words and thoughts can fathom. And if to have a warm interest in great national and public concerns, and to wish to help in them with our best work, is to be masculine, then let us be masculine, and be proud of being so. No virtue ought to be monopolised by either sex.

The debate of last session presented no such distinguished opponent as Mr Bright, and, as we have said, the state of mind of the House was not favourable to any calm and serious discussion of the claim. But of the speeches that were made, and the articles in the press that followed, all had this in common, that they ignored the Bill before them and its provisions, to dwell upon something that it did not contemplate. In fact, they could make out no case whatever if they did not do so. So they 'rose upon a wind of prophecy,' making general alarming assertions, which involved the three well-known assumptions – first, that women would form the absolute and great majority of the voters; second, that women, having, instead of human nature, a peculiar feminine nature, would always act as one woman, and opposed to men; third, that political arrangements can change nature itself.

The fears that may be entertained by good-hearted and reasonable men of a deterioration in that which they love and admire, though we may think them erroneous, are entitled to respect; but we cannot yield a like deference to that noisy majority which made one ask whether we were governed by brains or by strength of lungs, and suggested that painful doubt that 'masculine' and 'manly' were not always convertible terms.

But there was somewhat more of novelty in some of the newspaper arguments on the subject, and I propose to examine those of two of them, the *Spectator* and the *Times*. That of the *Spectator* is indeed the old one of physical force, but now formulated into a very distinct political principle. The writer in this journal, who appears as our regular opponent, at any rate never drops the character of a man of culture and a gentleman; I desire therefore to answer him as seriously and cogently as I can. I will first quote his argument; 'Women can only obtain the franchise by persuading men to give it them . . . and so long as men choose to refuse their demand, they have no means of enforcing it. This of itself constitutes, at all events, an initial difference between the cases of men and of women who are denied it. The nearer Parliament comes to a proportionate representation of the forces which, if there were no Parliament, would govern the country, the nearer it will approach to a perfect machine for its own purpose. . . . When the middle class was refused the vote they demanded, they could threaten a march from Birmingham to Westminster. When the artisans were refused the vote they demanded, they could demolish the Hyde Park railings.' It is assumed as usual, of course, that the women electors will be the majority, and that their vote will be given *en masse*, not divided like men's, and he further illustrates his point by a case which he assumes will be frequent, if not normal, in which it will be opposed to that of the majority of men's.

Put shortly, the above statement means that the paramount claim of any interests whatever to the attention of the Legislature is founded – not on force of reason, nor on the justice of the claim, nor on a numerical majority, nor on anything but the possibility of violence. The argument, then, leads to this or nothing – that no political class of measures may exist, save such as the classes disposed to violence (if such there be) may tolerate. On this showing, the government of England is, the rule of a Parliament tempered by fear of mob-violence. Our political condition, such as it would be if there were no Parliament, which pathetical condition the *Spectator* tells us is to regulate the actual representation of forces within it, would be, of course, either personal and despotic rule, or anarchy caused by the predominance of the brute-force element, an element which I thought Parliament was instituted, not 'proportionately,' that is preponderantly, to represent, but to control. Carry out the above argument, and it follows that we must live under a mob-tyranny. For, of course, the working classes – I name them because it is of them that it is assumed that they would menace violence – could threaten a demonstration when they believe their interests assailed, whether they have a vote or not; and in these cases, says the *Spectator*, 'it is wise to yield rather than have a state of permanent civil war.' Thus, if the lower classes were to demand Universal or Manhood Suffrage, they must have it because they can use force to insist on it. The *Spectator* admits that in that case we shall have a worse House of Commons, indeed he thinks it already worse in proportion to the lowering of the vote, but that it must be done because Parliament must 'accurately represent the forces out of doors.'[12]

I should have said that the allowing matters to come to such a pass as to necessitate hasty concessions to popular demands, in order to prevent civil war, exhibited not government in its normal action, but the absence of any real government at all. That our constitutional system is so framed as to exclude any such alternative, is shown by the fact that the lower stratum of society have not exercised this power of rule by intimidation even in days when they really had just cause of complaint. Had those demands of the people, which the *Spectator* has instanced as successful, not been just and reasonable, it was the duty of the Government to resist them, to resist, if necessary, lawless mob force with organised and law-sanctioned force. It was not because the people threatened to march from Birmingham to London or broke Hyde Park railings, but because those demands were just, and, being just, were backed up by a great force of opinion in the educated and influential classes that the Government felt they could not take the responsibility of refusing them. This principle, as embodied in our practice, will I think sufficiently guarantee the safety of a Constitutional system of which women's votes should form a part.

But the *Spectator* writer gives us a test, which he seems to consider crucial, of the mischievous working of female participation in politics. Here is the great Eastern Question, and the national feeling about it. All women, it is asserted, would vote for the use of force in aid of the oppressed Christians – most men would be for neutrality, and thus a dead-lock or a riot, or, at the very best, a simple nullification of the women's vote must ensue. 'For (he asks) do we suppose that in such a case the men would quietly submit to be forced to war by the women, the men who fill our armies and navies, and pay the taxes?' Does not this able writer forget that women too pay taxes, or have the same interest in the payment of them as men, that our armies and navies are voluntarily filled, and that *they* are not the classes that we find most averse to war? But, in short, it is utterly idle to talk of a direct opposition in this matter, or any like matter, between men and women; there is no such sharp division of opinion as it is, and not the remotest desire on any woman's part to go to war on one side or the other. Does he suppose that while the great mass of the nation is saying, 'Let us keep out of war,' a chorus of feminine trebles will rise in the midst to cry, 'No, let us rush into it!'

But supposing that in any disputed question the small contingent of the women's votes should help to turn the scale, and this could only be if the party were a very considerable one already – when then? Is a good measure nullified because women may concur with men in passing it? Is a bad one less dangerous because men only have had the passing of it? And what is this more than the usual course of constitutional action as now regulated? Does it not constantly occur that the views of one class of voters will help to determine the preponderance of some line of policy? Have not the illiterates and the public-house customers in great measure returned this Tory House of Commons? It is true that the *Spectator* writer must in consistency approve of this, because *they* are the classes from which violence is possible; women belong to the classes which have neither the will nor the power to make a disturbance – they belong to the propertied, the pacific, the educated classes; therefore, they must not have a vote. But does not this apply to classes of men just as well as to women? Might we not on this ground eliminate clergymen, old men, and sickly men? We can make a class of them at once for purposes of disqualification. Clergymen, especially, might be supposed likely to vote as a class, and not in accordance with working men, and are not likely to support their opinion by violence; yet we do not fear constitutional ruin from their vote. Nor surely are our working classes such wild animals as to trample down law and society whenever they do not get their way, and crush the women to begin with, as the *Times* kindly assures us they will. Before this happens, England will be no longer England, and whether men or women have a vote, will then little matter.

The *Times'* article is too long and declamatory, and, I must say, too little to the direct purpose to quote; briefly, its assumption is that we always are, or are going to be, in a violent state of conflict, of either external war, 'blood and iron,' or of internal fury, stormy meetings, and the like, when a rough vote, not a gentle one, is wanted, and women must be put aside altogether as having nothing to do with the matter. This, of course, is an argument concocted to suit merely the present moment, and could not have even the semblance of force at any other. Such a state of things (if it ever exists) must, one would think, be quite exceptional in our age, in our country, under our system of government, amidst our well-organised community. The very principle of the Constitution is to give all interests free play. We were once told (and I have shown) by the *Times* itself that property must be represented; now we are told that the vote should be not for property, but for bodily force. We had hoped that in our present stage of civilisation brain as well as force would have its influence, that old men, feeble students, men of peace, might give their votes safely, and yield their best help to their country's councils. But, no! it is absurd to take into account anything but passion and violence and brute force. This, then, is the age of 'Sturm und Drang' with a vengeance!

The *Times* further says, 'Here are men wrestling in rude arenas, in stormy passion, in daily and nightly excitement, and women in domestic calm, quietly and theoretically revolving the questions which are arousing the deepest passions and interests of men.' And it asks, 'Are both these classes to have votes alike?' and adds, 'We submit that such a division of labour is preposterously unfair.' Might we not paint the picture a little otherwise, as thus – 'Here are men rioting, raving, and roaring in public-houses and the like, in strong irrational excitement; and here are women feeling, thinking, and suffering at home on matters which are of equally deep and vital interest to *them*; and is it a fair division of labour that they should have no part in the question but to suffer, while the roarers and ravers are to decide?' It seems to me that if women can think and feel earnestly on these subjects without going into a passion or a public-house, they have, so far, a better claim to be heard.

We know, indeed, very well that the noisy brawlers do not represent the real governing forces, least of all on occasions of critical importance. But the *Times* has, it appears, a particular objection, on occasions like the present, to what it calls, 'gentle philosophical votes.' It is new to hear women's political characteristics thus described, we have generally heard complaints of their preferring sentiment to reason, and of the danger of 'hysterical' politics; but it seems we are to be hit hard on every side. Parties, it appears, are now furiously divided, some savagely disposed for war and bloodshed, others as fiercely bent on neutrality, for it is assumed that no men are, or ought to be, calm on this subject. Why we are to be especially given up to physical force on an occasion like this, which, as the *Times* justly observes, is 'a matter for statesmen, not armies, to decide,' I really do not know. We read of a Queen Elizabeth, who, like a statesman as she was, kept the balance between peace and war in far more perilous times.

But I am not the least disposed to admit that we are, or are going to be, in such a state of violent agitation and of discord between men and women, from expectation of a war which will drive all our peaceful civilians into the field, and turn the whole body of women into nuisances to be carted away. I see nothing in this, any more than in our normal state, that will make the vote of an orderly taxpaying law-obeying part of the community other than useful and proper.

The last point that I have to mention on the whole subject might as fitly have come elsewhere; it may be urged by others (as it is) as an objection to our claim, it may be urged by us as a social grievance. We are, it is said, not educated enough for the franchise. But what is the standard for a man? Not to be able to write his name, or even to read it when written, but to understand the mark made for it. That is all the education required for a male elector. Compared with this, the female standard will be that of high cultivation. No doubt women might be better educated (as well as men) but if in truth we are less fit than the humblest artisan, whose doing is it but that of the political and social legislation which has fixed our status for us, just as formerly the want of education of the lower orders, as they were termed, was the work of those higher orders who had undertaken to manage everything for them? The importance of education and of providing the means for it, whether for general culture or special training, has been recognised by public opinion for men, but not for women, otherwise than of the most imperfect and superficial kind. But women are not content with this, and are trying their best to improve it. They are struggling with immense difficulties – difficulties from that trades' unionism which shuts them out from established general institutions, from the means of special training, from the use of endowments lavishly applied for the other sex, difficulties from the indifference of the State, and still more from the indifference of the public. Yet, unhelped, at least[13] at first, save by the private exertions of some good and wise men, women have struggled on, showing alike in those who are working for others and those who are working to educate themselves, some of the most valuable qualities that could be applied to its own work by the State, such as will at least surely enable them to understand what they are doing when giving a vote.

I think the history of the long-continued, earnest, piteous struggles of women for an education which, for many, means absolutely bread to eat, which for all means usefulness, refinement, elevation, happiness, will justify me in saying that *not till women are of some political value will their education be regarded as a matter of national importance.*

The arguments that I have now dealt with singly, may, I think, be summed up together as the expression of a not unnatural, though unreasoning prejudice, shaped either into a robust denial of facts, or a contradiction to that common sense which is applied readily enough to other subjects, or a chain of purely speculative and fanciful hypotheses. But there is one argument that has been less touched on than any other, which yet is more worthy of reply as having a wider scope and being built on more rational premises. It may be said – Mr Bright, indeed, has said it – that a nation has a right to choose how it shall be governed, whether by one man, or by few, or by many. But the nation *has* chosen, long ago, and most decisively and permanently, that it shall be governed, not by one man, or by few, or even by many, but by itself – that is by *all*, as it understands the word *all*, which is, in fact, all who, as it is said, have a stake in the country; it remains then only to decide how that government by all shall best be organised. But the objectors, those who wish to regard all institutions as yet on their trial, will argue that the condition to be first sought in a system of government is the selection of the best powers in the nation for the purpose of governing, that the representative system has in its very nature a tendency to make such a discovery and selection difficult, and to expand itself beyond its nucleus of the fittest, and that the larger the non-selective admission of popular elements is made, the less effective is the governing power; and that the exclusion of women as a body is to be justified on this principle.

To which we answer first, that a still greater and more vital principle underlies all our ideas of government, and that is the liberty of the governed, which appears to be essentially connected with that expansion from which the exclusion of half the nation is a mere anomalous departure.

Secondly, that if our system had been designedly framed on the principle of the selection for government of the best powers in the nation, which includes of course the rejection of the worst, and the exclusion of women had been decided on as part of that method, whether as a legitimate deduction from the premises, or on proof of unfitness from experiment made, there would at least be consistency in this view. But, in point of fact, as I have said, the object of our Constitutional system was not to construct a machine for securing the best and choicest instruments of rule so much as to ensure to the ruled a share in the work with the rulers. And as no such principle of selection or construction was present at the first formation of national representation, nor in the further modelling and extension of it; as the exclusion of women has been an undesigned and accidental feature of the same, derived neither from reasoned conclusion nor from trial made, and inconsistent with its real first principle, the representation of property; as not exclusion but expansion has been the law of its growth, in accordance with all other national conditions – this exclusion of *one* element together with the ever-increasing admission of others still less select, to which the quality of the government resulting from their choice must more or less correspond, does not tend to the improvement of the representation, but does tend to the depression and depreciation of the one class that is thus marked as inferior to all classes of men, and so far to the unsatisfactoriness of the legislative result, and to the injury of national freedom.

Granting the inherent imperfections of a representative form of government, it is certain that it is the only one that the nation will recognise, that the result of all progress has been to strengthen and expand it, and that if the tendency of such expansion towards a democracy is regarded as dangerous, the exclusion of the only remaining element which would not be democratic is not more politic than it is just, anymore than is the deliberate rejection of social and civil powers which undoubtedly exist, from the field where they would have their highest as well as most defined and best limited exercise.

To go back briefly on the whole subject. These terrors expressed as to women's being in any way mixed up with men's affairs and with public business, all start from a point of view which we are passing away from. In fact, the barriers that once enclosed women are falling spontaneously and inevitably on every side, and what they *can* do, they will and must be allowed to do. When the ground has been conquered in so many other directions, when women have proved themselves worthy comrades of men in intellectual work; when they have a thought, a will, often a voice in large movements, beneficent organisations, social reforms, it really seems to be a kind of old-fashioned pedantry to refuse them this one sign of equality with men before the law – this proof that they too have a part in all that makes for a nation's greatness and prosperity.

And now to draw to a close. We have been told of women's indifference to politics, and especially to the possession of a vote. We hear of the 'few women who desire it.' I do not know that those who say so have taken any pains to ascertain whether they are few or many; I have already given some proofs that they are not a small number, and that they are growing.[14] I believe that those who think them few, and affirm that they find the 'best women' against it, have inquired – if they have inquired at all – only amongst the strictly drawing-room class, the ladies at ease, with every comfort and enjoyment, and knowing perhaps but little, at any rate taking no account, of the classes who have none of their advantages. Without disputing their merits, I should say they are the women who have in general thought least upon the subject. I find indifference co-extensive with ignorance, and obstruction the result of indifference. I find that the two classes whose opinion ought to have most value on the subject are most in favour of it. These are, first the women of cultivated thought and practical usefulness, who have given their attention and their powers of work to women's needs, and to public and social questions as connected with them; secondly, the women who from their social position suffer most from that man-made law of which the object has been to enforce the rights of men at the expense of theirs. For this is not a 'ladies' question, it is a 'women's' question, and I and many others know how the working order of women feel their practical grievances, and how they would hail any change that promised to amend them. And I am sure that those who are now indifferent, because uninformed, on the subject, will feel with me when they realise what is wanted, and what help can be given.

How can we help them? There are legitimate womanly ways by which women who have no desire, perhaps no power, to do what men call 'descending into the arena,' can further this movement for the benefit of their sex. They can sign petitions – this is the Constitutional method provided whereby individuals and classes can, without any kind of agitation, violence, or publicity, make the Legislature acquainted with their wishes. Again, they may use their social influence in a way no-one thinks unfeminine – they may persuade; I do not by persuasion mean coaxing, but appealing with our hearts in our words to men's reason, and best feelings. Let us remember the wife of Croke, one of the judges on Hampden's famous trial for his refusal to pay ship money. He would have yielded to fear, and given judgment for the King, but she adjured him not to sacrifice his conscience for fear of injury to his family, saying that she was content to suffer any misery with him rather than that he should violate his integrity. What she was in those fiery times that tried the metal of all hearts, let us be whenever occasion may arise – that is, helpers of others in the path of devotion to duty.

I conjure then all those, men and women alike, who have not thought much on this subject before, to think of it earnestly now. I conjure those who are already working to work on without discouragement, confident of the result. Let us think of the great causes that have been won by sheer hard struggling year by year, begun by one or two high-hearted men, carried on by a determined band, secured at last by the voice and sanction of the nation; all won by the same process that we are now pursuing – steady, peaceful, constitutional effort. The Abolition of the Slave Trade, perhaps the purest and noblest cause ever striven for, was a work in which women aided men; the passionate humanity which dictated their efforts was common to both. Again, the first Reform Bill was a people's success; this cause was fought for with more partisan violence from the strong class feeling which the struggle excited. But what was notable in it was that such an extension of the suffrage as the creation of a £10 borough franchise, and a £50 rent county franchise was thought at the time so revolutionary as to endanger our ancient Constitution, yet it proved so insufficient as to be changed in thirty-five years for our present ratepaying, and £12 tenant's franchise. But the most perfect example of a legitimate and successful agitation for a political object was that of the Repeal of the Corn Laws, an act which gave bread to starving millions. All these great causes were triumphantly and gloriously won, and the secret of the success was the intense, glowing, inspiring zeal of those who believed in them. Let us have faith and fervour like them.

I believe the heart of the country is with us; but after walking among these safe, smooth social fields, we have to knock at the iron gates and pass through the thorny paths of the two Houses of Legislature; and there we may again be baffled for the time, nay most probably shall be. But till we have conquered we must not relax our efforts. I shall be content, as one of our supporters has said, 'to die in harness,' certain as I am – as certain as that the sun will rise to-morrow – that the progress of enlightenment, liberty, and justice, will not long continue partial and one-sided, that ignorance, frivolity, and unreasoning submission will cease to be the portion of one sex and the delight of the other, and that this subjection of half the race will, like other barbarisms, melt away into the darkness of the past.

NOTES

1 Of this, if called upon to do so, I could give instances too many for citation here, but will only allude to the rules and regulations made and enforced by strikes or threatened withdrawal, all with the objects above mentioned, on the part of the workmen in various trades – as the wood engravers of London, the watchmakers, the carpet workers of Kidderminster, the factory weavers of Yorkshire and Nottingham, printers and type setters in Manchester, painters of pottery-ware in Staffordshire, not to mention such opposition as many members of the medical profession are still offering to women students.

2 The well organised efforts which have been lately made to increase the Irish vote by putting on the voting register a larger proportion of Irish lodgers and small householders in the Metropolitan boroughs and elsewhere, will, without the necessity of waiting for further legislation, have the effect of extending the franchise to large numbers of uneducated electors.

3 Mr Goldwin Smith says 'It must be remembered that the man remains responsible for the maintenance of his wife and children.' Not legally – as many a starved wife and child know, whose 'natural protector' is spending the money, which perhaps she has earned, at the public house.

4 These instances are taken from decisions by police magistrates.

5 I am told by a lawyer that a wife is not entitled to this release from a husband even in a case of ill-usage if he is subject to *delirium tremens*; because to constitute cruelty *will* and *intention* must be proved and where this malady exists there can be neither.

6 There has no doubt recently been legislative action concerning offences against the person; but this was immediately inspired by cases in which the violence had extended to men. The *Pall Mall Gazette* observed that the kicking to death of wives was often caused by the wives' own extreme ill conduct, 'but now that *men* also,' &c. &c.

7 The first limitation of the law which recognises the father as the only parent was enacted in 1833, empowering the Court of Chancery, on special application, to grant to the mother the care of her child, up to *seven* years only! The age is now extended to 16, but this remedy is to be secured only by the precarious process just named.

8 As a specimen of the arguments that are found to tell against us, I may mention the suggestion that a married woman, if she had her property in her own power, might leave her husband and set up in a shop or a business with a man whom she called her cousin for a partner. This argument, or whatever it may be called, seems to have a peculiar charm for our legislators, as it was repeated from a debate of some years ago in the Commons, where it met with equal success.

9 My readers must not think I am exaggerating. I have given the statement almost entirely in Mr Goldwin Smith's own words. His article is full of equally astounding assertions as to historic or existent

facts; but I have not space here to point them out. Nor is it necessary, for that piece of rhetoric is, I imagine, nearly forgotten. But the above theory may, and does, reappear in various shapes.

10 The results of the School Board elections have curiously falsified Mr Smith's vaticinations. The *Spectator* attributes to the disappointment of the reactionaries the increased acrimony shown by the Tory party in the House against Women's Suffrage.

11 It is obvious that till a practical test of the political tendencies of women is arrived at by admitting them to record their votes, such generalisation is incapable of proof, but remains in the region of assertion and speculation only – as, for instance, when the Liberal representative of a Welsh county said that, although he *had been told* that in Wales women were mostly Liberal, he *had been told* also that in England they were all Conservatives. The contrary assertion has lately been made by many Conservative gentlemen in London, who *have been told* that women would generally be Liberals.

12 May I suggest that certainly one element, that of the 'roughs,' was very 'accurately represented' by the majority in the debate I have been speaking of.

13 It is with pleasure that we notice the liberality of various public educational bodies in offering their advantages, as has recently been done, to women students.

14 Here, indeed, I might quote Mr Mill, who says: 'If only one woman in twenty thousand used the suffrage, to be declared capable of it would be a boon to all women.'

Helen Blackburn

Some of the facts of the women's suffrage question

1878

> Doth the desire for freedom rivet bonds
> Here, where thy boast is freedom?
> The Hon. Mrs Octavius Knox

TO
THE ELECTORS OF GREAT BRITAIN
AND IRELAND,

With whom it rests to return a House of Commons
in harmony with the needs of the time.

As the constitutional law of Great Britain formerly stood women
were not incapacitated, by reason of sex, from voting in
Parliamentary elections. As that law now stands women are
rendered incapable of exercising the franchise, and strange to tell,
their exclusion from this most important right and duty of
citizenship is due to this present century. Restriction of political
liberty is the last result which might have been anticipated from
an English Reform Bill, especially in a century when constitutional principles of Government are extending with unprecedented
rapidity. Yet the great Reform Bill of 1832 deliberately and for the
first time in our history, excluded women from the general
extension of political rights by using the term 'Male Persons' in all
the new franchises created by that Act instead of people. The term

'people' was, however, still retained in such of the old franchises as were untouched by the new legislation and women were not deliberately excluded from these older franchises until the decision of the Court of Common Pleas in 1868. Up to that time they might hope to break through the long growth of custom which hindered their exercise of the right and to record their votes quietly in company with all other duly qualified persons. Since that date this has become impossible without an enabling statute such as the Bill to Remove the Electoral Disabilities of Women.

In earlier and ruder ages when arms occupied the most prominent part of a man's existence, the exercise of electoral rights would seem to have been treated as a comparatively domestic concern, one which could be attended to by the non-combatant portions of adult society as well as by the combatant. But times have greatly changed since the days when our forefathers admitted ladies of rank and abbesses to an equal place in their Witenagmotes and on this point the change has been against, and not in accordance with the progressive growth of liberal institutions.

When Henry III and Edward I summoned abbesses to appear in Parliament and Edward III commanded peeresses to appear by proxy the idea of disqualification by reason of sex cannot have entered the common law of the land. No words occur in the early statutes regulating the elections of Knights to Parliament which can be construed as excluding women. The Knights of all counties (Henry VI x. c. II) are to be chosen by the *people* dwelling in the same, who have freeholds to the value of 40s. a year. 'These are extant,' says Mr Chisholm Anstey, 'many Parliamentary returns for counties and boroughs from the earliest times which were made by female electors and yet were received. Some of these are enumerated in Prynne's collection of Parliamentary writs, some of later date are mentioned in the Commons' Journals themselves, others are to be found in the repositories of the learned or the curious.'

Although women cannot be shewn to have been placed under any legal incapacity they fell under an incapacity almost as decided in its effects – that of custom. When home politics acquired a more absorbing interest these became more jealously guarded by men and although the right to vote remained unaffected, the inconsistency of allowing the civil law to treat women as subordinated to men while constitutional law left them equally independent acted insensibly on ordinary practice and told detrimentally on the general conception of their status. Persons treated by the policy of the law in the private relations of life as

317

perpetual minors could not be consistently regarded as fit to share any exercise of sovereign power; thus that which was 'contrary to the policy of the law' easily came to be esteemed as also 'contrary to decency.' The exercise of the franchise by women became so rare as to pass at last out of the current of ordinary ideas and Lord Coke's hasty inclusion of all women amongst non-electors was quietly acquiesced in though, as has been shewn by Mr Chisholm Anstey in a passage given below, the facts of his own time refuted the assertion.

Quoting Lord Coke, Mr Serjeant Heywood writes in 1790, 'and so the law is *understood* to be at the present day,' while Mr Hallam remarks, 'women have generally been supposed capable of no political right but that of reigning.' Nevertheless, this supposed incapacity rested, not on legislative enactment, but on custom, the first exclusion by statute law dating, as has been already said, from the Reform Bill of 1832.

The force of custom might encourage constitutional law to tarnish its own principles and approximate its practice to the policy of subordination which had been inherited as regards civil matters from an earlier stage of civilization, but custom however old and time-honoured, cannot withstand the tendency which draws political and social interests into closer relations. How was it possible that an agitation like that preceding the Reform Bill should sweep over the country and impart none of the excitement of the time to mothers, sisters and daughters, especially when the cry for reform was swelled by the cry for bread? It was the Corn Law of 1815 that first stirred Englishwomen into political combination, that made the women of the manufacturing centres form 'sister associations' to co-operate with the men. Reform came, heedless enough of them and of their part in the excitement; but the Corn Law still remained, bread was still kept back from their children's mouths, work from their looms, by that Parliament-made scarcity. Did men struggling for the Anti-Corn Law League tell women politics were not for them? – nay rather, they called on them to aid. 'This is emphatically a mother's question, it is a mother's duty to take it up' writes the Anti-Corn Law Circular and again and again refers to the help women gave. Then women learned to petition, a practice which hitherto had been generally confined to men, then women learned to attend public meetings, to watch closely the proceedings of debates and of elections. When the Corn Law was abolished the country returned to its usual quiet but the lesson learned could never be forgotten, politics had touched the inmost recesses of home, politics therefore had touched the women in the home and they knew now that the interests within and the interests without were closely interwoven together as they had never known it before. They had learned something of the power for good of combined effort and association. These were lessons which once learned both by women as they regarded themselves, and by men as they regarded women could not be forgotten but taught many to see that the time was fast approaching when, instead of discouraging the electoral rights of women, it was becoming socially imperative to encourage them. That apart from the injustice of creating an artificial distinction between persons equally fulfilling the test which should qualify for electoral power, such a distinction was discordant both with the much-prized principle that taxation should be accompanied by representation and with the tendency of modern times. That it was injuring society to teach women to cultivate an apathetic attitude of mind towards public affairs when so many interests of vital importance to every hearth were subjects of public policy. The course of women's education was extending beyond the narrow range within which a non-manufacturing, non-locomotive manner of life had held it for the majority of middle-class women, but instead of deepening that course was becoming dissipated on superficialities until it was worthless. The solid industrial occupations of a self-contained household of a generation or two ago which had become absorbed by large manufactories, instead of being replaced by solid intellectual occupations, were giving way to a pursuit of accomplishments which scarcely merited even so respectable a description as a dilettante pursuit, so unsystematic was the curriculum of a girl's education, bearing the same relation to true education that a patchwork of chance fragments does to a co-ordinated design. For was not the merest outer garnish good enough for those whom human law – at any rate – pronounced not good enough to be treated as helps meet (intellectually) for men? 'The constitution of States and Society, forms of Government, state of ancient nations, sources of wealth, many natural phenomena, the whole range of mathematical truths are generally presumed beyond her ken' – writes one of her Majesty's Commissioners for the Inspection of Schools in 1868. 'In a boy's school these points, whether taught or not, are treated as worth knowing, with a girl' continues the Commissioner, 'their importance is not even recognised, and the influence of school upon her mind is as far as it goes to discourage her from attempting to understand them:' and again, 'if the reproach be just that women do not reason accurately and their knowledge even when they possess it, is deficient in organic unity and coherence and in depth, there is no need to look for any recondite explanation of the fact. The state of the schools in which they are educated sufficiently explains it.' Well, might Mr John Stuart Mill say, in his speech in the House of Commons on 12 May 1867, 'The time is now come when unless women are raised to the level of men, men will be pulled down to theirs. The women of a man's family are either a stimulus and a support to his highest aspirations, or a drag upon them. You may keep them ignorant of politics, but you cannot prevent them concerning themselves with the least respectable part of politics – its personalities: if they do not understand and cannot enter into the man's feelings of public duty, they do care about his personal interests, and that is the scale into which their weight will certainly be thrown.'

Convictions like these work silently for a while, appearing in scattered pages of the press or the literature of the day, in occasional lectures and conversations, and then take shape at last in some enduring form. So it was with the Women's Suffrage question, which took coherent, organised shape with the approach of the Reform Bill of 1867. A preliminary Committee was formed in London in 1866 and that year the first petition with the signatures of 1500 women was presented by Mr John Stuart Mill. The Manchester Committee was formed in January 1867, followed by the Edinburgh Committee later in the same year.

The Representation of the People's Bill introduced before the House of Commons that year, gave the required opportunity of bringing the subject prominently before the attention of the country. Instead of the phrase 'Male Persons,' this Reform Bill of 1867 used the term *man* throughout all its provisions. By Lord Romilly's Interpretation Act passed in 1850 it had been enacted that in all future statutes words importing the masculine gender should include females unless the contrary were provided. The contrary was not provided in the Bill brought forward, it became a matter of some uncertainty whether this new Act was or was not framed with the intention of including women in its operations, and on 25 March Mr Denman raised the question in the House, whether it was intended by the use of the word *man* to come within the operation of Lord Romilly's Act and include women. The Chancellor of the Exchequer said in his reply that he believed the contrary had been provided in this case. This however was an error, the contrary was not provided and to place the question beyond all doubt, Mr Mill, on 12 May, moved his amendment which was supported by a petition signed by 13,000 persons 'to leave out the word man and insert person.' That amendment was rejected by 196 votes against 73. The Committees for women's suffrage in London, Manchester and Edinburgh were re-organized on a permanent basis. And thus was started an agitation which has continued to increase steadily from that time – an agitation about which Mr Mill said, when writing to a lady eminent in philanthropy who expressed some doubts to him whether the time had come for agitating – 'there are several reasons which concur to make me think it has. In the first place, to agitate for a change in the law is not to obtain it, and therefore even if any of us think that women are not yet prepared to exercise the suffrage, that will still not be a reason against agitating for it, because much smaller changes than this can never be obtained until after the agitation for them has lasted some time, and the agitation itself will be the most effectual means of preparing people for the change whenever it comes. The great change now taking place in the right of voting among men is, however, the main reason for bringing forward this question at this particular time. The subject of the right of voting is under discussion, and people's minds are comparatively open to receiving new ideas on the subject. If it is true that women ought to vote, it is wrong to lose the present opportunity of spreading this truth as far and wide as possible. By doing so, we are only sowing seed, to bear fruit in due time if it is good seed suited to the soil and climate.' In another part of the same letter Mr Mill wrote, 'the right of voting is in my opinion not only a power to be coveted (although it is a legitimate power which may be honestly coveted by an honourable ambition) but it is still more essentially an obligation to be dutifully fulfilled. You will see from this that I cannot agree in the wish you express that the right should rather be *given* to woman by those who deprive her of it, than from her own demand. Because even if any sentiment of generosity should make one feel that it is a more beautiful thing to receive a legitimate power unasked than asked, there can be no generosity and nothing noble or beautiful in waiting to have a duty thrust upon one, instead of asking to be allowed to take it upon oneself for the good of everybody concerned.' These words written in Dec 1867, just eleven years ago – express the feelings which animated the leaders in this movement; the Committees in London, Manchester and Edinburgh, formed themselves into one National Society, while each maintaining a separate organization; others followed quickly in Bristol and Birmingham and their first efforts were directed to finding whether it might not be even then possible for women to vote, since the Representation of the People's Act of 1867 had been passed without any change in its phraseology.

That same autumn, a lady – Miss Lily Maxwell – recorded her vote in favour of Mr Jacob Bright's election for Manchester, it is stated in the First Report of the Manchester Society for women's suffrage that 'the circumstance of this vote having been recorded, excited a great amount of public attention not only all over the kingdom but on the Continent of Europe and in America. It removed women's suffrage from the region of theoretical possibilities to that of actual occurrences, and therefore gave a powerful impetus to the movement.' The *Times* (29 Nov 1867) in a leading article on the circumstance, went so far as to say that women constitute in every sense more than half the British nation, 'nevertheless in violation of every principle of numerical and logical proportion they have no votes in the election of the national representation,' but concluded, 'we are afraid a legal scrutiny would deprive the sex of this momentary triumph and prove that we have been very absurd in writing a serious article on the subject.' Possibly, if a legal scrutiny had been ordered, the vote would not have been allowed, for the qualification under which Miss Lily Maxwell voted was one constituted by the Act of 1832. But so far as the fear of absurdity was concerned it doubtless had short duration, for during the weeks preceding the general election of December 1868, the *Times* records day after day, how women in large numbers and in many places entered their names on the electoral register, until on 3 Nov, commenting on the Second Annual Report of the Manchester Society, it wrote 'The present condition of the woman suffrage question is decidedly an odd one. It is not often that the glorious uncertainty of the law is so strikingly illustrated as it has been by the decisions of the revising barristers, as to whether a woman under certain assumed conditions may or may not vote for a Member of Parliament. . . . According to one view, the view of the majority, she may vote if her name is on the electoral register and is not objected to, the revising barrister himself remaining neutral; according to another, the barrister ought himself, if necessary, to start the objection; according to a third, the view taken in four Courts, her name ought to remain on the electoral roll even although objected to. . . . However this glorious uncertainty is soon to cease.' Pending the time when the question should come before the Court of Common Pleas and guided by the decision of the South West Lancashire Revision Court, which had held the women's votes as good, the liberal candidate for Chester issued his electoral address to the women as well as to the men inhabiting the constituency. On 6 November, the Court of Common Pleas heard the various cases for appeal, taking first an appeal from Manchester where 5,750 women had placed their names on the register. This case (Chorlton v. Lings) would govern all other cases before the Court which related to women's claims.

Mr (now Lord) Coleridge, QC, argued on behalf of the appellants; that in former times in all cases where men were entitled to vote, women were also; that women had, in point of fact exercised that right and no modern legislation had taken it away, although there might be cogent evidence to shew that the general understanding had been that no such right existed. Judgment was given on 9 November, when it was maintained by Lord Justice Bovill that the instances named had comparatively little weight as opposed to the usage of several centuries, and what had commonly been assented to as the law raised a strong presumption of what the law was. Mr Justice Willes concurred, and trusted that the unanimous decision of the judges in Scotland, as well as in England 'would for ever lay the ghost of a doubt which ought never to have been raised.' But as the *Times* remarked, 'there was not much of the spirit of prophecy in this prediction.'

The quarter to which prophecy should look was more safely indicated by the result of the Bill introduced by Mr Hibbert in 1869 to assimilate the Municipal and Parliamentary franchise: amendments extending the provisions of the Bill to women were proposed by Mr Jacob Bright and Sir Charles Dilke. Mr Hibbert readily consented to admit the amendments and they became law without opposition. This proved a great encouragement to the promoters of the Women's Suffrage movement and Mr Mill not having regained his seat, Mr Jacob Bright in 1870 introduced the Bill to remove the Electoral Disabilities of Women, supported by Sir Charles Dilke and Mr Eastwick. That Bill passed a second reading on 4 May, by 124 votes to 91, but in Committee the opponents of the measure, who had not troubled themselves to attend the second reading, rallied in great force and the Bill was thrown out by a large majority. However that same session of 1870 conceded another great step in women's political rights through the Elementary Education Act, framed with the express intention of admitting them to vote in elections for the Board and to sit themselves as members. Hence with some disappointment this session brought also a great encouragement. The Bill was re-introduced at each succeeding session by Mr Jacob Bright, supported by Mr Russell Gurney, Mr Stansfeld and Sir Robert Anstruther, and during the interval when Mr Jacob Bright was not sitting in the House, by Mr Forsyth, Conservative member for Marylebone. In the session of the present year (1878) Mr Jacob

Bright desiring to withdraw from the main burden of the conflict, the Bill was accepted, at the unanimous desire of all concerned, by the Liberal member for Liskeard, Mr Leonard Courtney, under whose leadership it passed through a division calculated to encourage its supporters, for it shewed that though death has lately thinned their ranks of many of their staunchest friends, new friends have not failed to replace them, in more than equal number. Subjoined are the words of the Bill,* which will have the effect of extending the system of interpretation provided by Lord Romilly's Act, to all Acts, relating to the Parliamentary franchise, to which, justly or unjustly, the decision of the Court of Common Pleas has ruled that interpretation shall not apply.

*Text of the Women's Disabilities Removal Bill
I That in all Acts relating to the qualification and registration of voters or persons entitled or claiming to be registered and to vote in the Election of Members of Parliament, wherever words occur which import the masculine gender, the same shall be held to include females, for all purposes connected with and having reference to the right to be registered as voters, and to vote in such election, any law or usage to the contrary notwithstanding.

Helen Blackburn

Comments on the opposition to women's suffrage

1878

THE inconsistency between the two theories which have co-existed in our jurisprudence, the Common Law treating women as without independent will, while Constitutional Law left them until 1832 (*de jure*) capable of the sovereign power of voting, has complicated the question of the admission of women to the suffrage, in itself a purely constitutional claim, with numberless points relating to domestic legislation and laws affecting special classes of persons, as in the various relations of wife, mother and independent earner, and this to such an extent that we frequently hear it said that if the laws which press heavily on women were repealed the claim to the suffrage would have no justification. But this is to regard the subject from a side-issue. The real question lies much deeper. For women as for men 'Freedom is a noble thing,' and though noble lives may be led without it, the standard of a nation's life must be higher where freedom is within reach of all. Those who are excluded from the share in sovereign power which the right to the franchise bestows are amongst the governed but not amongst the governing and no-one can deny that for any considerable number of the governed to find themselves absolutely excluded from all chance and possibility of becoming one of the governing, is utterly inconsistent with all theories of political liberty. 'It was the theory and it had been the practice in all times to adapt the representation to the state of the

325

country' said Mr Pitt in his speech on Reform in 1785. 'Now and in all future time to adapt the representation to the state of the country, was the idea of reform which he entertained.'

The supporters of the Bill to remove the Electoral Disabilities of Women believe that the time has come when this reform is adapted to the state of the country and will increase that conformity of sentiment between the representatives and the nation at large which the same great statesman calls 'the essence of a proper representative assembly.'

Even the most determined opponents of women's suffrage will probably allow that women form part of the nation at large. It is for them to show what there is in the state of the country inconsistent with a reform which will embrace a considerable fraction of law-abiding persons already acknowledged as citizens in respect to the duties they owe to local governments and state revenues, but not acknowledged as citizens in respect to the vital point of imperial representation. Or, what comes to the same thing; it is for our opponents to show what there is in the pursuits of women which unfits them for a duty laid theoretically on all except such as are 'in so mean a situation that they are esteemed to have no will of their own.'* The argument that elections are too tumultuous has been nullified since the ballot has made it easier to vote at an election than to attend her Majesty's drawing-room, as School Board elections have practically proved. The plea of intellectual inferiority has been abandoned, if not from a belief in absolute intellectual equality, at any rate from comparison of the average standard and the indignity of preferring to respectable women such drunken and illiterate voters as are at present occasionally channels of sovereign power. Again the mere superficial ridicule which buzzes about all new ideas, has almost subsided when eleven years of constant endeavour have worn off the novelty of the claim. Its opponents are at least conscious that they are called on to face the question on deep and serious grounds.

Here are numerous persons claiming an important national privilege with cogent arguments of logic, justice, expediency. Those who oppose the claim are bound to shew that it is illogical, unjust or inexpedient. The merely logical aspect of the question is little regarded by adverse thinkers, as one determined opponent, the *Pall Mall Gazette*, said so long ago as 1874, 'the argument that the power of voting ought to go with a certain amount of purely mental cultivation or with a certain amount of contribution to the

---

*Blackstone's Commentaries I p. 172, 15th edition.

public revenue, covers the case of women, *unless it be properly guarded.'* Conscious that they have not themselves unjust intentions towards women many men fail to conceive injustice that may nevertheless result from their legislative action, and the sense of injustice which many women feel strongly, is to them incomprehensible, consequently the opposition mainly guards itself on the presumption of inexpediency. Thus the contest is concentrated on the four points with which the question of expediency is alternately met, and which constitute 1, an assertion; 2, a prophecy; 3, a sentiment; 4, a suspicion.

First then, we are met by the *assertion* that law is based on physical force and therefore political power must rest with those who have physical power. Legislation must be masculine, lest at any time women should outvote men and an insurrection ensue when physical force would inevitably decide the conflict. This is the most serious difficulty that has been urged because it touches on the most fundamental point in legislation, the power of sanction. If the political equality of women means the weakening of order, women will be the last to desire it, they would rather continue to deserve the epithet bestowed by our Saxon forefathers of 'Peaceweavers,' than earn that of weavers of Chaos. But what ground has ever been shewn for the belief that days of law and order are less amenable to the force of peaceful influences than days of wars and turbulence?

Brute force is undoubtedly the substratum of society, for if we analyse civilization we come in the ultimate residuum to pure physical force. Strip off one by one the motives and the restraints with which civilization has surrounded human life and you find yourself at last reduced to the will of the strongest. In the absence of law the fist rules, but as law increases in power, that is to say as law creates additional motives to orderly self-controlled action on the part of men, the rule of the fist loses its force and each new principle of law is another layer intervening between us and the rude stage of no law.

It is easy to peel the rind off so lowly organized a growth as a mushroom, but try to strip the lawyers of bark off one so highly developed as a wide-branching oak tree and leave its woody fibres bared everywhere to the action of the elements, and it is a hard task. Similarly, every new motive, every new interest enveloping our complex civilization adds an additional hindrance in the way of returning to the ultimate residuum. It may well be true that the admission of women to political power is inconsistent with a society which depends on brute force for its maintenance, for such a society will simply fail to maintain itself at all, the societies which have maintained themselves are those which have travelled away from dependence on brute force. In the rudest forms of social life the will of the strong man dominates, overawes the mass into a chaotic sort of obedience, rough and uncouth in its forms and customs, step by step experience develops laws which tone down these customs and custom first, then law, interposes an ever broadening barrier between the brute force in the community and the motives impelling action. Civilization develops gradually accumulating interests, religion impresses nobler motives, and these the legislator inweaves into the daily national existence until they become a concrete part of it, sending the appeal to brute force further and further into the background. Those who believe that this process has been at work for ages must believe that it is still at work and that when men say the appeal to brute force makes it unreasonable to give women political powers, they have given the strongest possible motive in favour of giving them a share of such power, for by so doing they will be adding another influence to be overcome before the ultimate residuum can be reached, another element to be disintegrated before we get ourselves resolved back to anarchy. We can say nothing against the possibility of such a dissolution, the history of the earth shews times of retrogression as well as of progression, but those times of retrogression come when respect for law is relaxed and faith in brute force encouraged.

There was a time, as geologists teach us, when England was a mass of ice and glacier, and there may again come a time when ice fields will cover our land again, but meantime we sow and reap and build and weave confidently above the ice-worn rocks. Let us make our laws no less confidently, for if we know that it is possible for men to fall back to the lower type, we know also that it is in their hands to advance to the higher ideal and bring about a time when it shall as little enter into the heart of the civilized man to return to the rule of the strongest fist, as to return to the habits of the brute tearing and rending its prey.

To say that those who never fight (until their homes are attacked, their country perishing, and times of crises sink all ordinary duties in the one supreme duty of defence of the hearth) must have no share in legislation is to confess that legislation is a failure and its laws too weak to inspire the reverence which is stronger than arms – and such a confession would contradict all history and all civilization. If law did not obtain superior reverence armies themselves would be impossible, the cohesive discipline of an army is of comparatively early growth in the progress from the state of no law which is so often misnamed the law of force, yet that discipline is as truly the result of law, as that product of a complex condition of society, the organization of our electoral system.

The *prophecy* which forms our second point of difficulty, though unverified by experience, tells with the force of fact on many minds, declaring that women will practically nullify all their independence of will by delivering themselves over to the guidance of the clergy, so that a woman's vote will mean so much additional power given to the Church. No prophecy can stand the test of verification which is based on a solitary set of facts, and does not consider other modifying facts at work and in this instance, only one side of the case has been regarded. We must not only remember that for ages the Church has been the one organization which has provided women with systematic instruction beyond school days and with systematic work outside their own doors, reaping its reward in corresponding influence over women – but we must also remember that to extend political rights to women is symbolical of wider ranges of study, synonymous with more extended ranges of interests than the Church has ever provided. Hitherto sacerdotalism has flourished most where political liberty has been repressed. Hitherto political liberty has cultivated independent action and encouraged independent thought – and the common humanity of men and women is too deep-seated for any reasonable expectation that this order of things will be changed. We would beg those who are inclined to put faith in the prophecy of an increased clerical influence, to consider carefully whether they are not helping the evil they fear, by standing in the way of political liberty for women. We would remind them that it is one of the best attributes of human nature to give its chief reverence to those who have been the leaders of our intellectual lives. If statesmen, ignoring intellect in women, have left them to the guidance of the clergy until that guidance has assumed the narrowing tendency inseparable from limited horizons, then the more statesmanlike course would be to offer guidance to new horizons. A restricted mental horizon must promote an unintelligent conservatism: if priests promote such conservatism it is for politicians to counteract the evil and for these prophets of ill to watch, lest they stand in their own light.

The third difficulty which we have to meet is perhaps the most troublesome, because the least solid and tangible, point of attack. *Sentiment* is a shifting sand, and we are never sure where we have it. Sometimes it sternly confines women to their nurseries and store-rooms, ordering them to abandon all the solid studies which would enable them to connect the duties of these departments with the general facts of life. Sometimes it admits that it is right and good that women should earn money for their subsistence – when misfortune has depressed them – but is wroth if they begin, before misfortune comes, to follow the independent modes of life which ensue on power of self-support, nay which are essential to that power and for lack of which efforts begun too late fall inefficient. Our sentimental opponents will often grant that women should have the responsibility of property, while they steadily decry the correlative privilege. Occasionally they will advise women to study the newspaper, but with the warning not to take any deep interest in the politics they find there. Finally, sentiment will frequently take pains to encourage culture up to a certain point – the point which just falls short of making practical use of culture: rarely opposed the attentive and laborious study of the latest fashion books or even attendance at race-courses and hunting-fields, but ever and always reprehends such study as might help intelligent discriminations on the questions brought forward at an election: and should they desire to approach the polling-booth, sets up a lamentation over the grace which is departing and the sweetness which shall fill our homes no more.

We admit that women who value their dignity as citizens will be as little satisfied to be described as 'things of music and flowers' as Englishmen would be to hear themselves described as things of horses and dogs. They hold such descriptions to be as adequate as if one were to describe a book by its binding or a picture by its frame, and if the type of young gentlemen who think 'women are meant to look pretty and be amused' (*a bona fide* speech, oh incredulous reader) find themselves uncomfortably compelled to form another estimate of women after their aunts or sisters or mothers possess the franchise, we shall not deem it an evil to be deplored. We shall moreover esteem it to be a useful collateral advantage if the fact that his wife might have been the possessor of a vote before he married her, and may become so again should he die first, so operates as to modify the sentiments of people of the type of the gentleman who preferred that his wife should coax and wheedle him out of what she wanted, than that she should obtain it by a reasonable, sensible wish (and here again, oh reader we speak from actual fact). That the franchise will not be exercised by her while he lives, since the law has privileged him with the administration of the family possessions, is a matter of mere detail in presence of the paramount fact that the womanhood he professes chivalrously to honour shall no longer be pressed down among the non-governing governed and graciously permitted to have exemption from electoral duties along with minors and idiots, convicts and others, the most miserable of her Majesty's subjects. And let no man urge that this is an unfair application of a merely accidental coincidence. We are willing to acquit the law of having classified women, by malice afore-thought, with these unpleasant congeners, but the coincidence remains and while you, gentlemen, ply us with your sentimental objections to including us in the electoral body, we feel at liberty to indulge also in our sentimental objections to the exclusion, and now turn to the *suspicion* which is the last point of defence.

Many persons who profess themselves not averse to our claim for the franchise, and who readily admit that they see 'no harm' in women voting if they like, hold back nevertheless because they suspect ulterior ends and are haunted with the fear that to qualify women to elect is to qualify them also for election and straightway they will rush from the poll to the hustings, enter St Stephen's and accomplish mighty revolutions! That women have ulterior ends is perfectly true. The vote is valuable, not for what it is, but for what it brings – that sense of citizenship, that consciousness of progress which accompany political emancipa-tion; the means of more direct influence and increased power of usefulness which a recognized political position gives and which without the franchise is unattainable. These are ulterior ends which will work gradually ripening changes. We would remind the uneasy friends who suspect an imminent rush to Parliament, that to be an elector is not one of the qualifications essential for election – but let them be consoled, before any woman can enter Parliament, some one at least, must have been found ready to stand, friends must be ready to uphold her, and a constituency willing to elect her. As these conditions have not yet ripened into existence, it will be some time before all the three can meet in the necessary combination, and meantime, however essential that statesmen pay due regard to the ulterior consequences of legislation, suspicions like these do not prove that this may not be one of the points where a plain present justice calls more imperiously than far-off possibilities.

In justice to these cautious and doubtful friends, it is right to admit that their suspicion is not altogether unworthy of respectful treatment, for however unscientific in its operation it arises from a laudable motive, the fear that in some way or other the division of labour will become confounded, and the proper organization of duties obscured. Nature has from the most primæval days pointed out certain duties for the two co-ordinate sides of humanity, but civilization has gradually developed interests, sympathies, duties, where men and women meet as on common territory: the margin of that territory extends as culture extends: the man may still retain the general function of loaf-winner, the woman that of 'loaf distributor' and yet they may, without confounding their functions, find mutual consultation useful on the methods and organizations of their separate duties. The question to-day is whether the exercise of the electoral franchise is or is not one of those duties which culture has slowly brought to the shore of the common territory; we believe it is, and mere suspicion will not disturb that belief.

To those men and women who, while respecting the law as the expression of the national standard of conduct nevertheless believe that standard capable of frequent advance, the passing of the Bill to remove the electoral disabilities of the latter will bring no change of feeling, save the gladness that law is now on the side of the equality they prize for themselves.

To those who regard the law as the all-sufficient standard pointing out the whole duty of man, this Bill must add a new thought: but will make no change in the current of their lives; they will go on as before, following the lead of law and will quietly acquire the new idea that women are citizens in the full sense of the word and that therefore it is a duty for them also to give some thought to the service of the State.

To those who are below the law, by whom law is regarded as an enemy to be evaded and obeyed only from compulsion, this Bill will bring a new, unwelcome, but salutary command of respect for those whom now law marks as inferiors.

In days of old, the young man was invested with the sword as a sign of his manly activity and the young woman wore her keys as the sign of her household duties, but those keys should no more lock the thoughts of women within their cupboard doors, than the sword should cut off the men from domestic affections. Surely Home and Country are for all, and all for Home and Country.

Mrs Wynford Philipps

Women's suffrage

A GREAT writer has said that in a world that exists by the balance of antagonisms, the respective merits of conservator and innovator must ever remain debateable.

So many exquisite women have lived in the past that I do not wonder that some men wish to conserve the old feminine ideal, but when we look to future and see the developed intellect and the dignity, born of perfect freedom, added to every other charm, I do not wonder that others hasten to advance.

But the *ideals* of both ages are worthy sisters of one another; what reason then, makes us feel bound to come forward from our quiet and secluded homes to urge with energy, ardour, and enthusiasm that the condition of women needs to be changed.

It is this: we look at the condition of the *average* woman of our country, and see that the condition of her life urgently needs reform.

The ideal man or woman we need not legislate for, it is they who rule us, they can break the bonds of convention and grow and expand even in the poisoned air of bad institutions; but the ordinary average work-a-day mortals cannot develop, cannot do justice to themselves and to their fellow creatures if we shackle them with arbitrary restrictions.

What is a woman's duty in the world?

The Power that gives us power signifies by its very existence that it should be used, and it is a woman's duty, just as it is a man's duty, – it is a human duty, to develop every gift and make the most of all moral, mental and physical muscles.

Yet women, like the Chinese ladies who toddle helplessly on maimed perverted feet, have been taught that they should limit and dwarf their understanding, till the world at last comes almost to believe that they cannot support themselves, and cannot advance alone.

But I am not here to say what woman should do, but to tell you what they *do* do and must do, and then to ask you this: 'Since men are allowed a voice in the making of the laws, in order that the laws may be suited to their necessities, and in order that they may be able to secure and extend the rights and privileges on which their happiness and their prosperity depend, will you not allow these other human beings called women to have a voice in shaping the laws they are bound to obey, in order that they too may have a chance of bettering their condition, of giving voice to their necessities and of securing and extending their rights and privileges?

'But women should stay at home and grace their homes,' say the conservators; the innovators make the startling suggestion – 'Let us look at their homes!'

There are over three million women who work for wages in England who leave their homes early in the morning, and toil at honourable work till late at night. And what do they work at? According to the old idea, sewing was one of the few suitable feminine occupations. Yes, they might work as 'prisoners work for crime.'

> Band and gusset and seam
> Seam and gusset and band
> Till the heart is sick and the brain benumbed
> As well as the weary hand.

Have you ever heard of a sweater's den, or followed a poor needlewoman to her lonely garret, where she stitches her soul away to save herself from starvation?

But things are no longer so bad as they were, because the advocates of women's higher education, because the advocates of *women's rights* have opened up new fields for occupation of women in all directions.

There are thousands of women employed in the Civil Service, as telegraph girls, engravers, copyists, waitresses, hairdressers, law stationers, printers, publishers, painters, tradeswomen, &c. and women in a higher sphere have proved that they can be doctors, lawyers, landscape gardeners, lecturers and artists.

These women have had a highly technical training, these women live in a corporate body of fellow-workers and are affected in their work by all the stirring national questions. All questions of taxation, emigration, peace and war concern them. They *must* run in the race of life, and the race is not run with an equal chance, because the weaker competitor is handicapped by the heavy weight of Electoral Disability. The struggle grows daily more and more pathetic as women with the world against them earn their difficult wages, but the women who have won a position, help those who are struggling. Peaceful trade unions testify that women can unite in a common cause, that they understand that true spirit of self-dependence and inter-dependence that can make them useful members of a community working for a common cause.

Many men deplore the fact that women have to work at all, but work in itself is no calamity, women from the beginning of time have washed the wounds and wiped the tears of poor Humanity and it is a truth of creation that women go through long agony that men may live and work. Prevention is much better than cure, and when women with clear eyes see the cause of the world's suffering, can you deny them the right to help to make the laws that will prevent it?

It is a woman's duty to visit the dwellings of the poor, and it is her right to help to frame the laws that lessen poverty; it is her duty to nurse the sick, it should be her right to add her voice in favour of a measure that may cause disease to disappear; it is her duty to teach temperance, she should be allowed to vote with her fellow men and women to control the drink traffic.

Bacon says 'Without Philanthropie, Humanitie, Man is a busie, mischievous, wretched thing. In charitie there is no excess but errour.'

Now how can our benevolent women administer charity without error? Only by cultivating their minds and studying deeply the social questions of our day.

The benevolent lady of the good old times gave alms to the swarms of beggars at her gate; the woman of the future, with eyes as tender but with wisdom more profound, will seek to lessen the suffering in the world, not only to minister to the sufferers?

The great philanthropic institutions that assist our sister women have, many of them, been started and most of them supported by women who have had a so-called man's training and done a man's work. The National Health Society, which teaches poor women the laws of health and how to apply them in their own homes, was started by a woman who studied as a doctor, so was the East London Hospital for Children and the Public Dispensary for women and children.

Time is short and I am trying shortly to show that women by the circumstances of their very condition have a vivid interest in the Government of the country; by refusing them a vote you do not prevent them from feeling this interest, you do not prevent them from expressing it, but you do prevent them from expressing it in the legitimate, in the most effective – let me say in the most womanly – way.

The fine ladies who come together and say prettily 'We don't want the vote, we know nothing of politics, we can exercise influence in a more feminine manner' remind one of the French Princess who said that the poor need not starve for lack of *bread*, they could eat *cake*. That Princess heralded a revolution. There are thousands of wage-earning women who toil for their living and you tell them to eat the cake of an unwholesome back-stairs influence, when they want the honest sustenance that is a benefit to the Constitution, that crumb of legitimate political influence, the vote.

John Bright, the father of an extended franchise, thinks that women should not vote. He says if the husbands, fathers, brothers of the country do not legislate fairly and justly for women, it is the fault of our civilization and not of our laws. I agree with him. It *is* the fault of our civilization. There is a country where women, according to men, have no souls, and I daresay the laws are suited to soulless creatures. In our country it is assumed that they have no mind; they are classified with lunatics, paupers, and children, in order to be branded with electoral disability. But we are getting civilized very fast. And now that this error, by the effort of women and of men who believe in them, has been rectified, now that women are seen to possess souls and minds, the husbands, fathers and brothers *are* going to legislate justly, they are going to allow them a voice in making the laws they are bound to obey.

There are three hundred friends of the Women's Enfranchisement in the House of Commons and friends too in all parts of the House. It is not a party question only, but a human question that affects the welfare of more than half a nation. But there are party reasons too; many Conservatives will vote for women because they belong to the party of Law and Order, the Liberals will support them because they belong to the party of Peaceful Reform.

It has been well said the world can only remain uninfluenced by women so long as it is uncomprehended by women.

Much has been said of the danger of enfranchising married women, because of the domestic difficulties that would ensue. Ladies and gentlemen, once it was said that a man had a right to his wife's *person*, then it was held he had a right to her *property*, and it is still held that he has a right to hold his wife's *opinion* and should not allow her to hold her own. But men no longer wish their wives to be a mere 'mush of concessions' but wish them to give their devotion from the fulness and not from the poverty of their lives. You will not make unmarried people quarrel by Act of Parliament and you need not fear such a dumb method of expressing opinion as the vote confers.

The truth remains that when people feel strongly they fight, or they speak, or they vote. You get a Joan of Arc, a Maid of Saragossa, an Emily Plater of Poland, with whole nations to follow them. You get women of the Primrose League and ladies of the Liberal Federation, and a whole Parliament of men to make use of their services. The reform that we need is, that what *is* done, and what *is* recognised and accepted, should be ratified and made effective by law.

At first it may seem hard, because injustice is never fully realised until it is done away with. According to the old Bavarian Code a man was allowed to chasten his wife moderately. I can imagine how the supporter of women's rights in those days had to struggle before the word 'moderately' was inserted. According to our law at the present moment, (witness the recent police case at Bacup) a man can kick his wife nearly to death, and be sentenced to only two months' imprisonment for doing so. But men and women get accustomed even to bad laws; they will not quarrel with the law when it is good.

Now every argument for the enfranchisement of single women applies with intensified force to married women. But it is quite right for those who think domestic happiness would be interfered with to vote against the larger measure and advocate the extension of the franchise to single women only, just as it was quite right for the Bavarian to chastise his wife moderately if he really thought it was for her good. We must pray for more light.

We may be sure of this, when sex is no longer a political disability the relations which depend on sex alone will no longer be regarded as a cause for disfranchisement.

The real governors of the world, its greatest thinkers, have decided that women shall be free, and the time has come for the legislators to translate that great thought into action.

Augusta Webster

*Parliamentary franchise for women ratepayers**

1 June 1878

THE National Women's Suffrage Society, by announcing the
subject of its public meeting at St George's Hall, under, not the
familiar heading of Women's Suffrage, but the restrictive and
more explanatory title of 'Parliamentary Franchise for Women
Ratepayers,' has made so judicious an attempt at forestalling
criticism by definition that it is a pity it will be quite thrown
away. The Society's object manifestly is to place in unmistakable
prominence the exact claim they are making for their clients, and
to restrain their opponents from confuting their arguments for it
by replies against claims which they are not making. But it is not
the way of opponents in any matter to allow the other side to
limit attack to where it can most easily be met. Taken by itself, on
its own merits, a measure which would do no more than allow
certain women whom circumstances have placed in a position of
independent responsibility to have the vote by right of their
possessing the same legal qualifications as their male neighbours,
involves no particular principle but that of common-place justice.
If there is disturbance of the relation of the sexes, of the
Paradisaical, or Miltonic, subordination of women, it is in
allowing them to hold independent positions at all. The whole
mischief is done when once a woman is permitted to take control

*Originally published in the *Examiner*.

338

over herself, to manage her own affairs, to be mistress of a house without a master, to pay rates and taxes with her own money in her own name. The State, and society, have accepted her, Eve without an Adam to obey, as an authorised being, and made a citizen of her; the giving or withholding a vote in the election of a Member of Parliament for her borough can scarcely affect the relation of the sexes after that, though it may very much affect the worth of her citizenship to her and its use to her country. And in a country where, with not men enough to marry all the women and polygamy still forbidden, the women who are spinsters and widows cannot fairly be condemned for their solitary state, and where living is too expensive for men to take the cost of their female collateral relatives upon them and leave no woman unprovided with a man's house to live in under a man's guardianship, the majority of men would feel, if the case were allowed to go to them fairly, that the class of women whom Mr Courtney's bill would enfranchise are reasonably entitled to the help towards self-protection of the electoral vote. But the Society which exists for the purpose of getting this bill passed, charm it never so wisely with judicious headings to its cards and posters, will still find the deaf adders argue on their own themes. In a little while one member of Parliament will, in opposition to the bill, defend marriage, another the Bible, another the right of Man to have his dinner cooked by Woman; one will shudder over the feuds the bill's fatal gift would raise between man and wife, another be merry over the influx of lady-bishops to come of it.

It must always be well in taking any step to see what is the next step to which it naturally leads, and what again the next. But this form of wisdom may be pushed too far. Unless the subsequent steps are inevitable if the first be taken, we need not refuse to move at all because we do not want to go further than a certain point, or because, from where we stand, it is not possible to see round the corner, and we might not like the road beyond it. In our own small daily affairs we should never get any good done if we never dared make a useful change lest some other change we think not useful should afterwards seem to somebody its logical, though by no means its compulsory or necessary, sequence. We make the change so far as it is to our purpose, and we stop short of the point where we think it would begin to work amiss. English liberties, as we all know, have been established and legislated for in the same piecemeal but practical fashion, and there seems no earthly reason why the question of extending the franchise to a special class of women whom our laws and customs recognise as qualified citizens in all other respects should be treated as if the desire for it could pledge its supporters, or why its success could pledge the country, to even the smallest advance beyond it in the same direction – let alone to a seven-leagued-boot rush towards putting the men and the women in each others' places and governing England by the laws of the Amazons.

The women for whom enfranchisement is being asked have a definite and, all fair reasoners will admit, reasonable claim. It is a generally admitted principle that taxation and representation should go together, that those who put the money in the national purse should all alike have so much share in controlling the spending of it as comes of a voice in choosing the national representatives in Parliament. But these many women – about a seventh of the number of the present male voters, it is calculated – are, as householders and ratepayers, sharing their full burden of taxation with the male voters, and are politically helpless. Their case is manifestly a strong one. They have a right, and the country has a right, to require that it shall have due consideration. It is only proper that all objections there may genuinely seem to be against granting them the political privilege of their responsibilities should be brought forward and fully urged, and that, if on careful examination it should seem that this act of impartiality to them could be injurious to the commonwealth, it should continue to be withheld. But it is not fair to drown discussion of their claim in denunciations of revolutions in the airy future with which it has nothing to do; in arguments founded on the duty of the wife's submission to the husband – the women in question being husbandless; in combating a principle of the parity of the sexes in all points which the Bill not only does not seek to establish, but which it does not even insinuate. Nor is it fulfilling the duty of honest discussion to meet such a claim by assertions of the superiority of married women over single and of the reasons for believing that the wife's mental fitness to vote would be no less, or would be greater, than that of the spinster and the widow. Married women might, or might not, make better voters than the others, but this is not a question of a fancy franchise to be created on competitive examination principles, but of a claim to the existing franchise in virtue of the possession of the qualifications now established by law. It is no just answer to say 'You are women under your own control, recognised by the law as in the position of men, and you are householders and ratepayers and so have men's qualifications for the vote; but your betters, being wives, are not in this position and have not these qualifications: therefore you ought not to have the vote.'

It is quite true that the granting the women in question the vote, and so removing from them all legal stamp of inferiority on the ground of sex, must have effects reaching further than to themselves individually only, and no discussion on the subject would be complete which ignored this fact. We should not find so many married women prominent as workers in the Women's Suffrage Society if it were not generally felt among them that to remove the stamp of inferiority from the women on whom it is inflicted on the ground of sex alone, is to remove it from all women, and that the result must be favourable to the general position of women altogether. The disqualification of only married women would be of course felt in its true light, that is as one not of sex but circumstances only – no worse a stigma than is put upon a son living in his father's house on his father's income – and it would bring with it none of that sense of humiliation with which so many women now look upon the position given to women in a nation in which every man and no woman (Queens excepted, but then they are rare) is held to be capable of feeling an interest in the commonwealth. The disqualification of sex alone which presses on independent women is unquestionably a marked disparagement of womanhood, and it is not unnatural to suppose that its removal would gradually and indirectly have its effect on the general conception of the moral and mental position of women, and therefore on the position itself. If evil consequences can be apprehended from such a result, our legislators and those who seek to influence them ought to look into that part of the matter narrowly. No objection based on any result genuinely deducible from the proposed measure can be irrelevant or unfair. But to discuss, apropos of a Bill for not withholding votes from husbandless females who have achieved the masculine distinction of paying rates and taxes, the theory of marriage, Adam and Eve, ministering angels, Tennyson's Princess, physiology, psychology, and things in general, is – may be – honest.

Clever Alice went down to Hans in the beer cellar, and, while the beer ran, noticed a hatchet in what seemed to her a threatening place. Clever Alice at once perceived that, when she was married to Hans and had had a son and the son was grown up and just going to be married, the son might go into the cellar to draw beer for his betrothed, and the hatchet would tumble down on him and chop off his head. Clever Alice explained the danger, Hans listened and lamented, and the beer ran away unnoticed and left the barrel empty. Clever Alice was honest.

Helen Bright Clark

Speech at a women's suffrage congress, Bristol

23 January 1879

SOME people, I daresay, will be ready to think that this is an unfortunate time for holding a Women's Suffrage meeting. During the past two or three years, questions of useful home legislation have been almost entirely at a standstill. Measures that have been longer before the public than our Bill, and have excited a more widely spread if not a deeper interest, have made little or no onward progress. Almost all efforts for the good of the people, whether by way of reform or of economy or of education, have been baffled or overpowered by the opposition, or the apathy they have encountered; and the minds of the people have been diverted from the consideration of the pressing needs of this great population, in order that they might, shall I say, attack shadows and chimeras many thousands of miles distant from our shores.

Under these circumstances, it is perhaps not unnatural that we should be asked, Is it worth while to press the consideration of grievances which many people even yet look on as chiefly of a sentimental character? And so far as the question of peace or war is to the front, we must all admit that *that* overrides every other, for it carries the fate of every other question with it; and any government, or any party, that will keep the question of peace or war perpetually unsettled, will succeed in stifling discussion and checking progress to a very considerable extent. But I think that the suggestion, and the recapitulation of the burdens of men and women in this country, always affords one of the strongest arguments for those who are striving to maintain peace; and therefore that the holding of such meetings as these can never be out of place, even in the troubled times through which we have been passing, although they may perhaps not excite quite so much apparent interest as at other times. . . . But there seem at least to be some signs of what I should call a wholesome weariness, of a reviving interest in their own affairs, and to a great many people their own affairs have come to be very pressing indeed. The stagnation of almost every branch of trade, and the general and appalling distress which was increasing all over the country, especially in those places which were generally the most prosperous and active, are such as have not been known for a generation; and along with these distressing circumstances there is an increasing earnestness, and I hope a political searching of heart on the part of many who, in more prosperous times, might have remained in the state of apathy which is so fatal to progress. Now, women are often told that they lack imagination, and that the higher flights of genius are not for them, and that they are, in fact, a sort of humdrum creature who, to borrow the rather vague phraseology of their critics, ought just to stop at home. This sort of critic is very apt to forget that even the quietest home may be penetrated and instructed by daily newspapers, and that staying at home does not shield women from the operation of many of the unjust laws which they complain of. I am disposed to think that what is most wanted just now is a little more home virtue, and keeping at home nationally – a little more common-place honesty and economy – a little less flaunting about in scarlet – and a little more kindly consideration for the comfort of the toiling people of this country; and not for them only, but for those more helpless millions elsewhere, for whose welfare and for whose sufferings the Government and the people of this country are responsible. And however much men may be absorbed in more imaginative projects and alarms, shall we not look for something more tender, more home-loving, more practical and devoted to detail – more narrow, if you will – from women? I don't think that this time of general distress and suffering is an unfit time to appeal to women – to the thoughtful among them, to the majority, as I would hope, to let thought take practical shape in action – and to the frivolous to lay aside the weary pursuit of fashion or of emptiness, and to endeavour to devote whatever remains of life to nobler purposes. For this Parliamentary franchise for women, in itself so simple and moderate and a just measure, that it can hardly be attacked except through ignorance or misapprehension – this movement I take to be the symbol, and, as it were, the outward expression, of a great awakening, intellectual and moral, among women – and not only amongst the more scholarly, but among thousands of homely and religious women who have been especially impressed by the moral aspects of the political effacement of their sex. This moral awakening, which has not been effected without suffering, has been too little understood or appreciated; but it seems to me something to rejoice at. It has sometimes reminded me of the coming of the spiritual visitants whom Adam distrusted and fled from –

> A glorious apparition, had not doubt
> And carnal fear that day dimmed Adam's eye.

We are not only asking for the removal of a grievance which we feel to be heavy, and which acts as a barrier against the removal of other grievances that are perhaps more obviously harsh, but we ask all women everywhere to examine whether it is just or beneficial to anybody that they should be entirely overlooked and excluded in matters which so deeply affect them, equally with men, and in some cases even more deeply, because you must bear in mind that women are affected by almost all the legislation which touches men; and, in addition to that, there is a whole mass of special legislation which affects women only, which they have had no hand or share in making – which had been made for them entirely by men, and which men thought very little of. Some of that legislation was almost of a penal character; and it is a curious thing to reflect on, that, although so much is said about women not taking part in political affairs, and that their sole duties should be of a domestic character, it is a curious thing that when women come to fulfil those duties they are hampered in many ways – as, for instance, of a woman marries, she has to pay a very heavy fine to secure her own property; and then if she has children, over those very children, which are her first care and duty, she has no legal right or claim. These questions are very serious and painful often, and require a great deal of consideration. Three or four years ago I had the pleasure of attending an annual meeting of this Society, and I remember pointing out some of the great questions that were being discussed, and that I thought women were bound to examine. The time that has past since then has not lessened, but rather greatly multiplied, the number of important questions that are waiting for solution, and which I venture to say, if solved unwisely, will bring disaster and dishonour to Englishwomen equally with Englishmen. For we women, however we may try to wrap ourselves in a selfish seclusion, cannot evade the responsibilities that are thrown upon us, whether we will or not, in these days of widely-diffused information. We cannot evade responsibility by having no votes. Some timid members of the Liberal party think, or pretend to think, that women would be all Conservative. That does not seem to be an idea that has taken much hold of our Conservative friends, and it does not look as though these timid Liberals had much faith in Liberalism – or in women either. Some people have very little faith in anything that is good. It is a curious thing that, while the great Conservative reaction which took place at the last general election was a result, so far as votes went, exclusively of men's votes, the municipal and School Board elections, in which women take part freely, have shown no such general tendency, though they have been to a large extent political contests. I am willing to admit cheerfully that, for the election of the present majority of the House of Commons, and for its subsequent course, there is not one woman in the country who is directly or indirectly, through her vote, responsible. All the glory of that belongs to men, undoubtedly. All the peace, so long as it lasted – and all the honour, such as it was, and the garters and the ribbons – belonged to men. But you women *are* responsible for the influence you used, and for the influence you did not use, because you were too selfish or too idle to inform yourselves sufficiently to have any influence. And I maintain that, when you see a course pursued which you think hurtful to the true interests and the honour of the country, you are guilty if you do not use all honourable means to secure for yourselves that share of the representation which is the surest and most direct means of opposing that which you believe to be wrong.

I heard this afternoon of a well-known gentleman who said he could not be with us, because there were so many other more important things to be looked after. That may be a man's point of view, but it is hardly a woman's. That gentleman has a vote. I have no doubt he has two or three votes; and he can use them and the influence they give him to further those objects which he thinks so important. But the very point of the matter is, that women have no votes; and it is largely because we feel so keenly the importance of the questions before the country that we resent their exclusion from the representation of the people. For myself, I can truly say that it is from no capricious love of change, or from any desire for what may appear to some fantastic or new, but from an ardent love of liberty and of all that seems to me noble and Christian in the life of the nation, that I am here to-night to protest humbly, but with all my heart, against that unjust exclusion which denies to my sex the rights, and I may say also the sacred duties, of free citizenship.

Lydia E. Becker

*The rights and duties of women in local government**

24 January 1879

REPRESENTATIVE government is the fundamental principle which regulates the conduct of public affairs in this country. The principle had its origin in local government. The application of this principle in the supreme government of the country appears to be of comparatively recent origin. Before the reign of Egbert consolidated the Saxon kingdoms into a nation, all government might be said to be local government. During the reign of the Saxon kings, the representative assemblies had a real share in the government. Women took part in these assemblies. Gurdon, in his antiquities of Parliament, says the ladies of birth and quality sat in council with the Saxon Witas. The Abbess Wilde, says Bede, presided in an Ecclesiastical Synod.

The Norman conquest introduced the feudal system of government, in which the kings were little more than military chiefs. The various struggles for the crown from the death of Henry I to the accession of Henry VII were determined by military successes, and not in any sense by the choice of the people. A few hundred knights and men-at-arms, fighting hand to hand, gave the crown first to one prince, then to another, the people as a party standing aloof from a struggle which, in truth,

*Read at the Conference on behalf of extending the Parliamentary Franchise to Women, held in the Victoria Rooms, Clifton, Bristol.

concerned them very little. But local or municipal government was not dead. It survived in the government of parishes, cities, and counties, and it formed the basis of the more general representative government which first took definite form under the guidance of Simon de Montfort, the man who caused to be summoned the first House of Commons.

Women were not left out of consideration in the earlier forms of parliamentary government. We learn from Gurdon that in the times of Henry III and Edward VI, four abbesses were summoned to Parliament, namely of Shaftesbury, Berking, St Mary of Winchester, and of Wilton. In the 35th of Edward III were summoned to Parliament, to appear by their proxies, Mary, Countess of Norfolk; Alienor, Countess of Ormond; Anne Despenser Philippa, Countess of March; Johanna Fitzwater Agusta, Countess of Pembroke; Mary de St Paul, Mary de Roos, Matilda, Countess of Oxford; Catherine, Countess of Athol.

This indication of a sketch of the rise of parliamentary government, and of the connection between this and the earlier form of local government, is intended to prove that the annual local franchise, instead of being a secondary and subordinate vote of little or no importance politically, is in truth the foundation on which the whole of our system of government is built. Women have, and always have had, coeval rights with men in regard to local franchise; they have a share in the foundation, and they have a right to a corresponding share in the superstructure that has been reared upon it.

For an illustration of the proposition that local self-government, by means of representative assemblies, is antecedent to national self-government, we may turn to the condition of the village communities in Russia. Here representative government in imperial affairs is non-existent. The Czar is absolute autocrat. But local affairs are regulated by village communities named 'Mir;' these are described by Mr Mackenzie Wallace as 'a good specimen of constitutional government of the extreme democratic type.' The constitutional members are the 'Heads of Households.' The 'Mir' apportions the land of the community, regulates agricultural operations, and exercises authority over the taxes, and also over the movements of the villagers. Women are represented in these gatherings. Mr Wallace says: –

> In the crowd may generally be seen, especially in the northern provinces, where a considerable portion of the male population is always absent from the village, a certain number of female peasants. These are women who, on

account of the absence or death of their husbands, happen to be for the moment Heads of Households. As such they are entitled to be present, and their right to take part in the deliberations is never called in question.

Should parliamentary government come to be established in Russia, these village communities will in all probability form the basis of the electoral districts, and we may see representative government in imperial affairs accorded concurrently to women and men.

Men in this country obtained parliamentary representation in and through local government. They used the power they had, and they obtained more extended power. We urge women to follow their example – to take an interest in the local affairs in which they have a legal right to be represented, to make their votes felt as a power which must be recognised by all who would govern such affairs, and to be ready to fill personally such offices as they are liable to be nominated for, and to seek those positions to which they are eligible for election.

The parochial offices to which women may be nominated are churchwarden, overseer, waywarden or surveyor of roads, guardian, parish clerk, and sexton. Women now occupy, or have very recently occupied, all these offices. Recently, a parliamentary petition was placed in my hand signed by a lady as churchwarden of a parish in Wales. There are many parishes now in England where women are overseers. There is a parish in Cheshire where there are but six or seven farmers eligible for the office of overseer. One of these is a lady, and she takes her turn with the rest. Moreover, while many of the men employ a deputy, she performs the work herself.

The office of overseer is a very responsible one. When the guardians or other lawfully-constituted authorities require money for the relief of the poor or for other purposes, they issue a 'precept' to the overseers to furnish the required amount. The overseers are then personally liable for the sum. On the other hand, they are armed with stringent powers over the property of the ratepayers. They have to adjust the burden of the impost equitably among those who are to bear it, and they must collect the money from the people, either personally or by deputy. They have power to seize the goods of any person who does not pay the rate, and their own goods are liable to seizure if they do not collect the money from the parish. The office of overseer is unpaid, and the persons on whom the duties are imposed must discharge them under the penalty of a considerable fine. Women are not excused from these duties on account of their sex, and many women are now discharging these duties in various parts of the country.

A few years ago, Mrs Gold, a widow lady of sixty years of age, was appointed overseer of her parish in Montgomeryshire. She objected to serve, and applied to the Court of Queen's Bench to release her from the obligation to do so. Her application was refused; she would therefore be compelled either to fulfil an office entailing much trouble and no honour, or to pay a heavy fine.

A widow lady was recently appointed waywarden of a parish in Westmoreland. This lady had complained to the surveyor of the state of the roads, and at the next election he prevailed on the ratepayers to elect her to the office. Perhaps he imagined that she would decline to serve, and render herself liable to the penalty of twenty pounds for refusal. But the lady was equal to the occasion. She accepted the duties imposed upon her, and as she keeps a clerk and has ample means, she has no difficulty in obtaining a thorough supervision of the work. It is said that she has made some important discoveries as to the state of the accounts.

The conditions of local government vary greatly in different districts of England. They may be classified under three heads: –

1 Government of parishes by vestry meetings, in which every ratepayer had a right to vote, and which were convened for the imposition of rates and the election of parochial officers.
2 Government by vestries or other local commissioners under the provision of some local Act applying only to the particular district therein specified. This is the condition of the metropolitan parishes outside the city of London, and of large districts in the country.
3 Government by local authorities elected under a general Act of Parliament specifically applied – a kind of permissive Act, which may be extended on application by the ratepayers of any district in which it is not in force. Of this nature are the Public Health Act of 1848, the Municipal Corporations Act of 1833, with its amendments of 1869; and the Elementary Education Acts of 1870–6.

In all of these provisions for local government, the rights of women are recognised.

I have before me, as I write, a copy of an Act passed in the year 1774, when George III was King, for the local government of the parish of Clerkenwell. It is a quaint document, printed in black letter. The preamble sets forth that whereas the poor of the said parish are very numerous, and the present workhouse is not large enough to contain them, and a considerable debt for their relief has been unavoidably contracted; and whereas the present method of raising and applying money for the relief of the poor is attended with many inconveniences, &c. &c. &c. the Act proceeds to set forth the names of a number of gentlemen to act together with the ministers, churchwardens, and overseers of the parish as guardians or governors of the poor for carrying the Act into execution. The Act further provides that in the event of a death, or removal, or refusal to act of any of the before-named persons, it shall be lawful for the inhabitants of the parish paying to the rates for the church and the poor to assemble and meet together in the vestry-room of the said parish, on Tuesday in Easter week every year, or within one month after, to elect one or more persons to be guardians.

It is further provided that the inhabitants as aforesaid are authorised and required to assemble on the Tuesday in Easter week, or within ten days after, to nominate a list of eight persons to be overseers, and the persons so nominated shall be bound to serve under a penalty of ten pounds. It is further enacted that the churchwardens, overseers, and inhabitants are authorised and required to assemble on Tuesday in Easter week, or oftener, as occasion serves, to make a general equal pound rate or assessment for the relief of the poor, or for the other purposes of this Act.

The requirement to assemble in the vestry on the Tuesday in Easter week, for the election of overseers and the imposition of rates, is laid on all inhabitant ratepayers, without mention of sex. There is no doubt that women ratepayers are summoned equally with men, and that they may attend and vote.

In the clauses relating to the qualification of guardians masculine pronouns only are used; it is said no person shall be capable of acting as guardian unless *he* shall be assessed at the annual sum of twenty pounds, &c. Also, in the provision relating to the penalty for refusing to serve as overseers, the words 'if *he* or they shall refuse,' &c. are used. Notwithstanding this, it is probable that women might be guardians or overseers under this local Act, and it is certain that they may fill these offices in other districts.

But when it comes to the clauses providing for the payment of rates there is no possibility of mistake as to whether women are intended to be included. The pronouns he, she, or they, his or her house or houses, etc. occur. These feminine pronouns are not, however, introduced everywhere, and it would not be possible to construe the Act so as to exclude women in every case where masculine pronouns only are employed.

This old Act is the only one which I have had the opportunity of examining, but, as it is probably a type of many similar ones for other parishes, I have thought it worth while to describe its provisions.

I desire particularly to impress on women the fact that Tuesday in Easter week is the day for vestry meetings and parochial elections of churchwardens and other officials, that women ratepayers have equal rights with men in such elections, and I would urge them to assert these rights by taking part in the elections whenever practicable. Thus Tuesday in Easter week would in parishes become what the first of November is in boroughs, a day when thousands of women in different parts of England may be seen taking part in public affairs, forming a demonstration of women electors, and giving a practical proof that women desire and care for the suffrage.

The Public Health Act of 1848 contains an interpretation clause in virtue of which, to use the clumsy and ungrammatical phraseology of our legislators, 'words importing the masculine gender are deemed and taken to include females.' There seems to be nothing to prevent women from becoming members of Local Boards of Health; and I cannot help thinking that some of the energy which is successful in keeping the insides of our houses clean and well ordered might be usefully extended to the care of the outside arrangements for the same end.

The Municipal Corporations Act was originally intended to apply to men only. When its operation was extended to women in 1869 the extension was specifically declared to be to the right of voting for councillors, auditors, and assessors. It seems therefore probable, though not absolutely certain – because the question has never been raised in such a form as to call for a legal decision – that women are not eligible for election to Town Councils.

The Elementary Education Act, on the other hand, was from the beginning intended by its framers to include women in all its provisions. Women have not only the right to vote, but to sit on School Boards, and to be elected to any official position in connection with the work for which men are eligible. A woman may be chairman, vice-chairman, or clerk of a School Board, and ladies actually fill such offices.

The principle on which this part of the Act was based is that, as half the children to be educated are girls, women have an equal right with men to regulate the conditions of the education. But if this is allowed in the case of education, its application cannot be logically arrested here. Half the people to be taxed are women, half the people to be governed are women, half of the people whose interests are affected by the national policy are women; women therefore have as much right to a share in regulating these matters as they have to a share in the regulation of education.

Political freedom begins for women as it began for men, with freedom in local government. It rests with women to pursue the advantage that has been won, and to advance from the position that has been conceded to them in local representation to that which is the goal of our efforts – the concession of the right to a share in the representation of our common country.

Arabella Shore

*What women have a right to**

2 March 1879

I HAVE been asked to address you on the above subject, and I will at once begin by explaining what I consider to be included in that somewhat large and comprehensive title, 'What Women have a Right to.' They have a right to a livelihood, to a fair day's wages for a fair day's work, which means what it means with men, allowing for all the influences which necessarily affect its precise nature according to varying times and places; the means to live decently and with sufficient comfort and to bring up a family decently. It means also a right to just and equal laws, to have their interests, their persons and their property, as well protected, as completely their own, as those of men are. And finally it means, – because this last right is the guarantee of all the others, – a right to the position of citizens and the privileges belonging to such, which include a share in the regulation by law of their own affairs.

The key to this right, and consequently to all the others, is in one simple measure, that is, in the Bill for the removal of the Electoral Disabilities of Women, in one word for the admission of women householders to the Parliamentary Suffrage. The Suffrage is the right to vote for a Member of Parliament. Every county and

---

*A Lecture addressed to a meeting of members of Working Women's Unions at the Office of the Women's Protective and Provident League, 36, Great Queen Street, Lincoln's Inn.

every borough has the right to choose one or two men to represent them in the House of Commons. It is considered that every class in the community should have something to do with the making of the laws by which we are governed. This we have by having a control over the members who make those laws. Of course the chief immediate power is in the hands of the Ministers who direct all affairs, but when those Ministers depend entirely on having a majority in the House of Commons, that is on the greatest number of members being willing to vote for their measures. And that majority must attend to the wishes of the constituencies that return them. For, if they go against those views, that constituency will not return them again, but will choose someone who suits them better. This is what is called Representative Government and it is the principle acted upon in many other matters, in Municipal Councils, in School Boards and whenever any class have rights or interests which they desire to defend; that is, they choose some out of their body to manage their cause for them, and if it is not well done they choose others in their place. The people of England are in this case, and we come back to that, that they have or ought to have a voice in the management of the country's affairs.

But when we ask, who are the people? we are answered, why, almost all the men. The women? no, they have nothing to do, but to be governed, to submit and to obey. You know what the qualification which gives a man a right to vote, is. If he lives in a town, it is the being the head of a household and paying rates, if he is in the country, it is the having a freehold or paying £12 rental. Well, this brings down the right to vote very low indeed, to all but the agricultural labourers, and it is very likely that they will soon have it given them by an Act of Parliament; and then, this will be the state of the case, that the governing class will consist of all the men, and the governed of all the women. And a great number of these our rulers will be much less educated than you, less orderly and less law-abiding, and at all events they will not be as good judges as you of your own interests and your own wishes, and yet they will settle for you your dearest, your most domestic affairs, such as your relations with your husbands and your care of your children, and you will have no voice in it at all, no more than you have now.

I am often asked – and it is quite right in people to be careful that they understand what our meaning and our object is – do we ask the Suffrage for married women as well as widows and single women? I answer, certainly not. This must be particularly understood, because objections are founded on a misunderstanding in this matter. It is not of course that married women are not just as fit as single women and have not equally interests to be defended; but we can only ask it for those women who have the qualifications that give it to men. We go by the law just as it is, and householders' suffrage is the law of the land. Well, we ask why half the householders are excluded, why no amount of property gives women any right? Can any one tell me why? Do not women manage their property just as well as men? Do they not pay the rates and taxes? Is not the work they do in the world just as useful as that of men? Could this great community go on living and prospering without women, any more than it could without men? have they not their places, their work, their functions in it, and most important ones? They keep the home and regulate the household, they rear the future generation, they help to earn the bread, not unfrequently they are the principal bread-winners. To do all this requires faculties which fits a woman for larger spheres just as a man's work does him.

What then is the reason but *because* they are women? that is beings whom men, through prejudices handed down from ancient and barbarous times, regard as their inferiors and therefore think that they ought not to have the same rights and privileges. There *was* a time when women were treated just like animals and it is not to be wondered at therefore if they were then in many respects much inferior to men. And for a long while women were contented with this debased condition. It was just as with slaves, who were not regarded as human beings, and had no idea that they had rights and duties too, as human beings, like their masters. But men have grown more civilized, and women too have discovered that they are fit for something better than subjection and drudgery. Since they have had leave to use their faculties, they have used them well; and many a beautiful book, many a good work, many a wise thought and courageous undertaking, do we owe to women. I do not accuse men in general of undervaluing us; I think they have gladly accorded us this better social position and this liberty to use our faculties, and do us justice in their estimation of us, now that they see what we can do. But the law does not do so, for the law in these respects is the survival of old and barbarous notions. You see there is scarcely a class of men that the law does not put above women in this matter of the vote; and, from the strength of habit and dislike to change, even good men will maintain this state of things to be right. The law has pronounced no class of men to be ineligible for the vote save paupers, idiots, lunatics and criminals. But a man can hardly be enough of any of these things to disqualify himself;

for if an idiot just knows the names of the candidates or the parties, he can vote, or the lunatic in a lucid interval; the pauperism of course need not be a permanent disqualification; and an ex-convict, however often he has been convicted, may vote as soon as he is free from the penalties of the law. But you, however wealthy, sensible, virtuous or respectable, may *never* vote, because you are women. It is said that women are too silly, too ignorant, too I know not what, to vote. No doubt, many women do know nothing of politics, but then there are many men who do not either. And if women are too silly and ignorant to do what the silliest and most ignorant men are fit to do, they must surely be unfit to manage any business whatever. We should ask what *are* politics? They are the affairs of the nation, the mode in which it is governed, the laws that are made for it and the whole machinery by which that law-making is carried on. And these laws regulate our actions in many serious and important matters. The laws have to do with us in our houses, our marriages and children, our work and callings, our buyings and sellings, and are not women deeply concerned with all this? And there are between 300,000 and 400,000 women, widows and single, who pay rates and taxes, that is about the seventh part of the whole number of the ratepayers; all these are in exactly the same position as men, maintaining themselves or living on their property, and helping to maintain the State. If men desire the suffrage for themselves, may not the women who are in the same position as men desire it too?

Do you know the reason why men desire to have votes? It is a right which Englishmen have set themselves steadily to acquire and to maintain as the most precious of rights. It is in the first place because it is the best defence against a tyranny. There is the tyranny of a single man, the sovereign. In some countries he has absolute power to do what he likes with his subjects, but with us he cannot do so, for he is under the control of a Ministry, who owe their power to the consent of all the people. Moreover, it is a defence against the tyranny of a class or classes over the others. You know that in former days, and even now in some other countries, the nobility, that is the men of rank and the great wealthy landowners, have kept the other classes subject to them, making laws for their own advantage and exacting labour, military service and money from the working classes. But even now the classes that have most to do with making the laws may be apt to make laws too favourable to themselves, to neglect the interests of the classes below them and not look into their grievances. Well, through their possession of a vote, classes of men can look after their own interests in the manner I have told you, by selecting men who will undertake this duty in Parliament.

This leads us to the first reason why women ought to have the suffrage. They have various grievances to which men are not exposed. Of course in a general way the laws made for men affect women as well; in the matter of taxation women's interests are the same as men's, and in general the laws for the protection of person and property are the same. But there is an exception, that is in the laws concerning women in their special relation to men, that is as wives and mothers; and these laws are unjust and often even cruel. This is a grievance which affects all classes of women, the rich as well as the poor; because the law has decided that a woman, on marrying, forfeits all her rights and becomes entirely her husband's property, she and all that she has. It is true that in the case of rich persons there is a device called settlements which for the sake of the children, not the wife, will secure her property in some measure, but this is a very imperfect and uncertain arrangement, and it does not give her the real possession of it. Also, a few years ago a law was passed which gives a married woman a right to her own earnings. All you working women must feel what cruel wrongs were caused by that state of the law which enabled a bad husband who did not work but only wasted, to seize for himself all the hard earned money with which the wife was trying to maintain herself and her children. But all this has been badly done and though people allow that the law wants further improving and still causes many hardships, it is very difficult to get any alteration made in it.

Then with respect to children – you know that by law they belong to the father only, the mother has no right to them at all. The father is to decide how they are to be brought up, and if the mother objects they may be taken from her. Even if the father is dead, the mother is not their natural guardian; he may leave the care of them to any one he pleases, and the mother may be punished if she persists in retaining her own children. I have known mothers who rather than submit to this law which took their children from them and gave them to a stranger's charge, have run away to foreign countries and hidden themselves under false names with them.

Now, do you think that if women had any share in making or altering the laws they would allow such laws to stand?

These laws, as I have said, apply only to married women, but there are other laws that apply to all; and what we complain of is that women have not been consulted at all about them. There are the Factory and Workshop Acts for instance, meant kindly no doubt, in order to protect workwomen from being overworked by their employers, as it is supposed that women cannot protect themselves. But there is no real reason why they should not do so; it is treating them like children, and such legislation is the way to keep them still more dependent, more helpless, more unfit to take care of themselves. And the results of this interference are in many ways such as to make the women's case worse than it was; their work becomes less valuable and their wages are reduced, or they are dismissed, and men, who are not so restricted, are taken in their place. This happened once in Wales, all the women were dismissed from a factory on the ground that their work could not keep pace with the men's; so they had to find work in farms and public-houses where they had longer hours and less pay. And besides, these regulations are very minute, disagreeable and inquisitorial, their hours and places of work and meals are fixed for them and inspectors may come into a house where workwomen are employed at any hour of the day or night with a policeman to see that the rules are observed; refusal to admit them being punished by a fine of £5. A poor woman working in her own room with a single assistant is liable to this inspection. And a House of Commons composed of men settles all this, without regard to women's views on the subject. The women's delegates to the Trades' Congress protesting against restrictive legislation for grown-up women obtained no attention, the evidence given by women before the Royal Commission was disregarded and an audience was refused to a deputation of women by the Home Secretary. This and other facts of a like nature make one feel that, so far as special legislation for them is concerned, women are living under a despotism, not a free government.

But even worse than the hardships inflicted by law are the difficulties of women's economic position, the difficulty of gaining your bread, the difficulty of keeping sufficiently ahead in the struggle for existence. There are nearly a million more women in England than men; and there are upwards of three millions of women who have to work for their bread, and these require the power of self-protection as much as men do, in some respects even more.

We know that women's wages are very low, always much lower than men's, even when employed in the same business, in many occupations not enough to raise them much above destitution. We know that there is no fixed standard for women's wages, that they very capriciously, being pretty much what employers choose to give them, that the women are in many respects at the mercy of those employers, subject to sudden unfair reductions, that they have often to work very hard with long hours and inadequate pay. Various reasons are given for this. One is the excess of supply over demand, and this is no doubt true in certain kinds of labour, as for instance needlework, in which we know that unfortunate creatures may come down to twopence or threepence a day and be found at last dead of hunger on their garret floor. But this is not true in many kinds of work, for in some even of the worst paid there is a constant demand for women, bills and advertisements being posted up to that effect. Another reason given is the absence of skilled work in women, and no doubt it is part of their distressed condition that they cannot afford to get the early special training which men can procure, and so are obliged to overcrowd the callings that require less training and are less paid. But also even where they do such work as, from the peculiar delicacy of touch that it requires, is best suited to women, and in which long training has made them skilled, they yet receive but from 11s to 17s per week while the roughest most unskilled workmen have 18s. Want of strength is also alleged against them, but it has been testified by their employers that they make up for that by working quicker and having more energy of will to compress more work into a given time; and indeed, when women will work from twelve to eighteen hours a day, such endurance testifies to a strength which is something more than that of muscle. This is said to be the case in the cigar trade, in which they receive forty percent less than the men. We must look then for other reasons as well as those mentioned for this general low value of women's work and I think we shall find one cause to be the kind of prejudice which causes women to be regarded as naturally inferior, which causes far less account to be made of their work than men's, which makes all the high, honourable, well-paid callings to be kept for men. No doubt in early times it was considered that every woman would marry, and that, as her only business was to keep the home and rear the children while the man worked for them, there was no need of a calling for her. But this we know is now far from being the case; for besides the nearly a million of surplus women who cannot marry, many of whom have to maintain themselves, a great number of the wives have to work also to help to maintain their homes. Here then we have a strange state of things, a rapidly growing class of the community, sober and industrious, working with the greatest energy and application and yet with all their efforts unable to support themselves by the payment of their labour, as shown by the wages they receive. And I have shown you how little value is attached to their work, how often they are at the mercy of their employers who may be exacting, capricious or unjust, and we know that the too common alternatives for women who cannot live by the work of their hands are vice, the workhouse or destitution.

Now when men in the employment of others have been under like unfavourable circumstances they have as we know an organization ready which assists them in various ways. You all know the advantages of these Unions, and it has occurred to many of you that women might do the like, that if like men they combined to stand out for their rights they might secure better treatment and fairer pay. I shall not dwell on the benefit you derive from these Protective and Provident Unions, for you all know much more of them than I do; and all the advice and guidance you require, you can obtain from your excellent friend and Secretary, Mrs Paterson.

But what I wish to impress upon you is that these unions for your own protection, this organization of women's work, are a kind of beginning of political life; this is what men do who have resolved to protect their rights from any unfair law or any oppression by Government. It was by such unions that the people of England have obtained their freedom, a fair and just Government and the abolition of bad laws. It is not necessary fortunately to regard yourselves as fighting against tyrants or trying to force others to yield you advantages over them; because the evil comes in a great degree from ignorance on all sides, and you by understanding your own interests will help others to understand them too; and besides the good of all classes, of employers and workers, of governors and governed, is bound closely up together, and we are acting for the whole when we are acting wisely and honestly for a part. And by such action you are fitting yourselves for having a share in the general protection and defence of all the peoples' rights, which are yours too in a general way, just as the right to fair wages and just treatment from your employers is yours in a special way. Thinking and acting together for a common object is an inestimable political education. And if women, thus learning to organize themselves and act together for the good of each and of all, will bring those means to bear on the one great object of obtaining the suffrage, and if thus they obtain it, men will necessarily from that time regard them as equals; they will rise in social importance and they will value themselves more. And again when they have a part in the business of government – I mean as much part as all men who, like them, work and pay to maintain the Government have – the share this gives them in common action, the feeling that they help to form a public opinion, to give power to the public opinion, all this again will help them still more to a habit of union and co-operation. No class needs this habit and this training more than working women; they have interests as a class which they themselves must best defend when once they are roused to it and know how.

I have given you thus one reason why women should have the vote, that is to take care of their own interests, but there are other reasons of a more general nature which are of great importance to the well-being of the community. One is that they can help to advocate measures for the good of the country. There is much that sensible women can understand and can do in public matters without being at all required to interfere in what is beyond them. In all matters affecting the welfare of the people we have a right to an opinion and we ought to try to have one as far as our knowledge goes. Now there have been instances where women have shown such knowledge and acted upon it. In that great question of more than thirty years ago, the abolition of the Corn Laws, those laws that were meant to keep bread dear for the benefit of the landowners, the women did not fear to come forward in the cause they believed in. Ladies went canvassing for signatures to petitions from door to door in the depths of winter; working women attended public meetings in crowds. I remember at a meeting on the Women's Suffrage at which I was present a working man giving us one of the experiences of his childhood as an instance of the usefulness of women's counsel on important subjects: His father was a labourer on some great estate and at the time of the election when the contest about the Corn Laws was at the hottest, he knew that his employer expected him to vote in the farmers' interests, for keeping up the price of corn, and meant to do so. But his mother who had nine children pondered on the matter 'while looking after them and cooking the dinner' as our friend was careful to tell us, and she came to the conclusion that if corn was allowed to enter the country freely, its price would be lowered and there would be more bread to put in their children's mouths. So she worked on him till he had the courage to vote for the candidate who advocated the abolition of this unjust tax upon food.

In another very late question women have shown their interest in public matters and tried to influence them. This was when we believed our Government was desirous of going to war in favour of the Turks and a memorial to be signed by women only was drawn up addressed to the Queen praying her to use her influence in favour of Peace. It was signed eagerly by crowds of women, working women especially, who dreaded the misery and destitution that war would produce, and felt already the ill effect in their own homes of the disturbance of trade.

It was, I think, much to the credit of women that they came forward so decidedly to express a deep conviction on so important a question. But would not this action have been much stronger and more useful if it were known that these women had a vote; would not their petitions be more regarded if the Government and Members of Parliament had to pay the same respect to women that they do to men, as persons who help to return them to their seats and whose opinion therefore was of consequence to them?

A third and very important reason is that by this means women may promote morality in the nation. Women ought to bring into every business they have to do with a moral element. They ought to stand up, as much as they can, against cruelty and injustice, fraud and vice. On the first point, we had an opportunity lately of expressing our feelings in the same way as in the Memorial for Peace, indeed a year or so before that Memorial a petition was presented to the Queen signed by 40,000 women praying her to use her influence to stop the horrible cruelties that were then being inflicted by the Turkish authorities on their unhappy subjets in Bulgaria. This petition was in the cause of humanity, a cause in which I am sure women will never be indifferent. They showed this in a contest happily over many years ago, for the abolition of the wicked Slave Trade. All the country was stirred in this great question and women took a passionate part in it, working with all their might, giving money, time, labour, health to what they felt to be a sacred cause.

And there is another subject in which women are more deeply concerned than perhaps in any other, that is, that habit of drinking which produces at least two-thirds of the crime and two-thirds of the misery in England, some will say a great deal more. You all know how strong a body politically the publicans are and how much they had to do with returning the present Parliament which they believed would be favourable to their interests, that is unfavourable to yours, for you do not I believe wish that the facilities for drinking should be increased, but the contrary, if possible. There will always be danger of the drink interest predominating in the House of Commons as long as the persons concerned in it are so very large, so very wealthy, so very important a class. But if women had the Parliamentary vote they would join with a large number of good men who are working now, to make a very strong opposing force. A journal once said that women must not have the vote, because if they had they would get all the public-houses shut up. This we know is nonsense; but it shows which way the women's vote would go. And this is not mere guess-work; for it happens that we have an instance in America of the working of the women's suffrage. There is a small territory called Wyoming where for the last ten years men and women have had equal rights in voting. Well, the first thing the women did was to put a stop to the prevalence of drinking which manifested itself not only at the elections but in the House of Legislature itself. 'At our first election' says a Judge in the Supreme Court of Wyoming who was called to give evidence on the subject 'before women voted, we had a perfect Pandemonium. The saloons were all open. Whiskey was dealt out freely by the candidates to all who would vote for them. The streets were filled with men partly intoxicated, all armed with knives and pistols; it was dangerous to pass through them, bullets were flying at random. At the next election women voted, and perfect order prevailed;' and so it has been ever since. More than that, they have used the vote to defeat the saloon-keepers, who on one occasion we are told, fearing the return of candidates who would help to enforce the law against the Sunday sale of liquor, got up other candidates and sent out runners to meet the rough people coming up from the mines, gave free liquor and lunches and 'rolled up' a very large vote. The 'law and order' party alarmed, sent to every house to tell the women how the case stood, and they turned out in the afternoon, many of them being themselves wives of saloon-keepers and carried the temperance candidates by a large majority. So good has been the moral effect of the women's taking part in elections, that the men often set aside applicants for office because their characters would not stand the criticism of women. And the men of Wyoming themselves feel the advantage of this moral influence, so much that no-one now would repeal the law of women's suffrage if he could.

I must tell you one more thing about America. There is a State near Wyoming called Colorado, where from their having seen the success of this experiment among their neighbours, most earnest efforts were made to include in the universal suffrage, established there, the women's ticket as it is called. In the words of one who was present at the election 'Every man in Colorado had a voice in settling women's political rights. No woman in the State had any voice in the matter.' But the women were there eager to know their destiny. Grey-haired women and young girls sat at the polling tables, and offered their tickets to all who came in the hope and with the prayer that the men of Colorado would be just to the women. One proud mother said 'my three men will vote for the women's suffrage. My youngest son will give his first vote for his mother.' The young man's face was radiant with pride and pleasure that his first political act should be in his mother's interests. But though there was a large vote in their favour, the women were defeated, and the majority that beat them was mainly made up as we are told by very young men, by those without family ties and living in a loose manner, and by the party of the drink-interest who were without exception against them. Married men with wives who cared about the suffrage voted for them. Among their opponents were I am sorry to say coloured men, once slaves who had themselves known what it was to have rights denied them; and one said 'we want the women at home cooking our dinners.' A shrewd coloured woman asked 'whether they had provided any dinner to cook?' adding 'most of the coloured women have to provide the dinner as well as to cook it.' But the women of Colorado are not disheartened and they will try again, and perhaps get their vote before we do. But let us be equally determined, equally public-spirited with the American women. Let us remember the old saying that 'God helps those who help themselves.' You have proved this already in these Unions; you have shown that you can work together, that you can take care of yourselves, and maintain your rights without any violence or unseemly agitation or hostility against others. Now I want you to extend this mode of action to obtaining that which will be the great defence and protection of women, the suffrage. Do not let anyone frighten you from it by saying that it is not womanly to care about politics. It *is* quite womanly to care for what concerns women in general quite as much as men. Do not be ashamed of wishing for this thing, for it is wishing for the means of doing good to the country to which we belong. Our homes of course come first in our care and interests, but our homes cannot be happy if our country is not well-governed. And women who are themselves happy, safe and comfortable in their homes will feel for others and wish that they should share the same blessings. This is no question of setting women against men and men against women; we wish to be friendly fellow-workers with men. For there are many good men who are wishing and striving that we women should have the same advantages as themselves; but they say that they can only succeed by women showing that they want it. Will you now show that you do? Will you not sign the petitions which request the House of Commons to give the suffrage to women householders? This is a way of proving our desire that no one can object to; it is quiet and peaceable, it does not bring you a step out of your proper or your usual sphere, it does not make your names public, and it is the mode provided by our Constitution for all members of the community to make known their wants or their grievances to those who have the management of our affairs.

Louisa Bigg

Should the parliamentary franchise be granted to women householders? *

11 December 1879

I HAVE often heard it said that women do not care for politics. Unhappily, many of them do not, any more than they care for the laws of health or for real religion, but there is a large and increasing class who not only care for politics, but believe that it is their duty to do so. The questions affecting her own sex are of such vast importance to the community that the woman who takes no interest in their settlement must be very ignorant or very selfish; and beside these special questions, the laws of the land concerning Education and the Administration of Justice, the Home and Foreign Policy of the State, and all laws relating to Property, bear upon man and woman alike. This being the case, as long as no woman possesses a Parliamentary vote, a large and influential number of ratepayers are unrepresented, and it would only be fair if those considerate gentlemen who wish to relieve us of the trouble of voting, would also relieve us of the trouble of paying the rates and taxes. Surely no law can be sound which places such holders of property as Baroness Burdett Coutts or our own Lady of the Manor politically below the rank of their own footmen and day labourers, nor ought such a law to disgrace our Statute Book much longer.

*A Paper read at a Conference in the Council Chamber, Luton.

There is a well-known Latin maxim which lays it down that things which do not appear must be classed with things which do not exist, and as I have not met with any arguments against extending the franchise to women householders, which are based upon Justice and Right, I am inclined to treat them as non-existent and pass on to the objections founded on expediency. One great bugbear in the minds of politicians is that women will vote for somebody who does not agree with *them*. The Conservatives fear that women will be worked upon by agitators, and Liberals say it is certain that they will follow the clergyman; some are afraid to let women vote because they are so warlike; and the bloodthirsty party say it would never do for they would always want peace, and what would become of our national honour? Now I put it to any candid mind whether it is for a moment likely that women will all agree upon politics any more than men do, or that they themselves do upon every other conceivable subject. When all women are Ritualists, or all Evangelicals, or all Dissenters, or all Rationalists; when all admire the same book and picture, and wear the same dress, and go to see the same thing, then we may admit that this argument may have some weight, and the State be in danger of an overplus of votes for some party, though it hardly seems clear for which – till then we will continue to believe that women will vote as diversely as men, being subject to the same modifying influences of education, temperament, and surroundings.

Another objection brought forward is, that granting women a Parliamentary vote will, in some mysterious manner, make them unfeminine. It would appear that in the minds of certain people there is a great gulf fixed between a Municipal vote and a vote for a member of Parliament, but I have never been able to perceive it. Women are year after year quietly voting for town councillors and members of the School Board, and I am not aware that anything alarming has happened in consequence; but if the process of voting is indeed demoralizing to the feminine mind, what a weight of guilt rests upon the heads of our local representatives who not only accept the votes of female burgesses, but canvass for them with considerable vigour, and set especial value upon them as being less influenced by pints of beer than those of their brethren. Now these votes which women are constantly bestowing judiciously and successfully, are given far more frequently than could be the case with the Parliamentary vote, so that any mischief arising from the exercise of the franchise must be already at work, and one vote the more will scarcely make much difference, it is as well to be hung for a sheep as a lamb, and, to be consistent, the English Government should fill up the measure of its iniquity by giving women the only vote not granted them, and make their demoralization perfect.

But perhaps the most alarming idea of all is, that if women are allowed a Parliamentary vote they will covet Parliamentary seats, and the nation will fall under petticoat government. I wonder that these timid objectors do not forbid a woman to drive a pair of ponies for fear she should want to join the four-in-hand Club. The Common Sense of the nation will always condemn the woman who shall aspire to a place so unfitted for her as St Stephen's, and should such a woman exist, her own sex will be foremost in opposing her. We are not aware that any clergyman has attempted to break the law which forbids him to occupy a seat in the House of Commons, and undoubtedly women would be equally submissive.

Another fear expressed is that woman will be treated with scant courtesy by man if she ventures to take an interest in what most interests him! Men must have a very poor opinion of themselves. I was not aware that they were such ruffians, and I do not believe it. Could a man be found who would have insulted Madame Roland, because her genius inspired a great party; or Mrs Somerville, because she shone a leading light of science; or Miss Caroline Herschel, because she owned a gold medal of the Royal Society and discovered eight comets? Was Mrs Barrett Browning ever insulted because she wrote 'Aurora Leigh;' or George Eliot, because she is unsurpassed in fiction? The really cultivated woman (and, fortunately, there are many) who is neither a blue, nor a pedant, nor an *esprit fort*, but who with a matured intellect retains every feminine grace and charm, cannot fail to raise her sex in the estimation of every man whose goodwill is worth having, and need fear no lack of chivalry. We hear that the best women do not desire the suffrage, and this is a point which I cannot venture to decide, but I believe that nearly all the best men desire it for them, and that their claim to it is becoming more and more widely recognized by the general public. There still, however, exists a class which persists in considering the aspirations of women as a good joke, and treats them in the same spirit in which you would look at the attempts of a monkey to imitate a man. In one time-honoured witticism they find an ever-new delight, and always seem to feel that it settles the Woman Question for good and all – *Women, they say, should stop at home and mend the stockings.* You would really think, to hear these gentlemen talk, that the human family was a race not of bipeds, but of centipedes, and that darning was the whole duty of life for every wife and mother. But in reality there is a limit to the number of holes to be filled up, let there be never so many little feet about the house, and if a woman's life is to begin and end in household toil, Providence made a sad mistake in making her as she is. Let her darn the stockings by all means, but let her think while she darns. An Eastern Traveller, struck with the unbearable tedium and monotony of life in the Harem, asked a native gentleman whether he should like to be treated as he treated his wives who were shut up in their dreary prison from one year's end to another. 'Oh, no,' he answered, 'I am a man.' It is this spirit which dictated the Suttee, which prompted the Mahomedan to deny that woman has a soul, and which bids the Englishwoman stay at home and darn the stockings. It means in effect this – you shall drudge for me and fit your likings to my convenience, while I live the full life which befits an immortal creature. Such an Englishman as this does not deny woman a soul, only he thinks she had better not use it. Shylock in the Play asks for what reason his nation should be oppressed and despised. 'Hath not a Jew eyes,' he says, 'hands, organs, dimensions, senses, passions? Fed with the same food, hurt with the same weapons, subject to the same diseases, healed by the same means, warmed and cooled by the same winter and summer as a Christian is?' In a like spirit we would plead that woman is a reasonable being, endowed with energy and enthusiasm and varied gifts like her companion man; the common work of life is right for both, and for both alike a wider life is good and should not be denied; and in the words of John Stuart Mill – 'The suffrage is the turning point of woman's cause; it alone will ensure them equal hearing and fair play. With it they cannot long be denied any just rights, or excluded from any fair advantages; without it their interests and feelings will always be a secondary consideration, and it will be thought of little consequence how much their sphere is circumscribed, or how many modes of using their faculties are denied them.'

Jessie Craigen

*On woman suffrage**

14 February 1880

THIS demonstration puts a question to the justice of the English people. It is this – We women are taxed; why are we not represented? It is for those who, having their own share of political power, deny to us what they value for themselves, to give the reasons for this refusal. Certainly it will not be possible any more for gentlemen to stand up in the House of Commons and say that women do not want the vote. We do want it. We are asking for it in the plainest possible way. What more can we do than we are now doing to make our wish for it clearly evident? If they look for riot, for turbulence, for that pressure of threatened violence to which many political reforms have been conceded, these are proofs of our sincerity which it is not in the nature of things that we should give; and we hope also that the time for this mode of enforcing justice is passing away. The very claim that is being made to-night tells us that the reign of mere brute force is wearing to a close. I did not know till I came into the hall to-night that it is built on the spot which was the scene of the tragedy of Peterloo. On this ground, sixty years ago, the blood of women was spilt for freedom. On this ground to-night women lift up their voices in peace and security to claim their share of the liberty that has been won. This marks the progress of the people from

*Paper read at the great demonstration held in the Free Trade Hall, Manchester.

midnight to morning. The great fact that has impressed itself on me to-night is that of the unity of womanhood, in which our claim is made. We are separated by many barriers of caste, creed, and education. How vast is the interval which divides the rich lady from the poor mill-worker; but these divisions, though they are very real, are not deep or high. They are like the fences in the farmer's field that rail off the crops of barley from those of wheat or grass; but if you go down into the earth you pass along the gallery of the mine, the coal seam runs along unbroken and you never know when the boundaries overhead are passed, and above the sun shines on all alike. So these divisions of education, social position, and opinion divide us in our amusements, our employments, even sometimes in our churches. We are too much apart, but they do not separate the hearts of womanhood that beat in unity, nor the sunlight of God's justice that shines down upon the rich and poor alike. In the name of this common womanhood we are gathered here to-night, rich and poor, educated and untaught, to raise our voices altogether to ask for justice. Our sufferings have much in common. Gentlemen can be bad husbands as well as poor men. The money that should sustain a household can be melted in champagne as well as in beer or whisky; and though wife-beating is mostly confined to the poorer classes, yet educated men by cruel words, by cold unkindness, can strike blows on the heart which wound as deeply, and leave scars as hard to heal as any dealt by the hand. The mother's love also is one. The richest woman here to-night that is the mother of children loves them dearly; the poorest does no less. And the laws which wrong the mother's love are an outrage on the common womanhood by the bond of which we have all been drawn together here. Where I am lodging in Manchester I hear a clock strike with a slow, deep toned bell, and between the strokes other clocks of weaker sound and quicker utterance chime in, filling up the interval, making up a chorus of swelling sounds. These clocks are very various in tone and pitch, but they all say the same thing; they all tell the same story of the hour. So we have here to-night thousands of women whose voices are loud and strong – some of them with all the power of rank, wealth, education, social position. Others there are here, poor, hard-labouring women, who can bring us only their uprightness – their earnestness in our cause – but all their voices, from the loudest to the lowest, are saying the same thing. They all tell us that for us women also the morning hours are breaking. Far away in London the great clock of Westminster, 'Big Ben,' tells the time with his iron tongue; and in my girlhood – living almost under the shadow of the clock tower – I used to lay and listen to the solemn swell of his tone, telling to the revellers, and wanderers, and watchers, and all that wakened in the great city, the hours as they flew. But even that great clock has to strike at second-hand. At Greenwich they set the time for all the clocks in the country, and even 'Big Ben,' though he is so loud and so proud, has to take his orders from Greenwich. At Westminster also the clock of the empire strikes; every time it sounds it marks an epoch in the history of nations, and far and wide, to the very ends of the earth, men hold their breath and listen for the voice of England pealing out in power from Westminster. But the hands of that great clock of the empire move at the bidding of the people, and there is a political Greenwich as well as a scientific one. Here in the North is the political Greenwich; we in the North set the political time of day, and if the North shall say that this claim made to-night by women is set by the true sun of justice, then we shall soon hear 'Big Ben' strike the hour that makes women free citizens of their native land.

Emily Pfeiffer

*Woman's claim**

February 1881

HITHERTO when the women to whom the larger interests of
Society are dear, have expressed their desire for an extension of
the suffrage in their own direction they have very commonly been
met by the assurance that they belonged to an insignificant
minority, the sex being on the whole indifferent, if not averse to,
the active assumption of citizenship. The overflowing meetings
which have taken place successively at Manchester, in London,
and elsewhere, must at this stage of the discussion go far to silence
objections founded on a premise which every passing year is
rendering more erroneous. But, whatever might be the show of
hands if the issue were polled throughout the country, it is not so
much the amount as the quality of adherents which determines the
success of a movement, and it would not be impossible to show
that the greater part of all the force of intellect and character
known by public proof to exist among Englishwomen, is warmly
pledged to this woman's cause.

It may be conceded then as a fact, that the desire on the part of
the daughters of England to be no longer excluded from
participation in one of the rights which her sons hold dear, is a
genuine and increasing one; and in face of the manifest mental and
moral worth of its chief advocates, the assertion – a favourite

*Originally published in the *Contemporary Review*.

373

retreat of nonplussed disputants – that the 'best women' are still hostile to the change, must be acknowledged to be likewise untenable. I will not darken counsel by affecting to misunderstand what is meant in this connection by the 'best women.' They are the home-loving and tender creatures to whom fate has been good, and who find their highest joy – no very difficult strain, as it may be thought – in the performance of the duties of wifehood and motherhood, undeniably the most accordant to Nature of any that can plenish a woman's lot, and at the same time so bodily and spiritually engrossing, that those who well fulfil them may be forgiven if they tend to somewhat narrow the view and contract the sympathies. But whether the outlook of these fortunate sisters may happen to be narrow or wide, it is probable that the larger-hearted advocates of women's right to make their political judgments regarded, would think little of yielding the place of honour, in the estimate of the selfish or unthinking, to the happy band from whose ranks it is possible that chance or a more fastidious taste have exiled themselves. A circle which includes a large contingent of unpaid workers who are helping forward the best interests of humanity in many fields, and whose representative woman may be taken to be Florence Nightingale, will in any case be felt to be sufficiently select.

The men whose pleasure it is to affirm that 'good women' are in want of nothing, are far however from disclaiming the testimony to the same effect of beings who cannot be called 'good,' without putting an undue strain upon language, and who have of women neither the pitiful heart nor the helpful hand, but only the weakness and arrested development. These are the careless sisters of the millions who 'work and weep,' for working and weeping are only separately apportioned in a ballad, or in the quasi-poetical atmosphere which stagnates in places about masculine thought; these are the 'sitters at ease,' whose lives are given to self-pleasing as an end, and to flattering the humours of the men of whom they are the complement, as a means; who are callous to misery which they deem not likely to affect themselves, and have no aspiration higher than the false ideal which is the negative of manly vices. It is in the nature of such factions to be loud and prominent, and so to create a false notion of their numbers and weight; but happily for our hopes and for the prospects of humanity, those of the sex who, while neglecting their nearest ties, are utterly without what in the cant of science is now known as the 'tribal conscience,' are a minority, unworthy to be counted in the sum of opinion on a question of this nature and extent.

It may be taken, then, as a fact to be dealt with, and one which is presenting itself with increasing urgency, that a vast number of those who represent the noblest and tenderest womanhood among us, are dissatisfied with what has come to be the injustice of their position in view of the new social developments which have brought with them new needs. They are dissatisfied, that while they have no choice but to obey the natural law of development, the arbitrary laws under which they live remain rigid in their regard. It is no great thing that is required to put the lives of women in harmony with their altered conditions. The claim that widows and spinsters, when independent holders of property, should exercise the right of voting for Members of Parliament, carries so much of reason on its face, that it is difficult to see on what ground it could be withstood, other than that of a panic fear of results against which it might be supposed that Nature has sufficiently provided. This demand for the possession of the suffrage by widows and spinsters was the whole of the plea advanced at the meetings referred to, – a plea not simply put forward for the nonce, as we are sometimes warned, but one which there is reason to think honestly represents the extent of the claim as made by the majority of its female advocates. That widows and spinsters, as women, and possible wives, are in a better position for judging of the wants of women, whether single or married, than men, who must always view them chiefly in relation to themselves, few I think will contest. It is not asserted that the arrangement which would restrict the suffrage to single women householders would be a perfect one, but only that it appears to be the best which the nature of things permits of, and it may be presumed that a certain intuitive sense of fitness, together with a feeling of the sacredness of ideals possessed largely by women, would help them to cut the Gordian knot of a logic more tough than that presented by the limitations which marriage would be suffered to impose upon them.

Marriage is something more than a partnership – it is ideally a union; and if in the imperfections of all human relations, it fails in part, sometimes fails wholly, to fulfil its promise, it remains, fiction or truth, the lever which beyond all others has been effective in raising the moral nature of man to the height at which the sacrifice it enforces, can alone maintain it. Whatever may be the diversity of opinion in the domestic interior, however much the 'No,' pertinent or impertinent, may enliven the sameness of marital discourse, it will be felt I think as seemly, that while the marriage tie remains in force, no authenticated record of disagreement should go forth from the home to the world. But the sphere of a woman is so enlarged by marriage, her dignity so increased by motherhood, that it is little likely this renunciation of one of the rights of citizenship on accepting a partnership for life, would be accounted so deep a hardship as objectors would have us believe. The ear of the husband is found by most wives to be very conveniently within reach, and if the quickened interest in political questions which the change would inevitably spread among women, bond and free, should furnish another subject of possible variance, the same may be said of each one of those interests, intellectual or moral, which separate the cultivated women of our own clime and age from the odalisque and the squaw. That the too-tardily effected, and still very imperfect regulations in regard to the property of wives, imply a possible separation of interests incompatible with perfect union, is self-evident, but all our dealings are with an imperfect order of things, of which it is our difficult endeavour to make the best. This imagined union can, in Protestant countries, be openly dissevered, and the bitterest wrong has resulted in cases where the rupture of personal bonds has been confessed, while the legal tie maintaining the community of property – by which is meant its absorption by the man – has been held intact. When injustice, gross as that which can even now creep in under existing laws, has been rendered impossible, not by an invidious special act of the woman purporting to be married, or of her friends, but by the providence of a protecting law – no more than an honest confession will have been made, that we are seeking to provide against possible flaws in work which has to be built up of doubtful material. It is no part of the duty of society, in the abstract, to enforce upon its members by external means, the undeviating cultus of its purest ideals; the piety which exalts them must be the growth of the individual conscience.

Women are still sometimes roundly told that they have no grievances, and asked what it is they can want which it lies within the competence of the suffrage to give them. Like Shylock, 'I will not answer that.' There is little to be gained by going over that ground of old wrongs which has often led to bitter question. I will not even more than point in passing at the burning injustice which can wrest from the woman's grasp the child who, bone of her bone and flesh of her flesh, is the fruit of her labour and sorrow. It is, or ought to be, sufficient that women are awaking to a consciousness that their interests are unrepresented, and suffer in consequence; that they feel themselves aggrieved by their position – illogically maintained in the face of altered conditions – of a separate caste; and that they demand to join their judgment to the opinions of men on questions of social policy, and to add their experience to those same opinions on matters with which it is their special function to deal. To this end they seek to give weight to their views in the authorized fashion; they claim to count as an element in the constituencies with which members of the Lower House have to reckon. There are rocks ahead, no less than evils behind and abreast of us, and the dangers which threaten society in the shaking of the old faith, the loss of the old sanctions of conduct, and the overturning of the old ideals, are dangers which must press with something more than equal force upon its weaker half. If women must labour, and run risks with men, they demand to have something of their security, or at least to have free hands for the fight. They do not wish to struggle in bonds or to fall helpless into any pit which may open. They are not likely to exhibit a dangerous impatience, such as could be supposed to imperil the vessel of State, even if the share of power demanded by them were to be more than that fractional one of which there is now question. Their natural position in the scheme of things may be taken for a guarantee that the impact of their influence upon political questions would be consolidating rather than destructive. But if they presumably will not hurry on the wheels of progress, it is something that they may be expected to help in keeping them upon the rails. It is reasonably certain that the interests of marriage, for instance, would be more jealously guarded by women, single or widowed, than they would be by men; and is it too much to say that on the *maintenance of that institution rest the higher hopes of the race*? Life has this in common with Art: that the continent of a supreme law, to which voluntary obedience is rendered, is essential to its most perfect development. Time was when the praise of marriage would have been superfluous as the praise of sun-light; now it seems not wholly irrelevant to point out in what its essence consists, and what its observance has done for us. It has its source in the highest capacities of our nature, love and faith, of which last it is on the man's side the most signal human expression. The heirs to a man's worldly possessions and to the treasure of his affections, the beings for whom he works and strives, and for whose abundance he is contented often to go bare, he takes as his own upon the trust reposed in the woman of his choice. That this sacred trust is on the whole so rarely betrayed, that the marriage bond is so widely respected as to cause the sense of risk to pass practically out of view, is a circumstance which is adding, slowly and surely as the generations succeed each other, to the sum of that faith by which man as man must live. Let the elected partnership once lose its nobly sacrificial and sacramental character, let the caprice of man or woman claim to be its own law, the discordance of habit or opinion felt on the satiety of passion its own dispensation, let the man be free to shake off a yoke that irks, and the woman be emancipated from the guardianship of herself as the shrine, of his dearest hopes, and what becomes of the strength of individual will, increased by struggle and conquest, which has been lifting us higher and higher above the unregulated instincts of the brute? If the woman of the future is to be held, and rightly held, accountable primarily to herself for the preservation of her own truth, and if the notion that dishonour can come to any separate soul through other than his own act should be exploded, it can never be forgotten that the companion of man is the priestess of a temple whose desecration is his ruin. No State is known to have risen to greatness, that has not had 'the family' working to its own increase, and diffusing itself as a vital organic element within it, and the family can only exist with the definition necessary to its effective action, through the state of marriage. The woman alone will not suffice for its head; without the husband the circle of a family is incomplete, and without the family there can be no order in human relations, no permanence in human affections, no strength of self-restraint or forbearance – in a word, no virtue. The nomad of social institutions would spread disorder as a plague. As for love, the great regenerator, love which is

Half dead to think that he could die,

it is easy to conceive the sorry figure that he would be likely to make in any such time-bargain in place of marriage as that which finds advocates among certain moralists. In such a case there would be no lover's vows to move even the laughter of Jove; at which I think the earth no less than the heaven would be sadder. When the time shall come that we have cast away the marriage pledge to progress, it is presumable that we shall have commenced our downward course, and be on our way back to the ascidian, and through that to some wholly molluscous creature preparatory to the final extinction. It can hardly be doubted that the sentiment of love is deepened and exalted by the voluntary sacrifice brought to it by lovers in marriage. What is here contended is, that a human pair, in placing this seal upon love and faith, taken in its moment of efflorescence, are unconsciously drawn into the current of that stream which sets towards progress, and are making, unknown to themselves, an offering of individual liberty in the interests of the race. That a philosopher here and there, his vital energies having chiefly run to brain, should find rest by his own fireside with the companion of his experiment in life and their offspring, proves nothing for the probable permanence of unlegalized relations among the masses, with whom erratic fancy might be expected to be rather stimulated than controlled by culture, and who would in any case not be living under the check – stronger than law itself – of a thesis to uphold.

All women must deeply feel the plague-spot on our social system, for which, according to the moralists cited, the abolition of marriage is the remedy; it is a grief and shame to the best of them; but it is too vile a thing to be cured by *dispersion*. A French writer has said: 'The virtue of woman is the finest invention of man.' The thing is indeed so good, and men owe so much of the firmness of their moral fibre (by inheritance) to the particular power of self-restraint which goes under the name, that they would be entitled to high credit if it were of their making. Regarding it, however, not in the light of invention but discovery, we may hope that before humanity finally deflects from its upward course, it will be found that there exists a due capacity for its evolution in men; and every social movement crediting the authority of women would naturally tend to encourage the spread of such a growth.

It is possible that the men who have so long elected to be the visible providence of the other sex, have done what they could in its behalf; but it is difficult to estimate human needs wholly from the outside, and having always been legislated for as creatures apart, our common humanity has failed our 'keepers' as a serviceable guide to our requirements.

Women are dissatisfied not only with what has been done, and with what has been left undone for them, they are also dissatisfied that they, toilers and sufferers, should be left to the self-dependence of labour and sorrow without a voice in the Government to which they are accountable. Their right to labour on other fields than the barren patch into which they were until lately crowded, has been tardily conceded; they now demand to have a word to say in the making and administering of the laws by which the fruits of labour are protected. It is not well that there should be this widening breach, this growing sense of hardship.

If there is no class of men possessing to the full what they stand in need of, or with whom changing circumstances are not perpetually calling into play new requirements which demand to be met by new expedients, the conditions and necessities of women are even more fluctuating, and they feel that the time is come when light should be shed upon these intricate problems from within. They inherit faculties trained by household and educational cares, and know themselves fitted for the exercise of the function they demand to share. It is not a matter which calls for the employment of the comparative scale which men in our day seem so eager to apply to the endowments of their female companions. There is no earthly need that an intending voter should give proof of high dramatic or musical genius. It may be that the creative energy is less strong in women than in men, but that is quite beside the point at issue, and carries with it no implication that the female understanding is less proper than the male for nourishing the germs of thought, for forming a nidus for the ideas everywhere present in the air, and for presenting them clothed in shapes well fitted to act upon the material forces around us. As a matter of fact worth much theorizing, the women now employed in offices of trust, whether on the School Board or elsewhere, are proving themselves good administrators, steady workers, and as sober of judgment as their male coadjutors.

The evils of a complicated social system are great, and the difficulty of dealing with them sore. It may well be that such contingent of help as women could furnish, if they were more fully free to do so, would have a very inadequate effect in mitigating human ill. But many of those who are not called upon to bear the brunt of ills in their own persons, feel the burthen on them as pressing upon others; and it is waste of motive power, as it is pain and wrong to the modern woman, whose cultivated sympathy is often alive in every nerve to the shames and sorrows of society, to deny her right to put her untried strength to the wheel. If there be anything on which all noble-hearted human beings, whether men or women, are agreed, it is in a vast regret that the alleviation of social suffering, the purgation of social sin, is a work of such slow advance. It is folly in such a case to repudiate the help of willing workers, the folly becomes cruelty when the power to act upon circumstances is denied to those upon whom the suffering presses most hardly, and of whom the payment of sin is demanded with overwhelming interest. But while the women at the front of this movement, women who have long been fighting an unequal battle, and have had their training in a school of trouble and disappointment, are not rash enough to expect miracles from that partial possession of the suffrage by their sex for which they are contending, they are justified in looking for some appreciable result, which may increase with the growing time. If they do not conceive that the wilderness is to blossom as the rose when, in place of overt influence, they have come to the open exercise of a certain modicum of power, it is permitted reasonably to hope that feminine thought, practically directed to politics, may occasionally cast some glimpse of light on subjects which, not commending themselves to masculine attention, have heretofore remained obscure. And there is a further issue which, if more recondite, is of equally sure promise and of even deeper significance. I allude to the effect on character – on that character which the mothers and early teachers of mankind transmit to their descendants of both sexes, which may be looked for as a result of the recognized expression of woman's thought and will – in a word, from the exercise of the human right of freedom.

Speaking once with an Oriental of high mark, on the position of the women of his people, he said to me: 'In India women are all-powerful, even as they are here.' I believed and do believe him. The women of India are nimble-witted and acute, or they were no match for their husbands and brothers; and, smooth and subtle as snakes, they fold the limbless strength of their degraded souls about every question, which appeals with sufficient force to their passions or interest. Held by men in a condition of abject subjection, deprived by jealous supervision of all moral self-support, the Nemesis of the virtues which have been killed within them appears in the characters of craft and subtlety which they *print upon the race*. It is not too much to say of the women of a nation, that they are the moulds in which the souls of its men are set. Their very moods are reflected in the infant that is born into the world; the young child is surrounded by the mother's mind as by an atmosphere; her judgments are his code, her example his authority. Scarcely out of school, when the passions are in a state of fusion and make the whole being plastic, the youth falls under the operation of this law of life in another shape. The woman who is loved of boy or man, unconsciously prescribes the form of her own worship, and the character of the worshipper is modified, more or less, by the result. Let it never be dreamed that emotional contact can take place between two human beings without leaving a lasting impress on both. The frail creature who is believed to be the object of little else than scorn, is a factor in the sum of circumstances which determines a man's walk, and that which he seems to see in it, to the latest hour of his life. It is thus that society suffers throughout its length and breadth from wrongs which to the superficial thinker may seem to press only upon a part of it.

It will hardly be supposed that I am confounding the condition of women in our Western world with that of their cruelly crippled sisters in the East. The illustration they have furnished to me has been used only to give point to the argument that it is essential to the dignity of human character generally, that all voluntary forces which affect human action shall be duly accredited and openly applied. Nor is it in morals alone that the frank embodiment of opinion is of sound and invigorating effect; it is good also for the sanity of the intellect, that thought and action should suffer no divorce. The mind that is coquetting with questions to which it acknowledges no external ties, is less likely to form just views, than one which knows itself in responsible relation to them. It would seem that at the point of progress we have now reached, there is special need of some new inlet of ideas, stimulating to larger and more healthy interests. In view of our yearly increasing wealth and the perpetual additions which are thereby made to the idle and luxurious classes, every countercheck to corrupting frivolity is to be hailed as an element of salvation. It is this large amount of female energy run wild, disfranchised of the little active cares which formerly employed it, and having found no substitute for them but the daily round in the treadmill of pleasure, that is spreading a pernicious example at home, and lowering the character of our countrywomen abroad. The affairs of the world, under the name of politics, in which the withdrawal of the disqualifications of sex would give to women a more intelligent interest, may not be greatly more ennobling than those of the household, when they are viewed from the standpoint of party; but questions of wide, impersonal relation are involved in them, which could not always be shut out from the minds even of the narrowest partisans; and this widening of the mental horizon would be among the incalculable consequences of the removal of those arbitrary restrictions, which constitute an infringement of liberty. There can be no call to hymn the praises of freedom to English men or women; the former have always deemed it worthy of their struggle and sacrifice; and, for the latter, whatever virtues they possess are owing to the share they have enjoyed of it. But what was in a way freedom to women under the old order, is bondage now; and if even more women than men, standing in a position which should render them responsible, are wasting life and leisure on pursuits wholly selfish and trivial, it is that wealth has loosened the claims of former duties, before liberty has given authority to the new. It is thus clear that the continued refusal to women of their demands for a more active citizenship, is the denial to them of a sacred human right to perfect and harmonious development.

A great deal has been said, is still being said, about the alteration of the relations of the sexes which might be expected to result from any extension of the franchise in the manner demanded. I own I find it difficult to respond to these fears with becoming seriousness. If there be any one thing of which Nature is careful, she is careful of her types, and while that 'likeness in unlikeness' subsists, which is at the base of physical attraction, there is little fear of sexual relations being either reversed or annulled. So long as the maternal function continues tenderly to fashion the hearts of women, so long as the voices of men retain their resonance, and until their bodies lose their superior power of action and endurance, and their capacity for food and sleep, so long will there be little doubt that the saying of our neighbours, '*La barbe impose*,' will remain substantially correct. These quasi-material causes might be out of place in a system where abstract justice answered to a rigid logic, but in this world of incalculable movements, of checks and counterchecks, they present themselves as something more than the 'windage' for which in all reasoning we are bound to allow. It would seem that the alarmists above-mentioned are reckoning without that great primal force which binds together men and women, and for which the higher developments of reason are for ever forging stronger if more spiritual links. I would bid them take courage in remembering the comparative stability of the operations of Nature, judged by the shortness of the days of man; in any case, to plant a quiet hope in the largeness of those grants of time demanded for the changes she is supposed to effect. If men and women are finally either to grow into a dull resemblance or become inimical to each other, it will not presumably happen until the planet which they jointly inhabit has advanced far upon the process of cooling down; a contingency too remote for adjustment in regard to it, to come within the province of statecraft.

I am loth to accept as truly meant on the part of the men even most opposed to liberal views on this matter, the inconsiderate dictum that the possession of equal rights by those who can never be gifted with equal strength, should be held to exclude them from all chivalrous service and manly observance. If certain of those who have been the pioneers of this movement have used the rough and ready methods of speech and action which are perhaps proper to the nature of the work they have had to do in its beginnings, it affords no argument that those who enter upon tranquil possession of the good for which these others fought, would need to abandon any graces or gentlenesses which belong – let me say – to *contented* womanhood. But –

> A woman moved is like a fountain troubled,
> Muddy, ill-seeming, thick, bereft of beauty.

And, be it said, by the way, the poet who has best held the mirror to the nature he has left us to interpret for ourselves, has given us, in the play wherein these lines occur, a picture of the lying subservience resulting from acquiescence in despotism, which would furnish a keener sting than could be found in any words of mine, to some of the foregoing remarks.

Women are demanding a fair field wherein to labour and they make no claim for favour so far; but life is not all made up of labour and sorrow, and even labour and sorrow do not exclude mutual help.

Let it never be said that the daughters of Albion have had to choose between justice and mercy; the alternative would be hard, but the election could not be long doubtful. The grace which one sex arrogates to itself the right of according to the other, while its exercise has in all time been partial and self-regarding, has become, in relation to the exigencies of modern female life, little better than a sop to Cerberus. It is justice, simple, and, as is now scarcely denied, obvious justice, which the *femme sole* of our modern society, and through her womanhood at large, in such a degree as natural laws render expedient, is seeking to secure.

There was a time when physical force ruled the world, when law was feeble, and only the strong hand could make itself respected. A woman then who had got no man to marry her was forced to seek the refuge of the cloister; married or immured, in either case she was externally cared for and protected, as was needful in her unfitness to barbarous conditions; and in either case she gave herself wholly, and was swallowed up, whether of the Church or her liege lord, in return for shelter, suit, or service. It was an agreement, and when fulfilled according to the letter, it left no ground for complaint.

The laws which were made or redressed from time to time, were shaped in accordance with the demands of the ruling sex. That one of their chattels, which from the beginning has possessed a sad faculty of feeling, and was learning by degrees to think, was taken no heed of by the State, but left, with the rest of a man's personal property, entirely at his own discretion. And, perhaps on the whole, the possession of an object, if it happens to be of value to the holder, may be taken as a fair guarantee for its receiving a reasonable amount of care. But now a day has come when, if the 'seven women' of the prophet would not 'take hold on one man,' some of them must be resigned to belong only to themselves, and prepared to stand up and fight the battle of life alone. That they are to a certain extent handicapped by Nature in this struggle of opposing interests is not, cannot be, denied; but no one, I think, will say that any plea for undue allowance is put forward on this account by the brave women who are already in the arena. On the contrary, their demand is only that the terms of conflict shall be something like equalized where that is possible; and this is precisely the justice that is denied them. The rate-paying, law-abiding, property-holding, professional, or working woman, is suffered to have no voice in the regulation of the taxes or the laws under which she must live or die; and if she would influence them at all, must have recourse to the nearest man – possibly her butler, coachman, gardener, or the labourer in her fields – as the stalking-horse of her own unrecognized personality. It is no wonder if the moment has at length arrived when society, having outgrown the gross appetites which placed its physically weaker half in a state of dependent tutelage, women are showing themselves impatient of the persistence of limitations which, beneficial in their time and season, have now become as oppressive as they are unmeaning, and insulting to rational intelligence.

There is a divinity which shapes our ends.

Had it so continued that every woman in these isles could have 'dropped into the jaws' of some one man, and so 'ceased' as a social unit, it is highly probable that no word would have been heard among us of any further suffrage. But necessity has presented itself to the women of our generation with talons and beak more formidable than those of the eagle who drives the young one from the nest. They have not sought the shelterless strife with opposing prejudices and interests, but have been forced into it by the incontrovertible law which pushes the tribes of men over barren continents, and out upon stormy seas. It is *Hunger*, the mighty *Maker*, which is urging our women upon new paths, and driving them upon a way which they would not, to the fulfilment of a destiny which they know not. With this force behind them it is impossible that they should turn back, impossible that those before them should resist their impulsion. They have been crowded by their own numbers out of the penfold in which their activity was enclosed, and forced to seek the equivalent of their labour in an ever-widening sphere. In making the experiment of their fitness for untried work, they have had to face odium and abundant ridicule from those whose approval they hold dear. Their efforts to train themselves for higher and more remunerative labour have encountered the opposition of a jealously-guarded monopoly; and the claim for citizenship now formulated – though enforced independence has rendered it a right – may be met, seeing that it lacks the element of material force which still enters largely into human affairs, on many sides with indifference, and on some with scorn. It would not be thus if there existed a threat behind it. Meetings of men of any class, upon the scale of the women's meetings which have lately assembled, would be held sufficiently representative of their mind and will to enforce respect for their demands. But the stream of tendency which sets in the way of women's advance is irresistible, and the vital rational principles incorporated in her claim could in the end win alone in the struggle with material resistance –

> The soul of things is strong:
> A seedling's heaving heart has moved a stone.

The march of civilization is one sure, if slow, progression from the rule of the strongest to the equal right divine, and it will not stop short of its legitimate end. But with ends, as ends, we have nothing to do; our progress is step by step, our only guide the awakening conscience of humanity. It were vain to deny that seemingly moderate and wholly reasonable as is the demand now put forward, such exercise of reason would be a new and strange thing in the history of the already old world, and that some degree of faith in right is needed to enable men to commit themselves confidently to the unknown. We may win much, we must lose something, by this as by every other change; but change is a law of life, and this one has long been gathering force to make itself obeyed. Neither men nor women can finally resist the momentum of circumstances, but women at least could be made to suffer unduly by the presence of prolonged opposition.

I will not deal to my countrymen such scant measure of the justice often invoked, as to doubt that there are generous souls among them with whom the appeal of reason and feeling, gains more than it loses by the knowledge that it emanates from a region wherein the power to enforce it brutally, has no existence. It would only be entirely worthy of the men whose fathers have fought and died for liberty on many fields, to share the precious heirloom on the basis of moral right, with companions who could never wrest it from their unwilling grasp, or, prizing it however truly, baptize it with their blood in contact with such opponents. The place of a people in the scale of human development is determined by the condition of its women: it would be a meet crown to a long career of freedom, if the country of which it is the chosen home, should be the first among the nations to yield that which no one of them in the end may be able to withhold.

Laura E. Morgan-Brown

The census and women's suffrage

THE result of the census taken in April last is now before us, to discuss and digest with profit, for the number and general status of our vast population affect many different points of political and social interest, and for those who have eyes to see the census has comprehensive lessons to teach.

A woman, and especially an English woman, turns with natural interest to the paragraph which concerns the numerical proportion of her own sex, and this is the cardinal point, the importance of which I wish to press home to every woman in the land.

We read: – 'Of the total population at the census which has just been taken, 14,050,620 were males, and 14,950,398 were females. This excess of nearly 900,000 females would, of course, be considerably reduced had the army, the navy, and the merchant service abroad been included in the reckoning. The proportion of females to males has been *steadily increasing* at each census since 1851.'

So there are 900,000 more women than men in England and Wales?

Let us consider what sized town it would be if all these women, who have no other half with which their number can be paired, were to live together in a community. A vast territory would have to be set aside for the homes of these unattached women, who in spite of the 'protection' said to be so necessary for their sex are evidently out of court. They certainly have no male caretaker specially told off for their support, their comfort, their companionship, their credit! They are a vast concourse wholly and entirely unrepresented. They have no one man each, to seek to redress any personal wrong they may suffer. They must sow, they must spin, they must gather into barn themselves, for themselves, and by themselves. They are not the lilies of life neither do they lie on the roses, and there are 900,000! I turn to that most useful book, *Whittaker's Almanack*, to try to find out in imagination what kind of a city would be required to house the 900,000, and I find in the list of the population of great cities that, with the exception of London, Paris, Berlin, New York, and Philadelphia, there is not a city quoted large enough for the contingent. St Petersburg, with a population of 842,000, falls short, whilst Vienna, which most of us know better than St Petersburg, only houses 822,176 inhabitants.

Just conceive, then, our army of surplus women who are alone, i.e. without the direct care of one special 'lord and master,' for whose benefit we are so often told woman was specially created, though the natural corollary that, if this be so, man was created solely to look after her, is more often left to the imagination than expressed.

The Majority Neglected

Now, if the result of the census had shown a majority of 900,000 men I do not think I am wrong in asserting that in countless instances the fact would have been selected as a most significant one, pointing unmistakably to the natural preponderance and importance of men over women. It would be said, 'Men are stronger, better in every way to fight life's battle – to govern, to rule at home and abroad. They survive, you see, in greater numbers; the women die off. They, the men, are able to get their own living and struggle upwards by force of sheer numbers. Why, *of course* it is intended they should take the lead and keep it – and they mean to, that is very clear, *for they are in the majority*, so who shall say them nay?'

But the census tells a different story. It is the men who are the fewest. The army, the navy, emigration (of those who are often the most fit to do work at home), all these causes help to reduce men to the minority, and though from the 900,000 surplus women we should make a deduction of a good percentage of wives of soldiers, sailors, and emigrants, who are left behind and nominally protected, there yet remains a vast concourse of women who may safely be neglected because they have no vote. They have no voice whatsoever in the nation. If they lived in a city or county by themselves, no matter what the wrong, the injustice, the evil that might exist in that town or county, they could not themselves, although so numerically large a part of the nation, have one direct say in the nation on any point whatsoever. Now is this fair, is it right, is it just, is it wise?

It is so easy for women who are well off to be satisfied with everything that does not interfere with their own personal comfort – the welfare of themselves, and their children.

It is so much easier for a prosperous, well-dressed, amiable, school-instructed woman, who is married and fairly satisfied with a fairly pleasant life, to say, 'Oh! I really do not know anything about these things you mention. I leave all politics to my husband. I do not think women have the education or the time to understand things rightly.' It is so much easier to say all this than to say, 'Politics? Why do you ask *me* about them? You think women ought to know something about their nation and the way it is governed? Well, I suppose they ought, because, after all, the nation is only a big family, and I am sure I understand *my* part of the management of the family quite as well as my husband does *his* part. Ah! You are smiling – Well, to tell you the truth it never occurred to me in this light before. Will I join your society? No, I won't to-day, because I never do anything in a hurry, but I will tell you what I will promise to do. I will try to find out what you mean by the justice of the case – that a woman should have a vote, I mean – and I will learn all about the matter *for myself.* Yes, I promise you *I will not accept what other people tell me* is right or wrong, and when I have learned I will let you know my decision.'

Why, if women would only take that amount of interest, the 900,000 surplus women would not long have to complain of the greatness of their number, which only too briefly and graphically describes the helplessness of their condition.

Handicapped as we are, though, let us remember we are numerically the strongest. Men would think this something in their favour, and women must think so too.

Every kind of argument is used to show plainly and unmistakably the immense stake that we women have in the good of the country, and yet prejudice or ignorance blinds the eyes of women and deadens their hearts to their own interests in the most astonishing way.

Surely this result of the census will make women think of those less fortunate than themselves; those who *will* never be helped, *can* never be helped, raised and educated to a sense of their own individual responsibilities as citizens born into a State, unless women themselves help them with the right kind of help – help *to help themselves.*

Your power of good works, your power of money, your power of religious teaching, and the power of your prayers are deprived of half their efficacy because, though you are strong to *will*, you are politically powerless to *do.* Your wish to do all you can for your fellow creatures may be all that is holiest and best, but besides being a human being you are, like Paul, a citizen of 'no mean city,' and until you are politically recognised as such, you stultify your best efforts and you rob half its power from the inspiration to think and to do that which is right and for which you daily pray, because in spite of your education, your intention, your money, your power, or your religious zeal, you are one of the unprivileged classes – your accident of birth places you in the same category as lunatics, paupers, criminals, and children.

Millicent Garrett Fawcett

*Women's suffrage and the franchise bill**

14 January 1884

ON 2 January the *Pall Mall Gazette* contained an article written by a personal friend of M Gambetta giving, among other matters of interest, a short account of his view of the comparative rate of liberal progress in France and in England. It appears he thought that England was about ten years in advance of France in most liberal movements; but, he added, 'there is one thing you will have in England long before us – women's suffrage' – and he went on to say that he thought women's suffrage would be a good thing in England, but not at present in France, because of the degree to which the religion and education of Frenchwomen place them under the dominion of the priesthood. It is sometimes difficult to see the wood for the trees; and the opinion of an outsider, so well fitted as M Gambetta to gauge the weight of political forces, that women's suffrage is in the near future in England, is of special value. Many things have happened since the opinion was expressed which would have confirmed it had M Gambetta been still alive. The events of this autumn make it abundantly evident that the majority of Liberals are now in favour of giving the Parliamentary suffrage to women on the same terms on which it is or may be granted to men. To prove the truth of this it is necessary to go no further than the recent important

*Originally published in the *Pall Mall Gazette*.

conference of Liberals at Leeds. The conference represented between five and six hundred Liberal organisations, sending up about sixteen hundred delegates. The resolution in favour of admitting women to the suffrage was fairly put, and carried by an overwhelming majority; an eye-witness states that a perfect forest of hands went up in its favour, and only an insignificant sprinkling against it. The support which the rank and file of Liberals throughout the country give to women's suffrage, though strikingly exemplified at Leeds, was not there revealed for the first time. Among more recent events which tend to show that women's suffrage is part and parcel of the general programme of Liberalism at the present time, I may cite the great reform meeting on the Newcastle Town Moor last autumn, where at every one of the platforms allusions to the desirability of removing the political disabilities of women were received with cheers and general approval. The Liberal Associations of Manchester, Leeds, Birmingham, Edinburgh, Huddersfield, Nottingham, and many other important centres of political activity have adopted resolutions embodying the principle of women's suffrage; the movement is supported by nearly the whole Liberal press, both in London and the provinces. There is now little doubt that the Liberal members of Parliament are less advanced on this subject than the general body of Liberals in the country; but even in the House of Commons, if Liberal votes only had been counted, Mr Hugh Mason's resolution last session would have been carried by 44 (120 to 76), or if the Home Rulers are counted as Liberals the majority would have been 54 (135 to 81); whereas if Tory votes only had been counted the motion would have been defeated by 70 votes (99 to 29). In the foregoing figures the pairs and tellers on each side have been counted. One more piece of evidence which shows the hold which this question has taken among Liberals is to be found in the fact that, with all the feeling that has grown up respecting the importance of an immediate extension of the suffrage, 110 independent Liberals below the gangway last session sent a memorial to Mr Gladstone stating unequivocally that 'no measure for the assimilation of the borough and county franchise will be satisfactory unless it contains provisions for extending the suffrage, without distinction of sex, to all persons who possess the statutory qualifications for the Parliamentary franchise.'

The facts which have here been brought together prove, I think, conclusively that the mass of Liberal opinion is favourable to an extension of the suffrage to women; and this is almost necessarily the case now that the Reform question is uppermost in the minds of politicians. No politician can read with approval the speeches of Mr Gladstone, Mr Bright, Mr Chamberlain, and others in favour of an extension of the suffrage to the male householders in counties without being aware that every one of the arguments these speeches contain tells with equal force in favour of granting a similar privilege to women who possess the legal qualifications. The reasons which make it desirable that men should be represented make it equally desirable that women should be represented. Is it said that the rural labourers are loyal, law-abiding, peaceable, intelligent, and industrious? So are the women it is proposed to enfranchise. Is it said that the interests of the rural labourers are overlooked in the press and hurry of Parliamentary work in consequence of their want of representation? So are those of the women it is proposed to enfranchise. Is it said that it is desirable to place confidence in the people, and widen the basis of the Constitution? We can agree again, and only say, Extend your confidence a little further: 95 per cent of Liberal members of Parliament, according to the answers to the *Pall Mall Gazette* circular, are prepared, and quite rightly prepared, to trust the peasantry of Ireland with political enfranchisement – why not entrust it to women?

Considerations similar to the foregoing cannot be without their effect, except with those Liberals whose minds may be said to be built in water-tight compartments, and who can therefore admit a flood of conviction, enthusiasm, and eloquence into one compartment in favour of enfranchising householder A without its producing the slightest effect upon the dry crust of prejudice which is safely stowed in another compartment against enfranchising householder B.

I believe it will one day be considered almost incredible that there ever was a time when the idea of giving votes to women who fulfil the conditions which enable men to vote was regarded as dangerous and revolutionary. There is nothing apparently more subversive of reason and judgment than fear. The Duke of Wellington was afraid of the Reform bill of 1832, and honestly believed that it would bring down in general ruin property, the Crown, and the Church. Some of the most astute men of the world of the pre-Reform era were misled in a similar way. The author of the 'Greville Memoirs,' writing in 1831 of the scene in the House of Lords when William IV dissolved Parliament, speaks of the King with the 'tall, grim figure of Lord Grey close beside him with the Sword of State in his hand; it was as if the King had got his executioner by his side, and the whole picture looked strikingly typical of his and our future destinies.' The day for these extravagant hallucinations has passed. As Mr Bright said some time ago in speaking of household suffrage in Irish boroughs: 'Men are afraid of the first experiment of something which has a dangerous appearance; but if they find that their fears were altogether imaginary they make a second experiment without fear.' Some people seemed at one time to think that the whole order of society, the very laws of nature, would be reversed if household suffrage were made to include women; but a first experiment has been made in giving women the municipal and School Board suffrages. The fears at first expressed have proved altogether imaginary; society has not been turned upside down; the possession of a vote has not made women essentially different from what they were before; we still like needlework; we prefer pretty gowns to ugly ones; we are interested in domestic management and economy, and are not altogether indifferent to our friends and relations; and we ask, therefore, that a second experiment should be made without fear.

It is said sometimes that women themselves do not wish for the Parliamentary suffrage; a similar argument has been used against every extension of the suffrage and against almost every great reform. It was said that the slaves did not wish to be free, that Nonconformists did not wish for the repeal of the Tests and Corporation Acts. It is an old story. Those who say women do not wish for the suffrage are probably guided by the opinions of ladies whom they meet in society; but surely the last general election was a sufficient proof that 'society' and 'the English people' are not identical expressions. It cannot be denied that hundreds of thousands of women do wish for the Parliamentary suffrage, that they petition Parliament again and again to grant it to them; a smaller number devote a great part of their lives in working to promote it, and make real and deeply-felt sacrifices for it. Nearly all the distinguished women of the present time have wished for it and expressed their desire for it. Mrs Somerville, Miss Martineau, and Miss Florence Nightingale are the first three names that occur to me among the women who have made their names known in science, literature, and philanthropy who have been from the outset of the movement cordial supporters of women's suffrage. Coming down to the humble women of every-day life, it is found that a very large proportion now wish women-householders to have votes. A few months ago seven hundred women householders in Hyde, near Manchester, were canvassed to sign a petition in favour of women's suffrage, and of these seven hundred the petition was signed by 608. A straw shows the way the wind is blowing, and another little fact may be mentioned in this connection. A young women's debating society in Cambridge lately discussed women's suffrage, and rejected a resolution condemning it by 56 votes to 13. There are, of course, some women who do not wish for votes; the majority of these do not perhaps possess the qualification that would enable them to vote; but even if they do, no one wishes for a law to compel women to vote. I have sometimes heard men speaking with much satisfaction of having half a dozen votes in different parts of the country and never having used one of them. The type will probably be found among both sexes. But the women who do not want votes are not so zealous in their renunciation of what others want as were the Dissenters who petitioned Parliament against the repeal of the Five Mile Act and the Conventicle Act. Their petition was paraphrased by Burke in words that will not easily be forgotten: – 'We, say the Dissenters who petition against Dissenters, enjoy every species of indulgence we can wish for; and, as we are content, we pray that others who are not content may meet with no relief.' Some of us are not content; we are asking for freedom and for representation on exactly the same grounds on which our fathers and forefathers asked for it and won it.

Isabella M. S. Tod

Women and the new franchise bill: a letter to an Ulster Member of Parliament

March 1884

DEAR SIR, –

I am sure that as you listened to the speech of the Prime Minister in introducing the new Franchise Bill, you thought with interest and sympathy of the Irish friends of Women's Suffrage, and regretted that he who has listened to the cry for justice from men should not listen to the less loud, but far more anxious cry from women. You know how deep is the conviction of the best women in Ulster, of all religious and political opinions, that the possession of the franchise by those among them who have the usual qualification is an absolute necessity for the highest interests of the whole Kingdom, and peculiarly so for Ireland. You know that women in Ireland take a keen interest in politics, but that here, as elsewhere, their influence is a binding and uniting force in society, of priceless value. You know how, as our advocacy of this claim has reached all parts of the Province, all grades of society, all creeds and classes, serious opposition has gradually disappeared; and within the last few months nearly every political Association in Ulster, Liberal and Conservative alike, has expressed its approbation. You know also how strong a conviction of moral and social right is implied in such widespread approbation in a divided community like ours.

Allow me, therefore, as the chief pleader for women's suffrage here, and as a Liberal, and as one who has often experienced your help and friendship in fighting the battle of justice, to draw your attention to some reasons why we should press with the utmost determination our claim to be included in the present Franchise Bill. Mr Gladstone's sole allusion to our claim was not the allusion of one who saw anything undesirable in it. He simply indicated that in his view it was inopportune; that is, that he was anxious to secure the franchise for two millions of men who were householders, and so complete the circle of male household suffrage, and wished that other men should wait till this was achieved, and that all women should wait. Now, my first and greatest objection to this request to us to sit down silently with that 'hope deferred which maketh the heart sick,' is that there is no parallel at all between the cases of the women to be kept out, and the men to be kept out. I see clearly, as any one familiar with recent Parliamentary history must do, how immense is the difficulty of passing a great measure at all, and how desirable it is to simplify it for purposes of management. But to make household suffrage really complete, by admitting nearly half-a-million of women householders along with the two millions of men with whom the Bill deals, seems simple and reasonable on the face of it; and to admit these additional men, whilst leaving out all women, is not reasonable, and is only simple at the cost of a tremendous injustice. There is this intrinsic difference between our claim and that of any class of men, that the exclusion of any of them is not absolute, but our exclusion is. Any man left unpossessed of a vote by the new Bill, nay more, any man of those about to be enfranchised by it, has representatives among the men who are possessed of votes at this moment. An artisan living outside a borough has representatives of his own trade and standing among the present voters; a miner in a village has friends of his own occupation among miners in Parliamentary boroughs; a labourer, no matter how strictly rural his employment, has some fellow-labourers, though fewer than in the other cases, among the electors of some scattered constituencies. These men feel that there is much they need which cannot be attended to properly while they are unrepresented; but, for all that, their fellows, working not from philanthropic motives, but for their own needs, do nevertheless present *their* desires and necessities to the members of the Legislature.

But no woman has any virtual representative anywhere. No body of electors, doing their own work, and pleading their own cause, is unconsciously doing her work and pleading her cause. If women have a wrong to redress, a difficulty to remove, a mistake to prevent, a grave conviction to enforce, they must get up a special machinery of agitation, at once elaborate and clumsy, which absorbs strength and skill which ought to be spent directly upon the object to be gained. To push all women aside, while a fresh procession of men marches in through the gate of the Constitution, is inflicting upon them a far greater proportionate loss and injury than would be inflicted upon any class of men at present unrepresented, if they were similarly treated.

But the evil result of total exclusion is increased by another fact. Every enlargement of the franchise renders the position of a totally unrepresented class worse than before. You will remember that I am a firm believer in the wisdom of placing the power of the State on the broadest possible basis of representation. But by just so much as the welfare of the State is increased by the fuller development of true representation, by just so much is it lessened by the total and conspicuous exclusion of one large and valuable class of citizens. In the old days, when but a few men in each constituency had votes, an elector occupied somewhat the same place that a Member does now. He was virtually a trustee for all his unrepresented neighbours. He might, and often enough did, use his power for petty and selfish ends; but few ever wholly threw off the sense of responsibility, although they were very likely to come to a wrong decision as regards the rights of others. When the Reform Act of 1832 came, necessary as it was to make a real attempt to represent a nation instead of a class, one result was greatly to weaken the sense of responsibility in each elector. He thought of working along with his enfranchised neighbours, but not of watching over the interests of the unenfranchised. The Reform Act of 1867 effaced any such idea from the minds of electors altogether; for every man thought that every other man was as well able to look after himself as he was, and the interests of those who were not men receded into a very dim distance.

If the condition of women depended wholly upon the electors, the consequences to society would have been very evil. But providentially there has been a current of favourable as well as unfavourable circumstances. The energetic action of women themselves, first in the matter of higher education, and then in the matter of opening out more ways of earning a livelihood, – pursued in the face of all kinds of opposition, from airy sarcasm to trade-strikes and hostile votes in Parliament, – has had results for good extending throughout the whole framework of society. One marked result has been the determination of women already locally engaged in philanthropic and reforming work no longer to rest content with striving against secondary causes, but to unite their forces through the whole land, and work together for the removal of the root-causes of intemperance, impurity, juvenile crime and juvenile misery, and for the constructive work of elevating the classes who naturally come under their care. At this moment they have gained much; at this moment they are hopeful of gaining more; at this moment they feel that at the countless points where legislation intersects their work they are able partially to make themselves felt, though with difficulty and strain. But with the advent to power of another large body of men, a considerable proportion of them uneducated, all idea of responsibility to non-electors will be swept out of public life, the preoccupation of Members of Parliament will become more severe than ever; and the best women in the land, married, unmarried, and widows alike, will feel that their last hope of direct influence on the government of this so-called self-governed country will be gone.

I am not forgetting for a moment the influence of wives, mothers, sisters, and even friends upon the men who are electors. If that influence were not great and constant, the country could not be called a Christian country at all. That influence over the immense majority is the highest and best power in the land. But it is not exerted upon bad men, only upon good, – but the electoral power of women would reach both. It is not much exerted in the business and public relationships of life, only in the private and social relation-ships, – but the electoral power of women would go far to help justice in both. It is possessed in abundant measure by those women who are so surrounded by love that they need use it only for others, not themselves, and is absent from a host of others as good, but to whom Providence has allotted pain and hardship and struggle for life, – but the electoral power of women would to some extent redress the balance. These facts, of which men in power are so often quite unaware, because they naturally come in contact only with those who have power already, make this moment one of intense anxiety for women.

There is nothing revolutionary in the enlargement of the new household franchise scheme to take in the women who possess all the local franchises. They form a comparatively small body, about four hundred thousand in the United Kingdom; but they would place all other women in the position in which unrepresented men are, of having friends with the same interests as themselves among the electors. Every argument applied by the Prime Minister to the case of unenfranchised men applies equally to unenfranchised women. Mr Gladstone speaks of the position of the householder – his representative character – his share in industrial life – his capability of being a useful citizen. A woman householder holds the same place – shares also in one form or other of industrial life – has the same representative character towards members of her household and others – has the same capability of wise interest in civic concerns. It must not be forgotten either that whilst every man of influential local position, of wealth and generous helpfulness, of education and social leadership, is long since enfranchised, there is a very large class of such women waiting to be let in through the door which is at present shut in their faces. Upon these ladies, no less than upon the large body of middle-class and working women who are house-holders, rest many of the most onerous social duties, and those duties are performed by them at the least as well as the duties of any represented class in the community. Yet they have just now so little power to make themselves heard, upon any subject about which their masculine neighbours do not happen to care, that it is possible for those neighbours to forget the very existence of these women and their opinions, when matters are under discussion which affect their welfare. Writing lately on the difficulty of ascertaining some facts about the agricultural labourers, the *Spectator* observes, 'so completely have the rural majority been forgotten because they have no political importance.' For the same reason, women have found their opinions on matters of vital importance to them utterly overlooked. Even married women and others having near relations among electors find themselves unable to affect such legislation, from the mediæval notion that 'woman have nothing to do with politics,' though politics have so much and increasingly to do with them – a notion which would not last a day, if but even a few women were enfranchised. We ask that women who possess the local franchises shall have this wider and greater one – first, because they do obviously come within the scope of a household Franchise Bill – second, because they are composed of all classes, and can fairly represent other women – third, because they are independent citizens, having all the burdens and responsibilities of work and property, and yet without either a vote of their own, or the indirect power which a married woman has of being represented by her husband's vote.

I am afraid to trust myself to write as I feel upon some of the questions affecting women and girls, which can never be safely settled until women are represented. Well, indeed, I know the worth of some of our legislators – men whose religion is as present and as powerful with them in the House of Commons as in church – men to whom the honour and dignity and freedom of a woman are as sacred as the honour and dignity and freedom of a man. But I dare not say that these are the majority of any House of Commons that ever was elected. For the *average* MP really to remember how sacred these things are, he needs absolutely to have the fact present to his mind that he partly owes his seat to the votes of women, and that they, as constituents, are watching his legislative action. There is no more disrespect in such an assertion than there is in any argument for representation at all. A benevolent despotism is not a safe kind of government to entrust to average human beings, whether it is a class, or race, or sex, or creed that is ruled. Let those legislators who think their rule so good that women are stupid to want to have a voice in their own affairs, just try one experiment. Let them for a time, say a month, read each Bill or motion that comes before either House with such attention as women are likely to give it; let them read the newspapers in the same way, the lists of crimes and assaults, the police-news, and so on, trying to realise how women feel in regard to a large proportion of these matters; and they will quickly discern that every day the sun rises something is happening that sickens and tortures women who respect their own sex, and who want to lift up the poor. A week will be enough for a sensitive man with a conscience. He will know by that time that every day the sun rises adds a new reason to the fixed

conviction of women that they *must* have the franchise –
first, for the sake of their sex; next, for the sake of all honour
and goodness in the nation.

But it is not only in regard to women's questions that we
need the vote, that we may lay the facts of the case before
our legislators without the sense of intrusion which now
keeps many silent. Nor is it only in regard to those moral
questions which are equally binding on the consciences of
Christian men and women, but which women have taken up
as more continuous objects of effort. But every social
question suffers from the powerlessness of women. I shall
only instance two, which are attracting much attention here
just now, – the need of compulsory powers of education,
and of an improved administration of the Poor Law. Each is
of great importance to the welfare of Ireland, – each needs
special experience and wisdom to deal with it, – and in
regard to each a large proportion of the most competent
advisers are ladies. But they feel it impossible to take any
effectual step, as long as an impassable barrier stands
between them and any sufficient influence on legislation.
Why should that barrier be there? Why should they not enter
by the same gate as other citizens? To this question there is
absolutely no reasonable answer.

We cannot take the certainty of opposition to the inclusion
of women in this Bill as an answer. There will be opposition
to everything said or not said, done or not done. But among
our opponents are some whom good men should be chary of
being seen with. The worst of the publican interests has been
long arrayed against us. All profligate men are against us,
whether of the open or the decorous sort. It is quite true that
some good men oppose us still, in daily diminishing
numbers, some from habit and fear of change, and some
from ignorance of who the people are who ask for the vote,
– the members of Christian Churches, the active workers in
religious and philanthropic and educational movements. On
the other hand, our supporters are the best men. Of course,
in so large an army as ours has grown to be, our recruits are
not all alike, but the evil elements to which I have alluded
find no affinity there. You and I believe that Liberalism is
founded on the New Testament, – that as each soul is sacred
before God, it must be free before man, and that none can
have any rights which infringe on that equal right of others.
Representative government, as a human instrument for
securing these divine rights, is and must be imperfect. But

an imperfection so huge as to shut out from recognized representation the half of a nation brings into the system the principle of a fatal decay, a principle which cankers deeper with every increase of injustice. This is too grave a matter to be shelved for the mere chance of saving a few hours of time in the discussion of the Bill. I cannot but hope that the religious men in the House of Commons will feel this truth so strongly, as to make it clear that they not only desire but expect the recognition of the citizenship of women in this Christian land to be made by this Bill.

Of course, in speaking of religious men, I am thinking of the true religious spirit under whatever manifestation. But in writing to a member of the Irish Presbyterian Church, to which I am attached both by hereditary descent and personal conviction, I cannot but ask you and others who belong to Churches in which women possess the ecclesiastical franchise, whether it has been a source of strength or weakness to them. Has it not added to their stability and continuity of work – to their influence for good upon less firmly-built churches around them – to the completeness of their machinery for usefulness – to the wise and reasonable conduct of their internal affairs? It is more than a century since Henry Grattan, pleading in the old Irish House of Commons for some liberty for Presbyterians, declared that the British Constitution was built upon the same lines as the Presbyterian Church. Every change that has been made in the British Constitution since then has brought it nearer to that model which we believe to be so safe. It needs but this one more change, to enfranchise women who are heads of houses, to make the parallel complete!

I fear that some of our legislators do not realise that if our demand is a quiet and unexcited demand, it is also a persistent one. No class that has once decidedly asked for the franchise has ever accepted a defeat. The claim will be reiterated until it is granted; for it is not based upon caprice, but upon an assured conviction that it is impossible for women to do their duty, and to protect their interests and dignity, without the same weapon which men find essential for the same purposes.

Believe me,
Yours very truly,
Isabella M. S. Tod

Belfast

Elizabeth C.
Wolstenholme Elmy

The parliamentary franchise for women: to the editor of The Times

24 May 1884

THE subjoined letter was sent to the *Times* on 24 May in consequence of an article opposing the extension of the Parliamentary franchise to women, which appeared in that journal on 23 May. As the letter did not appear in the *Times*, and as it deals with some aspects of the question not, perhaps, sufficiently regarded, it is now submitted to those whom it may concern, and in particular to those gentlemen who will, in a few days, be called upon to decide whether this act of justice shall be done at once, while the concession will still contain an element of grace; or be delayed till it become simply a thankless matter of forced and surly deference to the invincible demands of an advancing humanity.

CONGLETON
24th May, 1884

Sir, –

In your leader of yesterday on the admission of women to the Parliamentary franchise you say, 'It is possible, as things stand, for the few women who have a call to public life to follow their inclination or impulse.'

I scarcely know what in this connection you mean by the phrases 'public life' or 'a call thereto,' but if I may understand you to mean that women even now can and sometimes do take a very active part in endeavouring to influence legislation, as they believe, beneficially – it is perfectly true; but, so far as it is conclusive on the point with reference to which you cite it, the question, that is, should women be admitted to direct representation in Parliament, and so to direct influence on legislation, it is conclusive in the affirmative, and not, as you would have it, in the negative.

No women know better than those who have given their lives to the work of so influencing legislation as to secure more of justice to women, how infinitely hard and difficult their task has been, because they were members of 'an unrepresented class.'

To take the illustration you yourself have given – the amended law relating to the property of married women, with regard to which I have, at least, some right to speak – none but those who toiled for fifteen years to bring about that change of sentiment and opinion, which at last found expression in the Married Women's Property Act, 1882, can know how slow, how all but impracticable was all legislative progress, and how, even down to the very last moment, all our hopes seemed at the mercy of the merest chapter of accidents.

> Full little knowest thou that hast not tried,
> What hell it is in suing long to bide;
> To lose good days, that might be better spent;
> To waste long nights in pensive discontent;
> To speed to-day, to be put back to-morrow;
> To feed on hope, to pine with fear and sorrow;
> To fret thy soul with crosses and with cares;
> To eat thy heart through comfortless despairs.

The pathetic words of Spenser but too truly pourtray the experience of all women who have endeavoured to influence legislative action for the benefit of their own sex, since they can only sue, and have no power to demand, remembering the while with an added pang that at every moment some heart is broken or some life undone by reason of the legislative injustice which they are helpless to remedy.

Turning to the present Session, we find that on 26 March last the House of Commons by the remarkable vote of 207 for and only 73 against the second reading of Mr Bryce's Infants Bill emphasised strongly the conviction long shared by all thoughtful women, that the law regulating the relations of every married mother to her own offspring is unjust and unsatisfactory. Yet, in spite of this consensus of opinion, nothing appears more certain than that, unless women can bring to bear upon Parliamentary action a force which as 'an unrepresented class' they do not possess, this most just and needful reform will either be indefinitely postponed or whittled down to a make-believe amendment which shall insult the motherhood of the nation by ignoring their most natural and sacred rights, and still hold them in the position of 'unpaid nurses of *their husbands'* children.'

That the course of modern legislation has *not* been uniformly 'favourable to women' is too certain for denial. To say nothing of the gross and shameful injustice between husband and wife, sanctioned and maintained by the Divorce Act of 1857, it is quite certain that the disgraceful legislation of 1866 and 1867, which placed the reputation of every poor woman in certain districts at the mercy of a spy police, could never have been proposed to, much less sanctioned by, a Parliament in which women were represented; but it seems hopeless to expect that this wrong will be set right until women themselves can directly influence legislation, rather would it seem – by the events of the present Session, and particularly by some of the proposals of the Criminal Law Amendment Bill – that our exclusively male Legislature is perfectly capable, under the guise and pretence of 'protection,' of exposing to the same insecurity and possible outrage every girl and woman in these kingdoms.

Many women, moreover, are apt to resent much recent legislation which, whilst affecting to protect them, does in reality interfere with their freedom, their convenience, and their means of earning an honest livelihood, and to look with distrust and suspicion upon further legislative proposals of a similar kind pressed on by exclusively masculine influence. In truth, in these and in all similar matters, where the interests of men and women conflict, or seem to do so, it is the great grievance of women that the masculine voice alone is listened to, the male interest alone considered by the majority of those who are not legally responsible to women. It is impossible that under such circumstances the predominant influence of sex bias should not cause great and grievous wrong.

And this predominant influence it is now proposed not only to maintain, but to strengthen and consolidate; for, should the Representation of the People Bill pass without including women within its scope, there will be an enormously increased male electorate controlling the destinies of the whole nation, whilst to not one woman, except to the lady on the throne, is permitted political voice, action, or influence. For this reason we claim *now* our political emancipation. It is not merely that we pay rates and taxes and ought to have a voice as to their distribution and expenditure, the far broader human truth remains, *legislation for the unrepresented is tyranny*. We suffer as women, as wives, and as mothers from evil laws, and we ask to have a direct voice in so reforming these laws that they shall protect, not the selfish interest of either sex or of any class, but the larger, deeper, more vital interests of humanity itself, of justice for to-day, of hope and progress for the future.

I thank you heartily for pointing to the wider issues of this question. It is beyond controversy that, if the claim of single and independent women to the franchise is recognised, the exclusion of married women possessed of the same qualifications will be absurd, illogical, unjust, and indefensible.

It is also true that some women are well fitted to give valuable aid in legislation and administration, and that it is not merely a dream, but a possibility of the near future, that such competence may be recognised and turned to account. But before a woman can take a seat in Parliament she must have won the confidence of a constituency; nor does it seem by any means clear that, if a constituency chose under the existing law to return a woman as its representative, she could, unless by special retrospective legislation, be prevented taking her seat in the House.

It is to the justice of men that we appeal; that sense of justice which has led many men to co-operate actively in securing what of recent ameliorative legislation has been effected. There are men, and many men, who loathe the possession of unjust prerogative; and as the co-operation of husbands and wives, brothers and sisters, fathers and daughters, mothers and sons has gained for women what vantage-ground they have already won, so will it ultimately secure this success also, no matter what the immediate issue.

It may well be that Mr Gladstone, who for a man of his rare gifts has marvellously little political far-sightedness, may be guilty now of the capital political blunder of refusing to women the recognition of their rights as 'capable citizens,' but such a blunder on his part can cause, at most, but a temporary delay. For what dignity, worth, or completeness can be claimed for a Representation of the People Bill which excludes from its provisions one half the nation? It will not be accepted, even for a single day, as a settlement of this grave question. Mr Gladstone's political opponents will not be slow to seize the great advantage of showing themselves more liberal than so-called Liberals, and more just than those who profess to base their political creed upon justice; and Mr Gladstone himself may find too late that, by insisting on the maintenance of the political disability of sex, he has fatally dwarfed and mutilated his best bit of statesmanship, and helped on the disintegration of his own political party.

I am, Sir, faithfully yours,
ELIZABETH C. WOLSTENHOLME ELMY

Mrs Humphry Ward *et al.*

An appeal against female suffrage

June 1889

WE, the undersigned, wish to appeal to the common sense and the educated thought of the men and women of England against the proposed extension of the Parliamentary suffrage to women.

1 While desiring the fullest possible development of the powers, energies, and education of women, we believe that their work for the State, and their responsibilities towards it, must always differ essentially from those of men, and that therefore their share in the working of the State machinery should be different from that assigned to men. Certain large departments of the national life are of necessity worked exclusively by men. To men belong the struggle of debate and legislation in Parliament; the hard and exhausting labour implied in the administration of the national resources and powers; the conduct of England's relations towards the external world; the working of the army and navy; all the heavy, laborious, fundamental industries of the State, such as those of mines, metals, and railways; the lead and supervision of English commerce, the management of our vast English finance, the service of that merchant fleet on which our food supply depends. In all these spheres women's direct participation is made impossible either by the disabilities of sex, or by strong formations of custom and habit resting ultimately upon physical difference, against which it is useless to contend. They are affected indeed, in some degree, by all these national activities;

409

therefore they ought in some degree to have an influence on them all. This influence they already have, and will have more and more as the education of women advances. But their direct interest in these matters can never equal that of men, whose whole energy of mind and body is daily and hourly risked in them. Therefore it is not just to give to women direct power of deciding questions of Parliamentary policy, of war, of foreign or colonial affairs, of commerce and finance equal to that possessed by men. We hold that they already possess an influence on political matters fully proportioned to the possible share of women in the political activities of England.

At the same time we are heartily in sympathy with all the recent efforts which have been made to give women a more important part in those affairs of the community where their interests and those of men are equally concerned; where it is possible for them not only to decide but to help in carrying out, and where, therefore, judgment is weighted by a true responsibility, and can be guided by experience and the practical information which comes from it. As voters for or members of School Boards, Boards of Guardians, and other important public bodies, women have now opportunities for public usefulness which must promote the growth of character, and at the same time strengthen among them the social sense and habit. All these changes of recent years, together with the great improvements in women's education which have accompanied them, we cordially welcome. But we believe that the emancipating process has now reached the limits fixed by the physical constitution of women, and by the fundamental difference which must always exist between their main occupations and those of men. The care of the sick and the insane; the treatment of the poor; the education of children: in all these matters, and others besides, they have made good their claim to larger and more extended powers. We rejoice in it. But when it comes to questions of foreign or colonial policy, or of grave constitutional changes, then we maintain that the necessary and normal experience of women – speaking generally and in the mass – does not and can never provide them with such materials for sound judgment as are open to men.

To sum up: we would give them their full share in the State of social effort and social mechanism; we look for their increasing activity in that higher State which rests on thought, conscience, and moral influence; but we protest against their admission to direct power in that State which *does* rest upon force – the State in its administrative, military and financial aspects – where the physical capacity, the accumulated experience and inherited

training of men ought to prevail without the harassing interference of those who, though they may be partners with men in
debate, can in these matters never be partners with them in action.

2 If we turn from the *right* of women to the suffrage – a right
which on the grounds just given we deny – to the effect which the
possession of the suffrage may be expected to have on their
character and position and on family life, we find ourselves no less
in doubt. It is urged that the influence of women in politics would
tell upon the side of morality. We believe that it does so tell
already, and will do so with greater force as women by improved
education fit themselves to exert it more widely and efficiently.
But it may be asked, On what does this moral influence depend?
We believe that it depends largely on qualities which the natural
position and functions of women as they are at present tend to
develop, and which might be seriously impaired by their
admission to the turmoil of active political life. These qualities
are, above all, sympathy and disinterestedness. Any disposition of
things which threatens to lessen the national reserve of such forces
as these we hold to be a misfortune. It is notoriously difficult to
maintain them in the presence of party necessities and in the heat
of party struggle. Were women admitted to this struggle, their
natural eagerness and quickness of temper would probably make
them hotter partisans than men. As their political relations stand
at present, they tend to check in them the disposition to
partisanship, and to strengthen in them the qualities of sympathy
and disinterestedness. We believe that their admission to the
suffrage would precisely reverse this condition of things, and that
the whole nation would suffer in consequence. For whatever may
be the duty and privilege of the parliamentary vote for men, we
hold that citizenship is not dependent upon or identical with the
possession of the suffrage. Citizenship lies in the participation of
each individual in effort for the good of the community. And we
believe that women will be more valuable citizens, will contribute
more precious elements to the national life without the vote than
with it. The quickness to feel, the willingness to lay aside
prudential considerations in a right cause, which are amongst the
peculiar excellencies of women, are in their right place when they
are used to influence the more highly trained and developed
judgment of men. But if this quickness of feeling could be
immediately and directly translated into public action, in matters
of vast and complicated political import, the risks of politics
would be enormously increased, and what is now a national
blessing might easily become a national calamity. On the one
hand, then, we believe that to admit women to the ordinary

machinery of political life would inflame the partisanship and increase the evils, already so conspicuous, of that life, would tend to blunt the special moral qualities of women, and so to lessen the national reserves of moral force; and, on the other hand, we dread the political and practical effects which, in our belief, would follow on such a transformation as is proposed, of an influence which is now beneficent largely because it is indirect and gradual.

3 Proposals for the extension of the suffrage to women are beset with grave practical difficulties. If votes be given to unmarried women on the same terms as they are given to men, large numbers of women leading immoral lives will be enfranchised on the one hand, while married women, who, as a rule, have passed through more of the practical experiences of life than the unmarried, will be excluded. To remedy part of this difficulty it is proposed by a large section of those who advocate the extension of the suffrage to women, to admit married women with the requisite property qualification. This proposal – an obviously just one if the suffrage is to be extended to women at all – introduces changes in family life, and in the English conception of the household, of enormous importance, which have never been adequately considered. We are practically invited to embark upon them because a few women of property possessing already all the influence which belongs to property, and a full share of that public protection and safety which is the fruit of taxation, feel themselves aggrieved by the denial of the parliamentary vote. The grievance put forward seems to us wholly disproportionate to the claim based upon it.

4 A survey of the manner in which this proposal has won its way into practical politics leads us to think that it is by no means ripe for legislative solution. A social change of momentous gravity has been proposed; the mass of those immediately concerned in it are notoriously indifferent; there has been no serious and general demand for it, as is always the case if a grievance is real and reform necessary; the amount of information collected is quite inadequate to the importance of the issue; and the public has gone through no sufficient discipline of discussion on the subject. Meanwhile pledges to support female suffrage have been hastily given in the hopes of strengthening existing political parties by the female vote. No doubt there are many conscientious supporters of female suffrage amongst members of Parliament; but it is hard to deny that the present prominence of the question is due to party considerations of a temporary nature. It is, we submit, altogether unworthy of the intrinsic gravity of the question that it should be determined by reference to the

passing needs of party organisation. Meanwhile we remember that great electoral changes have been carried out during recent years. Masses of new electors have been added to the constituency. These new elements have still to be assimilated; these new electors have still to be trained to take their part in the national work; and while such changes are still fresh, and their issues uncertain, we protest against any further alteration in our main political machinery, especially when it is an alteration which involves a new principle of extraordinary range and significance, closely connected with the complicated problems of sex and family life.

5 It is often urged that certain injustices of the law towards women would be easily and quickly remedied were the political power of the vote conceded to them; and that there are many wants, especially among working women, which are now neglected, but which the suffrage would enable them to press on public attention. We reply that during the past half century all the principal injustices of the law towards women have been amended by means of the existing constitutional machinery; and with regard to those that remain, we see no signs of any unwillingness on the part of Parliament to deal with them. On the contrary, we remark a growing sensitiveness to the claims of women, and the rise of a new spirit of justice and sympathy among men, answering to those advances made by women in education, and the best kind of social influence, which we have already noticed and welcomed. With regard to the business or trade interests of women, – here, again, we think it safer and wiser to trust to organisation and self-help on their own part, and to the growth of a better public opinion among the men workers, than to the exercise of a political right which may easily bring women into direct and hasty conflict with men.

In conclusion: nothing can be further from our minds than to seek to depreciate the position or the importance of women. It is because we are keenly alive to the enormous value of their special contribution to the community, that we oppose what seems to us likely to endanger that contribution. We are convinced that the pursuit of a mere outward equality with men is for women not only vain but demoralising. It leads to a total misconception of woman's true dignity and special mission. It tends to personal struggle and rivalry, where the only effort of both the great divisions of the human family should be to contribute the characteristic labour and the best gifts of each to the common stock.

Dowager Lady STANLEY OF ALDERLEY, Dover Street
Lady FREDERICK CAVENDISH, Carlton House Terrace
Lady WIMBORNE, Arlington Street
Lady RANDOLPH CHURCHILL, Connaught Place
Lady FANNY MARJORIBANKS, Piccadilly
The DUCHESS OF ST ALBANS, Bestwood, Arnold, Notts.
Lady ALWYNE COMPTON, The Palace, Ely
Lady LOUISA EGERTON, Piccadilly
Mrs GOSCHEN, Portland Place
VISCOUNTESS HALIFAX, Hickleton, Doncaster
Lady REVELSTOKE, Charles Street, Berkeley Square
Hon Mrs MEYNELL INGRAM, Temple Newsam
Mrs KNOX-LITTLE, The College, Worcester
Lady WADE, Cambridge
Mrs CREIGHTON, Cambridge, and The College, Worcester
Mrs WESTCOTT, Cambridge, and Abbey Gardens, Westminster
Mrs CHURCH, The Deanery, St Paul's
Mrs BOYLE, The Deanery, Salisbury
Mrs WOODS, Trinity College, Oxford
The COUNTESS OF WHARNCLIFFE, Wharncliffe House, Curzon
Street, W
Mrs MUNDELLA, Elvaston Place, SW
Mrs OSBORNE MORGAN, Green Street, Grosvenor Square
The COUNTESS OF MORLEY, Prince's Gardens, SW
Mrs HENRY BROADHURST, Brixton
Lady CONSTANCE SHAW LEFEVRE, Bryanston Square, W
Mrs T. H. GREEN, Oxford
Mrs LESLIE STEPHEN, Hyde Park Gate, SW
Mrs HUMPHRY WARD, Russell Square, WC
Miss BEATRICE POTTER, The Argoed, Monmouth
Mrs HOLFORD, Dorchester House, Park Lane
Mrs J. R. GREEN, Kensington Square, W
Hon Mrs JOHN TALBOT, Great George Street, Westminster
Mrs LOFTIE, Sheffield Terrace, Campden Hill
VISCOUNTESS BURY, Prince's Gate, W
Mrs SUTHERLAND ORR, Kensington Park Gardens
Lady LAYARD
Mrs FREDERIC HARRISON, Westbourne Terrace, W
Mrs HUXLEY, Marlborough Place, W
Mrs HENRY HOBHOUSE, Hadspen House, Somerset
Miss LUCY GARNETT, Upper Bedford Place
Hon EMILY LAWLESS, Eaton Terrace, SW
Hon Mrs CHAPMAN, Paul's Cray Hill, Kent
Mrs POYNTER, Albert Gate, SW

Mrs BALDWIN, Wilden House, Stourport
Miss CURETON, Matron, Aldenbrooke's Hospital, Cambridge
Miss SOULSBY, High School, Oxford
Miss OTTLEY, High School, Worcester
Miss TOPPING, Superintendent, St John's House, Worcester
Mrs BELL, The College, Marlborough
Mrs LYNN LINTON, Queen Anne's Mansions
Mrs BEESLY, Warrington Crescent, W
Mrs COURTENAY ILBERT, Gloucester Place, W
Hon Mrs ARTHUR ELLIOT, Cavendish Square
Mrs WYNNE FINCH, Charles Street, Berkeley Square
Mrs SIMPSON, Cornwall Gardens, SW
Mrs LATHBURY, Barkston Mansions
Mrs SEELEY, Cambridge
Mrs HORT, Cambridge
Mrs BRIDGES, Wimbledon
Mrs ROUTH, Newnham Cottage, Cambridge
Mrs PRIESTLEY, Hertford Street, Mayfair
Mrs KEGAN PAUL, Ashburn Place, SW
Mrs W. BAGEHOT, Hurd's Hill, Somerset
Mrs RATHBONE GREG, Melbury Road, W
Mrs LILLY, Michael's Grove, SW
Lady BUNBURY, Mildenhall
Mrs RUSSELL BARRINGTON, Melbury Road
Miss EDITH ANDERSON, Brighton
Mrs H. H. ASQUITH, Hampstead
Hon Mrs RALPH DUTTON, Halkin Street, W
Mrs D. CARMICHAEL, Sussex Gardens, W
Mrs SPENCER WALPOLE, Onslow Gardens, SW
Mrs MAXWELL LYTE, Portman Square, W
Mrs HIGFORD BURR, Eaton Place
Mrs ALMA-TADEMA, Grove End Road, W
Miss FRANCES POYNTER, Brompton Crescent
Mrs SHERLOCK WILLIS, Foulis Terrace, SW
Mrs R. WARD, Onslow Square
Mrs JOHN BALL, Southwell Gardens, SW
Mrs BISHOP, Prince of Wales Terrace, SW
Mrs MEREDITH TOWNSEND, Harley Street
Mrs ANDREW CROSS, Delamere Terrace, W
Lady WYNFORD, Grosvenor Square, W
Mrs BLUMENTHAL, Hyde Park Gate
Hon FREDERICA SPRING-RICE, Sumner Place, SW
Hon CATHERINE SPRING-RICE, Sumner Place, SW
Lady MONTEAGLE, Onslow Gardens, SW

Miss F. H. CHENEVIX TRENCH, Elm Park Gardens, SW
Hon Mrs J. R. ARTHUR, Queen's Gate Place
Mrs WM RAIKES, The Beeches, Farnborough
Mrs CECIL RUSSELL, Lowndes Square, SW
Mrs EDWARD O'BRIEN, Cahirmoyle, Limerick
Mrs T. WELLS, Manchester Square
Mrs W. E. FORSTER, Wharfeside, Burley
Mrs MATTHEW ARNOLD, Cobham
Mrs ARNOLD TOYNBEE, Oxford
Mrs MAX MÜLLER, Oxford
Mrs AGNEW, Great Stanhope Street
Mrs BUCKLE, Queen Square, WC
Mrs JAMES KNOWLES, St James's Park
Lady VICTORIA BUXTON, Grosvenor Crescent
Mrs CHARLES BUXTON, Fox Warren, Surrey
Hon Mrs EDWARD TALBOT, The Vicarage, Leeds
Mrs J. R. THURSFIELD, Montague Place, WC

[In furtherance of the foregoing Appeal – which has hitherto been only shown privately to a few persons – the accompanying proposed protest is laid before the readers of the *Nineteenth Century*, with the request that such ladies among them as agree with it will be kind enough to sign the opposite page and return it, *when detached*, to the EDITOR of this Review.

The difficulty of obtaining a public expression, even of disapproval, about such a question from those who entirely object to mixing themselves up in the coarsening struggles of party political life, may easily become a public danger. Their silence will be misinterpreted into indifference or consent to designs they most dislike, and may thus help to bring them about.

It is submitted that for once, and in order to save the quiet of Home life from total disappearance, they should do violence to their natural reticence, and signify publicly and unmistakably their condemnation of the scheme now threatened.

The deliberate opinion of the women readers of the *Nineteenth Century* might certainly be taken as a fair sample of the judgment of the educated women of the country, and would probably receive the sympathy and support of the overwhelming majority of their fellow countrywomen.

EDITOR, Nineteenth Century]

FEMALE SUFFRAGE:
A WOMEN'S PROTEST

The undersigned protest strongly against the proposed Extension of the Parliamentary Franchise to Women, which they believe would be a measure distasteful to the great majority of the women of the country – unnecessary – and mischievous both to themselves and to the State.

Millicent Garrett Fawcett

Home and politics

IT is now more than twenty years ago since I delivered the first lecture I had ever given in public, on a Brighton platform, in support of women's suffrage. Twenty years is a long time in the life of an individual; it is a very short time in the life of a great movement, and I think, as we look back over these twenty years, those who have devoted themselves to the cause of the enfranchisement of women have good reason to congratulate themselves on the substantial progress which has been made.

We have a direct increase of our strength in Parliament, and we have further cause for congratulation on side issues bearing upon the general position of women; their admission to the Municipal and School Board Suffrages; their activity in many invaluable efforts of social and moral regeneration; their work as Poor Law guardians; and their success in the higher fields of education. There is also the increased activity of women in political life. Each party now seems to vie with the other in its eagerness in calling upon the women within its ranks to come forward and work for what they believe to be the right side in politics. But, perhaps, more encouraging than any of these direct evidences of the progress the women's movement is making, is the general feeling that is beginning to prevail that women's suffrage is a thing that is bound to come. The tendency of public opinion is felt to be set in that direction, and even those who oppose us seem to know that they are fighting a lost battle. Mr Lowell used to say, 'There is a sort of glacial drift in English public opinion; you cannot see it move, but when you look again you see that it has moved.' I think there is no doubt that the glacial drift of English public opinion has moved and is moving in the direction of the active participation of women in politics. We have evidence of this in all parties.

With regard to the differences between men and women, those who advocate the enfranchisement of women have no wish to disregard them or make little of them. On the contrary, we base our claim to representation to a large extent on them. If men and women were exactly alike, the representation of men would represent us; but not being alike, that wherein we differ is unrepresented under the present system.

The motherhood of women, either actual or potential, is one of those great facts of everyday life which we must never lose sight of. To women as mothers, is given the charge of the home and the care of children. Women are, therefore, by nature as well as by occupation and training, more accustomed than men to concentrate their minds on the home and domestic side of things. But this difference between men and women, instead of being a reason against their enfranchisement, seems to me the strongest possible reason in favour of it; we want the home and the domestic side of things to count for more in politics and in the administration of public affairs than they do at present. We want to know how various kinds of legislative enactments bear on the home and on domestic life. And we want to force our legislators to consider the domestic as well as the political results of any legislation which many of them are advocating. We want to say to those of our fellow-countrywomen who, we hope, are about to be enfranchised, 'do not give up one jot or tittle of your womanliness, your love for children, your care for the sick, your gentleness, your self-control, your obedience to conscience and duty, for all these things are terribly wanted in politics. We want women, with their knowledge of child life, especially to devote themselves to the law as it affects children, to children's training in our pauper schools, to the question of boarding out, to the employment of children of tender years, and the bearing of this employment on their after life: to the social life of children and young persons of both sexes in the lower stratum of our towns and villages, to the example set by the higher classes to the lower, to the housing of the poor, to the provision of open spaces and recreation grounds, to the temperance question, to laws relating to health and morals, and the bearing of all these things and many others upon the home, and upon the virtue and the purity of the domestic life of our nation.'

Depend upon it, the most important institution in the country is the home. Anything which threatens the purity and stability of the home threatens the very life-blood of the country; if the homes of the nation are pure, if the standard of duty, of self-restraint and of justice is maintained in them, such a nation has nothing to fear; but if the contrary of all these things can be said, the nation is rotten at the core, and its down fall is only a question of time. Up to the present, my belief is that the home side and the political side of things have been kept too far apart, as if they had nothing to do with one another. We have before us the picture of the whole of Europe armed to the teeth, and the great neighbouring nations ready to spring like wild beasts at each other's throats, all for the sake of fancied political advantage, while the true domestic interests of the nations concerned would be almost as much injured by victory as by defeat. I confess that I think women are all too apt to forget their womanliness, even in such cases as this, and allow their aspirations to be guided by those of the masculine part of the society in which they find themselves. But by strengthening the independence of women, I think we shall strengthen their true native womanliness;* they will not so often be led away by the gunpowder and glory will-o'-the-wisp, which is really alien to the womanly nature, but will much more certainly than now cast their influence on whatever side seems to them to make for peace, purity, and love.

A large amount of opposition to Women's Suffrage is based on the fact that to women has been given, by nature, the charge of the domestic and home side of things, and there is also the fear that contact with political life would blunt the gentler qualities of women. Let us look at these two objections separately. To women, it is said quite truly, has been given the charge of the home and the domestic side of things. That is to say, most women's lives are wholly or almost wholly devoted to work for their husband and children within their home. I will apply myself to meet the argument against Women's Suffrage based on the fact that the daily business of most women's lives lies in the routine of domestic affairs. For the proper discharge of these duties many

---

*Mr R. L. Stevenson in one of his stories makes his hero refer to this, when a woman to flatter him repeats, parrot-like, what she conceives to be the man's formula on love and honour. 'My honour?' he repeated, 'For a woman you surprise me. . . . You speak, Madame von Rosen, like too many women, with a man's tongue,' – *Prince Otto*, p. 205.

very high and noble qualities are needed, and no insignificant amount of practical knowledge. Women who are immersed in domestic affairs should be good economists, knowing how to save and how to spend judiciously; they should know a good deal about the health and training of children, about education, about what influences character and conduct; no quality is more important in the management of servants and children than a strong sense of justice. In proportion as women are good and efficient in what concerns their domestic duties, they will, if they become voters, bring these excellent qualities to bear upon public affairs. Most men are as much taken up by some trade, business, or profession in their everyday life as women are by their domestic duties; but we do not say that this man is so industrious and experienced in his business that it is a great pity that he should be admitted to the franchise; we rather feel that all that makes him a useful member of society in his private life will also make him a good citizen in his public duties. I am well aware that there are some women who are not good for much in the home; in one class they think more of balls and fine clothes, than of home duties; cases have been known, I grieve to say, in all classes, where they have broken up their homes through drunkenness and idleness; though for one home broken up and destroyed by a drunken woman there are probably three or four broken up and destroyed by a drunken man. These women who are not good for much domestically will most likely not be good for much politically; but exactly the same thing can be said of the existing male voters. Taking women in the mass, I believe it can be claimed for them that they are faithful and conscientious in the fulfilment of the duties already confided to them, and if this be so, it is the best assurance we can have that they will be faithful and conscientious in the new ones that may be entrusted to them.

I think we may surely claim for women in general a high standard of goodness and virtue. Most of us are probably fortunate enough to know many women who live up to the ideal described by the late Poet Laureate.

> Because right is right
> To follow right, were wisdom in the scorn
> Of consequence.

In so far as conduct is a test of virtue, we have a rough test in the number of men and women respectively who are committed for trial, for serious offences against the law, and we find that the women thus committed are less than a fifth the number of the men, although women are more numerous than men by about four per cent. I do not stop now to enquire what the causes of this may be, but I think the bare fact is a strong evidence that the admission of women to the suffrage would raise rather than lower the average quality, as regards conduct, of the existing constituencies.

Duty is what upholds all the structure of national greatness; why then exclude from the responsibilities of citizenship a large number of women among whom the standard of duty as measured by their conduct is conspicuously high and pure?

Let us now consider the fear that has been expressed that contact with political life will blunt the gentler qualities of women. We know that a very similar fear has been expressed with regard to the extension of higher education to women. It was thought that if a woman knew Greek she would not love her children, and that if she learned mathematics she would forsake her infant for a quadratic equation. Experience has set these fears at rest. It was imagined that if women were admitted to the studies pursued by young men at Oxford and Cambridge, they would imitate the swagger and slang of the idlest type of undergraduates. Experience has proved that these fears were baseless; may we not also hope that the fears expressed by some of the effects of political life on womanly graces may prove to be equally unfounded? It seems to me very inconsistent and illogical to say with one breath Nature has made women so and so, and so and so, mentioning all kinds of graceful and delightful qualities, and then to add that all these qualities will disappear if a certain alteration takes place in the political constitution of the country. Nature is not so weak and ephemeral as this. All the Acts of Parliament that ever have been or even can be passed cannot shake the rock upon which the institutions of Nature are founded. To think that we can upset the solemn edicts of Nature by the little laws of human invention is the most grotesque infidelity to Nature that has ever been dreamed of.

If you descend from these general considerations to look at the experience we have thus far had of the result of political activity upon the gentler qualities of women, I think we cannot do better than cite the example which has now for more than fifty years been given us by Queen Victoria. She has been from her early girlhood immersed in a constant succession of political duties and responsibilities, and yet no woman, as wife, mother, or friend, has ever shown herself more entirely womanly in her sympathy, faithfulness, and tenderness. I like very much the story told of the Queen in the early years of her reign, when one of her ministers apologised for the trouble he was giving her in regard to public business. 'Never mention that word to me again,' she replied, 'only tell me how the thing is to be done, and done rightly, and I will do it if I can.' That is womanly in the best sense, and the very quality we want more of, not in politics only, but everywhere and in every department of life.

When we speak of womanliness and the gentler qualities of the feminine nature, we must be careful not to mistake true for false, and false for true. Is there anything truly feminine in fainting fits, or in screaming at a mouse or at a black beetle? Fifty years ago a female of truly delicate susceptibilities was supposed to faint on the slightest provocation; but there was, I venture to think, nothing truly and essentially womanly in this accomplishment: it was merely a fashion which has now happily passed away. Women don't faint now unless their heart or their digestion is out of order. Merely foolish foibles ought not to be dignified by the name of womanliness; their only advantage lies in their providing a cheap and easy means to persons of the other sex of establishing their own superiority. Those men who are not very sure, in the bottom of their hearts, of their own superiority, naturally like to be assured of it by finding a plentiful supply of women who go into hysterics if a mouse is in the room, know nothing of business except that consols are things which go up and down in the city, or of history except that Alexander the Great was not the son-in-law of Louis XIV. The world would wag on if this kind of womanliness disappeared altogether; what we cannot afford to lose is the true womanliness, mercy, pity, peace, purity and love; and these I think we are justified in believing will grow and strengthen with all that strengthens the individuality and spontaneity of womanhood.

In conclusion, I will only add that I advocate the extension of the franchise to women because I wish to strengthen true womanliness in woman, and because I want to see the womanly and domestic side of things weigh more and count for more in all public concerns. It is told in Nehemiah that when the walls of Jerusalem were rebuilt after the captivity, women as well as men shared in the work. Our country now wants the hearts and brains of its daughters as well as the hearts and brains of its sons, for the solution of many perplexing and difficult problems. Let no one imagine for a moment that we want women to cease to be womanly; we want rather to raise the ideal type of womanhood and to multiply the number of those women of whom it may be said: –

Happy he
With such a mother; faith in womankind
Beats with his blood, and trust in all things high
Comes easy to him, and though he trip and fall
He shall not blind his soul with clay.

Samuel Smith, MP

Women's suffrage

24 April 1891

THE question of the extension of the parliamentary franchise to women has not been debated in the present Parliament, but its advocates have at last been successful in getting the first place for their Bill on Wednesday, 13 May, and the question will then be discussed and a division taken, which will have momentous consequences. The question has slumbered for some time, partly owing to dissensions among the female suffrage party, who were divided on the point of giving married women the vote, but now it seems to be agreed that the question shall be argued on the ground of absolute electoral equality as between men and women. The Bills and resolutions on the subject all claim that the word man 'shall include woman' so far as political rights are concerned. This clears the ground, and enables us to see more plainly the final issues of this question.

I ask permission to offer some remarks for the guidance of public opinion, before the fateful decision is taken – a decision that will affect for weal or woe unborn generations. I premise by observing that the movement for women's suffrage springs out of a sincere desire to raise the status of the sex, and to redress woman's wrongs, real or supposed. It is advocated by many men of warm sympathies and earnest philanthropy; and if it be a mistake, as I consider it to be, it proceeds from excess of tenderness for the weaker sex. Let me here make the confession

that in the earlier stages of the movement I somewhat sympathised
with it, mainly on two grounds – first, that women were subject
to some injustices which men seemed unwilling to remedy; and
secondly, it seemed that the inclusion of women householders was
all that was aimed at; in other words, that an addition of some
800,000 women would be made to an electoral roll of say six
million men, all those women being single or widows, all
ratepayers and discharging the duties of heads of households, and
therefore presumably, fairly well qualified to take a part in public
life. They have the vote already for local affairs, such as town and
county councils, School Boards, &c. and it seemed to me that
perhaps some good would arise from the extension to them of the
parliamentary franchise. My opinion has changed since then, for
the two following reasons: – First, the injustices which women
suffered have been remedied one after another, the CD Acts have
been abolished, the Married Women's Property Act and the
Guardianship of Children Act have given to wives and mothers
reasonable control over their property and children. Parliament of
late years has shown itself most willing to remove any wrongs
under which women labour, and to legislate for their welfare as
far as it is practicable to do so.

Public opinion fully supports Parliament; and in the matter of
higher education, university training, medical education, literary
work, &c. we see that the door is steadily being opened wider and
wider. It is undeniable that women of ability can and do use their
talents just as much as men. They address public meetings,
conduct journals, and advocate their views as freely as in any
country of the world. It may be doubted whether in any country
or any age women have occupied as influential a position as they
now do in Great Britain. Therefore the claim of women to the
franchise, based upon unequal laws, is no longer tenable.

But the second consideration weighs with me more, namely,
the question of limiting the franchise to women householders.
Twenty years ago no one dreamed of going further than this, but
the whole situation has altered since then. The British Constitution
has been broadened again and again by the inclusion of large
classes of electors, and it is clear to those who can read the signs of
the times, that this country is going the way of all other countries,
namely, to the goal of manhood suffrage. I know that many are
opposed to this. I agree with them that household suffrage is a
sounder basis for government than manhood suffrage; and I do
not wish to see so extreme an extension; but one cannot shut one's
eyes to the signs of the times; it is as certain to come as that the
night follows the day. We cannot keep this island on a different

basis to the surrounding nations, our own colonies and the United States. The first political party which thinks it can make capital out of it will go for it; and with manhood suffrage will come womanhood suffrage, if we accept the principle of the Bill now before Parliament, namely, identical qualifications for men and women.

Even before manhood suffrage is reached, a great stride will be made in that direction by the next Registration Bill, which the Liberal party is bound to pass so soon as it comes into power. It will greatly shorten the term of residence, and make the lodger franchise effective by the appointment of paid public officers, whose duty it will be to get all qualified persons put on the register. A multitude of young men who are lodgers will be enfranchised by this Bill in the near future, and, if we adopt women's suffrage, a multitude of young women will also be enfranchised. Enormous numbers of shop girls, factory girls, sempstresses, barmaids, &c. are living in lodgings, especially in the Metropolis; in some parts of London they will preponderate over all other classes, and would completely swamp the women householders. I cannot forbear adding what every thoughtful person knows, that along with this class would come in an appalling number of fallen women, whose numbers have been estimated in London as high as sixty thousand. Need I point out what canvassing these women means?

It is obvious that no-one who reflects a moment can fail to see that any restriction of the vote to women householders is practically impossible. An unknown and enormous number of women, far less qualified, would be admitted along with them; and before very long there must come manhood suffrage, and with it, womanhood suffrage. Some eleven millions of women would be enfranchised, as against the ten millions of men who would also possess the vote. That is the question which we are invited to decide, and there is no use shirking it. As Mr John Morley said the other night, quoting Bishop Butler's aphorism, 'Things are what they are, and consequences will be what they will be' – in other words, mere hopes and wishes avail nothing against the inexorable forces of politics. I have spoken to many members of Parliament recently on this subject; several of them pledged themselves to women's suffrage long years ago, when no-one conceived of its extension beyond single women house-holders. They admit, most of them, that womanhood suffrage would be ruinous, but they still cling to the hope that somehow it could be averted. They are hampered by the pledges given before they foresaw the consequences of the principle; they would gladly escape the liabilities of their unwise promises, but hardly know how to do so. If these lines meet their eye, let me say that no-one is bound by an iron chain of consistency to vote for what he now sees to endanger the State, on account of old promises given when the question was in its infancy. We are bound to vote according to the best light at our disposal at the moment of action. I believe that there is the merest handful of members who believe *ex animo* that womanhood suffrage would answer. If the matter were decided by the mature consideration of Parliament, say by secret ballot, we should soon dismiss this question from the region of practical politics. Some still cling to the idea that married women could be permanently excluded. I would ask them to consider what election cries would be heard when an appeal was made to a constituent body of some ten millions of men, and, say, four or five millions of single women voters. It would be argued with overwhelming effect by female orators, reinforced by politicians, who meant to climb into power by their aid, that we made marriage a disqualification; that we emancipated the harlot but disfranchised the wife. Every candidate would be threatened with the loss of the female vote unless he removed this insult to marriage, and nearly every candidate would agree to it rather than lose his seat.

In the same way the cry would soon be raised that women must sit in Parliament and hold office on equal terms with men, and it would be impossible to resist it. Every fragment of political opinion in the country is now worked up by means of leagues and paid secretaries. Already candidates find it most difficult to resist the dictation of small coteries of faddists who threaten to cast their vote entirely on some petty issue dear to themselves. How could they resist the enormous combinations formed among women, most of them utterly ignorant of politics and practical administration, and who would be worked upon by demagogues and agitators to demand all kinds of ridiculous legislation. We should gradually find that our trained statesmen would disappear from politics, and their place would be taken by impracticable dreamers; and we should see social reforms tried more utopian than the world has ever known. 'Consequences will be what they will be.' You cannot lodge the final arbitrament with the women of a country without having in the long run feminine legislation and government.

Let us consider what are the qualifications of our future rulers. Let us say that there are eleven millions of adult women in the United Kingdom by the present census. What are their qualifications? How many have ever read a political speech, or know anything of the critical and difficult problems of government? Let any one investigate the ordinary reading and intellectual pabulum of maid-servants, shop and factory girls, working men's wives, &c. These will constitute nine-tenths of the ultimate female electors. I make bold to say that he will find not one in twenty ever reads a political speech or article, or has the slightest knowledge or concern for the staple questions that occupy Parliament. Nine women out of ten care less for principles than for persons; they reverence their clergyman, their priest, their political chief; they ascribe to him all kinds of imaginary virtues, and see no defects. Many Conservative women regard Lord Salisbury as the type of manly perfection, and Mr Gladstone as a modern anti-Christ. Many Liberal women just reverse the position. Women as a class prefer personal rule. Had women possessed the franchise in the time of the Stuarts, they might still have been on the throne; and the race of St Louis would have been on the throne of France; the Pope would still have held his temporal power, and Italy would be a geographical expression. I believe it is for this reason that the Conservative party rather favour woman's suffrage; they expect to gain support as against the levelling doctrines of Radicalism. But I would point out to them that they would put the State to a fearful risk for some small temporary party gain. Who could guess how the eleven millions of women would vote were womanhood suffrage to come? Among our dense population the man who would carry the day with the poorer women would be the man or woman (for undoubtedly women would then sit in Parliament) who would promise the wildest Socialistic legislation – such, for instance, as a fixed compulsory eight hours day for all kinds of work, and a fixed wage guaranteed by the State: one who would promise to build comfortable homes for all the poor, and to supplement their wages by grants from the State. How could the ignorant classes of women referred to comprehend the delicate and subtle machinery of our trade and commerce, the keen competition of foreign nations, and the commercial ruin that would ensue from insane legislation of this kind? Experience is the only teacher of democracies. It is hard enough to train the masses of men to comprehend the lessons of history, and to resist the temptation to seek present ease by mortgaging the future. How much harder would it be to educate the whole womanhood of a nation to understand such a difficult science? I say it would be wholly impossible. The mass of women do not have, and never will have, the opportunities that men, even the roughest, have to study politics. Men usually work together, frequent clubs or public houses, and discuss the events of the day. Women cannot undertake this without destroying their domestic life. A good wife and mother cannot leave her home to attend clubs and public meetings, and if she does she will soon cease to be a good wife and mother.

This question is often argued on the ground of the rare and exceptional political woman. We admit there are highly gifted ladies who can address large audiences as well as any man; but in conferring the franchise we have to consider the average woman as contrasted with the average man. The average man in a free country naturally takes to politics; but the average woman does not. Some argue that because there are many ignorant male electors we should not be afraid to emancipate ignorant female electors. They say that the ship of State can be navigated fairly well with a considerable deck cargo of male ignorance on board; why not with female ignorance as well? A ship of five thousand tons may carry a deck cargo of five hundred tons in addition, and though very perilous, it may ride through the storm; but put on a deck cargo of five thousand tons and it will certainly founder. We have six millions of male electors, of whom say five millions are fairly intelligent, and perhaps one million ignorant; but under manhood and womanhood suffrage our electoral body would consist of about twenty-one millions, nearly eleven millions being women, of whom ten millions at least are absolutely ignorant of politics, and perhaps two or three millions of the men. No ship of State could avoid being capsized with such a cargo. It is said that the franchise itself educates men, and therefore it would educate women. That is a question of degree; most men rapidly and easily take to politics, most women will never do so, because the Creator has made them different.

Let me glance for a moment at what may be termed the religious argument. It is allowed by all that Christianity has wonderfully raised the condition of women. Contrast the women of England and America with the women of Mahomedan, Hindoo, or Buddhist countries; the superiority of our civilisation is indisputable. Yet it is undoubted that the framework of human society as laid down in the Bible gives to men the place of authority and power. Woman was created to be 'a helpmeet' for man; the wife was appointed to be subject to her husband. 'The husband is head of the wife, as Christ is head of the Church.' Such passages may be quoted by scores. They rebut the idea that Christianity affirms absolute equality between the sexes. It does nothing of the kind, and I allege that much of the present movement to attain absolute equality springs from the denial of the authority of Revelation. Of course there are many exceptions to this statement. Some of the leaders in this movement are among the best of women, but I think, all the same, that they are mistaken in their interpretation of the Scriptures.

This too lengthy letter must be brought to a close by glancing at the social effects of the change. Already we can form some opinion from the effects of the Primrose League, and the countervailing Liberal women's leagues. Does anyone believe in his heart of hearts that this interference of women in politics has raised and purified their nature? Are the women who go round canvassing at election times more scrupulous and ladylike than those who abstain? Is it not a fact well known to all that the dirtiest election work is often deputed to women; that they are allowed to deceive and intimidate voters in ways that men could not do without punishment? If there is anything certain, it is that 'political women,' as they are called, are usually bitter partisans, and their intrusion into political life has added to its acrimony, not lessened it. Women feel far more keenly than men: they take matters in a more personal way, and they provoke enmities where men would laugh and shake hands next day. The reason is that woman has a finer and more highly-strung constitution than man; she was never meant for this rough and dirty work, and her very virtues turn to vices when she is pushed into man's place.

But all the evils we now experience are a trifle to what we must endure were all women to have votes. None need take part in politics now, unless they are inclined; but then every one will be pressed to do so whether they will or not. Incessant canvassing will force every woman to declare herself on one side or another. The wife will often be brought up to the poll by her friends, while the husband goes the contrary way; the peace and quietness of home will be exchanged for a turbulent, excited life, out of which will spring innumerable scandals. Let it be remembered that the more democratic a country grows the more numerous elections become. In the United States they are constantly occurring, and it will be the same here in the course of time, and the women voters will be pushed into this stormy sea *per fas aut nefas*, and kept in a constant whirl of excitement. Ask any medical man what will be the effect on the children of the future of this nervous excitement on the part of the mothers. Already it is well known that a sad physical deterioration of the children is the penalty of a mother exhausting her nervous powers in public life. No physiological fact is more certain than that febrile excitement in a mother is ruinous to the unborn babe, and nearly all great men are children of mothers who have led wholesome, quiet lives. Nothing is more certain than that we shall have an enfeebled race just as we draw the mothers aside from the sacred duties which God and nature have assigned them.

I would say finally that the United Kingdom is the last country in the world to institute so hazardous an experiment. It has never been tried in any age or clime up to this time. Surely if it had been practicable it would have been tried in little republics like Switzerland, or young democracies like the United States or the British colonies. The problems of these countries are few and simple compared with what we have to solve here. Their women are far better educated than they are here. Yet the idea is scouted in those countries, and their women do not desire it. It is true that there is one small exception in the United States, which proves the rule. The small state of Wyoming, just admitted into the Union, has womanhood suffrage: it was adopted by accident, and is looked upon as a practical joke by the rest of the country. But, as is well put in Mr Bryce's masterpiece on the American Commonwealth, public opinion is entirely opposed to it, and the great bulk of educated and cultivated women are dead against it. Such is also, I believe, the case in this country, if it could be fairly tested: the advocates of women's suffrage are but a small minority of women, and they persist in pressing on their sisters a boon they do not covet.

Never had any country in ancient or modern times such complex problems to solve as our own now has. More than half of our food is drawn from abroad, and most of the raw materials which supply our factories, a vast and highly refined mechanism of capital and credit, keeps all this machinery in motion; any fatal blow inflicted on it would cause famine and social chaos at home. Then we are the centre of a prodigious empire embracing a fifth of the human race, and involving the tremendous problem of the government of India with its two hundred and eighty millions of people. We are surrounded by jealous and often hostile States, armed to the teeth, and we need more wariness and trained skill in piloting the ship of State than any country since the world began. Our success is largely owing to the inherited instinct for government which centuries of freedom have developed. A sober, cautious race of statesmen have evolved a wondrous machine for government at home and abroad. Its success is the envy of mankind. It relies in the last resort on the trained experience of the electorate of the United Kingdom. That electorate has been slowly formed by concentric rings like the growth of a tree; no addition has been made till it was clear it could safely be added to the parent stock. Let that cautious course be followed in the future, and we may still breast many a storm; but if we abandon the caution of the Anglo-Saxon race, and plunge into wild experiments like woman's suffrage, I much fear that dark days will befall this nation, and that the splendid fabric of centuries will totter to its fall.

Samuel Smith
7, DELAHAY STREET, WESTMINSTER

Millicent Garrett Fawcett

A reply to the letter of Mr Samuel Smith, MP, on women's suffrage

1892

MR Samuel Smith, MP for Flintshire, has given notice of his intention to move the rejection of Sir Albert Rollit's Women's Suffrage Bill, which is down for second reading on 27 April. It seems, therefore, not inopportune to consider some of the objections urged by Mr Smith against women's suffrage, which were printed and widely circulated among Members of Parliament and the public during last session.

It is obvious at the first glance that Mr Samuel Smith's criticisms do not apply to either of the Bills introduced by Sir Albert Rollit or Mr McLaren, but to an entirely different measure which exists only in the clouds. Mr Smith's objections apply to a Bill which would have the effect of enfranchising eleven millions of women; he recurs to the figures again and again: eleven million women, he says, would be enfranchised, and we regret to notice that his experience of women leads him to believe that they would be animated by a practically unanimous desire to destroy the commerce, the credit, the empire and the greatness of England. Against this horde of eleven million malignant women, he says that the fortress of the Constitution would only be defended by ten million men; and the inevitable consequence, in his opinion, would be that 'the splendid fabric of centuries will totter to its fall.' Trust women with the franchise, he says, in effect, and their first act will be one of matricide.

> This blessed plot, this earth, this realm, this England,
> This land of such dear souls, this dear, dear land,
> Dear for her reputation through the world

is according to Mr Samuel Smith worthily served by her sons, but would be hated and betrayed by her daughters. He says that our success as a nation is due to the 'inherited instinct for government which centuries of freedom have developed;' but he appears to believe that this 'inherited instinct' is strictly tied up in tail male. He does not, however, explain why he thinks women would be insensible to the claims of patriotism, for he claims for women superiority in matters where heart and the power of affection enter, and also says that 'woman has a finer and more highly-strung constitution than man.' Now patriotism is very much a matter of the heart, and of susceptibility to the emotion of gratitude and the sense of indebtedness to what others have wrought for us. It is therefore to be expected that if women are really more developed on the side of the affections, and if they really have finer and more highly-strung constitutions, they would be more susceptible to love of country, and more keenly sensitive in regard to those actions which might prove either injurious or beneficial to national interests.

The curious mixture in Mr S. Smith's mind of sentimental homage and practical contempt for, and distrust of, women, must not, however, lead us aside from combating the fundamental error upon which the whole structure of his argument is founded. He assumes throughout that universal womanhood suffrage is what is aimed at; and that every political disability of women will be swept away. Having made this fundamental (and false) assumption, he is able to conjure up at will his horrific pictures of the eleven million women destroying the Constitution; wives being brought up to vote against their husbands; wives and mothers neglecting their babies and their husbands' suppers to attend clubs and political meetings; the physical health of unborn generations being destroyed by 'febrile excitement' of politics on the part of mothers, and all the rest of it. It could hardly be believed, if it were not a patent fact, that all these things are said in criticism of a practical proposal which, if carried out, would enfranchise not eleven million but less than one million women, heads of households, ratepayers and property owners, who have already exercised, during some twenty-two years, all the various local franchises without producing any symptom, however infinitesimal, of the evils Mr Smith so confidently predicts. It is true that Mr Smith says that if once Parliament enfranchises women householders, it must necessarily go on to universal womanhood suffrage. But that is not for Mr Smith nor any of us to decide; the decision as to how far exactly future Parliaments will go in the direction of female enfranchisement is one for those Parliaments, or rather for the nation as then constituted, to determine. All that can be with certainty predicted is perhaps that Parliaments in the future, like Parliaments in the past, will be more influenced by practical considerations than by any desire to attain exact logical consistency. That is really the strength of the women's suffrage question at the present moment; we are not asking Parliament to give legislative expression to any theory or doctrine of equality between the sexes, but we ask Parliament to weigh the practical expediency of giving Parliamentary representation to a certain class of women who, as heads of households and ratepayers, have already had experience of voting in other elections, where much good and no harm whatever has resulted from including them in the lists of persons entitled to vote.

Mr Smith confesses at the commencement of his letter that he was once in favour of extending the parliamentary suffrage to women householders, but that his opinion has changed for two reasons: – the first is that 'the injustices from which women formerly suffered have been remedied,' and the second is that if there is women's suffrage at all, it must be universal womanhood suffrage.

I have already attempted to show that the English Parliament can stop just when it chooses to stop, or rather, just when the constituencies choose to stop, in the process of enfranchisement. The principle of popular election has existed in England for some six hundred years without as yet landing us in universal suffrage. Parliament does not, as a matter of fact, labour under the necessity of riding to death any principle which it sees fit to adopt. When Catholic emancipation was carried, certain exceptions were made. Three of the highest offices of State were reserved and cannot be held by Catholics. To some minds this may be illogical; but it commends itself to the judgment of the majority of Englishmen as a reasonable precaution, and the reservation will be maintained, logic or no logic, as long as the political safety of England appears to require it. In the same spirit, it may be confidently anticipated, Parliament will act in regard to the political emancipation of women; it will enfranchise the nine hundred thousand women householders and property owners without being bound therefore to go on and enfranchise the whole adult female population of England. In a country where for so many hundred years women have been allowed to reign but not to vote, no mere logical exigency will control the freedom of Parliament. It is true that most of the advocates of women's suffrage hope and believe that additional experience of it may encourage future Parliaments to go further in the direction of enfranchisement than this Parliament is asked to go; but this hope and expectation is a very different thing from an assertion that future Parliaments will be bound to go on to universal womanhood suffrage, no matter what experience may teach us as to the effects of a more limited measure.

There is a very curious inconsistency in Mr S. Smith's position in regard to manhood suffrage. He says that he is opposed to it; that he wishes to prevent it; that he believes household suffrage to be a sounder basis for Government than manhood suffrage. Holding these views, it might be expected, especially from one who thinks legislation is controlled by logical necessity, that he would endeavour to strengthen household suffrage by making it a reality, and including all householders, whether men or women. If he did this and helped to secure the enfranchisement of women householders, he would then be in a position logically to use all those arguments based on the numerical majority of women in this country, which he now attempts to apply, although they are totally irrelevant, to the practical question raised by the Bills before the House.

Let us now glance at the other reason which Mr Smith gives for changing his views on the question of women's suffrage. 'Women,' he says, used to be 'subject to some injustices, which men seemed unwilling to remedy,' but these injustices he apprehends, have been remedied one after another, therefore he thinks there is no reason to give women the protection of representation. Mr Smith's calm assumption that the legal injustices under which women labour have all been removed, is an instance of the fortitude with which one of the kindest of men is prepared to endure the misfortunes of others. It is hardly an exaggeration to say that there is scarcely an instance in which the supposed interests of men and women come into conflict in which the state of the law is not flagrantly unjust to women. The law in regard to the relation of parents to their children appears to have been framed in practical infidelity to the Divine law which gives to every child two parents, a father and a mother. The man-made law regards this as more than enough, and it therefore endeavours, in a bungling way, to deprive each child of one of its natural protectors. Where the birth of a child is legitimate, that is where it brings nothing but happiness and credit with it, the sole parent, the sole fountain of authority in the eye of the law, is the father; but where the child is illegitimate, where the birth means disgrace and shame, the sole parent recognised by the law, except under special conditions which it is easy for the father to evade, is the mother. The inequality of the divorce law is well known and need not be expatiated on. The law in regard to the protection of children and women from criminal immorality is studded with provisions which seem framed with the express purpose of protecting the criminal and making his detection and punishment far more difficult than they ought to be. The law for the protection of property (e.g. the protection of infants from money-lenders), is tenfold more stringent and more vigilantly executed than the law for the protection of the persons of young girls and women from the pursuit of vicious men. The law at present deals most inadequately with persons who trade in vice. Parents who bring up their children to send them on the streets in order to live on the proceeds of their infamy, are well known in every town and in many villages. Little or no effectual attempt is made by our law-makers to restrain them. Husbands send their wives on the streets by actual personal violence or by threats of it, and are hardly touched by the law unless they happen to complicate their villainy by mixing it with blackmailing of their male victims. Every man is a possible victim of blackmailing, and everything that law can do to stop it has, very properly, been done. What we wish to see is equal vigilance for the repression of offences of which every woman is a possible victim. The law in all cases deprives a divorced wife from access to her children, but a divorced husband is not invariably treated in the same way; the heir to a ducal house was taken away a few years back from his innocent mother and made over to the charge of his guilty father, although it must have been obvious that the best hopes of moulding the child's character for good were thereby seriously endangered.

Many cases might be mentioned in which English law is unjust to women or grossly inefficient. A leading member of the late government at Melbourne, writing the other day about his probable return to this country, concludes his letter by saying, 'I shall try to keep my Victorian domicile for the sake of my daughters. I hope if they marry they will have good husbands, but if one of them is unlucky I should not like her to be under the tender mercies of the English law.' And yet Mr Smith flatters himself that all the injustices which he appears to have been aware of a short time ago have been removed, or are rapidly being removed by the action of Parliament.

With regard to avenues of remunerative employment, every woman of the professional classes who has to get her own living knows that every profession that can be closed to women is closed. The medical profession has been at last opened after years of conflict; but the opportunities for professional study in it are very much more restricted and hampered than they are in the case of men. The older universities admit women to their examinations, but rigidly exclude them from any kind of membership. The Vice-Chancellor's certificate that women have passed tripos or other honour examinations gives them no status whatever in the university. Of course no university prizes or positions are open to them; they are permitted to use the museums and libraries of the universities only on sufferance, and they are liable at any moment to be turned out of them.

The way in which women of the industrial class are restricted in their choice of employments by the rules and political power of trades' unions is well known. Hardly a session passes without new legislative restrictions on the labour of women. The efforts of trades' unions are constantly being directed against women's labour: – 'Female labour is not at present a crying evil in our trade: it would be worse than folly to allow it to become so,' is a passage from the report of one of the London Bookbinders' Unions of 1891. This union succeeded in turning women out of the employment of gilding and marbling the edges of books in which they had been employed for many years. Among the working class the opinion is almost universal that it is justifiable to forbid by law or forcibly prevent the labour of women wherever their labour comes into competition with that of men. A witness before the Labour Commission was describing a strike that had taken place against employing women in one of the Army Clothing factories in Ireland. Mr Courtney asked the question: 'Have not the women the privilege of living?' to which the witness replied, 'They have the privilege of living as long as they do not interfere with the men.'

What this witness was guileless enough to put into words is the spirit that animates nearly the whole of men's trades' unions. They exert themselves to keep women out of all except the most unskilled and worst paid trades: they combine to prevent the natural growth of industrial efficiency among women: and in so far as they are able to do this, they swell that great army of 'fallen women' whose ranks are so much recruited by industrial inefficiency and want of steady employment. The Rev G. P. Merrick, late chaplain of Millbank, in an address recently published (Ward, Lock & Co) made an analysis of the life-history of 16,022 'fallen women' who had passed under his care; he speaks of 'want of industrial efficiency' as being very prominent among the causes of a vicious life among women. He also says, 'I am continually coming across cases where the street is resorted to only during the time when more reputable work fails. . . . When their trade revives they gladly forsake the streets.' Those engaged in rescue work constantly refer to the necessity for an increase of female industrial employment, and to the difficulties presented by the low wages of women in ordinary industry.

It cannot for a moment be doubted that the possession of Parliamentary representation would immensely strengthen the position of women industrially. We have only to look at what the possession of the Parliamentary franchise has already done for the agricultural labourer, to be sure that if women had votes, all parties would be eager to prove their zeal in remedying any legal, educational or industrial incapacity from which they may suffer.

Mr Smith in one passage of his letter appeals to the religious argument and to the authority of St Paul. In this matter we appeal from Paul to a greater than Paul, to Christ. No words ever fell from His lips which were inconsistent with that elevation of womanhood which is so marked a feature of practical Christianity. That women were among the last at the cross, that they were the first at the tomb, that when all forsook Him and fled, they remained faithful; that our Saviour honoured them by specially addressing to them several of His most important conversations; that He proclaimed, what the world has not yet accepted, that there is but one moral law for the man and the woman; all these things afford indications that work for the uplifting of the lives of women from a position of subordination is in accordance with the spirit of His teaching. With regard to St Paul, we may remember this: – that if we take his teaching about women with its context, it is obvious that he was expressing to the best of his capacity his judgment about the circumstances of his own time; and he particularly and definitely asserts in more than one place that this is so. 'I have no commandment of the Lord, yet I give my judgment.' Much therefore, of St Paul's teaching about the position of women and other social matters is not accepted by any Christian Church as a practical guide for conduct at the present time. St Paul taught and believed that celibacy was a higher state than marriage, both for men and women; but I do not think that even in the Roman Catholic Church celibacy is recommended, except for the priesthood and for sisterhoods. St Paul thought it unseemly for a woman to pray with her head uncovered; but I have never heard of any one regarding this as having any application at the present time, and the most devout Christian women attend and conduct family worship bareheaded, just as they braid their hair, wear gold, pearls and costly array on fitting occasions without any inward accusations of conscience in the matter. If we are now to be tied by the exact letter of St Paul's opinions on the social questions of his own time, we may expect Mr Smith and those members of Parliament who agree with him to move, when the education estimates come in, to reduce the vote by the amount of the salaries of the women teachers, for St Paul said, 'I suffer not a woman to teach.' It is no exaggeration to say that one who did so would be considered very near the confines which separate sanity from insanity. Then why in other social matters, must we not merely accept St Paul's words in their simple natural meaning as expressing his best judgment in the special circumstances of his own time, but twist them into something quite different, viz. into an argument for voting against the second reading of Sir Albert Rollit's Bill for enabling women ratepayers to vote for members of Parliament?

I have already encroached too much on the limits of your space, but Mr S. Smith makes such an astounding statement about women's suffrage in Wyoming and in the British Colonies, that I must trespass a little further on the patience of your readers. He says, 'the idea' of women's suffrage 'is scouted in these countries.' A women's suffrage Bill was carried last autumn in New Zealand by large majorities in the Chamber of Representatives, and was only lost in the Upper House by the narrow majority of two. It is not a little instructive that two Maories voted in this majority and therefore it may be said that they turned the scale against women's enfranchisement. Those long resident in the colony inform me that in their opinion women's suffrage is absolutely certain to become law there within a very few years. Women's suffrage has been supported by a majority several times in the South Australian Legislature, but the majorities have not been sufficiently large, as an absolute majority of the whole House is required there for any law amending the constitution. In 1890, the women's suffrage measure only failed at the third reading by one vote of this sufficient majority. In Victoria and New South Wales the promoters of women's suffrage have more than once come very near success. It is supported in New South Wales by Sir Henry Parkes, probably the most influential of our colonial statesmen. He embodied women's suffrage as an integral part of his scheme for the confederation of the Australian colonies. And yet Mr Samuel Smith boldly asserts that the idea of women's suffrage is 'scouted' in the Australian colonies. One is tempted to imagine that, like Mr Brooke in *Middlemarch*, his pen runs away with him sometimes. Now for the scouting of women's suffrage in

Wyoming: – Mr Smith quotes Mr Bryce as having said in his book on the American Commonwealth that it was adopted there by accident, and is looked upon as a practical joke by the rest of the country. It is true that people who have had no practical experience of women's suffrage are apt to regard it as a joke and to produce ancient Joe Millerisms in reference to it, such as that if women's suffrage were restricted to women over forty, not a single woman would be found to claim it; but these very humorous comments do not generally survive practical experience of women's suffrage. The people of Wyoming, having seen it at work for twenty-five years, take it quite seriously, and recently confirmed it (though they were told that their adhesion to it would imperil the success of their claim to be admitted as a State of the Union), by a majority of 8 to 1.

Mr Smith has lately taken a prominent part in favour of Church Disestablishment. I do not do him the injustice of supposing that in opposing women's suffrage he is influenced by the impression that the majority of women would be against him on this question. As Mr Courtney said the other day, such a reason for opposing a measure of enfranchisement is too shameful to be avowed, and, he hoped, too cynical to be secretly acted upon. The importance of the question of Church Disestablishment gives a fresh weight to the claim of women to enfranchisement. Whether we are for establishment or for disestablishment, surely this is a question in which women are as vitally interested as men, and have at least as great a claim to be heard. In his last speech to his constituents, my husband, himself a supporter of disestablishment, placed this issue plainly before them. 'If the Church is to be disestablished,' he said, 'the wishes of women on such a question are entitled to the fullest consideration.' Mr Gladstone has said that to withhold the franchise from any section of the community on the ground that their political views may not be in accordance with our own is a 'sin against first principles.' I therefore earnestly hope no one will be guilty of this sin on 27 April, but that all who believe that a case for the enfranchisement of women householders has been made out, will vote for Sir Albert Rollit's Bill.

W. E. Gladstone, MP

Female suffrage: a letter to Samuel Smith, MP

11 April 1892

1, CARLTON GARDENS

DEAR Mr Samuel Smith,

In reply to your letter, I cannot but express the hope that the House of Commons will not consent to the second reading of the Bill for Extending the Parliamentary Suffrage to Women, which will come before it on the 27th instant.

The Bill is a narrow Bill, inasmuch as it excludes from its operation the entire body of married women; who are not less reflective, intelligent, and virtuous, than their unmarried sisters, and who must I think be superior in another great element of fitness, namely the lifelong habit of responsible action. If this change is to be made, I certainly have doubts, not yet dispelled, whether it ought to be made in the shape which would thus be given to it by a halting and inconsistent measure.

But it is a change which obviously, and apart from disputable matter, ought not to be made without the fullest consideration and the most deliberate assent of the nation as well as of the Parliament. Not only has there been no such assent, but there has not been even an approach to such consideration. The subject has occupied a large place in the minds of many thoughtful persons, and of these a portion have become its zealous adherents. Just weight should be allowed to their sentiments, and it is desirable that the arguments on both sides should be carefully and generally scrutinised: but the subject is as yet only sectional, and has not really been taken into view by the public mind at large. Can it be right, under these circumstances, that the principle of a change so profound should be adopted? Cannot its promoters be content with that continuance and extension of discussion, which alone can adequately sift the true merits of their cause?

I offer this suggestion in the face of the coming Election. I am aware that no legitimate or effectual use can be made of it for carrying to an issue a question at once so great and so novel; but I do not doubt, considering the zeal and ability which are enlisted in its favour, that the occasion might be made available for procuring an increase of attention to the subject, which I join with them in earnestly desiring.

There are very special reasons for circumspection in this particular case. There has never within my knowledge been a case in which the franchise has been extended to a large body of persons generally indifferent about receiving it. But here, in addition to a widespread indifference, there is on the part of large numbers of women who have considered the matter for themselves, the most positive objection and strong disapprobation. Is it not clear to every unbiassed mind that before forcing on them what they conceive to be a fundamental change in their whole social function, that is to say in their Providential calling, at least it should be ascertained that the womanly mind of the country, at present so largely strange to the subject, is in overwhelming proportion, and with deliberate purpose, set upon securing it?

I speak of the change as being a fundamental change in the whole social function of woman, because I am bound in considering this Bill to take into view not only what it enacts, but what it involves. The first of these, though important, is small in comparison with the last.

What the Bill enacts is simply to place the individual woman on the same footing in regard to Parliamentary elections, as the individual man. She is to vote, she is to propose or nominate, she is to be designated by the law as competent to use and to direct, with advantage not only to the community but to herself, all those public agencies which belong to our system of Parliamentary representation. She, not the individual woman, marked by special tastes, possessed of special gifts, but the woman as such, is by this change to be plenarily launched into the whirlpool of public life, such as it is in the nineteenth, and such as it is to be in the twentieth century.

So much for what the Bill enacts: now for what it involves, and involves in the way of fair and rational, and therefore of morally necessary, consequence. For a long time we drew a distinction between competency to vote and competency to sit in Parliament. But long before our electorate had attained to the present popular proportions, this distinction was felt to involve a palpable inconsistency, and accordingly it died away. It surely cannot be revived: and if it cannot be revived, then the woman's vote carries with it, whether by the same Bill or by a consequential Bill, the woman's seat in Parliament. These assertions ought to be strictly tested. But, if they cannot be confuted, do not let them be ignored.

If the woman's vote carries with it the woman's seat, have we at this point reached our terminus, and found a standing ground which we can in reason and in justice regard as final? Capacity to sit in the House of Commons now legally and practically draws in its train capacity to fill every office in the State. Can we alter this rule and determine to have two categories of Members of Parliament, one of them, the established and the larger one, consisting of persons who can travel without check along all the lines of public duty and honour, the other, the novel and the smaller one, stamped with disability for the discharge of executive, administrative, judicial, or other public duty? Such a stamp would I apprehend be a brand. There is nothing more odious, nothing more untenable, than an inequality in legal privilege which does not stand upon some principle in its nature broad and clear. Is there here such a principle, adequate to show that when capacity to sit in Parliament has been established, the title to discharge executive and judicial duty can be withheld? Tried by the test of feeling, the distinction would be offensive. Would it stand better under the laws of logic? It would stand still worse, if worse be possible. For the proposition we should have to maintain would be this. The legislative duty is the highest of all public duties; for this we admit your fitness. Executive and judicial duties rank below it: and for these we declare you unfit.

I think it impossible to deny that there have been and are women individually fit for any public office however masculine its character; just as there are persons under the age of twenty-one better fitted than many of those beyond it for the discharge of the duties of full citizenship. In neither case does the argument derived from exceptional instances seem to justify the abolition of the general rule. But the risks involved in the two suppositions are immeasurably different. In the one, individual judgment and authority plainly would have to distinguish between childhood and manhood, and to specify a criterion of competency in each case, which is now more conveniently fixed by the uniformity of law. In the other, a permanent and vast difference of type has been impressed upon women and men respectively by the Maker of both. Their differences of social office rest mainly upon causes, not flexible and elastic like most mental qualities, but physical and in their nature unchangeable. I for one am not prepared to say which of the two sexes has the higher and which has the lower province. But I recognize the subtle and profound character of the differences between them, and I must again, and again, and again, deliberate before aiding in the issue of what seems an invitation by public authority to the one to renounce as far as possible its own office, in order to assume that of the other. I am not without the fear lest beginning with the State, we should eventually be found to have intruded into what is yet more fundamental and more sacred, the precinct of the family, and should dislocate, or injuriously modify, the relations of domestic life.

As this is not a party question, or a class question, so neither is it a sex question. I have no fear lest the woman should encroach upon the power of the man. The fear I have is, lest we should invite her unwittingly to trespass upon the delicacy, the purity, the refinement, the elevation of her own nature, which are the present sources of its power. I admit that we have often, as legislators, been most unfaithful guardians of her rights to moral and social equality. And I do not say that full justice has in all things yet been done; but such great progress has been made in most things, that in regard to what may still remain the necessity for violent remedies has not yet been shown. I admit that in the Universities, in the professions, in the secondary circles of public action, we have already gone so far as to give a shadow of plausibility to the present proposals to go farther; but it is a shadow only, for we have done nothing that plunges the woman as such into the turmoil of masculine life. My disposition is to do all for her which is free from that danger and reproach, but to take no step in advance until I am convinced of its safety. The stake is enormous. The affirmation pleas are to my mind not clear, and, even if I thought them clearer, I should deny that they were passing.

Such being the state of the evidence, and also such the immaturity of the public mind, I earnestly hope that the House of Commons will decline to give a second reading to the Woman's Suffrage Bill.

I remain, dear Mr S. Smith,

Very faithfully yours,

W. E. GLADSTONE

Anon

Female suffrage: the letter which ought to have been written by *the Right Hon W. E. Gladstone, MP, to Samuel Smith, MP*

24 April 1892

London

DEAR Mr Samuel Smith,

In reply to your letter, I cannot but express the hope that the House of Commons will consent to the second reading of the Bill for Extending the Parliamentary Suffrage to Women, which will come before it on the 27th instant.

The Bill, it is true, is a narrow Bill, inasmuch as it excludes from its operation all those married women who do not happen to be on the register adopted as the basis of enfranchisement – women, who are not less reflective, intelligent, and virtuous, than their unmarried sisters, and who must, I think, be equal in that great element of fitness, namely, the lifelong habit of responsible action. But if this change is to be made – a change which the growing enlightenment of the age renders of increasing urgency – I certainly have doubts, not dispelled by my experience of former great constitutional changes, whether it could be begun by any measure that would not appear halting and inconsistent.

It is a change which obviously, and apart from disputable matter, ought not to be delayed without the fullest justification and the most deliberate hostility of the nation as well as of the Parliament. Not only is there no such justification, but during the last twenty-five years of continued discussion there has not been even an approach to reasonable and influential hostility. The subject has occupied a large place in the minds of many thoughtful persons for the last twenty-five years, and of these the major portion have become its zealous adherents. It is time that just weight should be allowed to their sentiments, and it is desirable that the arguments on their side, and the want of argument on the side of their opponents, should produce their inevitable and proper results; the opposition, of late years at least, has never been other than sectional, the movement finding many and influential supporters in all parties of the State, while those who opposed it have signally failed to impress the public mind at large. Must it not be right, under these circumstances, that this change, based upon fundamental principles of the Constitution, should be adopted? Must not its opponents be deemed to be answered by the evident failure of such arguments as they have seen fit to advance – a failure which of itself alone has adequately demonstrated the true merits of the cause?

I offer this suggestion in the face of the coming Election. I am aware that no legitimate or effectual use can be made of it for carrying to an issue a question at once so great and so simple; but I do not doubt, considering the want of zeal and lack of seriousness which are arrayed in its despite, that the occasion might be made available for procuring a definite pronouncement in favour of a wider and more catholic enactment upon the subject, which I earnestly desire.

There are very special reasons for putting an end to delay, misnamed circumspection, in this particular case. There has never within my knowledge been a case in which the franchise has been extended to a large body of persons without the alleged indifference of those about to receive it. But here, in spite of this alleged indifference, there is, on the part of large numbers of women who have considered the matter for themselves, the most positive demand and strong desire for enfranchisement. Is it not clear to every unbiassed mind that before continuing to maintain as against them what they conceive to be a fundamental disability in their citizenship as women, that is to say, in their Providential calling, at least it should be established, as it certainly cannot be established, that the womanly mind of the country, at present so deeply sensible of the injustice of their position, is in overwhelming proportion, and with deliberate purpose, set upon retaining that disability?

The opponents of female suffrage assert that it will produce a fundamental change in the whole social function of woman, not so much on account of what the Bill enacts, as by reason of what it involves. But I will not admit that the removal of the electoral disability from womanhood will produce any fundamental change in the social function of woman. The possession and the exercise by women of the local and municipal franchises have not wrought any such fundamental change, and there is no ground either in history or in logic for supposing that the Parliamentary franchise will falsify that experience. I make this assertion, taking into view not only what the Bill enacts, but what it involves.

What the Bill enacts is simply to place the individual woman on the same footing in regard to Parliamentary elections as the individual man. She is to vote, she is to propose or nominate, she is to be designated by the law as competent to use and to direct, with advantage not only to the community but to herself, all those public agencies which belong to our system of Parliamentary representation. She, not the individual woman, marked by special tastes, possessed of special gifts, but the woman as such, is by this change to be allowed, if she herself should so desire it, to plenarily launch herself into the whirlpool of public life, such as it is in the nineteenth, and such as it is to be in the twentieth century.

So much for what the Bill enacts. Now for what it involves in the way of fair and rational, and therefore of morally necessary consequence – i.e. according to the opponent's view of the case. Some of these opponents argue to the effect that for a long time we drew a distinction between competency to vote and competency to sit in Parliament. But that long before our electorate had attained to the present popular proportions, this distinction was felt to involve a palpable inconsistency, and, accordingly, it died away. 'It surely cannot be revived,' they urge; 'and if it cannot be revived, then the woman's vote carries with it, whether by the same Bill or by a consequential Bill, the woman's seat in Parliament.' These assertions ought to be strictly tested. If they cannot be confuted, at least they ought not to be ignored. But they can be confuted. The distinction still exists. It is sufficient to mention that no clergyman or civil servant is eligible to sit in Parliament, although possessing the vote. Therefore, while we may admit the accuracy of these assertions as a matter of abstract logic, yet this is very far from admitting their practical probability. 'The woman's vote carries with it the woman's seat,' say the opponents; but even then it would only be where the electors so desire it. 'Nor is this all,' they continue; 'capacity to sit in the House of Commons now legally and practically draws in its train capacity to fill every office in the State.' Admitted; but, again, only where, along with legal capacity to fill the office, there exists actual capacity to fulfil the duties of that office. But perhaps nothing more clearly indicates the weakness of their case than that these same opponents should gravely construct an argument against woman's suffrage on the admitted impossibility of having two categories of Members of Parliament, the potential necessity for which could only arise – following their own line of argument – out of a contingency not only remote in theory, but still more remote, not to say most improbable, in practice.

Opponents have found it impossible to deny that there have been, and are, women individually fit for any public office however masculine its character; they have attempted to discount this fact by arguing that there are persons under the age of twenty-one better fitted than many of those beyond it, for the discharge of the duties of full citizenship. In no case does an argument derived from exceptional instances justify the abolition or the retention of a general rule. But here the implications involved in the two suppositions are immeasurably different. In the one, individual judgment and authority plainly would have to distinguish between childhood and manhood, and to specify a criterion of competency in each case, which is now more conveniently fixed by the uniformity of law. In the other, a permanent and vast difference of physical functions, it is true, has been impressed upon women and men respectively by the Maker of both; but their differences of social office rest mainly not upon causes physical, and in their nature unchangeable, but upon legal disabilities enacted by a privileged and opposite sex, and in their nature essentially removable. I for one deem it irrelevant to inquire which of the two sexes has the higher and which has the lower province, if indeed there be a higher and a lower. I recognise willingly the subtle and profound character of the differences between them, but I must again and again, and again, deny that the complete removal of the electoral disability from womanhood, already accomplished in part, would be, in the fanciful phrase of the opponents, 'the issue of an invitation by public authority to woman to renounce as far as possible her own office, in order to assume that of man.' I do not entertain the fear that in thus enormously benefiting the State, we shall eventually be found to have injured what is yet more fundamental and more sacred – the sanctity of the family; or shall dislocate, or injuriously modify, the relations of domestic life.

As, owing to the paucity of serious opponents, this could not be made a party question, or a class question, every effort has been made to render it a sex question. I, however, have no fear lest the woman should encroach upon the power of the man. The fear I have is, lest the political domination of man should too long exclude from our public life the delicacy, the purity, the refinement, and the elevation of woman's nature, which are the present sources of the regeneration of the race. It is admitted that men, as legislators, have been most unfaithful guardians of woman's rights to moral and social equality. And I most firmly believe that full justice never can, and never will, be done to women until female suffrage shall enable women themselves to protect a woman's rights, and to redress a woman's wrongs. In the Universities, in the professions, in the secondary circles of public action, we have already gone so far as to leave no shadow of plausibility to the present opposition to women's enfranchisement, and this shadow is not made more tangible by the statement that the Parliamentary franchise, as such, will plunge the woman, as such, into the turmoil of masculine life. My disposition has always been to do all for her which is free from danger and reproach, but to take no step in advance until, as in this juncture, I am convinced of its safety. The case is urgent. There is nothing more odious, nothing more untenable, than an inequality in legal privilege which does not stand upon some principle in its nature broad and clear. The opposing arguments are to my mind not clear, and, even if I thought them clearer, I should deny that they were sufficient.

Such being the state of the evidence, and also such the growing maturity of the public mind, I earnestly hope that the House of Commons will not decline to give a second reading to the Woman's Suffrage Bill.

I remain, dear Mr S. Smith,
Very faithfully yours,
The Author

Elizabeth Martyn

The case of the helots

1894

THE last class to be enfranchised in this country – last, so long as representation is based upon taxation – is that of the helots. For a quarter of a century helots have been asking for the Parliamentary vote, and they are asking for it still. They have seen class after class enfranchised, sometimes with very little trouble and after slight demand, but the time for the helots is not yet.

Why do they want the vote? The simplest answer to this question is another question; why does anyone want the vote? This sets the first questioner thinking; and thought is good.

A great statesman, speaking of another class, once used words like these: 'They had no votes, and therefore they could be safely neglected.' And it is a fact that grievances are not easily redressed, and usually remain unredressed, while those who suffer are unrepresented in our Parliament.

An exasperated helot sometimes says to an adversary, 'Am I not a householder? do I not pay rates and taxes? have I not property of this, that, and the other kind? have I not to keep the laws as well as you? and is it not true that laws are made on purpose to arrange my affairs for me? Why should I not have a voice in the making of them?'

'Yes, oh, yes!' hurriedly and impatiently, 'I grant all that, but – oh, it would never do.'

'Why not?'

'Well, you see – er – you are only a helot!'

On which the helot has much ado not to lose her temper – on some occasions, alas, she loses it – and begs to know what the fact of her helothood has to do with the question of the franchise.

'Here am I,' she cries, 'living next door to a man who pays exactly the same rates and taxes as myself. He has a vote; I have not. How is that?'

'Well, don't you see? It is as plain as possible. Of course he is not a helot!'

There is no other argument. Yet the men who use it are accounted sane.

Helots are scolded for wanting class-legislation. 'You are making divisions in the body politic,' they are told; 'you are setting class against class. No one would dream of wrongs, rights, jealousies, grievances, if only you would keep quiet.' Then helots humbly submit that as long as they are left out in the cold there is division, but not of their making. Some people have votes, others have none; some have rights, to others these rights are denied. And they throw the accusation of class-opposition back upon the law-makers, which, if one thinks of it, seems only reasonable.

There are at present signs that the old method of representation, based upon taxation, is coming to an end, and that manhood suffrage is to take its place; but here comes in another inequality. An outsider might naturally consider that manhood signified humanity; but no, the helot part of humanity is still to be excluded.

Helots are in a minority, then, in this country? On the contrary, they number nearly a million more than the privileged persons. If the figures happened to be reversed we should hear them quoted continually as proof positive of the survival of the fittest.

For twenty-five years the majority has been asking for the franchise. Twenty-five years: is that all? Helots knew these grievances years, centuries ago, but they were taught to believe that they were heaven-sent, and therefore good, and good-producing. Submission was enjoined upon them, and beauteous self-abnegation. They were apt scholars, all the more apt because they could not help themselves; and they carefully impressed their beliefs upon their children. Little by little, however, one here, and another there, they began to ask, 'Is it right? is it just? Why should we bear tamely all our lives what our brethren, our masters, would not bear for a day?'

The first important book written in vindication of the rights of helots appeared about a hundred years ago; a second was produced in this century by a man who was not a helot, and to whose memory, therefore, helots owe undying gratitude.

And what were the wrongs which exasperated helots at last to claim their rights?

They were many, and of various kinds. Helots who had to earn their own living knew that their work was often harder than other people's, and never commanded the same remuneration. Some helots were teachers, others were household servants, others again, were in business; but every one of them who was employed by anyone else had to take small pay, on the one ground – so simple, so easy to comprehend – that she was a helot.

The Universities were shut against them, and so were many trades, and all professions.

Preach! oh, dear no. There is something dreadful, even blasphemous, in the thought! But act, sing, recite in public, by all means; you do it so well, and it amuses Us. The ornamental and amusing is distinctly your mission in life, 'O Helot, in Our hours of ease!'

As for being lawyers, helots had not brains enough; and, as for being doctors, it was so indelicate, don't you know, even if a helot desired to practise only upon other helots. It was not indelicate or out of place to be a hospital nurse. There was, and is, a great demand for helot-nurses, the more highly educated, the more perfectly refined, the better. Not forty years ago, however, the pioneer of helot-nurses was treated with contempt, and had to fight her way against great opposition. To volunteer to nurse wounded soldiers was thought to be so 'unhelotic' as to argue something like depravity of nature. But the pioneer had courage and the consciousness of right, and accomplished so grand a work, that she was put upon a pedestal for all time, and praised as being 'most helotic,' and an example to the whole body of helots.

The way was prepared, and the pioneer's sisters began to walk in it, and, as men blessed them more and more, to press into it in crowds. The path was widened for them, and all stones were taken out of the way. Here was an opening, here at last was something to be done, here an escape from frivolity and idleness!

Many helots were so greatly interested in their new work that they desired to go further, and be surgeons and physicians. But they found a 'thus-far-and-no-farther' barrier, a dead wall of opposition. 'Stay where you are,' was said to them; 'you are in your sphere; it would be unhelotic and indelicate in the highest degree to seek to go beyond it. Here we will shelter you in our hospital wards. You shall smooth pillows, and sit up at nights, and wash up after operations, and scrub floors, and all for twenty pounds a year, and a most becoming uniform. Your refinement is such that we could not bear to see you among things that are coarse and vile; your fragility of constitution would not stand the strain of a doctor's life. Besides, you could not do it – no helot ever did; your mental capacity is known to be inferior to ours.'

The would-be doctors sat down to consider their position, and thought that they made sure of four things concerning it: –

1   The work of a nurse was harder, physically, than that of a doctor.
2   Many more 'indelicate' things had to be done by a nurse than by a doctor.
3   There was little possibility, either of liberty or leisure, in hospital life.
4   And the pay was very small.

Then a gleam of light illumined the darkness of the nursing mind.

Some helots were well-to-do in the world, and had not only money, but houses and lands in their own right. When they married, however, everything that they possessed became the property of their husbands. If the marriage were a happy one the injustice was not felt, because there was love, and, therefore, unselfishness on either side; but many marriages were unhappy, and very many more were decidedly uncomfortable. It often happened that a helot was married solely for what she possessed, and then was not allowed to touch a morsel of her property, and might be left at her husband's death with nothing which she could call her own. As this was the law of the land, and as no helot had any share in law-making, there was no redress, and those who went into the law courts were told that nothing but submission was possible. The great majority of cases never came before judge and jury at all. The wrong was suffered in silence, and unquestioned.

In the case of a married helot, who had to work for her living, things were even worse. She had not even a right to her earnings. This, again, did not matter in a marriage of love and sympathy, but it acted terribly where husband and wife were pulling different ways, and especially where the husband was lazy and unprincipled. Case after case was reported in the newspapers of drunken husbands who would not work for themselves, but seized upon the earnings of their wives, spent all upon themselves, and left their families to starve; of husbands who deserted their wives, and then came back upon them just as they had started a little shop or saved a little money, sold up everything, and left the helots once more destitute, and with the despairing conviction in their minds that, whatever they did and wherever they might hide, the persecutors would swoop down again and exact the uttermost farthing. Neither police, nor magistrate, nor judge could do anything. Most of them seemed surprised that they were expected to do anything: was it not the law of the land?

Again, a married helot had no right to her own child after the child had reached the age of seven years. It might be brought up in a form of religion which the helot disliked; it might be cruelly treated, and the helot was powerless; it might be taken away, and the helot never see it again.

Then as regarded divorce. The husband could free himself from the wife on the one charge; the wife could not be free unless she could prove besides that her husband was cruel to her in the presence of witnesses.

No wonder that many a helot said to herself, 'It is bad enough to be a helot, but to be a married helot is worse than all!' No wonder that at last a few helots, both married and unmarried, banded together and said, 'These things must come to an end. Those who make the laws may possibly mean well, but they clearly do not understand us, and they legislate for us from their own point of view. We must have the franchise.'

A cry of horror arose from one end of the country to the other. The poor helots were argued with, shouted at, hustled and badgered. Worse than all, they were laughed at.

'What wrongs have you, my dears?' asked one.

'Ho, ho!' laughed another; 'only a helot, and wanting a vote! Why, you will be wanting to sit in Parliament next!'

'I don't believe in "Helot Rights," ' was a growl from another quarter; 'all moonshine! fudge!'

They were called 'strong-minded,' under the impression that this was a term of reproach, and in utter obliviousness of the fact that the antithesis of 'strong' is 'weak.'

They were told that home was their sphere, their only sphere, and they had quoted to them such sweet sayings as 'The hand that rocks the cradle rules the world,' the quoters forgetting that the world is not always in its cradle, and that many and many a helot never has a chance of rocking. There was also thrown at them a nice little poem which begins –

> The rights of helots, what are they?
> The rights to labour and to pray.

'That is all very well,' said one helot after another, 'we are willing to labour, and we are thankful that we can pray; but you do the same? And, if you don't, why don't you? The

457

has nothing to do with what we are talking about.'

Their opponents drew pictures of the helots who wanted to vote, and they made them as ugly as they could, with blue spectacles and big umbrellas, so that people should laugh; and they had their reward, for the laughter was loud and long. It was so long, indeed, that some of it can be heard to this day.

And they drew beautiful pictures of the dear, sweet helots who did not want the vote; for, unfortunately, there were some so very comfortable that they did not realise that their fellows were suffering, and so selfish that they did not care even when these sufferings were described over and over again. Some of them would say – parrot-like, for they could only repeat what they had been taught – 'It is so unhelotic, don't you know, so unfashionable, too! Nobody likes a helot who goes in for helot's rights.'

And people who knew them were fond of making, on platforms, such speeches as these:

'I have asked several helots whether they desired the suffrage, and they have invariably said, "No, not on any account;" and I am quite convinced, for I know them very well, that they have no wrongs, and that, therefore, no helot has any. All the best helots are with us.'

The helots whose eyes were open to see the way in which unjust and unequal legislation pressed upon them, grieved greatly over the attitude of their rich, comfortable sisters. For they were drags upon the wheels. They lived sheltered lives, and never thought of anything but themselves, their relations and friends. They talked a great deal about 'their sphere,' and all the men who petted and admired them talked about it too, but no-one knew exactly what it meant.

So the 'best' helots sat still, and came not to the help of the 'shrieking sisterhood.' But these worked on, worked harder and harder, and yet did not gain what they wanted – the Parliamentary franchise.

In consequence, however, of their continuous demand, statesmen were at last driven to ask, 'Why do you want the suffrage?'

The answer was the recital of a whole chapter of grievances.

'Stop!' cried the great men, putting their hands to their ears. 'What shrieking this is! you deafen us.'

And they retired to consult. They then agreed to redress one small grievance rather than have this clamour go on any longer: and an Act of Parliament, hedged about with many restrictions, was thrown to them as a sop. In the course of years one or two other things were bestowed upon them with a 'take-this-and-be-satisfied' kind of air. Behind the scenes, grave politicians said to each other,

'If those stupid helots want the franchise because of all the things they call grievances, let us redress the "grievances" one by one, as far, of course as is compatible with the preservation of our own interests, and then they will have nothing to complain about. Anything, anything, rather than give them the vote!'

'*The* vote' was not granted, but several lesser ones were granted as the years went on. Helots began to vote councillors into Town Councils, and soon found that people treated them with a little respect when they complained of the state of the streets, for instance, or the way in which the rates had gone up. The franchise for the Board of Guardians was also given, and helots were allowed, besides, actually to sit upon these Boards and watch over the interests of those poorer than themselves. And when the School Boards were formed, a friend of helots managed to put a word or two into the Parliamentary Act, which allowed helots from the first not only to vote for members of the board but to be members themselves. Then came the County Council, with a vote for householders all round, helot-householders included. But may helots sit in these Councils? Oh, no, that would be too shocking; it would be almost like going into Parliament.

It is only fair, however, to say, that the members of the greatest County Council in the kingdom would welcome helots as fellow-members if the law would but allow them to come.

But, to-day, though so much has been gained, helots are still unsatisfied, are still asking for the Parliamentary franchise. Why? For the simple reason that they are taxed exactly as their fellow subjects are taxed, and ought to have the same right as they to say how the money shall be spent. They see their money taken to build an unnecessary ironclad, or to promote an unrighteous war against barbarians; and many a helot grudges her money for such purposes, and wishes to say so with effect.

In these latter days, another and more insidious danger has arisen. Helots have come more and more to the front, and their fellow-men, speaking generally, have discovered that they really have the brains that were so long denied, and that they can, in consequence, be made of very great use. It was often said at first when helots began to creep out into public life, 'How well the get on, considering that they are only helots! It is really qu' surprising!' But after a time people began to acknowledge t' helots could speak on platforms, and conduct business-meeti as admirably as themselves; and they often complimented ther their most astonishing success.

Then, when the helots turned upon them with the old der 'Give us the suffrage,' there was a look of shocked solemr many faces, and a sudden slipping away at side doors, and the helots were left alone to wonder why, *why*, WHY their brethren were so much afraid of them.

Both political parties are every day making more and more use of helot-labour. It is not 'unhelotic' now to speak from platforms, or to canvass for votes; and helots who will do either, especially the latter, are courted and caressed. Nothing is too good for them – except the franchise.

The Conservatives will not give it because they are certain that all helots are Liberals; and the Liberals cannot see their way because they are quite sure that all helots are Conservatives. Helots often complain to both parties that this behaviour is based on mere expediency, but they complain in vain, because the average political mind rather loves expediency than otherwise, and has not yet risen to the comprehension of abstract justice.

Many helots do not see that they are engaged in merely pulling chestnuts out of the fire for other folk to eat. 'We must just put in this candidate,' they say, 'and then the next – and the next:' and when the election is over, the new member will thank them in the most graceful and grateful way, but it will not occur to him that they, after all, have no political rights, and that he is now in a position to work for them. On the contrary, it often happens that, if distinctly questioned on the subject he replies with the fervour of conviction that helots' suffrage is perfectly impossible; it would create a revolution, wreck the homes of England, and be disastrous in its effects on helots themselves.

When helots formed their own Conservative and Liberal associations they should, as a matter of course, have made the demand for enfranchisement the fundamental part of their programme. Was it ever known in all the history of our past that any other class of men who had no political standing banded together to help those who had, and yet forgot to ask for their own rights? The old habit of subjection has been too strong. Fear of offending 'the powers that be,' combined with humblest abnegation of self, have made helots again and again stand on one side till this, that, and the other measure has been passed; and so victory is still delayed. Bit by bit, after long and severe struggle, and with sad expenditure of strength, justice on several points has been gained, which would have been readily granted if the petitioners had had votes at their backs, and, thus, a recognized standing in the country.

The root-mistake which has caused helots to be treated differently from other people has been the regarding of Helothood as a special, and greatly inferior, variety of Humanity, not

Humanity itself, but created to wait upon Humanity. Thus a great French writer of the last century uses words like these:

'The education of helots should always be relative to that of men. To please, to be useful to us, to make us love and esteem them, to educate us when young, and take care of us when grown up, to advise, to console us, to render our lives easy and agreeable: these are the duties of helots at all times, and what they should be taught in their infancy.' And a modern German writer thus 'takes up the wondrous tale:' 'Man desires a being that not only loves but understands him, a being whose heart not only beats for him, but whose hand smoothes his brow, a being that, wherever it appears, irradiates peace, rest, order, silent control over itself and over the thousand trifles that make up his daily life; he desires a being that diffuses over everything that indefinable odour of helothood which is the vivifying warmth of domestic life.'

These extracts may be paralleled by scores, hundreds, in ancient and modern literature. There is no thought that the helot can be 'of like passions' with other men. No-one is 'to please, to be useful to' her, no-one is to render her life 'easy and agreeable;' she never wants some one 'that not only loves but understands her,' or, if she does, she must 'go without': and where is she to procure that 'peace, rest, order, and silent control' which 'man', it appears, admires but cannot attain? She must manufacture them herself and then supply her masters. The masters in return do not propose to smoothe her brow or 'irradiate' anything for her benefit: why should they, when they are Humanity and she only a helot, with neither feelings, nor interests, nor individuality of her own?

We often see book or lecture advertised with some such title as this: 'Helot: her place and power', 'Helot's Work in the Church', and so on: and people gravely discuss such subjects much as they would discuss the position of cats or cows in the social system.

The productions of intellect are discussed on their merits until an instance appears which is due to a helot. Then the laws of art, music, literature, drop out of sight; and the work is 'very good for an helot', or 'a striking illustration of the kind of thing a helot can be brought to do'. 'The defects of helotic work are here very apparent', we read; or, 'we must compliment the artist on having quite surpassed her sister helots'.

('Impossible to surpass Us', is not added, but is understood.)

Pope said long ago –

> Most helots have no characters at all,
> Matter too soft a lasting mark to bear,
> And best distinguished by black, brown, or fair.

461

Poor Pope!

Condescending editors often reserve one little column in their newspapers which they call 'The Helots' Column'. It is supposed to suit exactly the humble range of the helotic mind. It deals almost invariably with cookery and clothes, and with the doings of the Royal Family. Many of its appointed readers peruse this column and the lists of births, marriages, and deaths, and nothing else in the paper. Why meddle with matters that are known to be too high for them: politics, the state of trade, the prospects of the crops, and the election of Mr Brown as vestryman? I cannot blame these people. The power of thinking for themselves has been drilled out of them. Their food has been not only selected but cut up for them on their plates, and they have never yet seen the absurdity of the thing. Let us admire those helots who have dared to think for themselves (how they ever began to do it I cannot imagine), whose sense of humour and strength of originality have broken through the tradition of the elders. And let us be patient with the readers of 'The Helots' Column', and do our best to enlarge their vision. Let us also remember that a very great many people who are not helots, and have never been shut up in a sphere, but have always had full liberty of thought and action, prefer *Titbits* and *Scraps* to politics and metaphysics, and a glass of beer and a pipe to anything else in the wide world. Yet no kind editor provides a column for these lowly minds.

Then there are sayings which are accepted without question, and passed on from mouth to mouth, in parrot-fashion, generation after generation. More evil is done by unreflective, unquestioning people than can be calculated. 'Helots are such talkers', 'so fond of dress', 'always looking at themselves in the glass', 'always gossiping', 'never able to keep a secret', etc. It is very seldom that anyone stops to ask, Are these sweeping assertions true? and, if they are, are they not true of humanity in general and not of one species only? There are helots who are uninterested in dress, others who rarely open their mouths, others again who will keep a secret to the death. And there are people who are not helots who look long at themselves in the glass, and are fastidious about the breadth of a hat-brim and the set of a coat. There are also people, not helots, who sit for hours in public-houses, or stand at street-corners with their hands in their pockets, gossiping, gossiping, chattering, chattering, yet no-one calls attention to their behaviour at being peculiar to one section of humanity; and no one sneers.

The very word 'helotic' is a question-begging word. What does it mean? Used by you, dear sir, it simply means your idea of what a helot ought to be. We do not speak of 'a sheeply sheep', or 'a pigly pig'; and I do not know that our conception of either sheep or pig would be enlarged if we did. Why go on talking, then, of 'helotic helots'?

It may be worth while to imagine a country where only helots live, a circumscribed area – oh, most circumscribed! – which may be called, for want of a better name, Helot's Sphere. Outside the boundary line people are doing, thinking, saying anything they please. Inside, there is restriction in the air, repression, artificiality. It is not proper, for instance – though everything is being rapidly modified by self-assertion – for a helot to be out late at night alone, to go unattended to concert or theatre, to ride outside an omnibus, or to be carried about in a hansom. A young helot cannot live alone in rooms without losing caste, even though she has to earn her own living, and has no home. A well-to-do young helot is thought to be more than peculiar if she attempts to inhabit her own house alone. She is always expected to hire a 'companion', or find some elderly relation, who will 'play propriety'. As for travelling alone, especially in 'foreign parts', such a thing is shocking to the Grundy mind. Did you ever hear a youthful helot say anything like this: 'I think of running over to Paris for a few days'? did you ever see her pack her portmanteau and depart, just to look at Paris and 'enjoy herself', with no protecting, chaperoning friend at her heels?

Again, a helot must dress, not so much for considerations of suitability, or convenience, but to 'look nice' in the eyes of those outside the sphere. If they are pleased, all is well. Many a helot would like to be clothed so as to be able to go about easily and in all weathers. She is often taunted with not walking much, and laughed at for being easily fatigued, but the regulation garb is rigidly enforced, and any modifications thereof are denounced as 'fast', 'eccentric', 'advanced'; worse than all, 'unhelotic'; and the small boy laughs in the street.

It used to be the fashion in the sphere to be physically delicate. Pale faces and languid movements were cultivated, and appetites that could scarcely be seen. Outdoor exercise of any kind, riding and a little walking excepted, was not to be thought of. Perhaps the idea was that weakness of body would help to promote that gentle dependence of mind so sweet to the feelings of the governing class.

There are all sorts of curious little unwritten regulations for the decorous conduct of the helot-world. A helot must keep her hat on in church and at a public meeting. Everybody would sit and gaze at her if she took it off. She may, however, go without it to concert, theatre, or opera, if in what is called 'full dress', which, being interpreted, means less dress than usual. If in ordinary dress the hat must be carefully kept on, as in church. At balls a helot must uncover shoulders and arms. No one can give a reason for this regulation. Other people never have to do it, and it would be thought 'not quite the thing' if they did. The Lord Chamberlain would most certainly turn anyone back who came to Court in such guise – anyone, except a helot; and the rules for helots who attend Court are very severe, and are written and printed so that even she who runs may read. No helot can appear before her sovereign except with bare, exceeding bare, shoulders, neck and arms. Within the last few years, however, a slight concession has been made. If a helot will bring a medical certificate stating that her lungs or throat are likely to suffer from exposure, or if she choose to proclaim herself advanced in years, court-etiquette will grant her absolution. But the latter part of the concession accomplishes little because it is accounted somewhat disgraceful in a helot to be elderly. Curiously enough it does not greatly matter if she be married; but, if unmarried, the helot who is approaching middle age is made to feel in many ways that she is a failure and ridiculous. And so helots in general are driven to pretend that they are younger than they are, to avoid reference to birthdays, and to dread the coming of the census.

Of late the sphere has widened.

Much, very much, has been changed. But nothing would have been changed if helots themselves had not had some little originality, some perception that whatever is is not necessarily right, some love of freedom, some determination that right shall be had, and justice shall be done, had by all, done for all, though the skies come down upon our heads.

It reminds me of nothing so much as the life in seed and tree, the life that is so strong that overlying mould, nay, even overlying stone, is pierced to make way for its coming, so strong that all the strength of gravitation cannot pull it back or hinder it from standing in uprightness; so calmly, silently, grandly triumphant that air and sunshine, and rain and dew are but its ministers. And it grows: it will not lie low upon the ground, though that mysterious force ceases not for one instant its strain; winds shall not tear it from the earth, rain shall not beat it down, for its roots take fast hold in the darkness, and do but cling the firmer for the storm; upwards it will go, and sunwards. Breadth is gained, and all-roundness, and solidity, by this over-mastering life; branch after branch, twig after twig is put out, and, as for the leaves – it may be that the leaves are for the healing of the nations.

Gwenllian E. F. Morgan

The duties of citizenship: the proper understanding and use of the municipal and other franchises for women[★]

*The duties of citizenship: the proper understanding and use of the municipal and other franchises for women**

27 October 1896

> Political freedom begins for women, as it began for men, with freedom in local government. –
>
> LYDIA BECKER

THE motto I have chosen for the opening of this paper sums up in a sentence all the thoughts, which have suggested themselves in connection with this subject. Whether we agree or not as to the justice and wisdom of women being given the Parliamentary franchise, on one point we must all agree, and that is, that there can be no training so excellent for the women, who may in the future be called upon to vote in Parliamentary elections, as the thoughtful, intelligent use of the municipal and other franchises which they already possess. At every election that takes place, in every paper that a woman marks and drops into the ballot-box, a formative influence is going on that is silently building up the character of women as citizens, and the more women can be interested in the local government of their parishes and towns, the fitter they will be for taking part in the government of their country when the time comes for them to do so.

My attention has been drawn to some very remarkable words by Mr Toulmin Smith, which so admirably describe that freedom

*A Paper read at the Annual Conference of the National Union of Women Workers, Manchester.

which is dear to the hearts of English citizens, women as well as men, that I cannot resist quoting them. He says: 'True freedom consists in the continual active consciousness of the position and responsibilities of a free man, a member of the State, and a positive item in it. The free man will feel that he has something to live for beyond the attainment of mere personal ease and comfort; that he has, as member of the State, certain important and active rights and duties and responsibilities coextensive with them in relation to his fellow-men; that he has faculties beyond the mere sensual ones – the strength of which he is bound to put forth in order to help the great works of human happiness and progress.'

The oldest form of local government, that of the parish, with its privileges and responsibilities, has been very ably defined by the same writer when he says: –

> The parish is with us the institution through which the inner life of the people is developed, and in which it should be habitually exercised. The subject of the parish is not, then, a matter of mere local taxation, a question of how to get rid of troublesome burdens. In the exercise of the functions of this institution consists the truest fact of freedom; and the mode of that exercise, the jealous guardianship of those functions from encroachment, and the conscientious discharge of them constitute the test of whether free institutions truly and practically exist and are appreciated, or whether the reality has been or is being lost under vague names and declining forms. . . . The parish is the truest school that can exist; it is the school of men in the active business of responsible life – it is the school for the highest moral training. Men may be educated by book-teaching, they can only become men and members of a free state, and true neighbours one to another by the practical school, which such institutions as the parish keep continually open. The true philanthropist and the real statesman will seek to keep these schools in the highest state of continual efficiency. Each of these will seek not to cramp, but to develop the activity and scope of these institutions. –
> *The Parish*

The local elections at which women may now vote are those of Parish and District Councils, Poor Law Guardians, County Councils, Town Councils, London Vestries, and School Boards, and though the limitations of time will not allow me to deal fully with each of these as I should like to do, I must, in alluding to their powers, briefly emphasise the fact, that the carrying out the duties of each of these bodies affects the welfare of women as closely as that of men, and that a very solemn responsibility rests upon us as women to use our votes aright at every election.

Parish Councils perform the duties hitherto belonging to vestries, with the exception of specially ecclesiastical duties. They also hire land for allotments, and have power to carry out what are known as Adoptive Acts: viz. The Lighting and Watching Acts, 1833; The Baths and Washhouses Act, 1833; The Burials Act, 1852 and 1885; Public Improvements Act, 1860; and the Public Libraries Act, 1892.

District Councils combine the duties of the Sanitary Authorities and Highway Boards, and, in rural districts, the District Councillors are also Poor Law Guardians. They perform sundry duties which were carried out by Justices of the Peace, viz. licensing pawnbrokers, gangmasters, dealers in game, and persons having charge of infants under the Infant Life Protection Act.

Poor Law Guardians administer the Poor Law locally, are responsible for the good management of the workhouse and its inmates, and give out-door relief.

County Councils have many and varied duties, amongst the most important being the assessing and levying of country rates and police rates, and the application and expenditure thereof, also the borrowing of money.

They license places for music, dancing, and stage-plays, and are entrusted with the provision, maintenance, and management of pauper lunatic asylums, and the establishment of reformatories. They have also the administration of the fund granted by the Local Taxation Act of 1890, with a view especially to further technical education. Since 1891 there has been a rapid extension of technical teaching for boys and girls in connection with County Councils. To name those subjects more especially connected with women's work, grants have been made in a great many counties for dairy-work, cookery, laundry-work, horticulture, domestic economy, and bee-keeping.

Town Councils appoint the police and regulate the markets. They must see that the town is properly lighted, paved, cleaned, supplied with gas and water. Further, the Corporation has powers, under the Artisans' Dwellings Act, to buy lands for building proper dwellings for the people. Under the Free Libraries Act it can establish free libraries, museums, schools of art, and open spaces for the recreation of the people may all come under its jurisdiction.

The *London Vestries* are the Sanitary Authorities for their respective areas. They also superintend the lighting, paving, watering, and cleansing of the streets. They control common lodging houses, and can suppress houses for improper purposes. They manage, either directly or through Commissioners whom they appoint, the public libraries, the cemeteries, and the baths and wash-houses. They can acquire and manage open spaces. Certain charities are under the control of the Vestry, managed by Trustees whom it appoints. The Vestry has the construction and management of public lavatory accommodation. As regards workshops, it enforces the sanitary regulations embodied in the Factory and Workshop Acts. The London Vestries deal with areas in which the population is as great as that of a large provincial town.

School Boards deal with the elementary education of boys and girls.

The enumeration of even a few of the duties of these public bodies shows us that the health and comfort, and even the moral welfare of our towns and villages, is largely dependent on good government; and such government can only be attained by choosing men and women of the highest character and ability to carry it out. The ratepayers have it in their choice, by the exercise of their votes, to decide whether they will seek for high-minded, public-spirited members to represent them on the various councils and boards, or leave their municipal independence to drift away from them, and their towns and villages to stagnate for lack of improvements.

Surely these considerations appeal as strongly to women as to men, and all women, who think over their duties as citizens either from a personal, a domestic, or a public standpoint, must deeply feel the responsibility and the privilege of making use of their right to vote.

I would deprecate party politics being made the paramount influence in local elections. Whilst fully recognising the value and help of party organisation from an electioneering point of view, I think the standard of local representation will be lowered not raised (as the introduction of women into the conflict should raise it) if character and ability are not put before any mere party qualification in the choice of a candidate.

It is a subject for rejoicing to know, that every year women are awakening more and more to a sense of their responsibility as citizens, and that the result which was anticipated by some, i.e. that women would not take the trouble to vote, being utterly indifferent to the issues at stake, has *not* been realised.

It would be extremely interesting to have a return of the women who voted at the elections, which followed the Local Government Act of 1894, but nothing short of a Parliamentary return could procure such figures; all that is possible is to record some experiences from different parts of the country. Writing from Bath, Mr S. Hayward, who has had long experience in electoral matters, says: 'From inquiries I have made, I gather that the women voters in the rural parishes took an intelligent interest in the election of parish councillors, and especially that the poorer class appeared to pay more attention to the social and moral character of the candidates than to mere party considerations, and this independently of class. In Bath we have found a general disposition to ignore party considerations in the choice of lady guardians even amongst active political workers.'

Very similar experience has been furnished from Bristol by Mr W. H. Elkins, who had good opportunity of knowing the course of the elections in that city. He writes that in Redland ward, where there was a contest, fully one-third of the votes polled were those of women, and as there were 450 women on the register out of a total of 1,620, this shows a higher percentage amongst the women voters than the men. In those wards of Clifton which were contested, the proportion of women is said to have been still higher. A correspondent in a rural part of Cornwall remarked that the women who were on the register nearly all voted, but that they were so few. Thus in the parish where she herself resided there was but one.

In a Sussex parish, out of nineteen women on the register, twelve came to the poll, and in five rural parishes of the Tunbridge Wells Union, in which there were contests, it appears that the women voted in rather a larger proportion than the men; i.e. out of a total of 165 women on the register 114 (or 69 per cent) voted. Out of a total of 976 men on the register 514 (or 67 per cent) voted. Stray facts like these could no doubt be multiplied, and we should find that, take it all in all, the women of the rural districts did not ignore the new opportunities that had come to them.

I will now quote the opinion of competent judges as to the extent and manner in which women have used their votes in towns, and as types I will take Cardiff, which has the lowest percentage of women voters of any town in the kingdom, and Bath, which has one of the highest, Cardiff having a percentage of nine, and Bath of twenty-five.

Miss Sanders, of Cardiff, writes: 'My father (Mr Alderman Sanders) wishes me to say, that he thinks few men have a wider experience of municipal contests than he has had, which experience extends over thirty years. It may be perfectly true that some women vote as they are told, but not the majority. It is equally true that many men vote as they are told, but on the whole he is convinced, that the majority of women voters use their suffrage with a higher and nobler purpose than do the majority of the other sex.'

The next letter is from Mr S. Hayward, of Bath, who has before been quoted: 'An experience of thirty years in municipal elections in Bath (where the women voters comprise 1,700 out of 7,000) enables me confidently to contradict the assertion "that the great majority of female voters have the strongest dislike for independence" (a statement that had recently been made in the *Speaker*). The municipal elections here have been fought generally on political grounds (I think unfortunately), and hence both male and female voters have been influenced in various ways; but I have found that the women voters have generally attached more importance than the men to the personal moral character and social usefulness of a candidate, and certainly have shown more independence than the majority of the lower class of male voter.'

I will conclude with the words of one whose whole brave, beautiful life has been a protest in favour of the freedom of women, political and otherwise, – I allude to Miss Frances Power Cobbe. She says:*

'We now turn directly to consider how stands the duty of women in England as regards entrance into public life and development of public spirit. What ought we to do at present as concerns all public work wherein it is possible for us to obtain a share? The question seems to answer itself in its mere statement. We are bound to do all we can to promote the virtue and happiness of our fellow men and women, and, therefore, we must accept and seize every instrument of power, every vote, every influence which we can obtain to enable us to promote virtue and happiness. . . . We know that the individual power of one vote at any election seems rarely to effect any appreciable difference; but this need not trouble us, for little or great, if we can obtain any influence at all, we ought to seek for it, and the multiplication of the votes of women bent on securing conscientious candidates would soon make them not only appreciable, but weighty . . . we must come to these public duties – whenever we may be permitted to fulfil them – in the most conscientious and disinterested spirit, and deter- mined to perform them excellently well. . . . This, after all,

*Duties of Women.

is public spirit – in one shape called patriotism, in another philanthropy – the extension of our sympathies beyond the narrow bounds of our homes; the disinterested enthusiasm for every good and sacred cause. All the world has recognised, from the earliest times, how good and noble and wholesome a thing it is for men to have their breasts filled with such public spirit; and we look upon them when they exhibit it as glorified thereby. Is it not just as ennobling a thing for a woman's soul to be likewise filled with these large and generous and unselfish emotions? . . . with indignation against wrongs and injustices and perfidies, and with the ardent longing to bring about some great step of progress, some sorely needed reform?'

Eva McLaren

The civil rights
of women

ALTHOUGH the Parliamentary franchise has not yet been granted to women, they are entitled to vote at all elections for local governing bodies and are eligible for election on most of them.

It is impossible to over-estimate the importance to the whole community of a right exercise of the duty of voting, and in agitating to obtain the vote for Members of Parliament we should not overlook the fact that women have already very extensive powers in the matter of local self-government.

However vitally important legislation is, it is hardly more vital for the actual life of the people than those functions of Government which are exercised by Town and County Councils, School Boards, Boards of Guardians, and other local authorities. The levying and expenditure of the rates is entirely in the hands of these bodies, and it extends to something like one-third of the whole public charge of the country. The whole internal government of towns is in the hands of their elected councillors, whose powers everywhere, except in London, extend to the Control of the Police, the care of Public Order and the Public Health, the Drainage and Sewage of the Town, the Management of the Streets and of all Improvement Schemes, the Provision for the Housing of the Poor, and the Management of the Great Public Services, such as the supply of Gas and Water, to which is added, in some cases, the Management of Markets, and in others, the

Management of Tramways. Besides these wide powers, there are various special matters, such as the Licensing of Places of Public Entertainment, the Acquisition and Management of Open Spaces, and the practical control of any action as to Free Libraries or Baths and Wash-houses, which intimately concern the moral condition of the people. It is obvious that it is of the highest importance that women should assist in placing upon the Town Councils of the country, men, who can be relied upon to take an upright and a moral view of these great responsibilities, the more so as the constitution of these Councils also affects the question of the Licensing of Public Houses. Powers almost exactly analogous, except as regards the Public services and the Police, have lately been conferred upon the County Councils as regards the rural districts of the country. For places of an urban character, which have not yet grown to the rank of corporate towns, there are Local Boards and Improvement Commissioners, endowed with similar authority. In the metropolis there is as yet no full municipal government, but the powers above mentioned, with the exception of gas, water, markets, tramways, and police, and with other restrictions not necessary to be here described, are divided between the London County Council and the various Metropolitan Vestries and District Boards of Works.

Side by side with all these municipal and quasi-municipal bodies, there are the School Boards, controlling the immense mass of the non-sectarian elementary education throughout the country, and administering an enormous revenue: and there are the Boards of Guardians who are responsible for the treatment of thousands of paupers, for the management of workhouses, infirmaries, pauper schools, boarding-out schemes, casual wards, and out-door relief, besides discharging a large number of nondescript statutory functions, for which no other convenient authority was found. The School Boards, the Boards of Guardians, and the School Attendance Committees have to perform a vast and very delicate work in relation to the remission of school fees, and it is unnecessary to insist upon the evident fact that the administration of the Poor Law and the Education Act must be of vital concern to women and children.

It will be seen from the summary which follows, that women are still excluded from some of the bodies exercising municipal powers although they are free to vote in every case. However, as regards School Boards and Boards of Guardians they can not only vote, but they can be, and have frequently been, elected. It is not now denied by anyone that the evidence in favour of the participation of women in public affairs, so far as it has gone, is overwhelmingly strong. It cannot be said that they have failed to exercise such franchises as they possess with at least as much judgment as men. The offices to which they have been elected they have occupied with zeal and success, and when women have once been elected their assistance has almost always been afterwards sought for as a matter of course.

The exclusion of women from a share in the management and control of these various institutions has frequently resulted in worse accommodation, and less care and attention in the internal administration in those departments provided for the women and girls than in those for men and boys.

Many instances might be quoted of the inevitable bad management of workhouses, where the Board of Guardians consists entirely of men. One will suffice. In a metropolitan district a newly-elected lady Guardian, on her first visit to the workhouse school, was struck by the number of children incapacitated by chilblains. She was informed that this was the normal condition of the children during the winter, and neither the doctor nor the male guardians had ever been able to discover the cause. After considerable resistance on the part of the matron and her assistant, she succeeded in getting the children's boots removed, when she found that few if any of the children had feet to their stockings – the explanation being that when a stocking needed darning the foot was simply cut off.

Another case referring to the County Council which may be given is that of Miss Alderman Emma Cons, who in the exercise of her duty as a Councillor visited the dressing-room of a large place of amusement, where she found that owing to insufficient lighting the girls were bringing candles and small paraffin lamps and setting them down on the floor. The dressing-rooms were for the most part built of wood, and the girls were in light inflammable dancing dresses. The importance of women inspectors of music halls and theatres is the more obvious because men are not permitted to visit this part of the theatre.

The machinery of government is so complex that even the bodies already mentioned are not the only ones to which the functions of citizenship extend. Apart from the London Vestries, holding municipal powers, there is the organization of the Parish Vestries throughout the country, with their machinery of Parish Officers and Churchwardens; there are the Overseers and Assistant Overseers; there are the Highway Boards formed by the local Waywardens, with their Road Surveyors; there is the army of Inspectors, from the powerful officials chosen by the Local

Government Board, to the Inspectors of Baby Farms nominated by the London County Council.

It is unfortunate that in many cases, either by intention or by oversight, the privileges conceded to women do not appear as yet to be legally extended to married women, even where they are possessed of separate property. The Law upon this subject is extremely complex and uncertain, and in some places a usage has tacitly arisen by which the invidious distinction is practically neglected. It is hoped that the present summary may serve to call the attention of many women who have not hitherto considered the subject, to the powers and consequent duties which they already possess. The rights of a citizen carry with them the responsibility of a public trust: and those who are qualified to exercise a franchise on which the health, the happiness, the morals of a community may depend, are answerable if by their neglect misgovernment is rendered possible. No less is it a duty upon those women whose circumstances make it possible, that they should take an active part in the service of the country, and train themselves for the further responsibilities they claim, by filling such elective or other offices as may be open to them. The help and influence of women is needed as much in public affairs as in private life, and the work already done by women on County Councils, School Boards, and Boards of Guardians testifies to their fitness to be entrusted with the duties and responsibilities of local government.

When so much power is already possessed by women, and when they have so great a responsibility, it becomes every day more clear that they are fitted to be entrusted with the Parliamentary franchise.

Until this disability is removed, women should never rest satisfied. It is as much their duty to take an interest in the good government of their country as of their town; and the active part which many women do already take in Parliamentary contests will make it increasingly difficult to prevent them any longer from exercising their proper and legitimate influence by means of the ballot.

The Parliamentary franchise is the only franchise which is not open to women in Great Britain. Women are, however, not excluded from it by any Act of Parliament, but merely by the decision of the Court of Common Pleas; and it has been stated by lawyers that the correctness of the judgment was open to doubt. In ancient times it is reasonably certain that women could vote, and until the Reform Act of 1832, had women claimed the franchise, it would in all probability have been conceded by the Courts of Law. There is one well-known case in which Dame Dorothy Packington was the sole elector for the Borough of Aylesbury. In the 14th year of the reign of Queen Elizabeth, she acted as both elector and returning officer, and certified that she had 'chosen, named, and appointed my trusty and well-beloved Thomas Lichfield and John Burdon to be my Burgesses of my said town of Aylesbury' for the purpose of serving in Parliament. The Reform Act of 1832 used the words 'male person' and these were held to exclude women. The Reform Act of 1867 on the other hand used the word 'man', and according to the Act known as Lord Brougham's Act, which provides that words importing the masculine shall include the feminine, this would have enabled women to vote. When the Bill was passing through the House of Commons, Mr J. S. Mill endeavoured to amend it by changing 'man' into 'person', with the avowed object of including women. He was defeated by 194 to 73, but though this vote showed the intention of Parliament, it did not settle the technical and legal meaning of the word 'man' in the Act as passed. Accordingly several revising barristers in the autumn of 1867 placed the names of women on the Register. In Manchester the revising barrister refused to do so, and on an appeal (Chorlton v Lings) his decision was upheld by the Court of Common Pleas. The evident intention of Parliament as shown by the above vote largely influenced this judgment, and it seems probable that had the words of the Act been interpreted by themselves, the decision would have been in favour of the women. In spite of this, however, women have occasionally voted in Parliamentary elections when their names have by accident been placed on the Register. Another and still greater anomaly exists with regard to the University franchise. Women may now obtain degrees in the University of London, but in the supplementary charter which conferred this right upon women, a clause was added providing that women-graduates should not be entitled to vote in elections for members of Parliament for the University. The London University is the only one which confers degrees upon women, and therefore this peculiar grievance has not been felt elsewhere.

The only legislative franchise possessed by women in the British Islands is in the Isle of Man. The Constitution was reformed in 1880, when the franchise entitling persons to vote in elections for the House of Keys was extended to women who are owners of property: and since that time women have voted in large numbers at all elections.

In addition to the general injustice of excluding from the

franchise those women who possess the qualifications necessary to entitle men to vote, a curious and special form of hardship arises from time to time in connection with bribery and corruption at elections. When an Election Judge on a Petition reports that very great corruption has prevailed, the Government appoint a Special Commission to go to the place and thoroughly investigate the matter with a view to the possible disfranchisement of the constituency. Such a commission costs several thousand pounds, which have to be paid by a rate levied on all the ratepayers, male and female. In 1872 for example, the ratepayers of Bridgewater paid a rate for this purpose of 3s in the pound. In 1881–2 the ratepayers of eight boroughs had similar rates of varying amounts levied on them. Thus the women ratepayers have to pay for the expenses incurred owing to the corruption of the men voters, though they themselves have no votes.

A similar grievance is likely to arise if a Bill passes to which most Liberal Members are pledged. It is proposed to pay the Returning Officers' expenses at a Parliamentary election out of the rates. If this be carried into law, women will be unjustly obliged to pay for the costs of elections in which they have no votes.

By the Allotments Act of 1887, all persons who possess the Parliamentary franchise may vote for the election of Managers of Allotments, a Board which is probably the humblest of all local governing bodies. Women therefore are excluded from voting in these elections.

By the Municipal Franchise Act of 1869, Section 9, it is provided 'In this Act and the said recited Act of the 5th and 6th years of King William IV, Chapter 76, and the Acts amending the same, wherever words occur which import the masculine gender, the same shall be held to include females for all purposes connected with, and having reference to the right to vote in the election of Councillors, auditors and assessors.'

This was an amendment inserted on the motion of Mr Jacob Bright in the Bill as introduced by the Liberal Government of the day. It was considered for several days by the Government and then accepted by Mr Bruce (afterwards Lord Aberdare) then Home Secretary. It was again discussed in the House of Lords and supported by the Earl of Kimberley on behalf of the Government, and by Earl Cairns on behalf of the Conservatives. These particulars are mentioned because it is often erroneously stated that this important alteration in the law in favour of women was made either accidentally or was slipped through without the knowledge of Parliament.

A woman may therefore vote in Town Council elections if she

is on the Burgess List. A person has the Burgess qualification who on 15 July in any year, is and has been for the then last preceding twelve months in occupation, joint or several, of any house or shop. A house includes any part of a building which is separately occupied as a dwelling by a person who is not receiving some form of household service as a lodger. The Burgesses must also have been rated either by themselves or through their landlord during that period, and have paid before 20 July all rates levied up to the preceding 5 January, and in addition must not have received Parish relief, during the qualifying period.*

Sub-letting a whole residence for not more than four months does not break the occupation, but part may be sub-let always.

A married woman living with her husband cannot vote for their joint house, and though it has been decided by the superior court in parallel cases that a married woman may not vote for separate property which she may occupy and pay rates for, yet she is sometimes put on the Burgess List, and if so, she may vote, subject to the chance of a scrutiny.

A woman cannot be elected to the Town Council, as the above clause is expressly limited to the right of voting.

By the Municipal Elections Amendment (Scotland) Act 1881, Section 2, it is provided that:

> Whenever words occur which import the masculine gender, the same shall be held for all purposes connected with and having reference to the right to vote in the election of town Councillors, and also to nominate candidates for election to the said office, to include females who are not married and married females not living in family with their husbands, such females shall not be eligible for election as Town Councillor.

This Act, which was brought in by Dr Cameron, MP, differs from the English Municipal Franchise Act, in so far as it specially provided that only unmarried women, and married women not living in family with their husbands, shall be permitted to vote; whereas the English Act merely removes the disability of sex, and leaves in uncertainty the position of married women.

Women do not possess the municipal franchise under the ordinary law in Ireland. In Belfast, however, votes were given to

---

*Medical Relief, Vaccination Fees, Payment of School Fees by Guardians or Remission of Fees by School Board do not disqualify a voter. Removal of any of the family to a Workhouse, Infirmary or pauper Lunatic Asylum does qualify, but (in London) treatment in one of the Metropolitan Asylums Board Hospitals is no disqualification. If a person becomes a pauper after the Register is made up, he may continue to vote so long as that Register remains in force.

women a few years ago, by a Local Improvement Act which greatly extended the franchise in that city.

The Bill brought forward for several years by the Irish Nationalist Members for assimilating the Irish municipal franchise to that of England would have the effect of enfranchising women.

County Councils were created for England by the Local Government Act passed in 1888, and for Scotland in 1889. For England the qualification is set out in the County Electors' Act 1888. The Burgess qualification already described under Town Councils has been extended to all parts of the country. The result is that the County Electors' list practically contains men and women possessing the occupying householders' qualification for the Parliamentary franchise, with the addition of Peers and Peeresses occupying or owning property in the County.

In Scotland the qualification is the same as for Town Councils. Women may therefore vote. By the Scotch Act they are expressly prohibited from being elected. The English Act left it doubtful and several ladies stood, two being elected in London, viz. Lady Sandhurst for Brixton, and Miss Cobden for Bow and Bromley. Miss Cons was subsequently elected an Alderman by the County Council for London. Lady Sandhurst was however unseated on an election petition brought by Mr Beresford Hope, her defeated opponent, on the ground that she was a woman, and that women were not eligible for election. In future, therefore, no women can be elected, without an alteration in the law. (Hope v Sandhurst, LR 23, 2 BD, p. 79.)

Committees of Visitors of County and Borough Lunatic Asylums are appointed by County Councils under the Act 16 and 17 Vic c. 97, and the amending Acts. Women are apparently eligible.

Coroners are now elected by the County Councils, but previous to the creation of these bodies, they were elected by the freeholders of the Counties under one of the oldest franchises in the country, established by an Act passed in the 28th year of Edward III. By an Act passed in 1887 it was provided that 'Every Coroner for a County shall be a fit person having land in fee sufficient in the same county whereof he may answer to all manner of people.' There is nothing in the Act to render women ineligible, and the County Council could probably therefore, elect a fit woman.

The Elementary Education Act of 1870, enacts in Section 29, that 'The School Board shall be elected in manner provided by this Act – in a borough by the persons whose names are on the Burgess roll of such borough for the time being in force, and in a parish not situate in the metropolis, by the ratepayers.' And Section 37 runs – 'The members of the Board shall in the city of

London be elected by the same persons and in like manner as Common Councilmen are elected, and in the other divisions of the metropolis shall be elected by the same persons and in the same manner as vestrymen under the Metropolis Management Act, 1855, and the Acts amending the same.'

According to this women cannot vote within the limits of the city of London, as they do not vote for Common Councilmen. There is no clause in the Act enfranchising women, or rendering them eligible for election on School Boards. There is no reference to women from beginning to end. There is a scrupulous and exclusive use of the masculine gender throughout the clauses, and no interpretation clause to declare that such words shall apply to women.

During the discussion on the Bill, Mr Peter Taylor asked the Vice-President of the Committee of Council on Education, Mr Forster, whether the words 'he' and 'his' would include women. Mr Forster replied that they would, because by Lord Brougham's Act, words importing the masculine gender are deemed to include females unless the contrary is expressly provided. Thus women are included in the operation of the Act as persons, without reference to sex. They have therefore received votes, not because they are women, but simply as ratepayers. They can also be elected. Ever since the formation of School Boards women have been elected in numerous places, both in England and Scotland. The method of voting in School Board elections differs from that of every other election. It is called cumulative because an elector may accumulate all his votes on one candidate, or may distribute them in any way that he thinks fit among the various candidates, provided that the total number of votes given by the voter does not exceed the number of members to be elected. Although married women do not vote in School Board elections, they may be elected. No property or other legal qualification is needed for election.

In districts where there is no School Board, School Attendance Committees are appointed by the Local Authority. If the district is a borough the Committee is appointed by the Town Council. In other places, the appointment rests with the Urban Sanitary Authority. In rural districts, it lies with the Board of Guardians. The governing statute is 39 and 40 Vic, Chapter 79, and women appear to be eligible in all cases unless it be in Municipal boroughs. The School attendance Committee has also the power of appointing Local Committees under the same act.

Committees of Management of School Boards are nominated

by the School Boards. Women are eligible and are frequently
appointed.

The Guardians are elected by the ratepayers. Every ratepayer,
male or female, may vote who has been rated to the relief of the
poor for the whole of the year immediately preceding the voting,
and who has paid the rates, and who is not in receipt of parish
relief.★ Also owners of property may vote, if they occupy the
property themselves or are rated for it. The number of votes
which each ratepayer may have for each candidate depends on the
rateable value of his or her property. The scale is one vote for less
rateable value than £50; but if rated at £50 for one rental, then two
votes are obtained. One additional vote is obtained for every £25
extra rateable value, up to a maximum of six votes for each
tenement. The voting is by means of voting papers left at each
voter's house on one day and collected on the following day. The
Guardians are generally elected for one year only, but in some
Unions they are elected for three years. There is no provision in
the Acts on this subject respecting the right of women either to
vote or to be elected. They have obtained these rights as
ratepayers. The first woman Guardian was elected in 1876 and
since then a great number have been elected. The qualification for
election as a Guardian is being rated to the relief of the poor at
amounts varying from £15 to £40 a year. In London the amount is
£40 in the richer parishes and £25 in the poorer. A married
woman who is rated can be elected a Guardian, and married
women who are ratepayers also vote occasionally, as no legal
decision has been given against the practice. The reason for this
seems to be that here they vote as ratepayers, whereas in Town
Council elections it is the Burgesses who vote, and a married
woman may not be a Burgess in England.

Registrars of Births, Deaths, and Marriages and Collectors of
Poor Rates are elected by Poor Law Guardians, subject to
approval by the Registrar General. In numerous cases women
have been elected and the election has been duly confirmed. The
first appointment of a woman was in 1874, when the Guardians of
the Poor for Martley Union, Worcester, nominated Miss M.
Lipscombe to be Registrar for the district, and the election was
confirmed.

Women have also been appointed members of Dispensary
Boards by Boards of Guardians.

The qualification for voting for Local Boards of Health and the

★See note, page 478.

method of voting is in every respect the same as for the Boards of Guardians. Women may vote, but no woman has been elected, and it is generally supposed they are not eligible, but a dictum is quoted in the case of Chorlton v Lings (LR 4, CP 374, at p. 379), which seems to indicate that there is no disqualification.

Improvement Commissioners are similarly appointed in several of the smaller towns, and the same observations apply as in the case of Local Boards of Health.

The Waywardens, whose duty it is to attend to the repairs of the roads, are elected annually in rural districts by the ratepayers, including women, under the same franchise as that for the election of Guardians. The Waywardens for the various townships form the Highway Board for a larger area, and in most cases, they elect the Road Surveyor. In some cases, however, the Road Surveyor is elected annually by the ratepayers, and that office is sometimes paid and sometimes honorary. Women may vote in all these elections, and may themselves be elected and compelled to serve. There are cases on record in recent years of women having been appointed.

A widow lady was appointed surveyor of roads in a parish in Westmoreland not long since. She had complained of the state of the roads to the surveyor, and at the next election he prevailed on the ratepayers to elect her, probably imagining she would decline the honour. She accepted it however, engaged a clerk, and having much energy and plenty of means she had no difficulty in obaining a thorough supervision.

As the Municipal Elections Amendment (Scotland) Act of 1881, to which we have already referred, merely conferred on women the right to vote in Town Council elections, Dr Cameron, MP, in 1882, introduced and carried the General Police and Improvement Act (Scotland), by which votes were also given to women in Police Burghs, which are analogous to non-corporate districts in England. They may not only vote for Burgh Commissioners, but may vote whether a populous place shall be constituted a Police Burgh or not. Women may not however be elected to the office of Commissioner. By the Local Government (Scotland) Act of 1889, however, it is probable that women may be elected members of District Councils. These Councils are elected partly by Parochial Boards (i.e. Boards of Guardians) from among their own members; and as women may be, and are frequently elected to Parochial Boards, the members of these Boards might elect their women colleagues to serve on the District Councils.

Parochial Boards are equivalent to Boards of Guardians in England. During recent years many women have been elected members of them, and women can vote in these elections.

The Inspector of the Poor, analogous to the relieving officer in England, is appointed and paid by the Parochial Board. In 1872 a lady in Stromness was appointed to fill the office and also to be collector of poor rates. The Board of Supervision (which corresponds to the Local Government Board) refused to confirm the appointment, first on the ground that they did not consider it expedient for a woman to fill the office, and then that she was unfit. A long correspondence followed, but though the Board of Supervision maintained its refusal, and induced the Parochial Board to give way and appoint a man, it never alleged that the appointment of a woman was illegal. The Parochial Board obtained an opinion from an advocate of high standing that a woman may be legally appointed Inspector of the Poor; and this is doubtless the law.

The Vestries of the 25 larger parishes in the metropolis have to a large extent municipal powers. The remaining 53 parishes have Vestries with limited powers which nominate the members of the 14 District Boards of Works. At elections for London vestries, when a poll is demanded, the Metropolis Local Management Act, 1855 (Section 17), provides that 'each ratepayer shall have one vote and no more for the members of the Vestry, and one vote and no more for the auditors or auditor of accounts to be chosen for the said parish.'

Section 6 of the same Act provides 'The Vestry elected under this Act in any parish shall consist of persons rated or assessed to the relief of the poor upon a rental of not less than £40 per annum' subject to a proviso for reduction to £25 in parishes containing a certain proportion of poor property.

Women may, therefore, vote if they are ratepayers, provided they have been rated in the Parish for the relief of the Poor for the year before 15 July preceding the election, and have paid all Parochial rates, taxes and assessments then due. Apparently they may also be elected, because the word 'persons' includes both men and women. No instance has, however, occurred in which a woman has been elected. A few years ago a lady was nominated for the Paddington Vestry, but the deputy returning officer took upon himself to refuse her nomination. He probably acted illegally, but the matter was not carried further.

Inspectors of Nuisances who may be men or women, and either paid or honorary, are appointed in London by the Vestry or District Board, and elsewhere by the Local Sanitary Authority under the provisions of 38 and 39 Vic c. 55, ss. 189–90.

Commissioners of Public Libraries are appointed under the Free

Libraries Act (18 and 19 Vic c. 70, 29 and 30 Vic c. 114 and the amending Acts). They are generally elected by the Vestry, and women appear to be eligible.

Commissioners of Baths and Wash-houses are appointed by the Local Sanitary Authority (which in London is the Vestry) under 9 and 10 Vic c. 74 and the later Acts, and women are presumably eligible.

Burial Boards are elected by Vestries or Urban Authorities under the Act 15 and 16 Vic Chapter 85, and the Acts amending the same. Women are understood to be eligible.

Overseers are nominated annually by the magistrates and may be compelled to serve. During the last two hundred years down to the present time women have occasionally been appointed to fill the office, their eligibility under the terms of the Poor Law of 43 Elizabeth having been decided by the case of R v Stubbs, 2 Term reports, p. 395, in 1788.

Assistant Overseers are elected by the ratepayers, including of course women. Women may also serve as Assistant Overseers themselves. During the last ten years several have been elected. The qualification for voting is the same as for the election of Guardians, but the election is differently conducted, as the voters go in person to record their votes by open voting.

Churchwardens are elected annually in Easter week by a show of hands at the Vestry Meeting of a civil parish. All ratepayers whose names appear on the last rate, and who are also parishioners, including women, may attend the Vestry meeting and vote. Women may be elected as Churchwardens, and numerous instances have occurred during the last fifteen years where they have filled that office, for which they have been judicially declared eligible. There is no legal religious qualification for Churchwardens, and Nonconformists have at various times been elected.

In London and other Urban Districts the civil parishes which elect Churchwardens with control over local management are only the older parishes, as distinguished from the newer ecclesiastical districts, where Churchwardens are purely congregational officers.

It was decided in an early case that a woman might be a Sexton, and she is probably eligible for the office of Parish clerk and other similar appointments.

Women Local Government Board Inspectors, including Inspectors of Poor Law Schools, and of children boarded out, have been twice appointed – first Mrs Nassau Senior by Mr Stansfeld, and afterwards Miss Mason.

Postmistresses, and Civil Service Clerks in the Post Office and

Telegraph Department. Great numbers of women fill such offices as County Council Inspectors of Baby Farms, Weights and Measures, Noxious Trades, &c. There is nothing to prevent women from being appointed. The Colonial Office has also appointed a woman to be the Postmistress and Superintendent of Telegraphs at Gibraltar, with a salary of about £800 a year.

Factory and Workshop Inspectors are nominated under the Act of 1878 (41 & 42 Vic, c. 16, s. 67) which empowered the Home Office to appoint 'inspectors, clerks and servants', which by the effect of Lord Brougham's Act clearly includes the power to appoint women.

Women were employed by Government in the Census Work for 1881 in Ireland.

An Official declaration was made by the President of the Local Government Board in 1884, that there was nothing to prevent a lady being placed on a Royal Commission. In spite of this when the Royal Commission for enquiring into the housing of the poor was appointed, to the surprise of everyone Miss Octavia Hill's name was not in the list of members of the commission. Commenting upon this the *Times* said: 'A correspondent to-day suggests a doubt whether Miss Hill may not be omitted from the Royal Commission because no female Royal Commissioner has yet been known. The exclusion of her unsurpassed experience on so foolish a ground is almost incredible. We shall not believe it until the list appears without her name.'

It will be seen from the foregoing pages that every local franchise is now open to women; that the disability of sex is removed, though the disability of marriage remains. But the law is less satisfactory with regard to the right to be elected than it is with regard to the right to vote, imperfect even as that is. It is only certain that women may be elected to Boards of Guardians and School Boards. As to most of the others the law is doubtful, though probably favourable to women's claims; while with regard to the two most important, the Town and County Councils, the law is decided in the negative. The following table will show at a glance the votes which women may give, the public Bodies on which they may either certainly or probably serve and the offices to which they may be appointed. The field is already wide, but we hope to see it much wider. Meantime it is greatly to be hoped that women will come forward as candidates for all such elective bodies as may be open to them, both that the law may be made clear, and still more that the public may have the benefit of the skill and care which women bring to the discharge of such duties as they are called upon to perform.

Part IV
Text of the Women's Franchise Bill

1892

Text of the
Women's Franchise Bill

1892

[55 VICT] Parliamentary Franchise (Extension to Women)
A BILL TO Extend the Parliamentary Franchise to Women
BE it enacted by the Queen's most Excellent Majesty, by and with
the advice and consent of the Lords Spiritual and Temporal, and
Commons, in this present Parliament assembled, and by the
authority of the same, as follows:

1 This Act may be cited as the Parliamentary Franchise
(Women) Act, 1892.

2 Every woman who –

(1) In Great Britain is registered or entitled to be registered
as an elector for any town council or county council; or

(2) In Ireland is a ratepayer entitled to vote at an election for
guardians of the poor;

shall be entitled to be registered as a parliamentary elector,
and when registered to vote at any parliamentary election for
the county, borough, or division wherein the qualifying
property is situate.

(Prepared and brought in by Sir Albert Rollit, Sir A. Borthwick,
Viscount Wolmer, Mr W. McLaren, Mr Penrose FitzGerald, Mr
T. D. Sullivan, Mr T. W. Russell, Mr Burt and Mr Ernest
Spencer)

Index

Aberdare, Henry Austin Bruce,
  1st Baron, 477
Adoptive Acts, 467
Allotments Act (1887), 477
America: Colorado, 364–5;
  position of women, 201;
  rejection of women's votes,
  59–60, 81, 85–6, 365; slaves, 27,
  145; Spanish policy, 57; system
  of representation, 76, 254;
  Wyoming, 364
Anstey, Chisholm, 317, 318
Anstruther, Sir Robert, 323
Artisans' Dwellings Act, 467
Australia, 67, 137, 441
Austria, 42, 147, 150

Bacon, Sir Francis, 335
Baillie, Joanna, 97
Ballot Bill, 56
Baths and Workhouses,
  Commissioners of, 484
Beale, Dorothea, 161
Becker, Lydia, 5, 287, 465
Bede, 347
Berkeley, Mr and Mrs, 135
Berry, Mary, 97
Blackburn, Mr Justice, 123
Bodichon, Barbara, 1–2, 6
Bookbinders' Union, 439
Borthwick, Sir Algernon, 489
Bouverie, Edward Pleydell–:

opposed to Bill, 52, 66, 71, 78,
  81, 82; speech in Commons,
  58–65; views of women, 176–7,
  190
Bovill, Mr Justice, 323
Bowring, Sir John, 169
Brett, Mr Justice, 138
Bright, Jacob: defeated, 4; elected,
  322; municipal franchise, 323,
  477; on voting procedure, 67;
  speeches in Commons, 49–54,
  87, 276; support for women's
  suffrage, 2–3, 64, 158, 179, 271,
  287, 294, 323; on 'women's
  sphere', 297
Bright, John: illness, 114; letter to,
  257–63; on freedom, 173;
  opposed to women's suffrage,
  2–3, 302–4, 336; oratory, 102;
  political leadership, 103; speech
  in Commons, 247–56, 264–5,
  267; support for male household
  suffrage, 393, 394
Bright, Ursula, 2
Brougham, Henry Peter, Baron,
  476, 480, 485
Browning, Elizabeth Barrett, 368
Bryce, James, 405, 432, 442
Burdett-Coutts, Angela Georgina,
  Baroness, 42, 179, 366
Burdon, John, 476
Burgesses, 367, 478, 479, 481